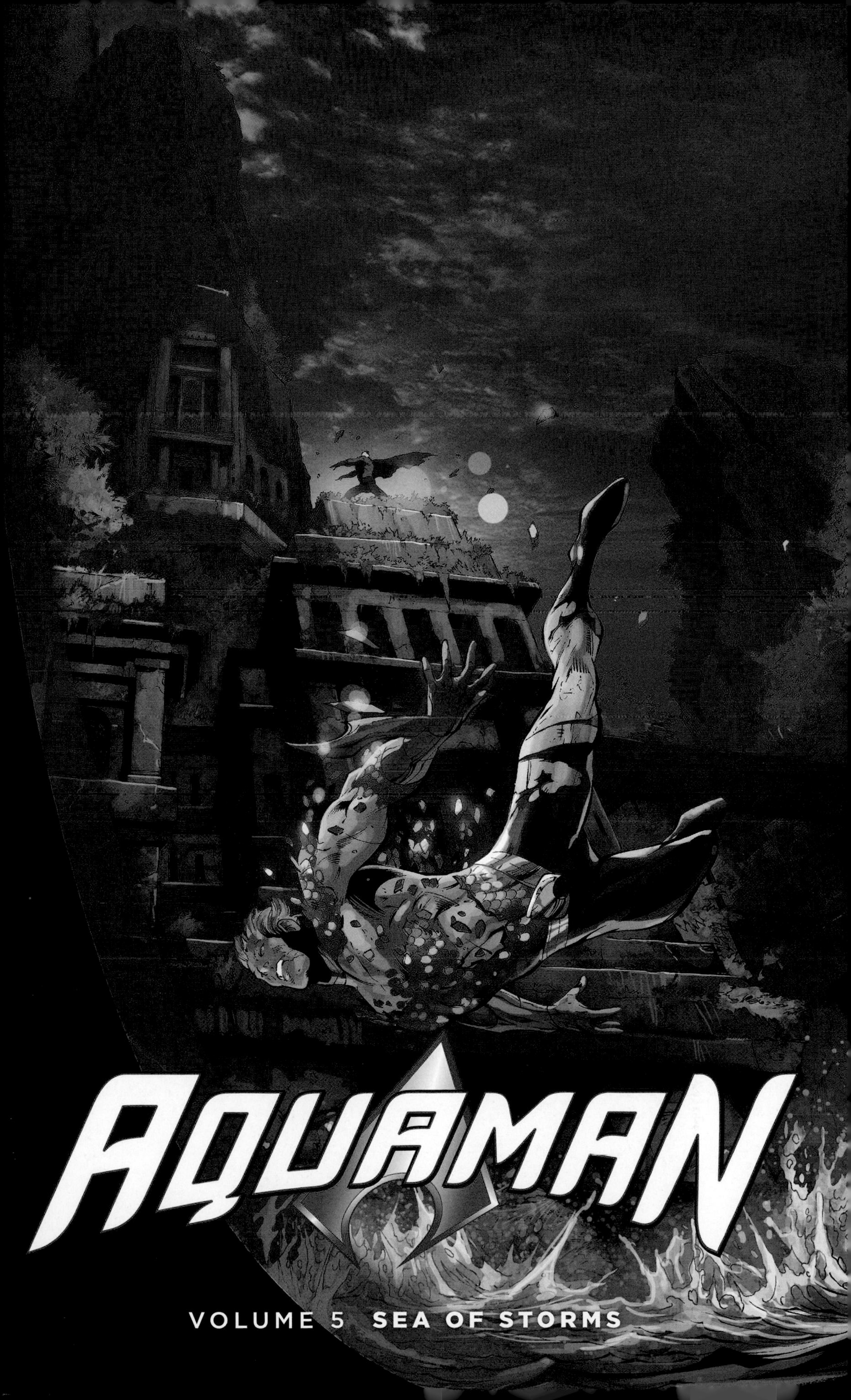
AQUAMAN
VOLUME 5 SEA OF STORMS

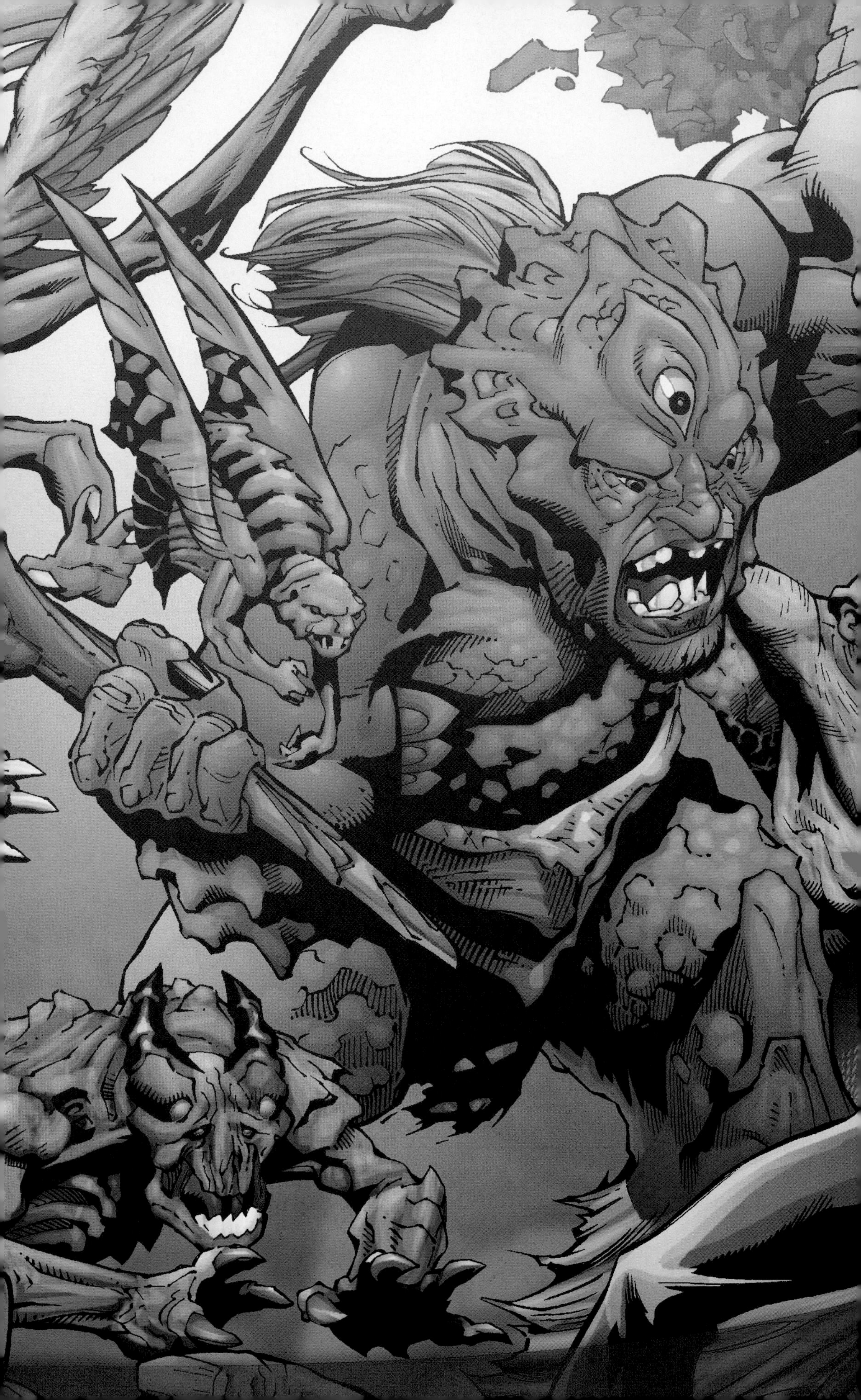

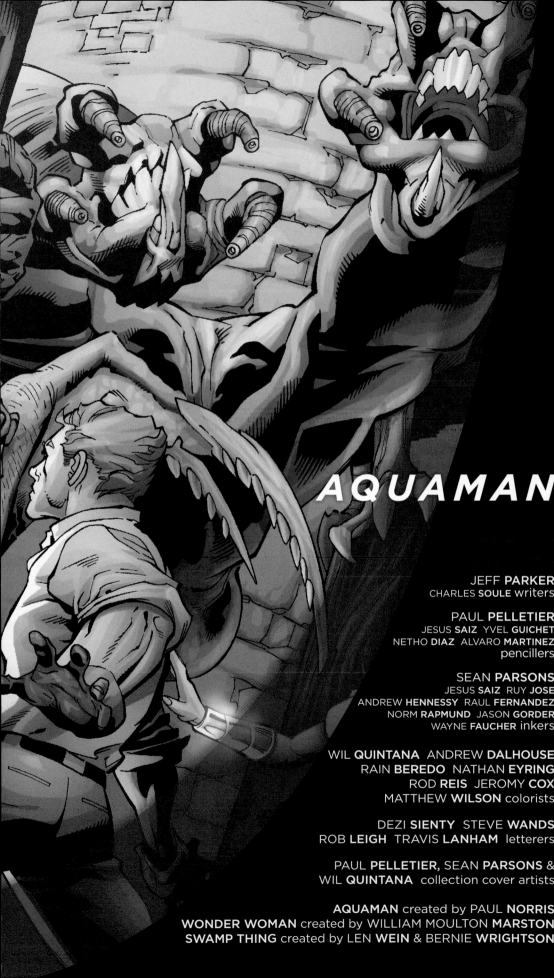

AQUAMAN

JEFF **PARKER**
CHARLES **SOULE** writers

PAUL **PELLETIER**
JESUS **SAIZ** YVEL **GUICHET**
NETHO **DIAZ** ALVARO **MARTINEZ**
pencillers

SEAN **PARSONS**
JESUS **SAIZ** RUY **JOSE**
ANDREW **HENNESSY** RAUL **FERNANDEZ**
NORM **RAPMUND** JASON **GORDER**
WAYNE **FAUCHER** inkers

WIL **QUINTANA** ANDREW **DALHOUSE**
RAIN **BEREDO** NATHAN **EYRING**
ROD **REIS** JEROMY **COX**
MATTHEW **WILSON** colorists

DEZI **SIENTY** STEVE **WANDS**
ROB **LEIGH** TRAVIS **LANHAM** letterers

PAUL **PELLETIER**, SEAN **PARSONS** &
WIL **QUINTANA** collection cover artists

AQUAMAN created by PAUL **NORRIS**
WONDER WOMAN created by WILLIAM MOULTON **MARSTON**
SWAMP THING created by LEN **WEIN** & BERNIE **WRIGHTSON**

CHRIS CONROY Editor – Original Series
HARVEY RICHARDS DARREN SHAN Associate Editors – Original Series LIZ ERICKSON Editor
ROBBIN BROSTERMAN Design Director – Books ROBBIE BIEDERMAN Publication Design

BOB HARRAS Senior VP – Editor-in-Chief, DC Comics

AQUAMAN VOLUME 5: SEA OF STORMS

DC Comics, 1700 Broadway, New York, NY 10019
A Warner Bros. Entertainment Company.
Printed by RR Donnelley, Salem, VA, USA. 10/17/14. First Printing.

Library of Congress Cataloging-in-Publication Data

Parker, Jeff, 1966- author.
Aquaman. Volume 5, Sea of storms / Jeff Parker, writer ; Paul Pelletier, Sean Parsons, artists.
pages cm. — (The New 52!)
ISBN 978-1-4012-5039-3 (hardback)
1. Graphic novels. I. Pelletier, Paul, 1970- illustrator. II. Parsons, Sean P., illustrator. III. Title. IV. Title: Sea of storms.

PN6728.A68P37 2014
741.5'973—dc23

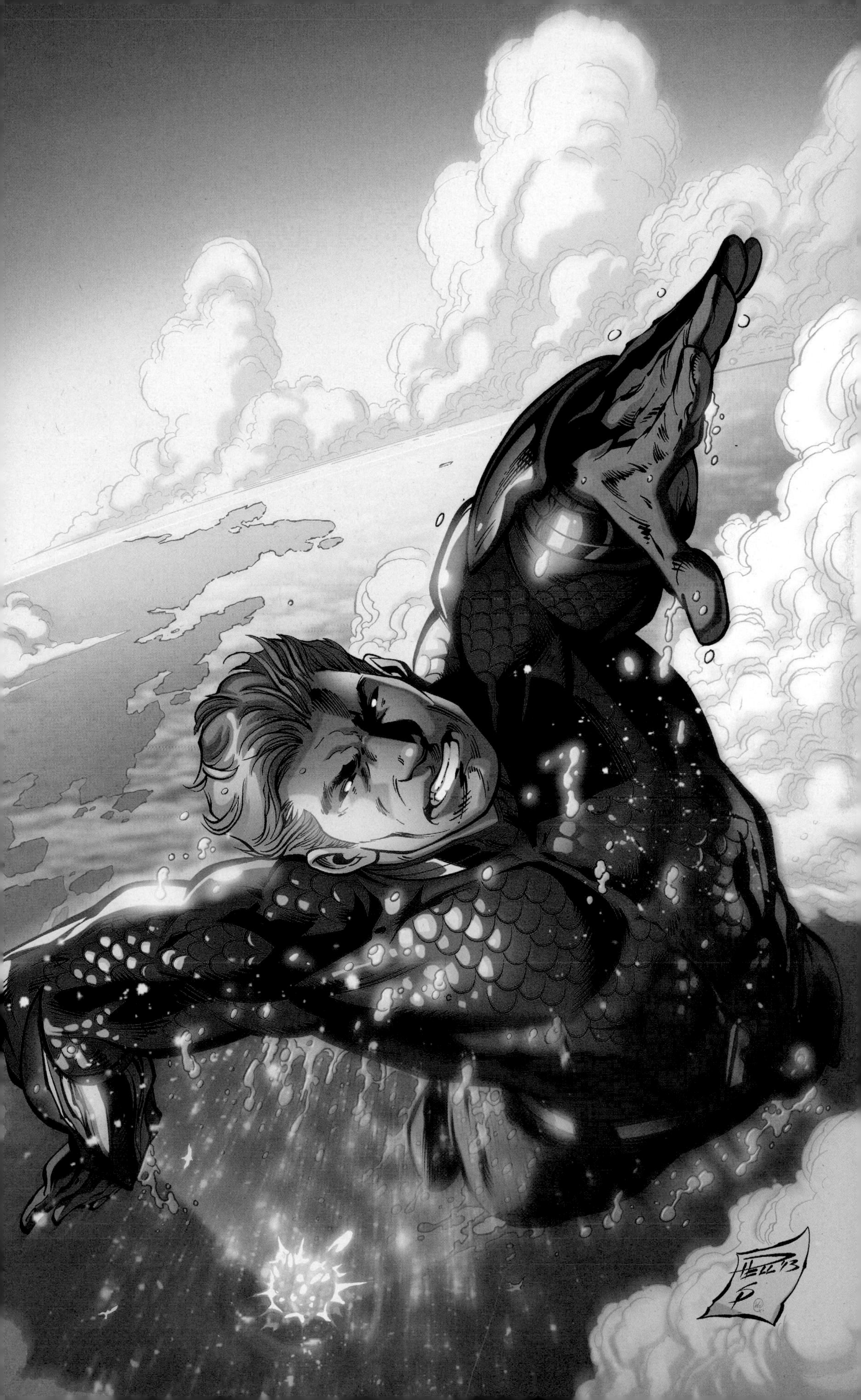

PRESSURE

JEFF PARKER writer **PAUL PELLETIER NETHO DIAZ** pencillers **SEAN PARSONS RUY JOSE** inkers
WIL QUINTANA ANDREW DALHOUSE colorists **DEZI SIENTY** letterer cover by **PAUL PELLETIER, SEAN PARSONS** and **WIL QUINTANA**

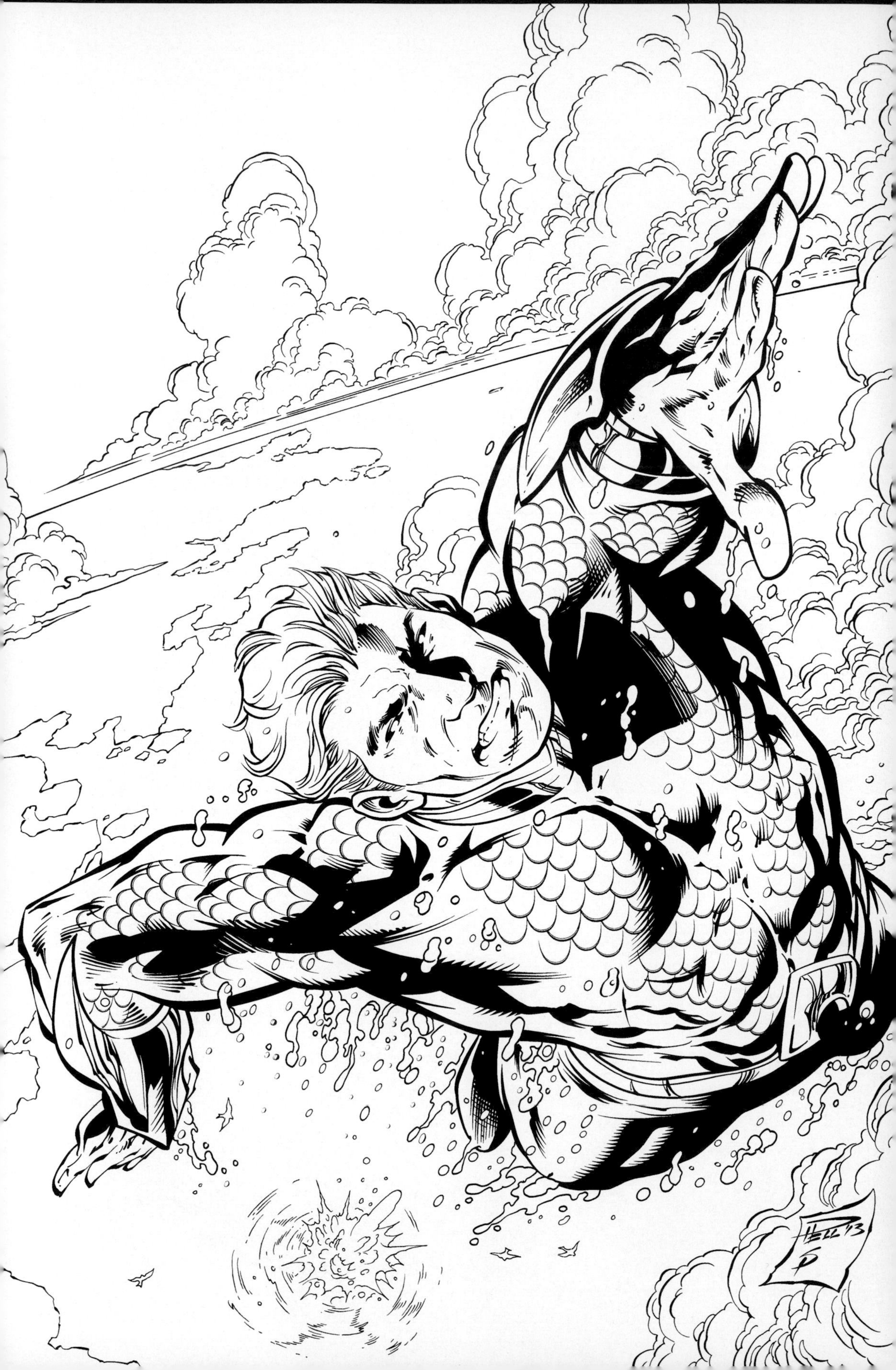

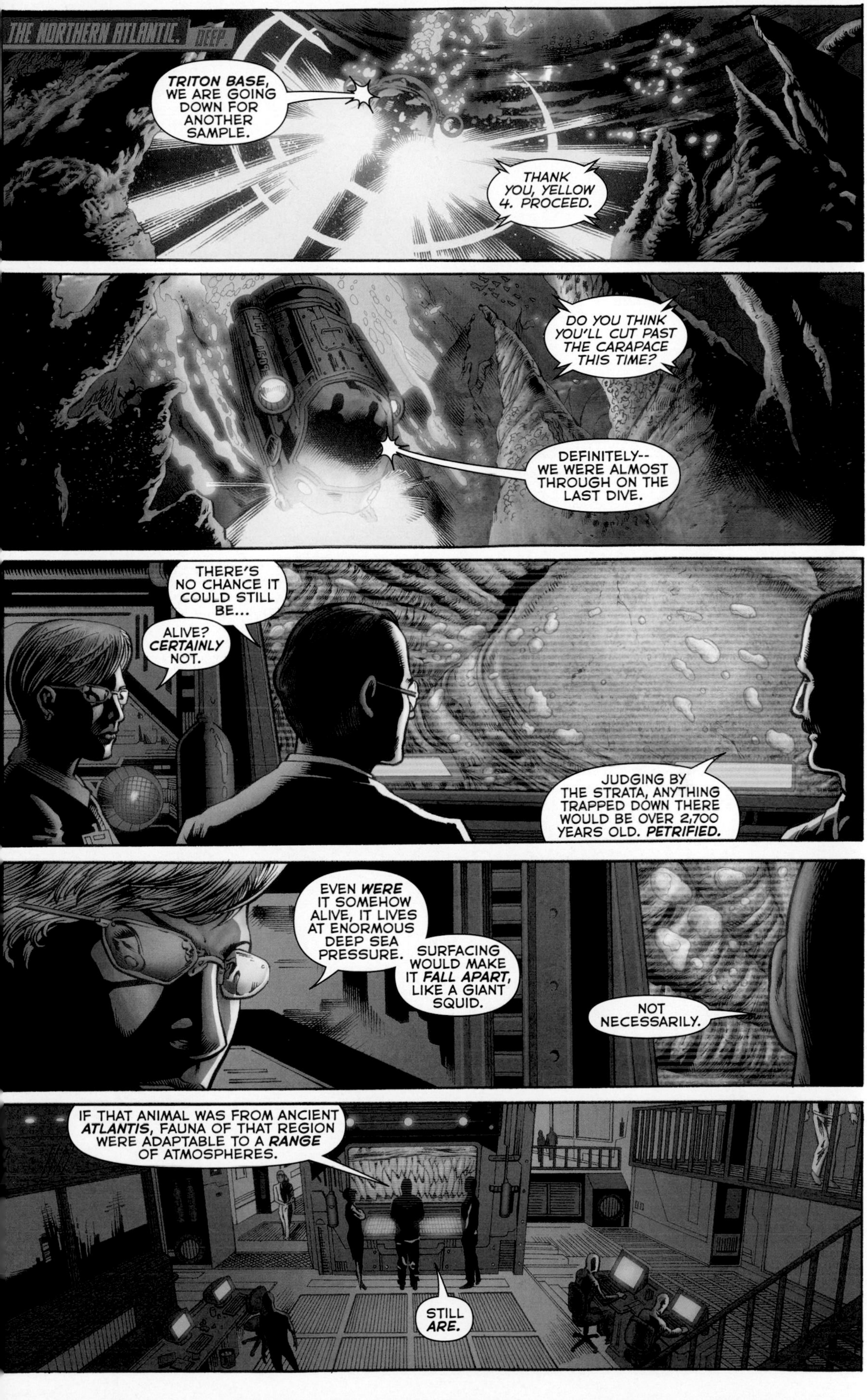
THE NORTHERN ATLANTIC. DEEP.
TRITON BASE, WE ARE GOING DOWN FOR ANOTHER SAMPLE.
THANK YOU, YELLOW 4. PROCEED.
DO YOU THINK YOU'LL CUT PAST THE CARAPACE THIS TIME?
DEFINITELY-- WE WERE ALMOST THROUGH ON THE LAST DIVE.
THERE'S NO CHANCE IT COULD STILL BE...
ALIVE? CERTAINLY NOT.
JUDGING BY THE STRATA, ANYTHING TRAPPED DOWN THERE WOULD BE OVER 2,700 YEARS OLD. PETRIFIED.
EVEN WERE IT SOMEHOW ALIVE, IT LIVES AT ENORMOUS DEEP SEA PRESSURE.
SURFACING WOULD MAKE IT FALL APART, LIKE A GIANT SQUID.
NOT NECESSARILY.
IF THAT ANIMAL WAS FROM ANCIENT ATLANTIS, FAUNA OF THAT REGION WERE ADAPTABLE TO A RANGE OF ATMOSPHERES.
STILL ARE.

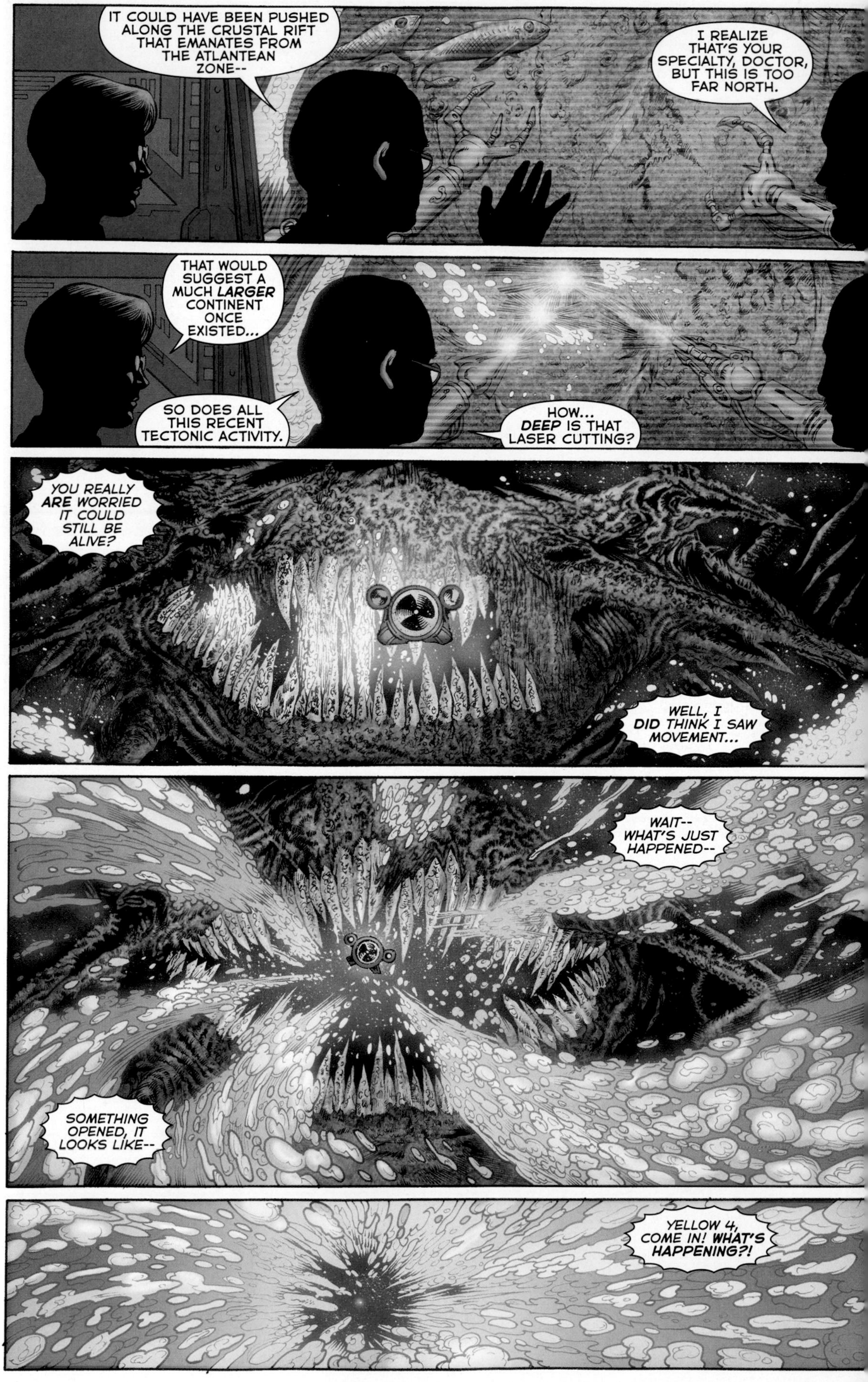

IT COULD HAVE BEEN PUSHED ALONG THE CRUSTAL RIFT THAT EMANATES FROM THE ATLANTEAN ZONE--
I REALIZE THAT'S YOUR SPECIALTY, DOCTOR, BUT THIS IS TOO FAR NORTH.
THAT WOULD SUGGEST A MUCH LARGER CONTINENT ONCE EXISTED...
SO DOES ALL THIS RECENT TECTONIC ACTIVITY.
HOW... DEEP IS THAT LASER CUTTING?
YOU REALLY ARE WORRIED IT COULD STILL BE ALIVE?
WELL, I DID THINK I SAW MOVEMENT...
WAIT-- WHAT'S JUST HAPPENED--
SOMETHING OPENED, IT LOOKS LIKE--
YELLOW 4, COME IN! WHAT'S HAPPENING?!

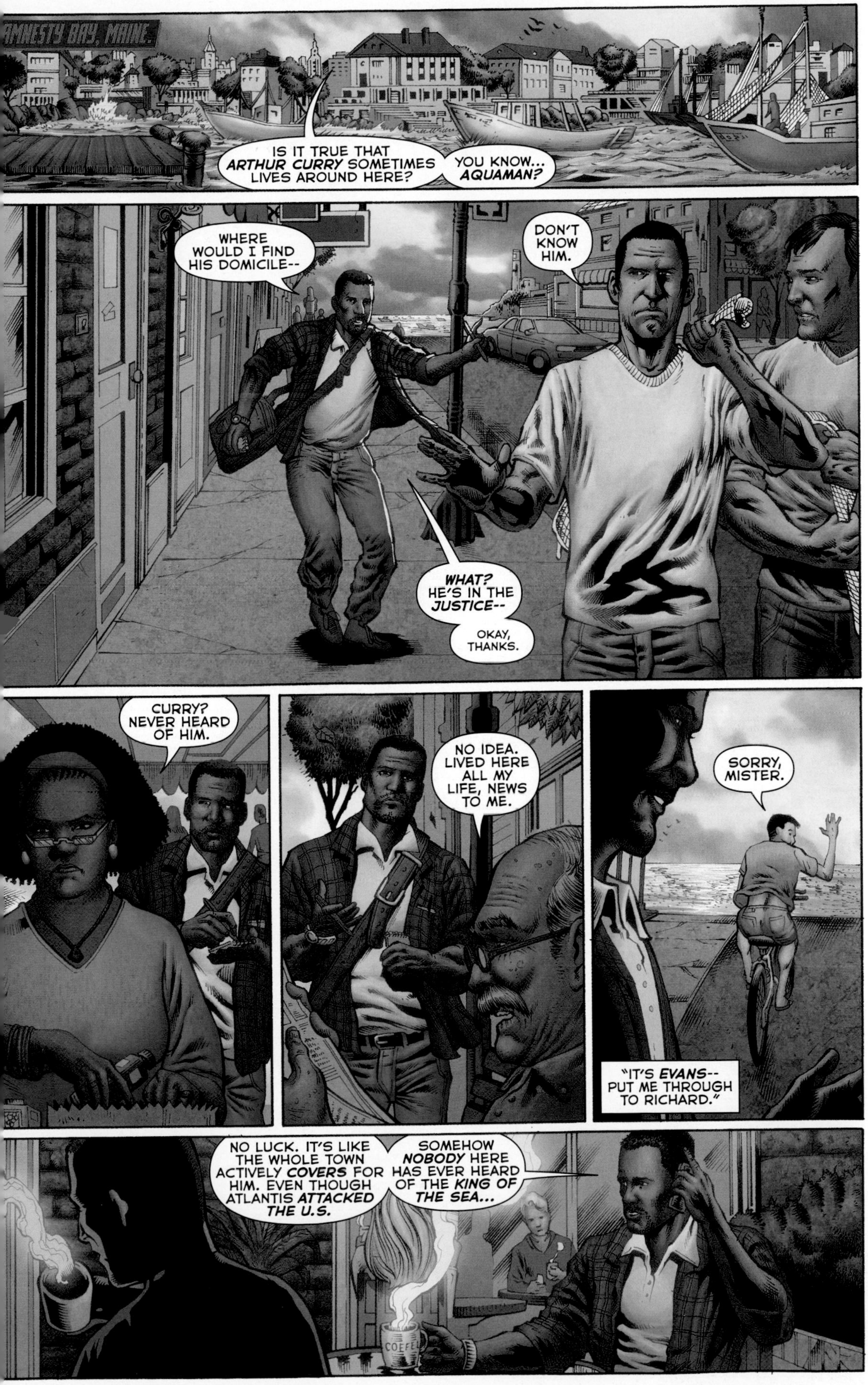
AMNESTY BAY, MAINE.
IS IT TRUE THAT ARTHUR CURRY SOMETIMES LIVES AROUND HERE?
YOU KNOW... AQUAMAN?
WHERE WOULD I FIND HIS DOMICILE--
DON'T KNOW HIM.
WHAT? HE'S IN THE JUSTICE--
OKAY, THANKS.
CURRY? NEVER HEARD OF HIM.
NO IDEA. LIVED HERE ALL MY LIFE, NEWS TO ME.
SORRY, MISTER.
"IT'S EVANS-- PUT ME THROUGH TO RICHARD."
NO LUCK. IT'S LIKE THE WHOLE TOWN ACTIVELY COVERS FOR HIM. EVEN THOUGH ATLANTIS ATTACKED THE U.S.
SOMEHOW NOBODY HERE HAS EVER HEARD OF THE KING OF THE SEA...
COFFEE

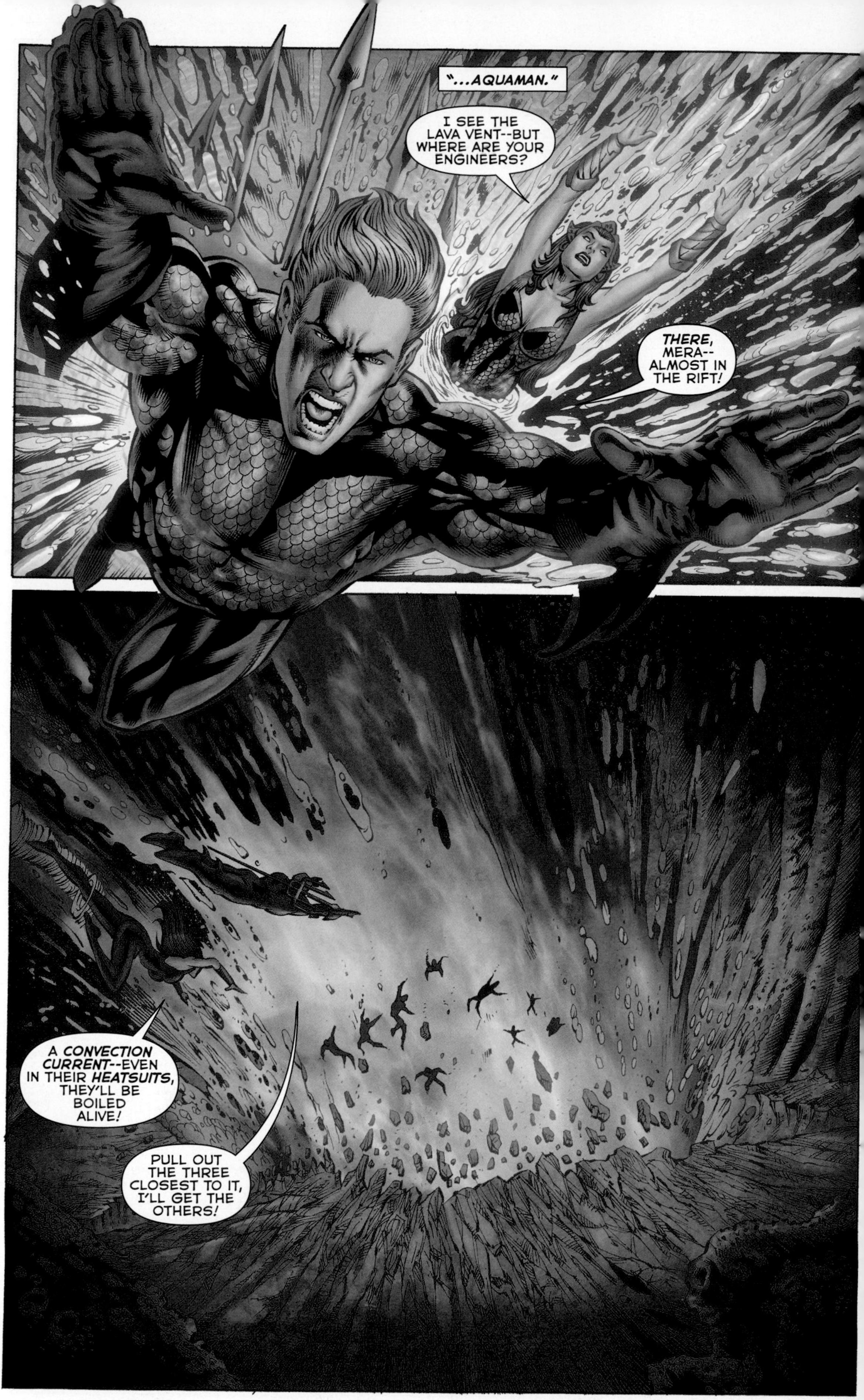
"...AQUAMAN."
I SEE THE LAVA VENT--BUT WHERE ARE YOUR ENGINEERS?
THERE, MERA--ALMOST IN THE RIFT!
A *CONVECTION CURRENT*--EVEN IN THEIR *HEATSUITS,* THEY'LL BE BOILED ALIVE!
PULL OUT THE THREE CLOSEST TO IT, I'LL GET THE OTHERS!

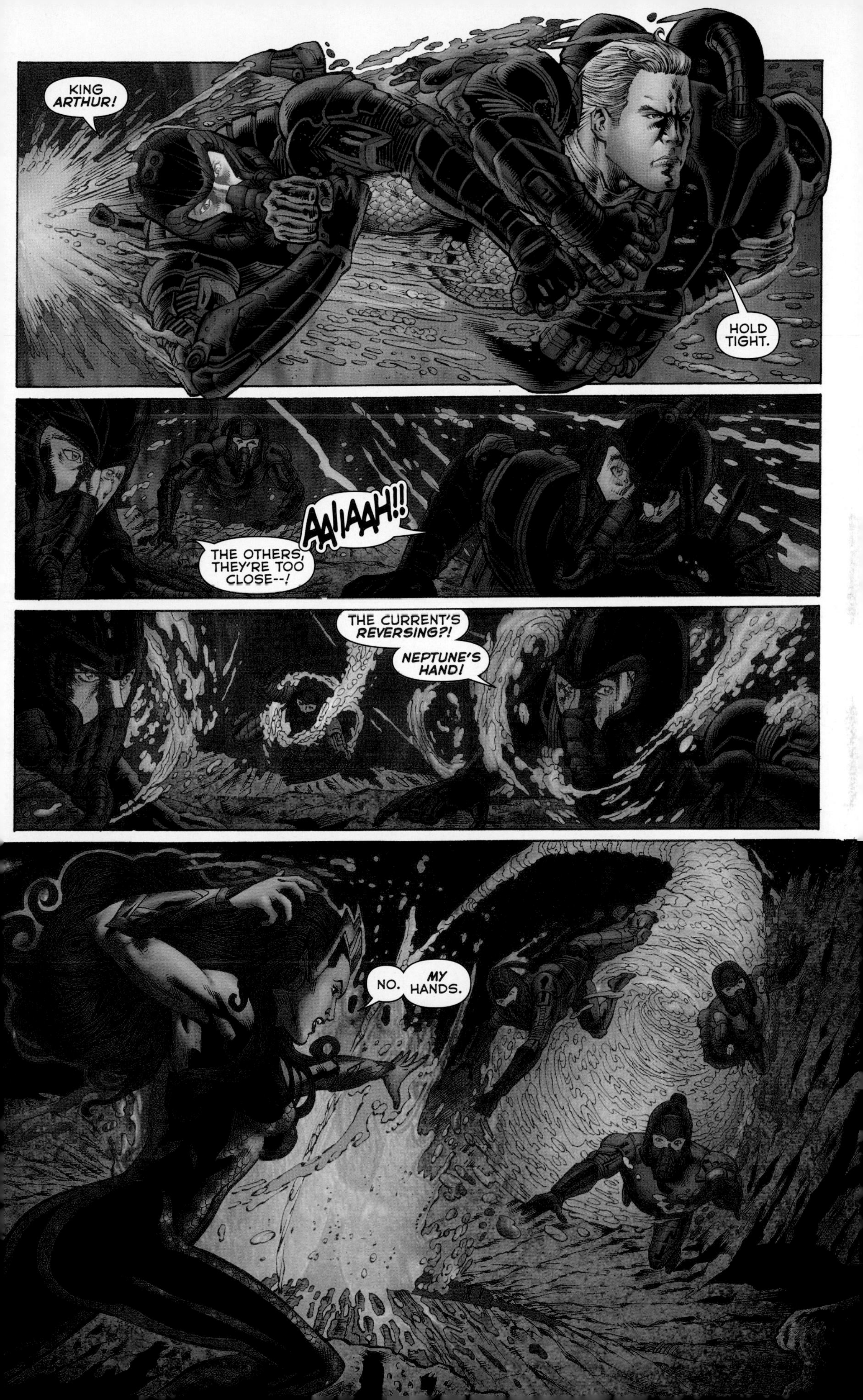
KING ARTHUR!
HOLD TIGHT.
AAIIAAH!!
THE OTHERS, THEY'RE TOO CLOSE--!
THE CURRENT'S REVERSING?!
NEPTUNE'S HAND!
NO.
MY HANDS.

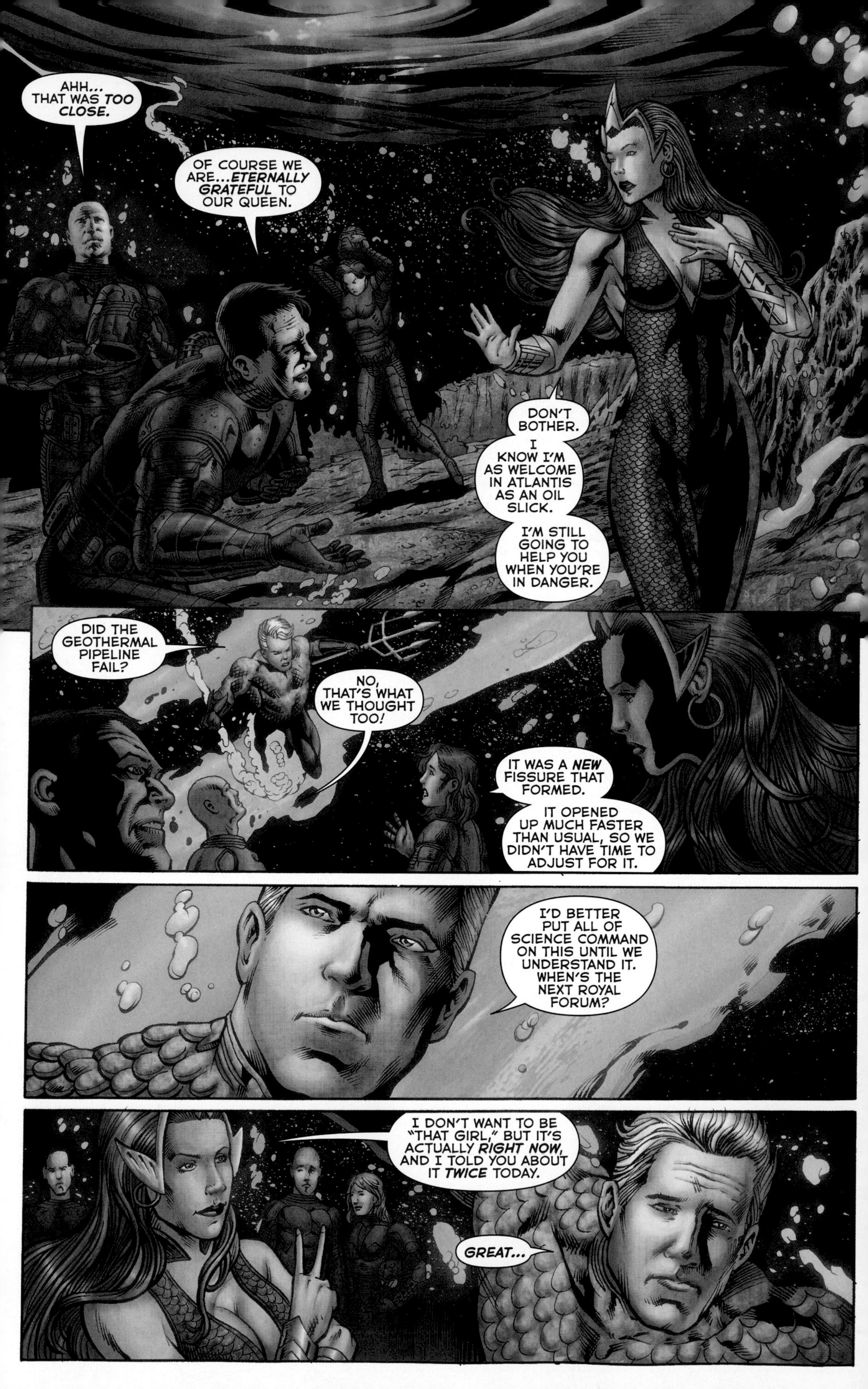
AHH... THAT WAS TOO CLOSE.
OF COURSE WE ARE...ETERNALLY GRATEFUL TO OUR QUEEN.
DON'T BOTHER.
I KNOW I'M AS WELCOME IN ATLANTIS AS AN OIL SLICK.
I'M STILL GOING TO HELP YOU WHEN YOU'RE IN DANGER.
DID THE GEOTHERMAL PIPELINE FAIL?
NO, THAT'S WHAT WE THOUGHT TOO!
IT WAS A NEW FISSURE THAT FORMED.
IT OPENED UP MUCH FASTER THAN USUAL, SO WE DIDN'T HAVE TIME TO ADJUST FOR IT.
I'D BETTER PUT ALL OF SCIENCE COMMAND ON THIS UNTIL WE UNDERSTAND IT. WHEN'S THE NEXT ROYAL FORUM?
I DON'T WANT TO BE "THAT GIRL," BUT IT'S ACTUALLY RIGHT NOW, AND I TOLD YOU ABOUT IT TWICE TODAY.
GREAT...

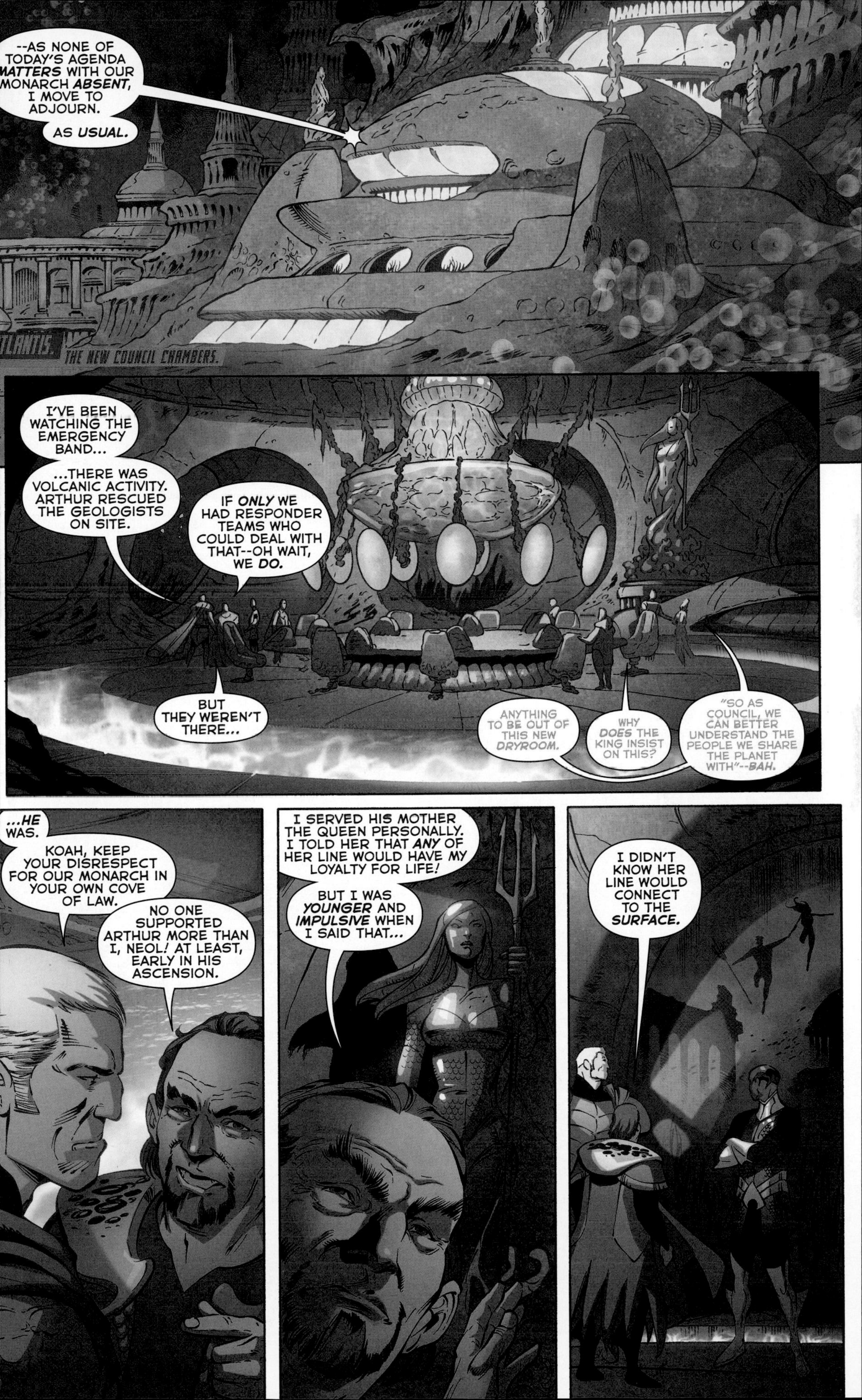
--AS NONE OF TODAY'S AGENDA MATTERS WITH OUR MONARCH ABSENT, I MOVE TO ADJOURN.
AS USUAL.
ATLANTIS. THE NEW COUNCIL CHAMBERS.
I'VE BEEN WATCHING THE EMERGENCY BAND...
...THERE WAS VOLCANIC ACTIVITY. ARTHUR RESCUED THE GEOLOGISTS ON SITE.
IF ONLY WE HAD RESPONDER TEAMS WHO COULD DEAL WITH THAT--OH WAIT, WE DO.
BUT THEY WEREN'T THERE...
ANYTHING TO BE OUT OF THIS NEW DRYROOM.
WHY DOES THE KING INSIST ON THIS?
"SO AS COUNCIL, WE CAN BETTER UNDERSTAND THE PEOPLE WE SHARE THE PLANET WITH"--BAH.
...HE WAS.
KOAH, KEEP YOUR DISRESPECT FOR OUR MONARCH IN YOUR OWN COVE OF LAW.
NO ONE SUPPORTED ARTHUR MORE THAN I, NEOL! AT LEAST, EARLY IN HIS ASCENSION.
I SERVED HIS MOTHER THE QUEEN PERSONALLY. I TOLD HER THAT ANY OF HER LINE WOULD HAVE MY LOYALTY FOR LIFE!
BUT I WAS YOUNGER AND IMPULSIVE WHEN I SAID THAT...
I DIDN'T KNOW HER LINE WOULD CONNECT TO THE SURFACE.

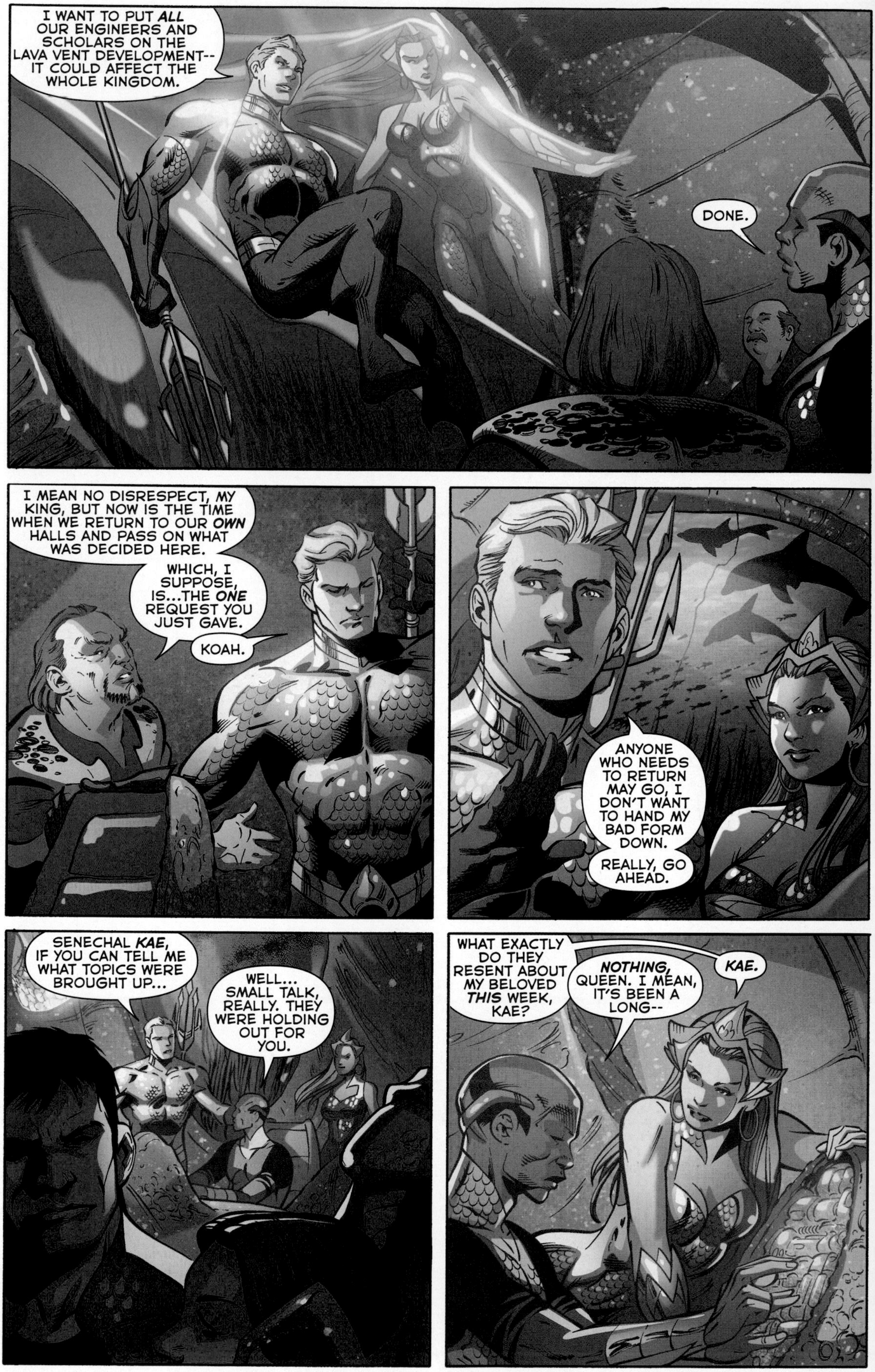
I WANT TO PUT ALL OUR ENGINEERS AND SCHOLARS ON THE LAVA VENT DEVELOPMENT-- IT COULD AFFECT THE WHOLE KINGDOM.
DONE.
I MEAN NO DISRESPECT, MY KING, BUT NOW IS THE TIME WHEN WE RETURN TO OUR OWN HALLS AND PASS ON WHAT WAS DECIDED HERE.
WHICH, I SUPPOSE, IS...THE ONE REQUEST YOU JUST GAVE.
KOAH.
ANYONE WHO NEEDS TO RETURN MAY GO, I DON'T WANT TO HAND MY BAD FORM DOWN.
REALLY, GO AHEAD.
SENECHAL KAE, IF YOU CAN TELL ME WHAT TOPICS WERE BROUGHT UP...
WELL... SMALL TALK, REALLY. THEY WERE HOLDING OUT FOR YOU.
WHAT EXACTLY DO THEY RESENT ABOUT MY BELOVED THIS WEEK, KAE?
NOTHING, QUEEN. I MEAN, IT'S BEEN A LONG--
KAE.

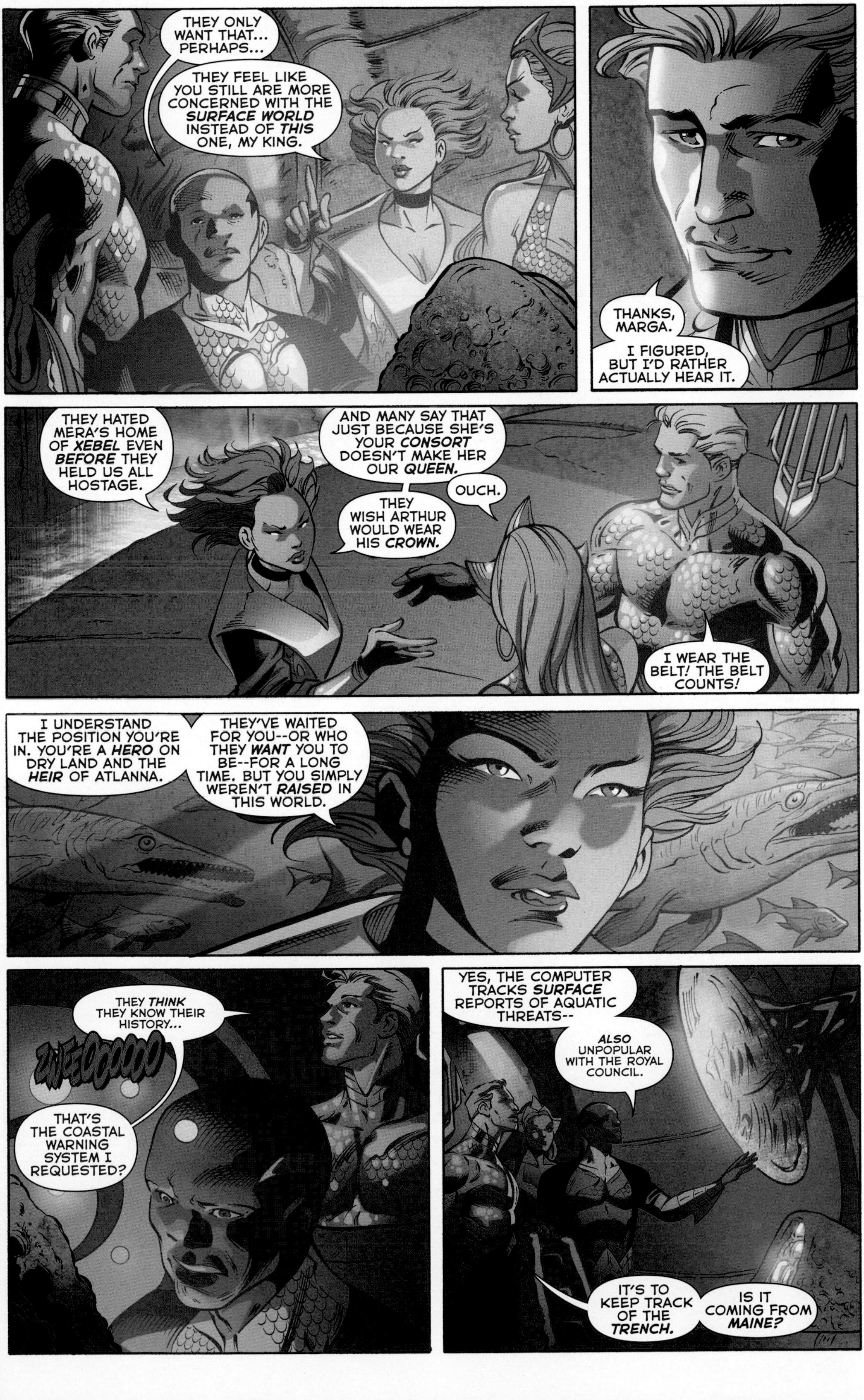
THEY ONLY WANT THAT... PERHAPS...
THEY FEEL LIKE YOU STILL ARE MORE CONCERNED WITH THE SURFACE WORLD INSTEAD OF THIS ONE, MY KING.
THANKS, MARGA.
I FIGURED, BUT I'D RATHER ACTUALLY HEAR IT.
THEY HATED MERA'S HOME OF XEBEL EVEN BEFORE THEY HELD US ALL HOSTAGE.
AND MANY SAY THAT JUST BECAUSE SHE'S YOUR CONSORT DOESN'T MAKE HER OUR QUEEN.
THEY WISH ARTHUR WOULD WEAR HIS CROWN.
OUCH.
I WEAR THE BELT! THE BELT COUNTS!
I UNDERSTAND THE POSITION YOU'RE IN. YOU'RE A HERO ON DRY LAND AND THE HEIR OF ATLANNA.
THEY'VE WAITED FOR YOU--OR WHO THEY WANT YOU TO BE--FOR A LONG TIME. BUT YOU SIMPLY WEREN'T RAISED IN THIS WORLD.
THEY THINK THEY KNOW THEIR HISTORY...
THAT'S THE COASTAL WARNING SYSTEM I REQUESTED?
YES, THE COMPUTER TRACKS SURFACE REPORTS OF AQUATIC THREATS--
ALSO UNPOPULAR WITH THE ROYAL COUNCIL.
IT'S TO KEEP TRACK OF THE TRENCH.
IS IT COMING FROM MAINE?

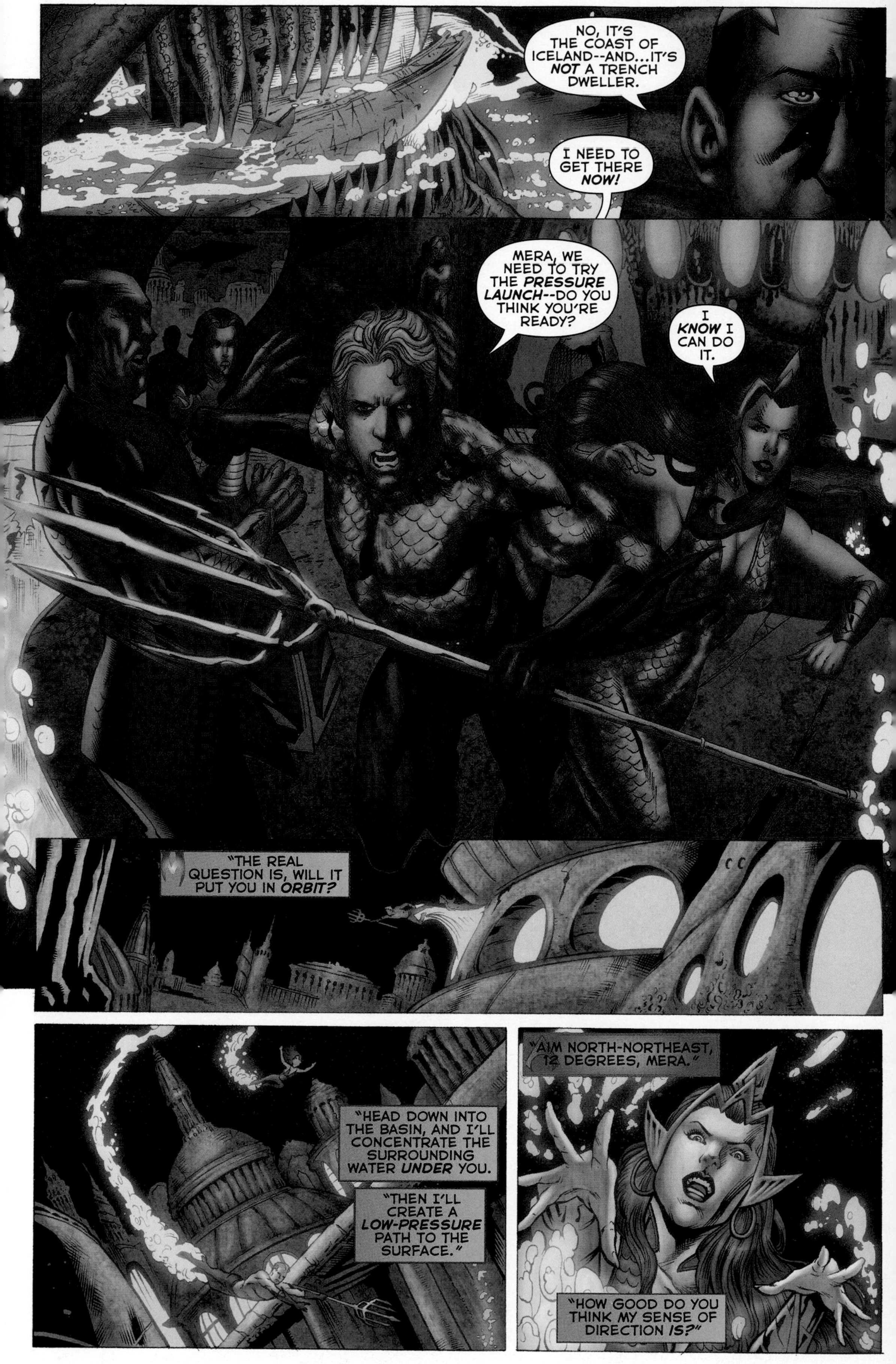
NO, IT'S THE COAST OF ICELAND--AND...IT'S NOT A TRENCH DWELLER.
I NEED TO GET THERE NOW!
MERA, WE NEED TO TRY THE PRESSURE LAUNCH--DO YOU THINK YOU'RE READY?
I KNOW I CAN DO IT.
"THE REAL QUESTION IS, WILL IT PUT YOU IN ORBIT?
"HEAD DOWN INTO THE BASIN, AND I'LL CONCENTRATE THE SURROUNDING WATER UNDER YOU.
"THEN I'LL CREATE A LOW-PRESSURE PATH TO THE SURFACE."
"AIM NORTH-NORTHEAST, 12 DEGREES, MERA."
"HOW GOOD DO YOU THINK MY SENSE OF DIRECTION IS?"

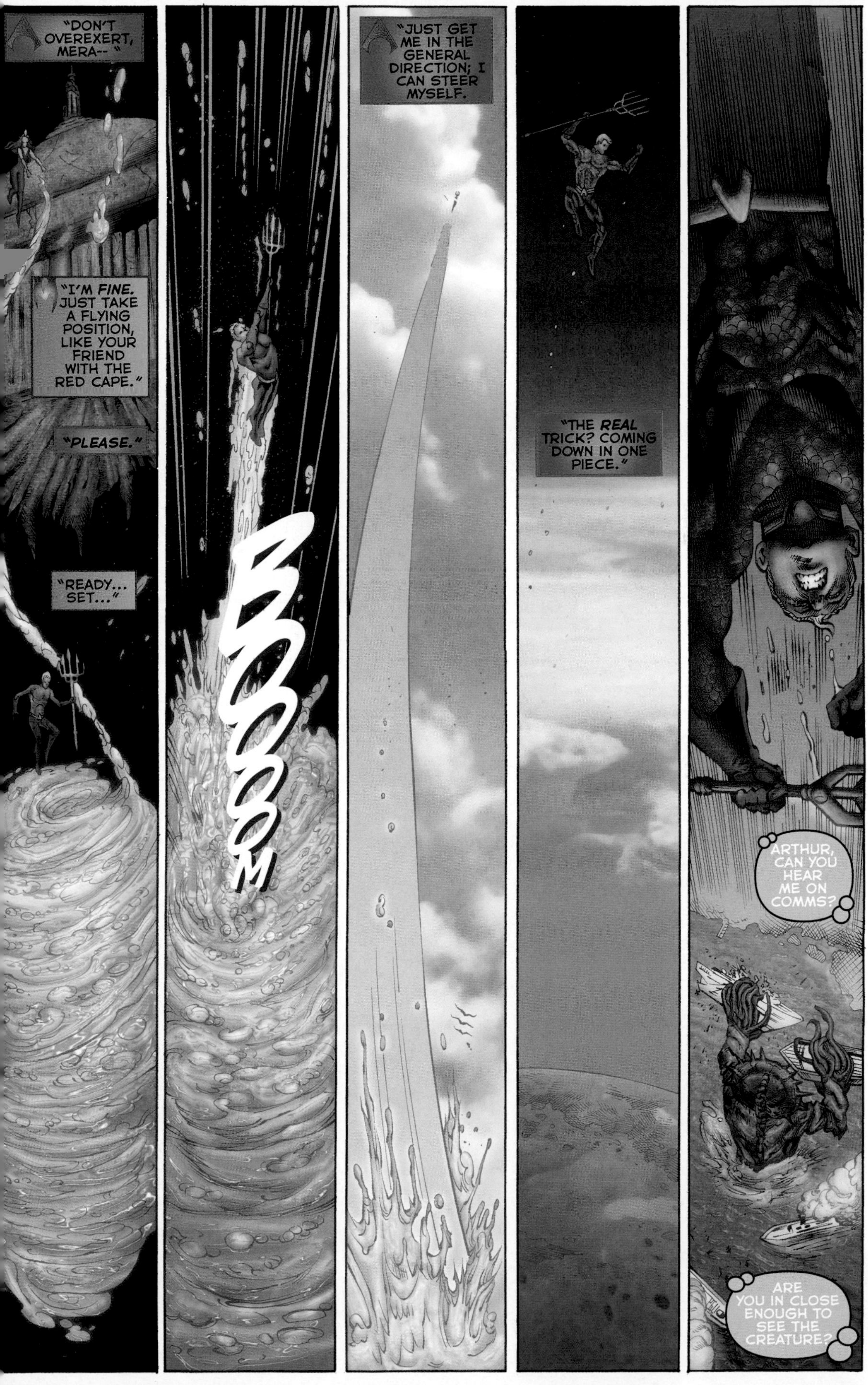
"DON'T OVEREXERT, MERA-- "
"I'M FINE. JUST TAKE A FLYING POSITION, LIKE YOUR FRIEND WITH THE RED CAPE."
"PLEASE."
"READY... SET..."
BOOOOOM
"JUST GET ME IN THE GENERAL DIRECTION; I CAN STEER MYSELF."
"THE REAL TRICK? COMING DOWN IN ONE PIECE."
ARTHUR, CAN YOU HEAR ME ON COMMS?
ARE YOU IN CLOSE ENOUGH TO SEE THE CREATURE?

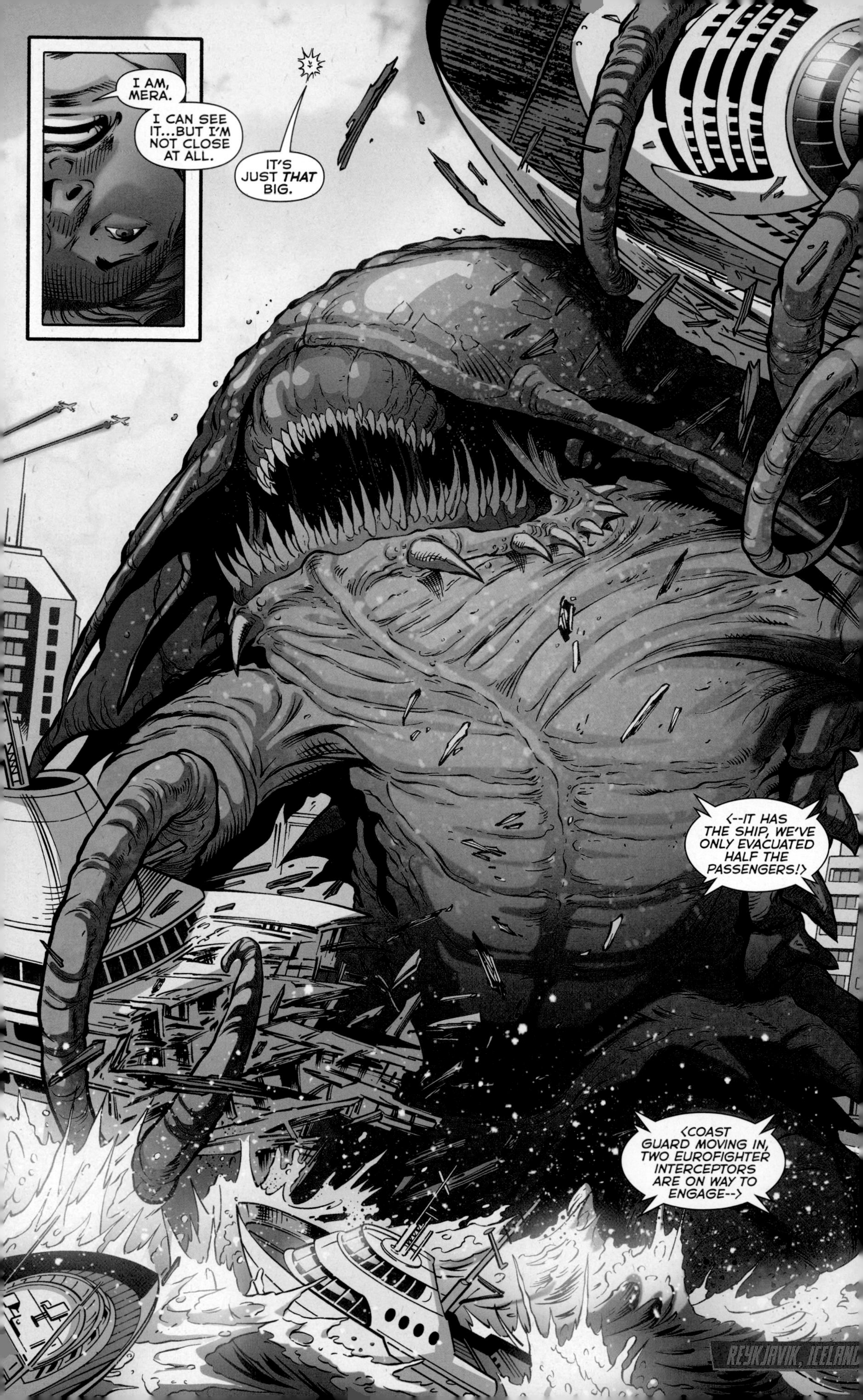
I AM, MERA.
I CAN SEE IT...BUT I'M NOT CLOSE AT ALL.
IT'S JUST THAT BIG.
<--IT HAS THE SHIP, WE'VE ONLY EVACUATED HALF THE PASSENGERS!>
<COAST GUARD MOVING IN, TWO EUROFIGHTER INTERCEPTORS ARE ON WAY TO ENGAGE-->
REYKJAVIK, ICELAND

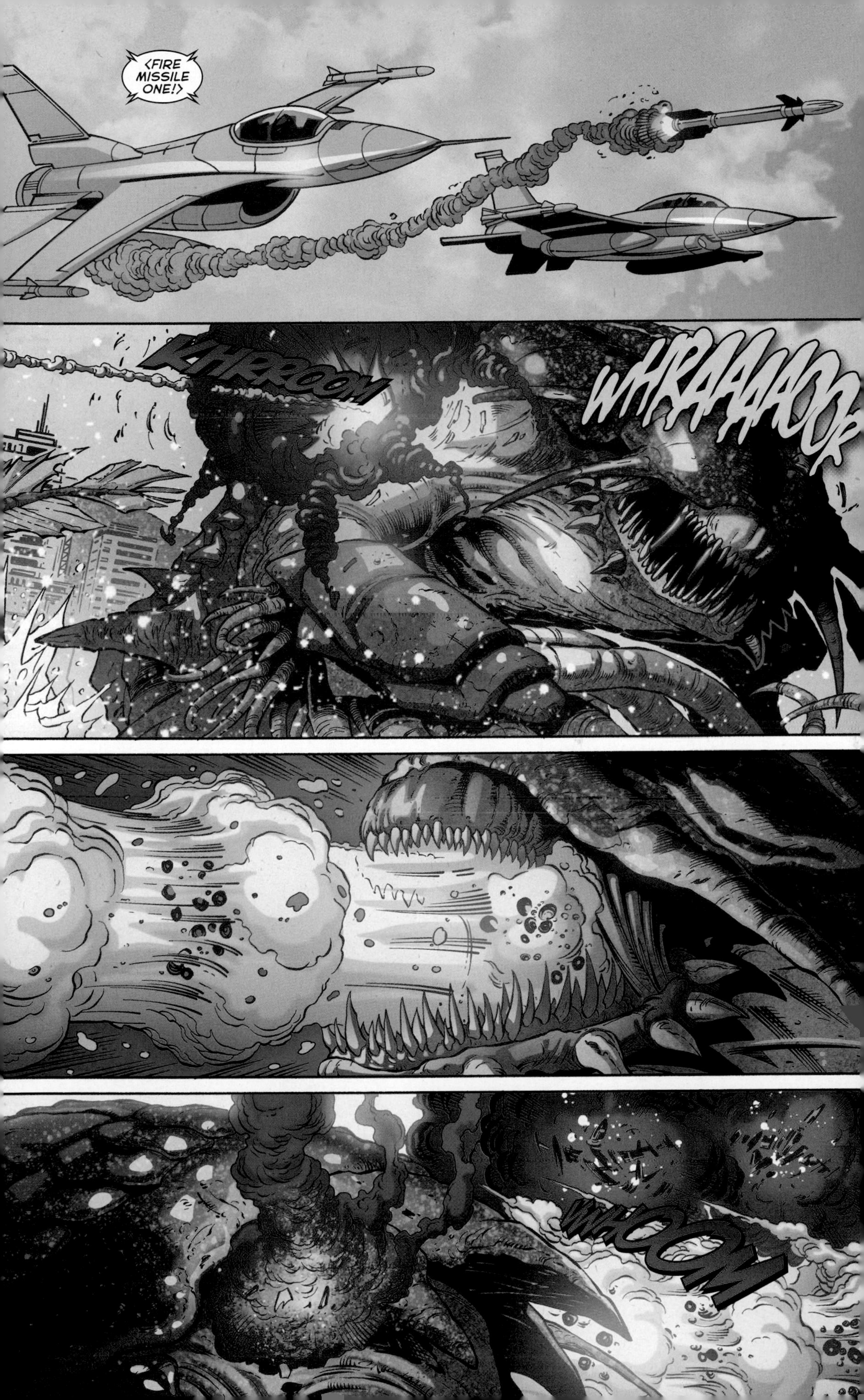
<FIRE MISSILE ONE!>
KHRROOM
WHRAAAAOOK
WHOOOM

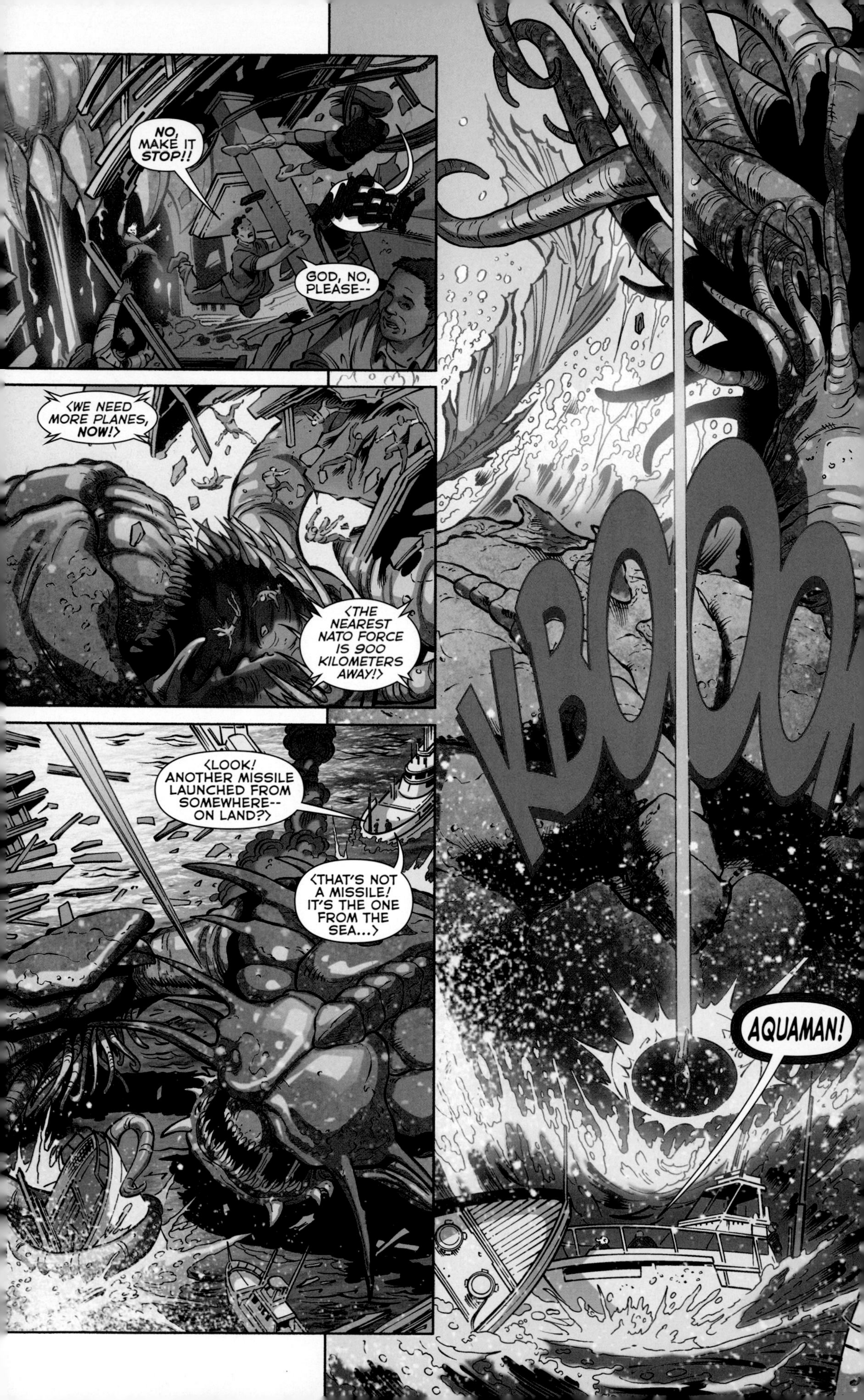

NO, MAKE IT STOP!!
GOD, NO, PLEASE--
<WE NEED MORE PLANES, NOW!>
<THE NEAREST NATO FORCE IS 900 KILOMETERS AWAY!>
<LOOK! ANOTHER MISSILE LAUNCHED FROM SOMEWHERE-- ON LAND?>
<THAT'S NOT A MISSILE! IT'S THE ONE FROM THE SEA...>
KBOOO
AQUAMAN!

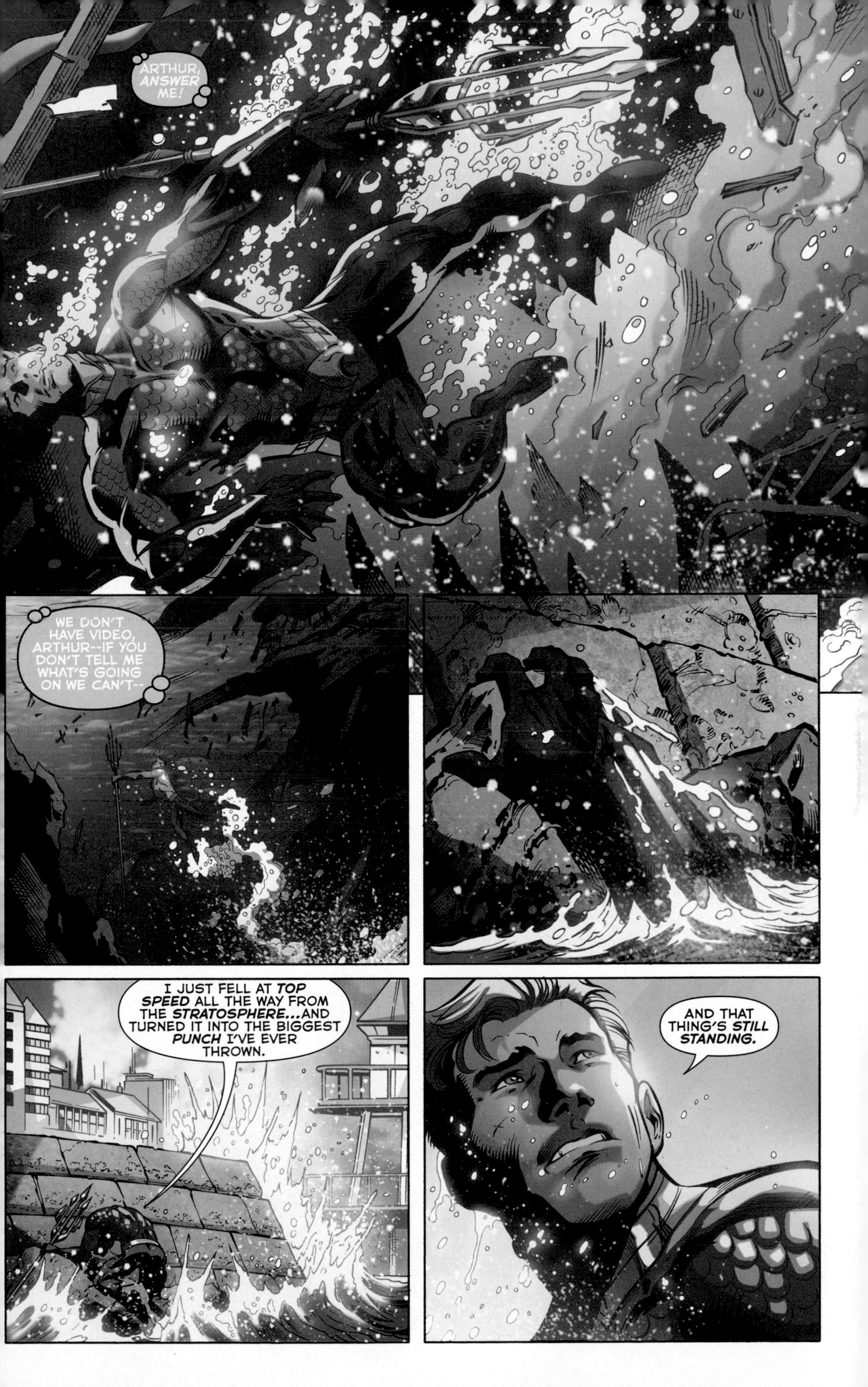
ARTHUR, *ANSWER* ME!
WE DON'T HAVE VIDEO, ARTHUR--IF YOU DON'T TELL ME WHAT'S GOING ON WE CAN'T--
I JUST FELL AT *TOP SPEED* ALL THE WAY FROM THE *STRATOSPHERE...*AND TURNED IT INTO THE BIGGEST *PUNCH* I'VE EVER THROWN.
AND THAT THING'S *STILL STANDING.*

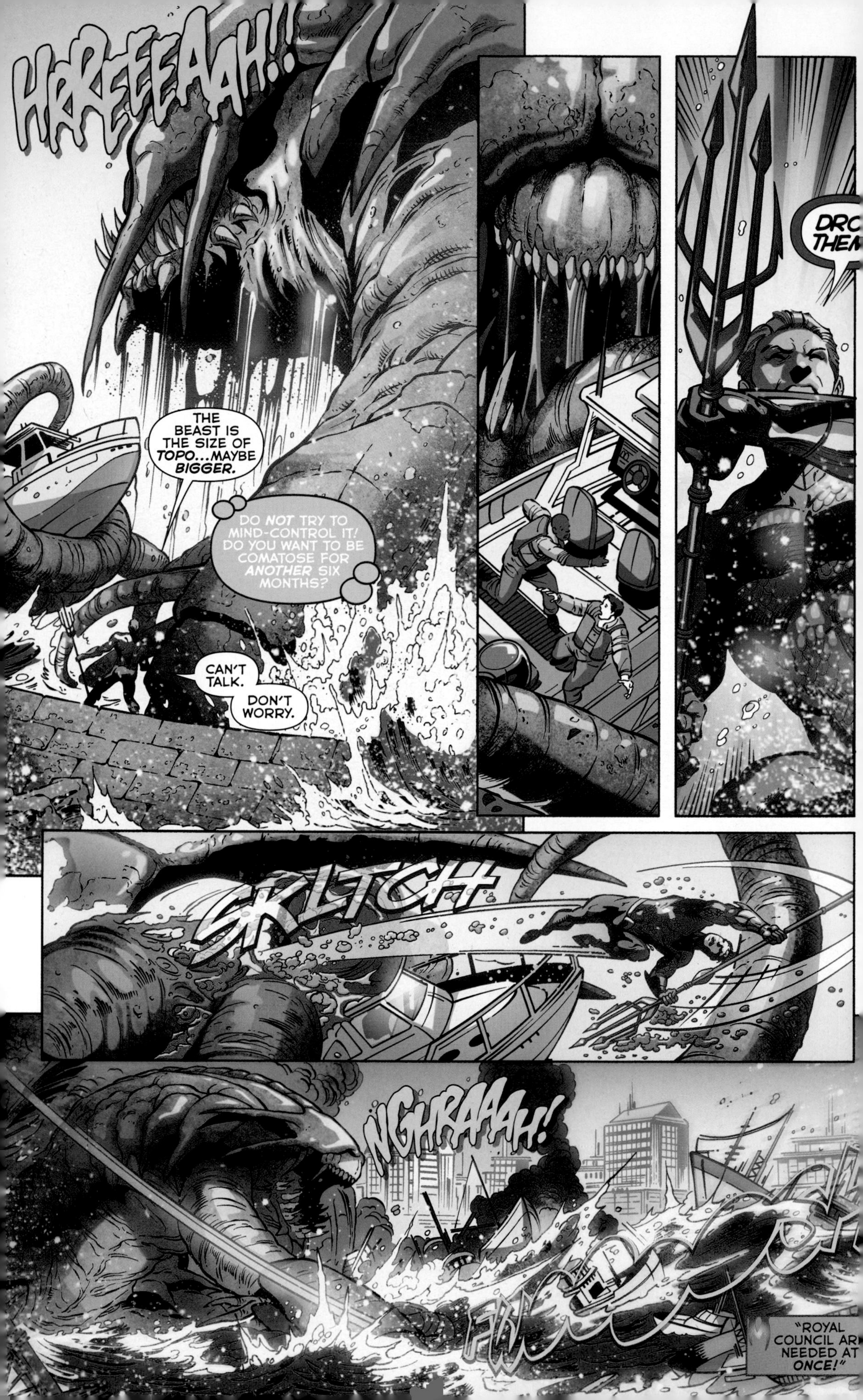
HRREEEAAH!!
THE BEAST IS THE SIZE OF TOPO...MAYBE BIGGER.
DO NOT TRY TO MIND-CONTROL IT! DO YOU WANT TO BE COMATOSE FOR ANOTHER SIX MONTHS?
CAN'T TALK.
DON'T WORRY.
DRO THEM
SKLTCH
NGHRAAAH!
"ROYAL COUNCIL AR NEEDED AT ONCE!"

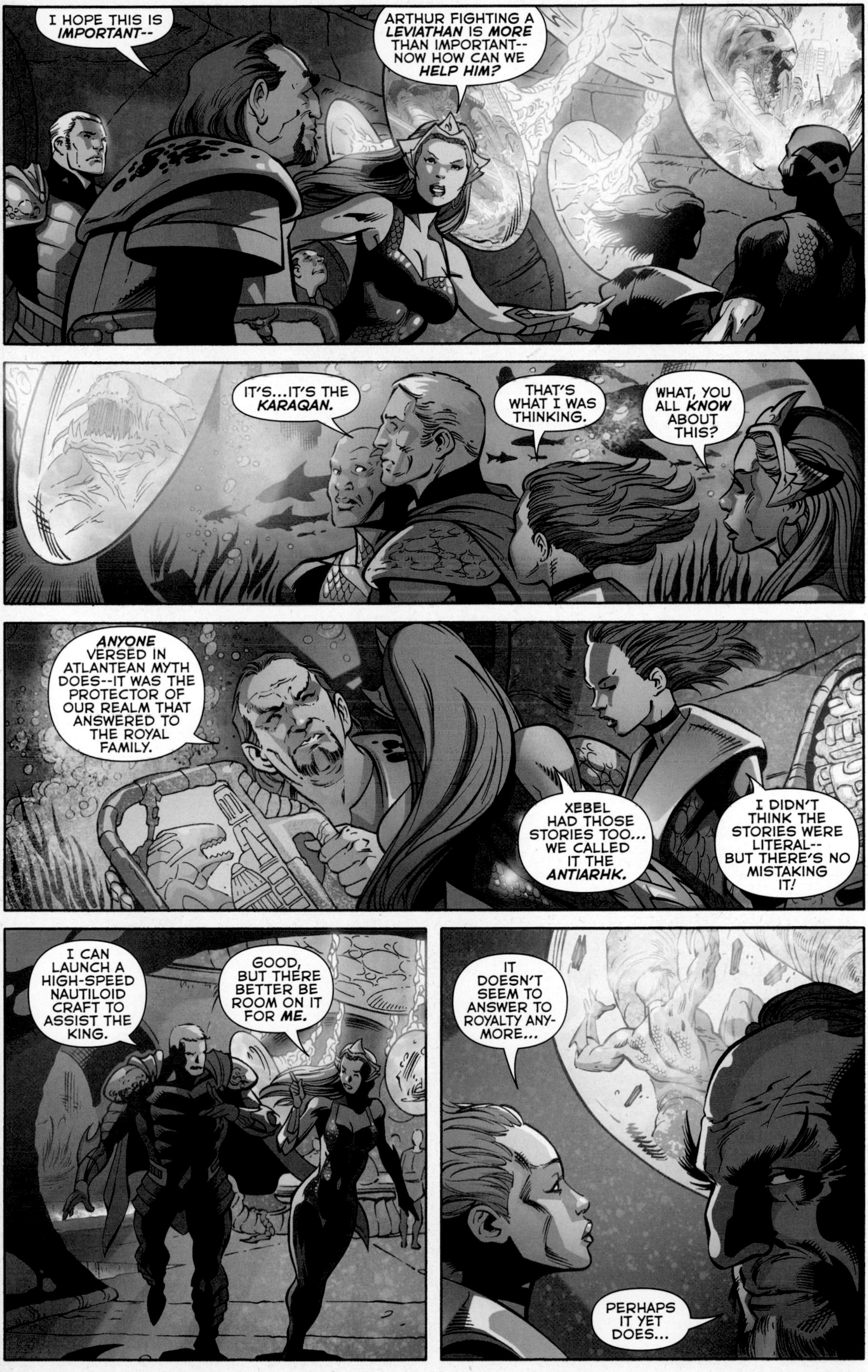
I HOPE THIS IS IMPORTANT--
ARTHUR FIGHTING A LEVIATHAN IS MORE THAN IMPORTANT-- NOW HOW CAN WE HELP HIM?
IT'S...IT'S THE KARAQAN.
THAT'S WHAT I WAS THINKING.
WHAT, YOU ALL KNOW ABOUT THIS?
ANYONE VERSED IN ATLANTEAN MYTH DOES--IT WAS THE PROTECTOR OF OUR REALM THAT ANSWERED TO THE ROYAL FAMILY.
XEBEL HAD THOSE STORIES TOO... WE CALLED IT THE ANTIARHK.
I DIDN'T THINK THE STORIES WERE LITERAL-- BUT THERE'S NO MISTAKING IT!
I CAN LAUNCH A HIGH-SPEED NAUTILOID CRAFT TO ASSIST THE KING.
GOOD, BUT THERE BETTER BE ROOM ON IT FOR ME.
IT DOESN'T SEEM TO ANSWER TO ROYALTY ANY-MORE...
PERHAPS IT YET DOES...

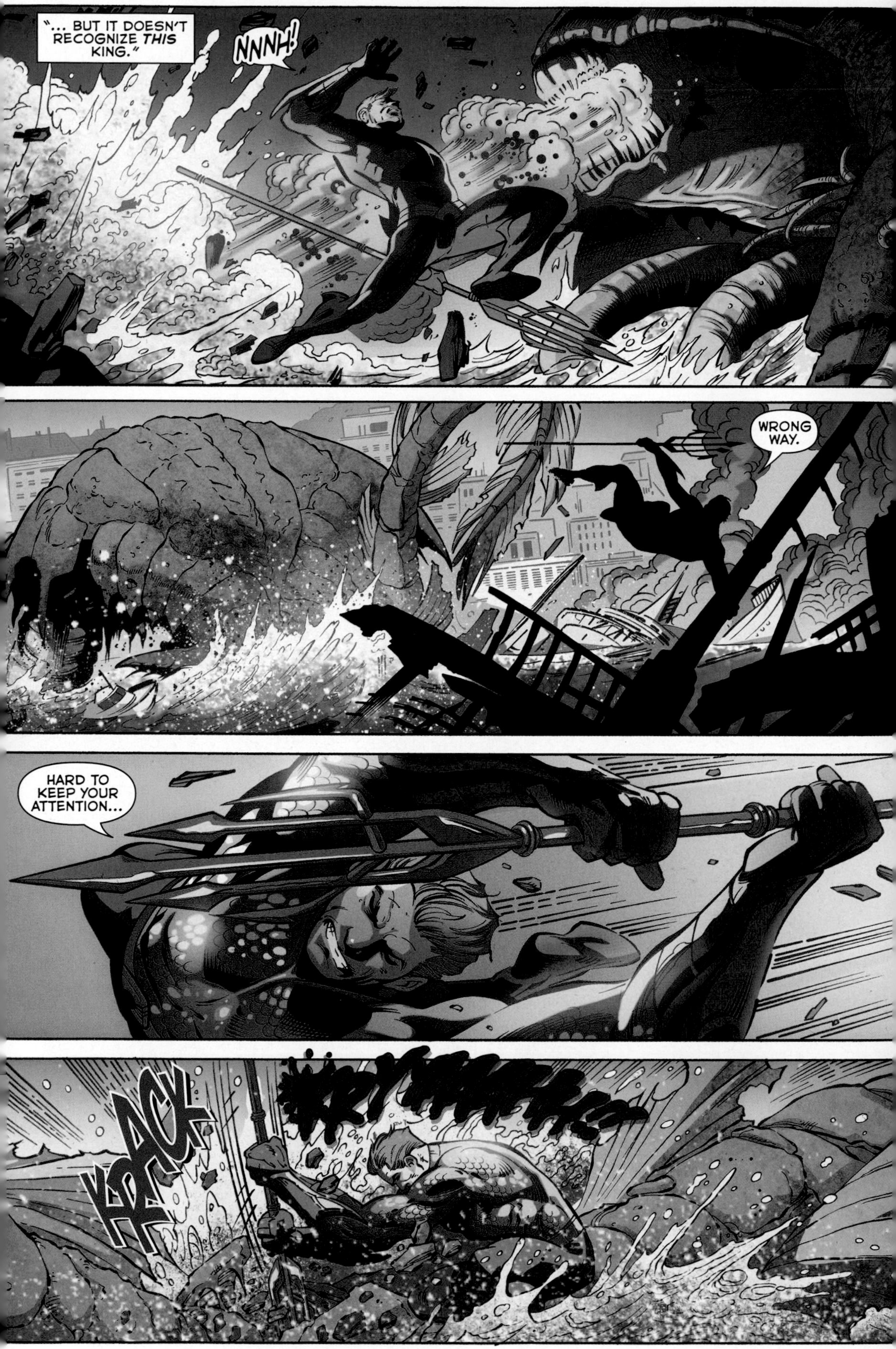
"... BUT IT DOESN'T RECOGNIZE *THIS* KING."
NNNH!
WRONG WAY.
HARD TO KEEP YOUR ATTENTION...
KRACK

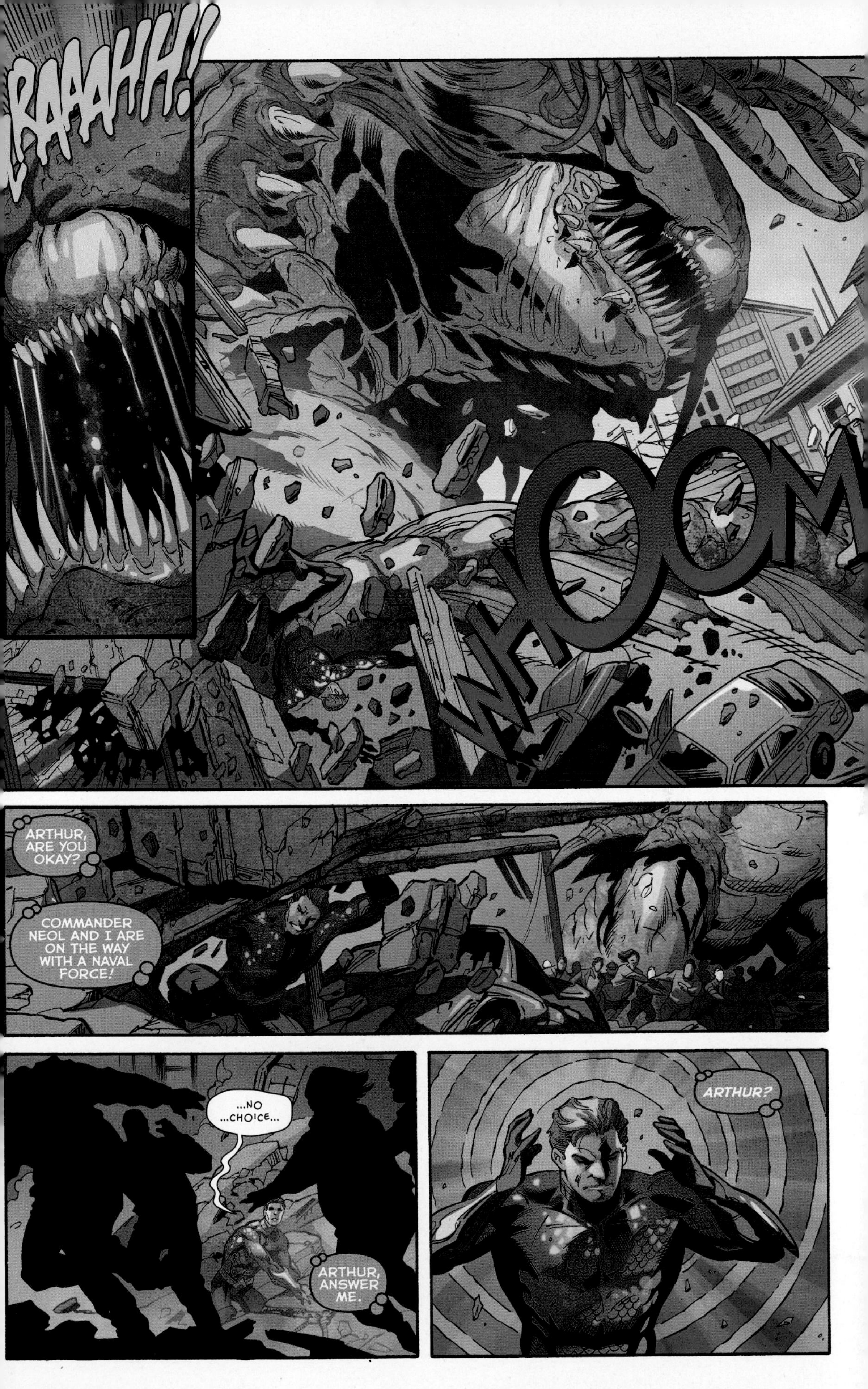
RAAAHH!!
WHOOOM
ARTHUR, ARE YOU OKAY?
COMMANDER NEOL AND I ARE ON THE WAY WITH A NAVAL FORCE!
...NO ...CHOICE...
ARTHUR, ANSWER ME.
ARTHUR?

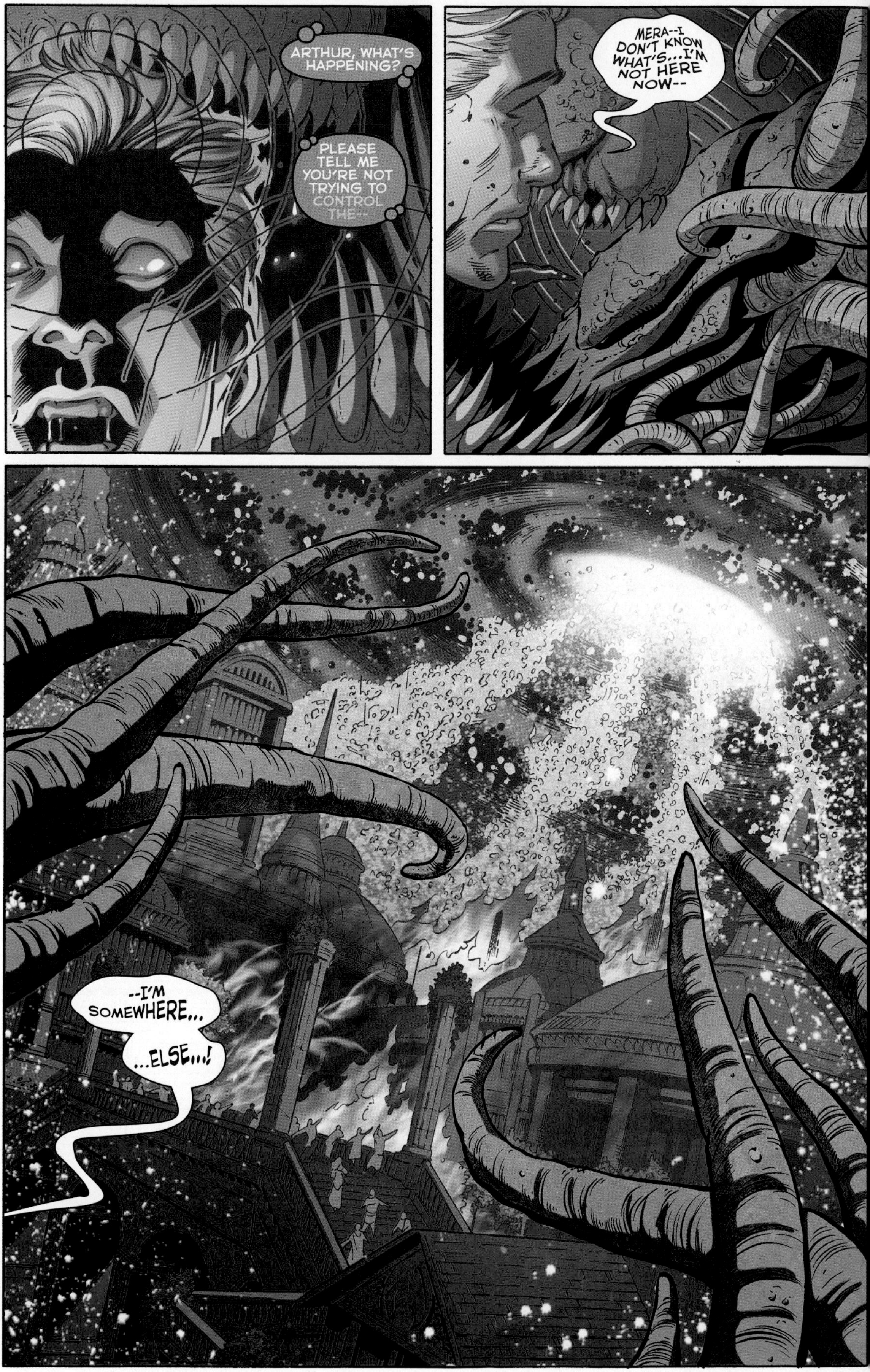
ARTHUR, WHAT'S HAPPENING?
PLEASE TELL ME YOU'RE NOT TRYING TO CONTROL THE--
MERA--I DON'T KNOW WHAT'S...I'M NOT HERE NOW--
--I'M SOMEWHERE...
...ELSE...!

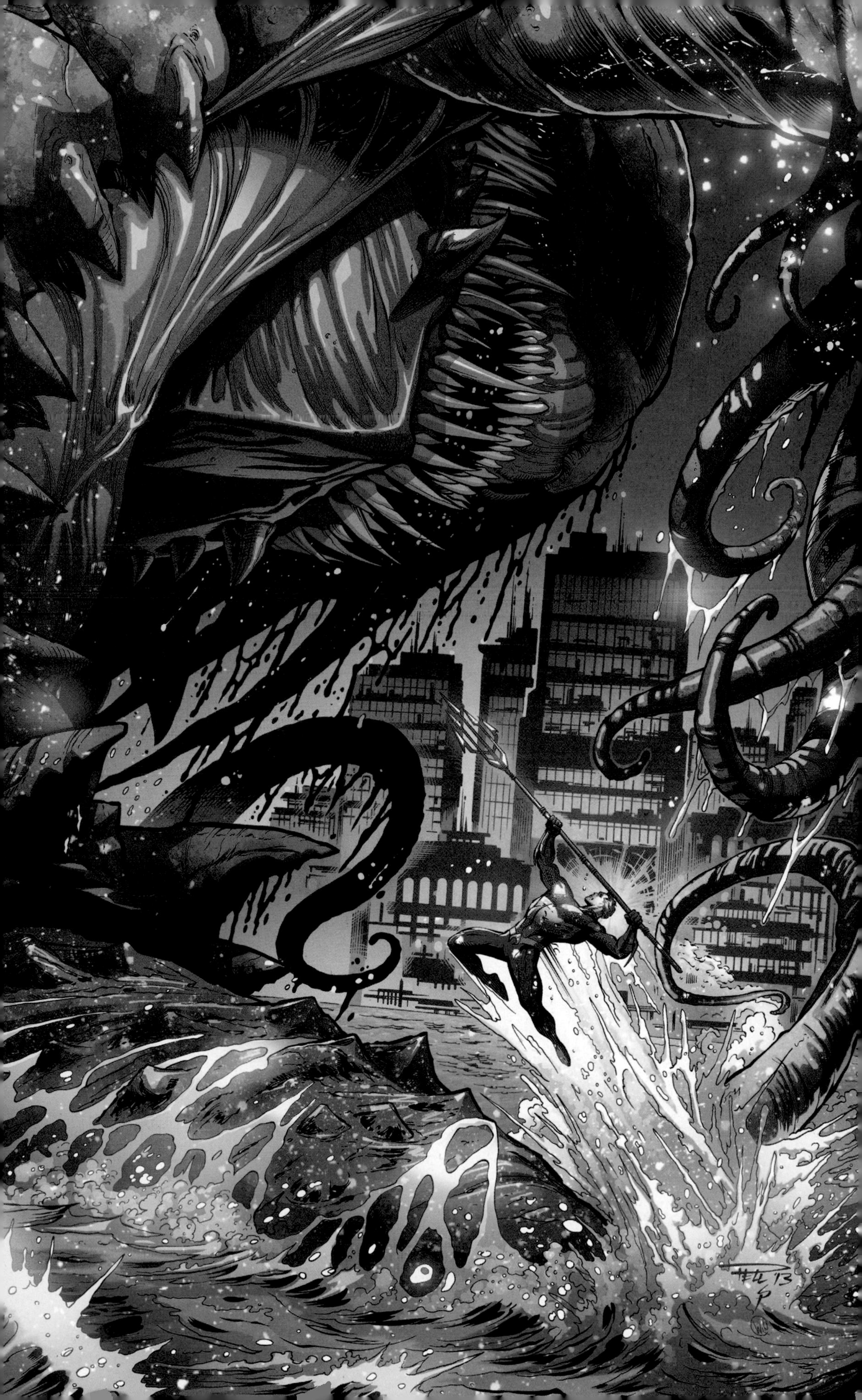

LIFE & DEATH

JEFF PARKER writer **PAUL PELLETIER NETHO DIAZ** pencillers **SEAN PARSONS RUY JOSE** inkers
ROD REIS colorist **STEVE WANDS** letterer cover by **PAUL PELLETIER, SEAN PARSONS** and **WIL QUINTANA**

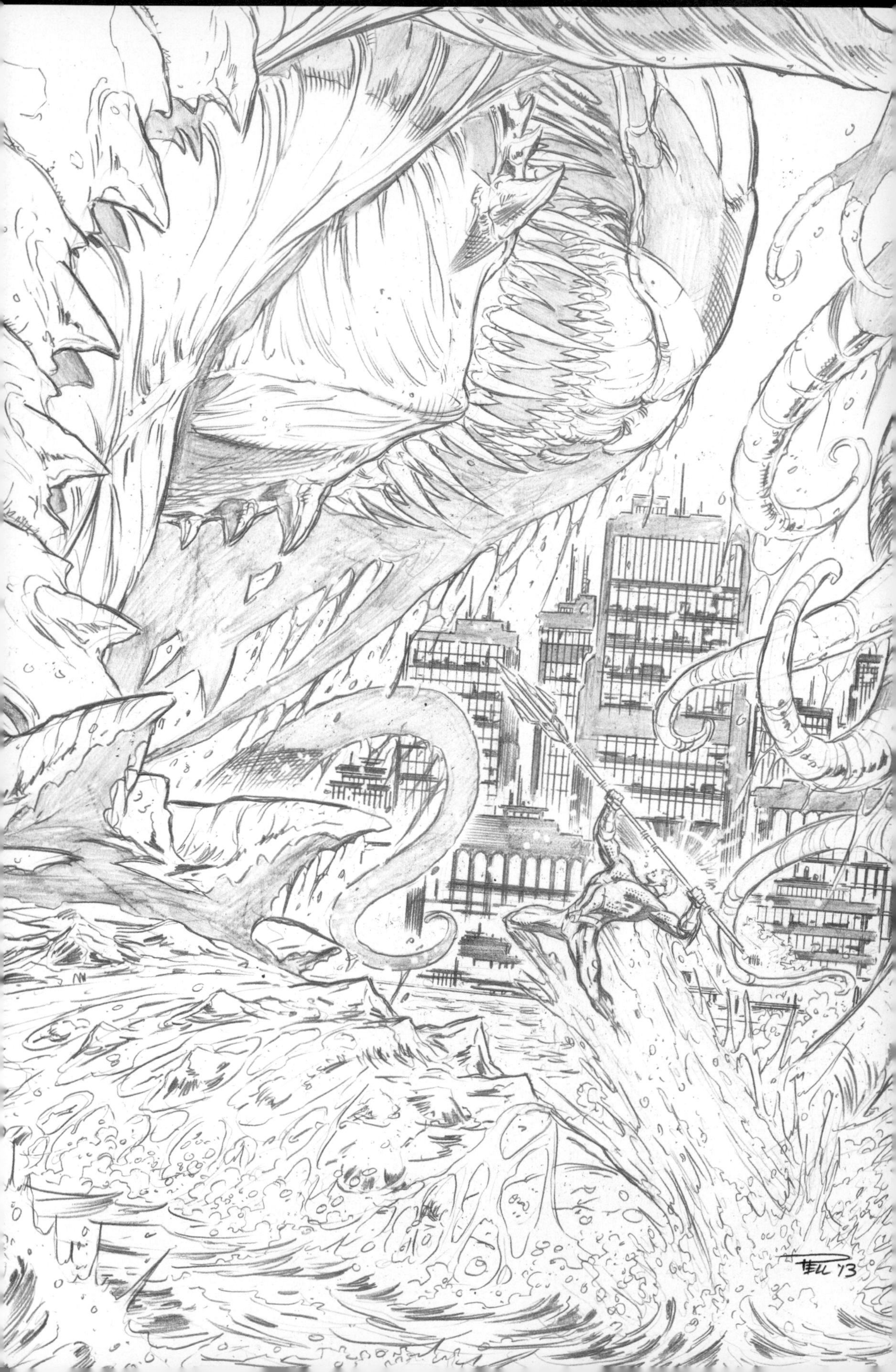

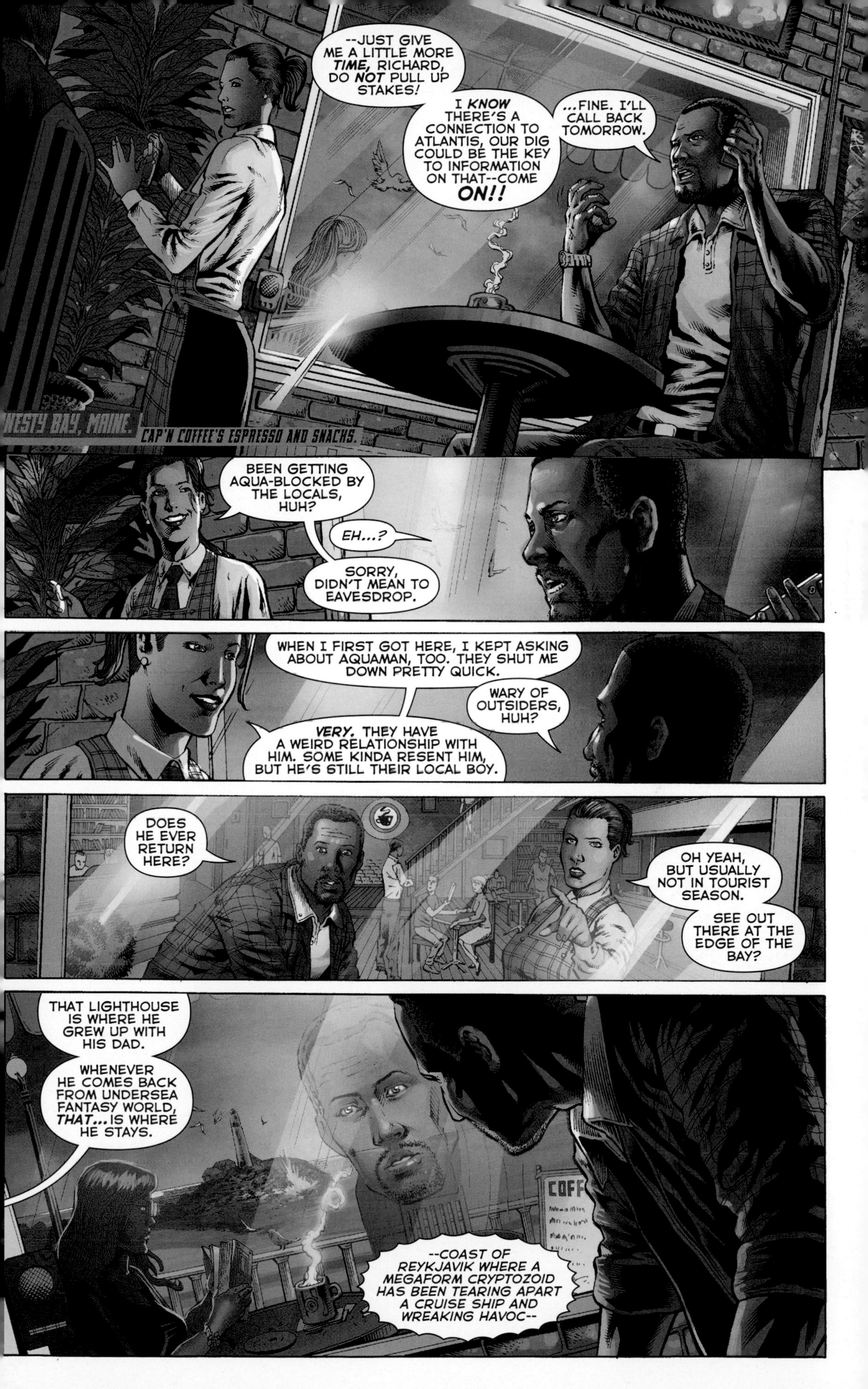

--JUST GIVE ME A LITTLE MORE TIME, RICHARD, DO NOT PULL UP STAKES!
I KNOW THERE'S A CONNECTION TO ATLANTIS, OUR DIG COULD BE THE KEY TO INFORMATION ON THAT--COME ON!!
...FINE. I'LL CALL BACK TOMORROW.
NESTY BAY, MAINE.
CAP'N COFFEE'S ESPRESSO AND SNACKS.
BEEN GETTING AQUA-BLOCKED BY THE LOCALS, HUH?
EH...?
SORRY, DIDN'T MEAN TO EAVESDROP.
WHEN I FIRST GOT HERE, I KEPT ASKING ABOUT AQUAMAN, TOO. THEY SHUT ME DOWN PRETTY QUICK.
WARY OF OUTSIDERS, HUH?
VERY. THEY HAVE A WEIRD RELATIONSHIP WITH HIM. SOME KINDA RESENT HIM, BUT HE'S STILL THEIR LOCAL BOY.
DOES HE EVER RETURN HERE?
OH YEAH, BUT USUALLY NOT IN TOURIST SEASON.
SEE OUT THERE AT THE EDGE OF THE BAY?
THAT LIGHTHOUSE IS WHERE HE GREW UP WITH HIS DAD.
WHENEVER HE COMES BACK FROM UNDERSEA FANTASY WORLD, THAT...IS WHERE HE STAYS.
COFF
--COAST OF REYKJAVIK WHERE A MEGAFORM CRYPTOZOID HAS BEEN TEARING APART A CRUISE SHIP AND WREAKING HAVOC--

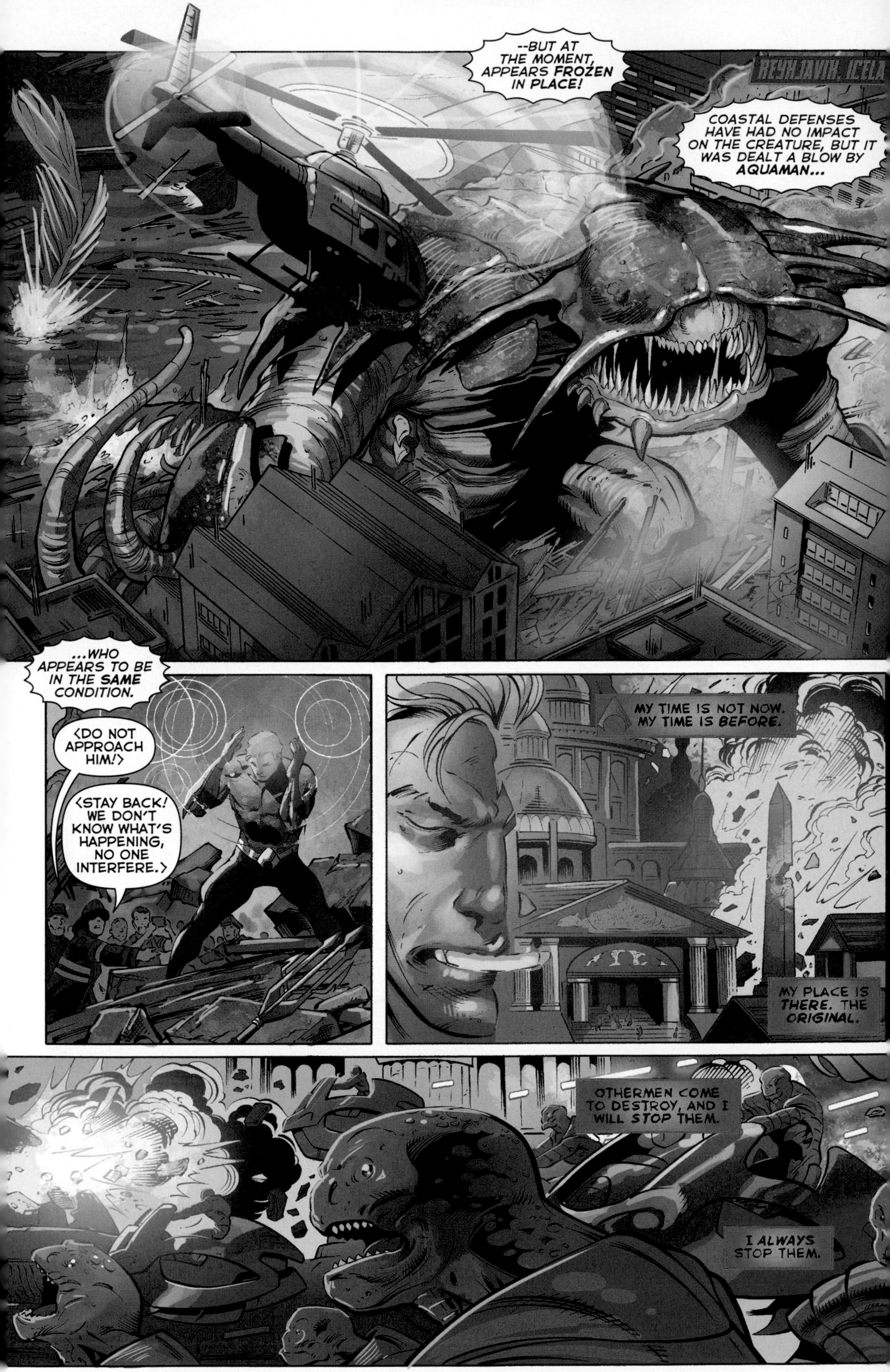
REYKJAVIK, ICELA
--BUT AT THE MOMENT, APPEARS FROZEN IN PLACE!
COASTAL DEFENSES HAVE HAD NO IMPACT ON THE CREATURE, BUT IT WAS DEALT A BLOW BY AQUAMAN...
...WHO APPEARS TO BE IN THE SAME CONDITION.
<DO NOT APPROACH HIM!>
<STAY BACK! WE DON'T KNOW WHAT'S HAPPENING, NO ONE INTERFERE.>
MY TIME IS NOT NOW. MY TIME IS BEFORE.
MY PLACE IS THERE. THE ORIGINAL.
OTHERMEN COME TO DESTROY, AND I WILL STOP THEM.
I ALWAYS STOP THEM.

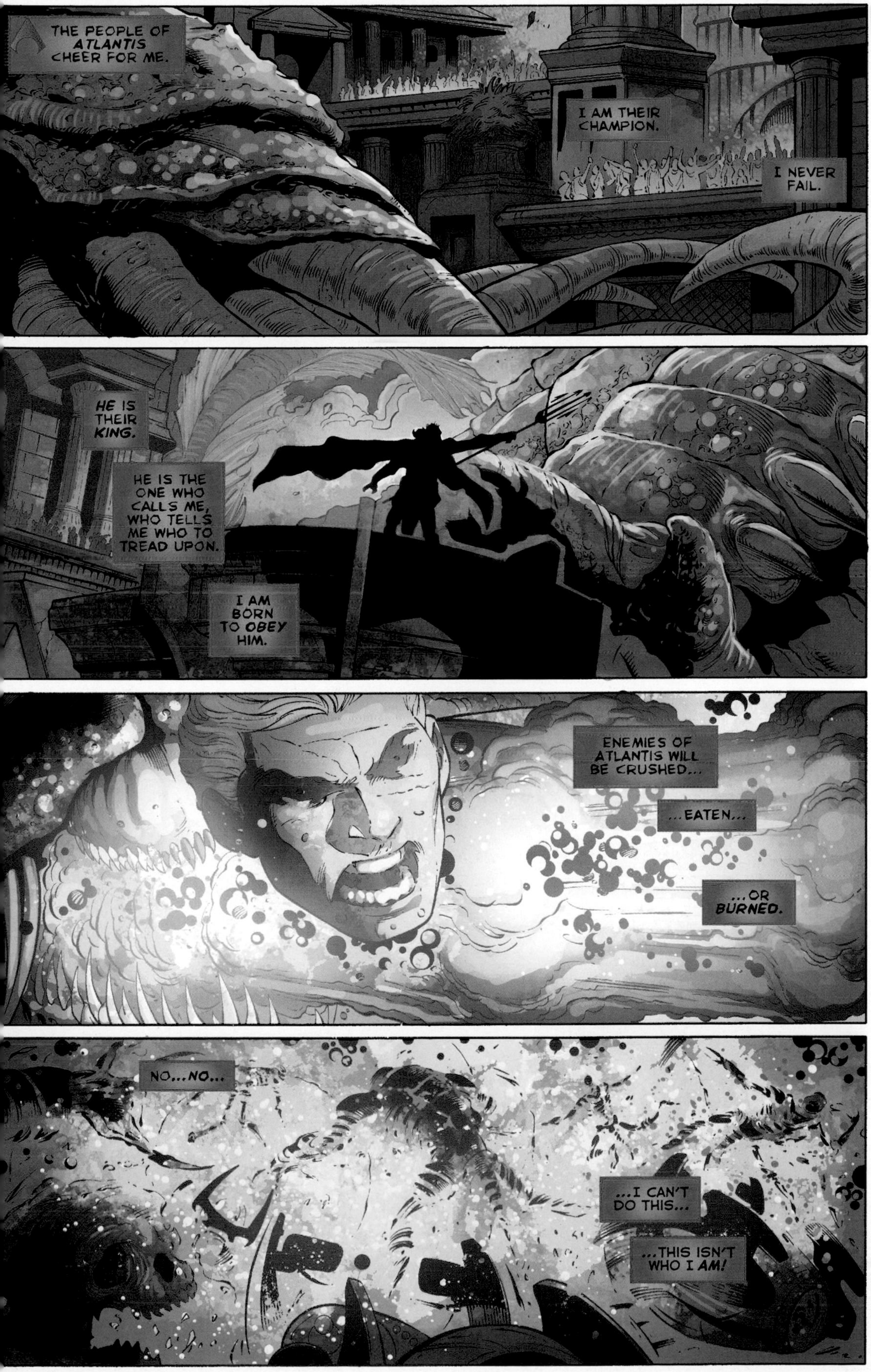
THE PEOPLE OF ATLANTIS CHEER FOR ME.
I AM THEIR CHAMPION.
I NEVER FAIL.
HE IS THEIR KING.
HE IS THE ONE WHO CALLS ME, WHO TELLS ME WHO TO TREAD UPON.
I AM BORN TO OBEY HIM.
ENEMIES OF ATLANTIS WILL BE CRUSHED...
...EATEN...
...OR BURNED.
NO...NO...
...I CAN'T DO THIS...
...THIS ISN'T WHO I AM!

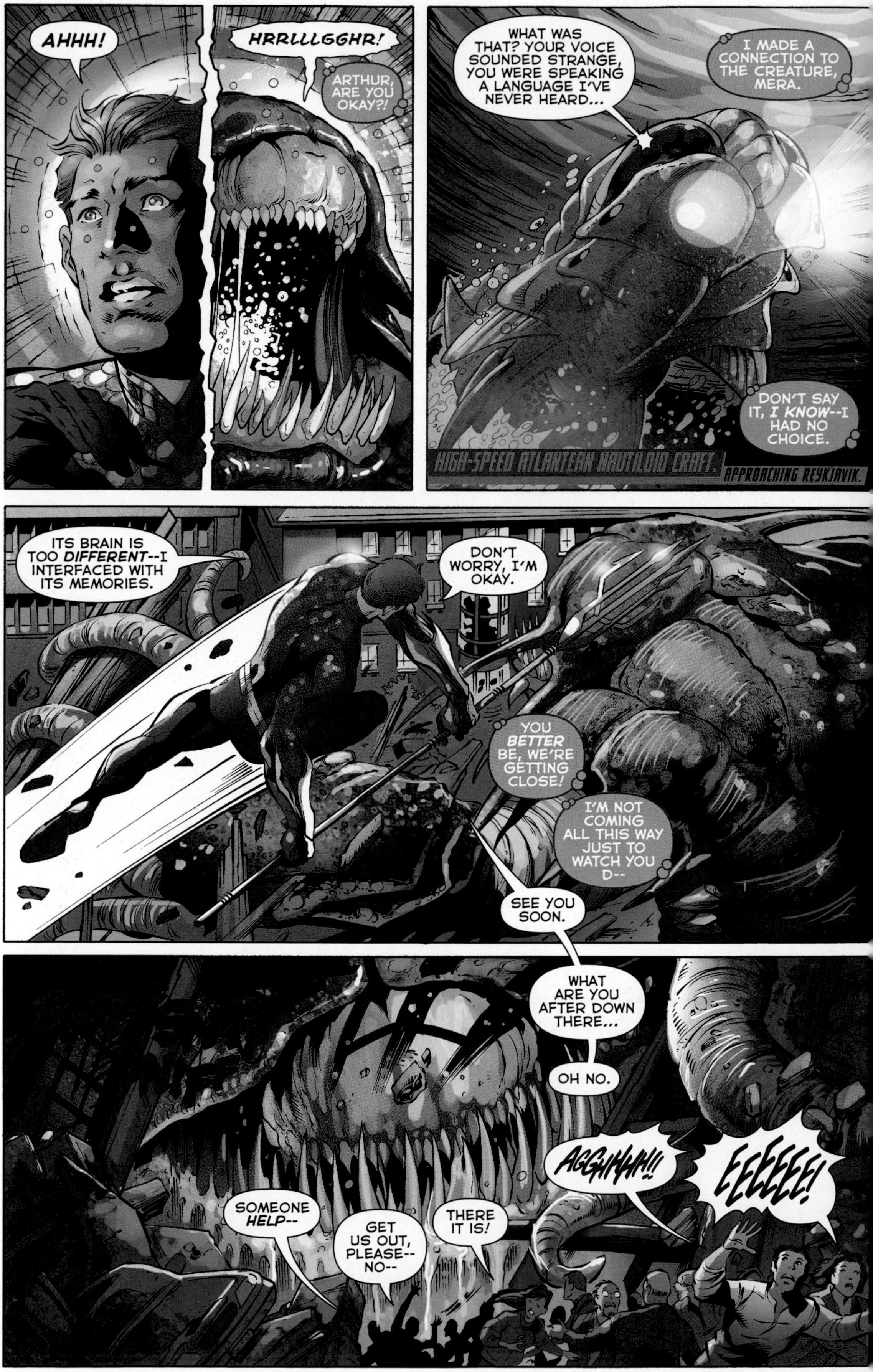
AHHH!
HRRLLLGGHR!
ARTHUR, ARE YOU OKAY?!
HIGH-SPEED ATLANTEAN NAUTILOID CRAFT.
APPROACHING REYKJAVIK.
WHAT WAS THAT? YOUR VOICE SOUNDED STRANGE, YOU WERE SPEAKING A LANGUAGE I'VE NEVER HEARD...
I MADE A CONNECTION TO THE CREATURE, MERA.
DON'T SAY IT, I KNOW--I HAD NO CHOICE.
ITS BRAIN IS TOO DIFFERENT--I INTERFACED WITH ITS MEMORIES.
DON'T WORRY, I'M OKAY.
YOU BETTER BE, WE'RE GETTING CLOSE!
I'M NOT COMING ALL THIS WAY JUST TO WATCH YOU D--
SEE YOU SOON.
WHAT ARE YOU AFTER DOWN THERE...
OH NO.
SOMEONE HELP--
GET US OUT, PLEASE-- NO--
THERE IT IS!
AGGHHHH!!
EEEEEE!

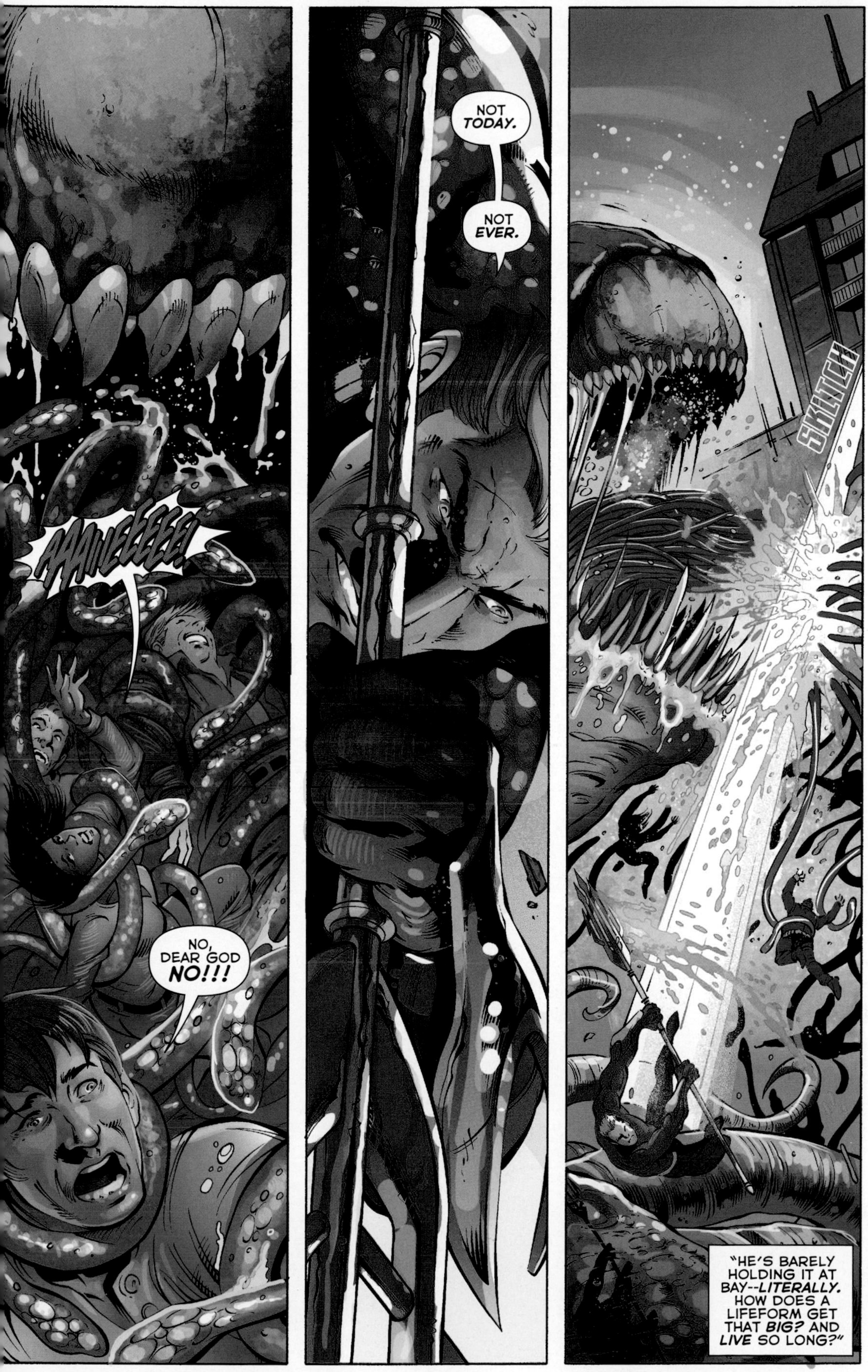
AAAIIEEEEE!
NO, DEAR GOD NO!!!
NOT TODAY.
NOT EVER.
SKLTCH
"HE'S BARELY HOLDING IT AT BAY--LITERALLY. HOW DOES A LIFEFORM GET THAT BIG? AND LIVE SO LONG?"

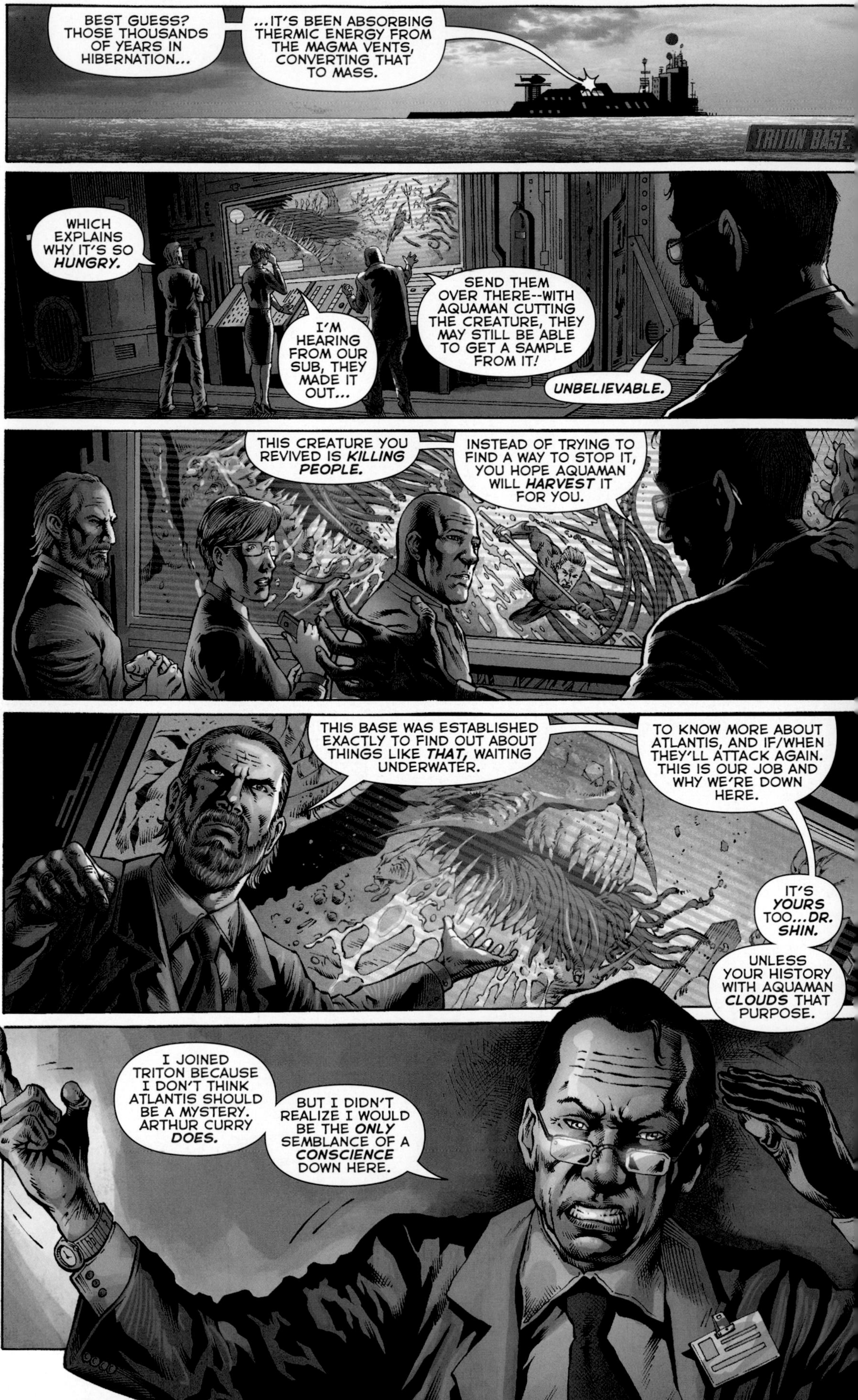
BEST GUESS? THOSE THOUSANDS OF YEARS IN HIBERNATION...
...IT'S BEEN ABSORBING THERMIC ENERGY FROM THE MAGMA VENTS, CONVERTING THAT TO MASS.
TRITON BASE.
WHICH EXPLAINS WHY IT'S SO HUNGRY.
I'M HEARING FROM OUR SUB, THEY MADE IT OUT...
SEND THEM OVER THERE--WITH AQUAMAN CUTTING THE CREATURE, THEY MAY STILL BE ABLE TO GET A SAMPLE FROM IT!
UNBELIEVABLE.
THIS CREATURE YOU REVIVED IS KILLING PEOPLE.
INSTEAD OF TRYING TO FIND A WAY TO STOP IT, YOU HOPE AQUAMAN WILL HARVEST IT FOR YOU.
THIS BASE WAS ESTABLISHED EXACTLY TO FIND OUT ABOUT THINGS LIKE THAT, WAITING UNDERWATER.
TO KNOW MORE ABOUT ATLANTIS, AND IF/WHEN THEY'LL ATTACK AGAIN. THIS IS OUR JOB AND WHY WE'RE DOWN HERE.
IT'S YOURS TOO...DR. SHIN.
UNLESS YOUR HISTORY WITH AQUAMAN CLOUDS THAT PURPOSE.
I JOINED TRITON BECAUSE I DON'T THINK ATLANTIS SHOULD BE A MYSTERY. ARTHUR CURRY DOES.
BUT I DIDN'T REALIZE I WOULD BE THE ONLY SEMBLANCE OF A CONSCIENCE DOWN HERE.

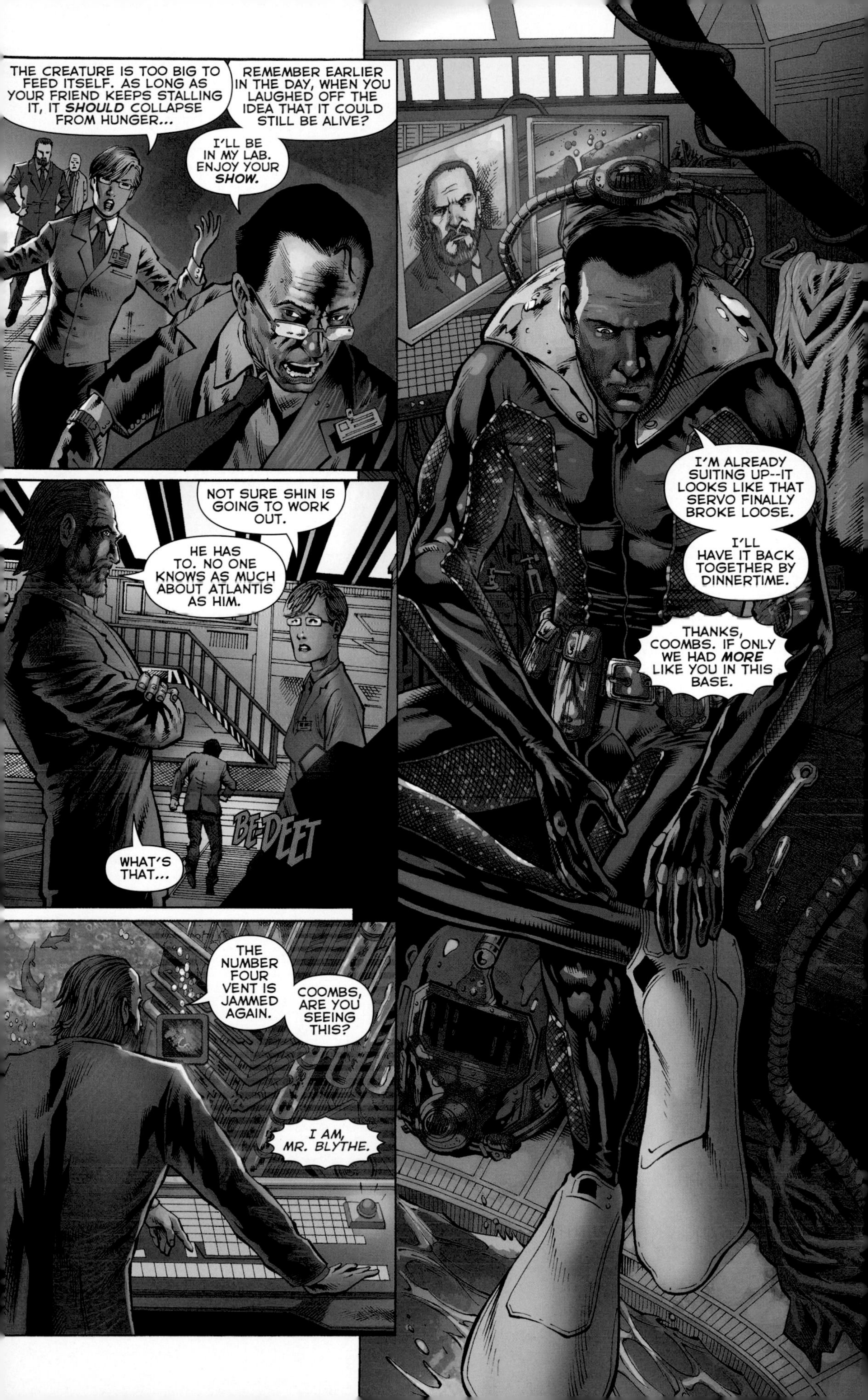
THE CREATURE IS TOO BIG TO FEED ITSELF. AS LONG AS YOUR FRIEND KEEPS STALLING IT, IT SHOULD COLLAPSE FROM HUNGER...
REMEMBER EARLIER IN THE DAY, WHEN YOU LAUGHED OFF THE IDEA THAT IT COULD STILL BE ALIVE?
I'LL BE IN MY LAB. ENJOY YOUR SHOW.
NOT SURE SHIN IS GOING TO WORK OUT.
HE HAS TO. NO ONE KNOWS AS MUCH ABOUT ATLANTIS AS HIM.
BE-DEET
WHAT'S THAT...
THE NUMBER FOUR VENT IS JAMMED AGAIN.
COOMBS, ARE YOU SEEING THIS?
I AM, MR. BLYTHE.
I'M ALREADY SUITING UP--IT LOOKS LIKE THAT SERVO FINALLY BROKE LOOSE.
I'LL HAVE IT BACK TOGETHER BY DINNERTIME.
THANKS, COOMBS. IF ONLY WE HAD MORE LIKE YOU IN THIS BASE.

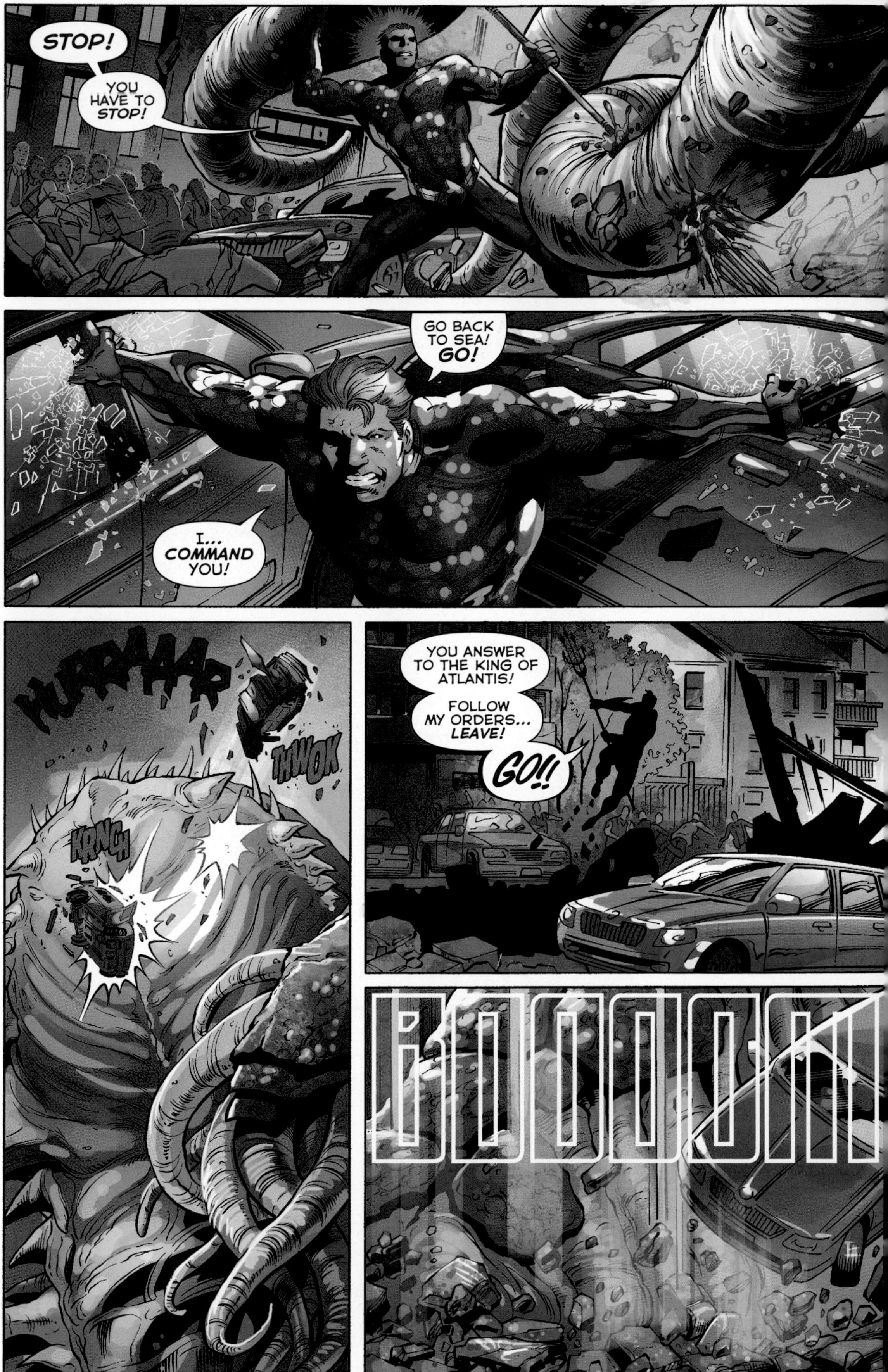
STOP!
YOU HAVE TO STOP!
GO BACK TO SEA! GO!
I... COMMAND YOU!
HURRAAAR
THWOK
KRNCH
YOU ANSWER TO THE KING OF ATLANTIS!
FOLLOW MY ORDERS... LEAVE!
GO!!

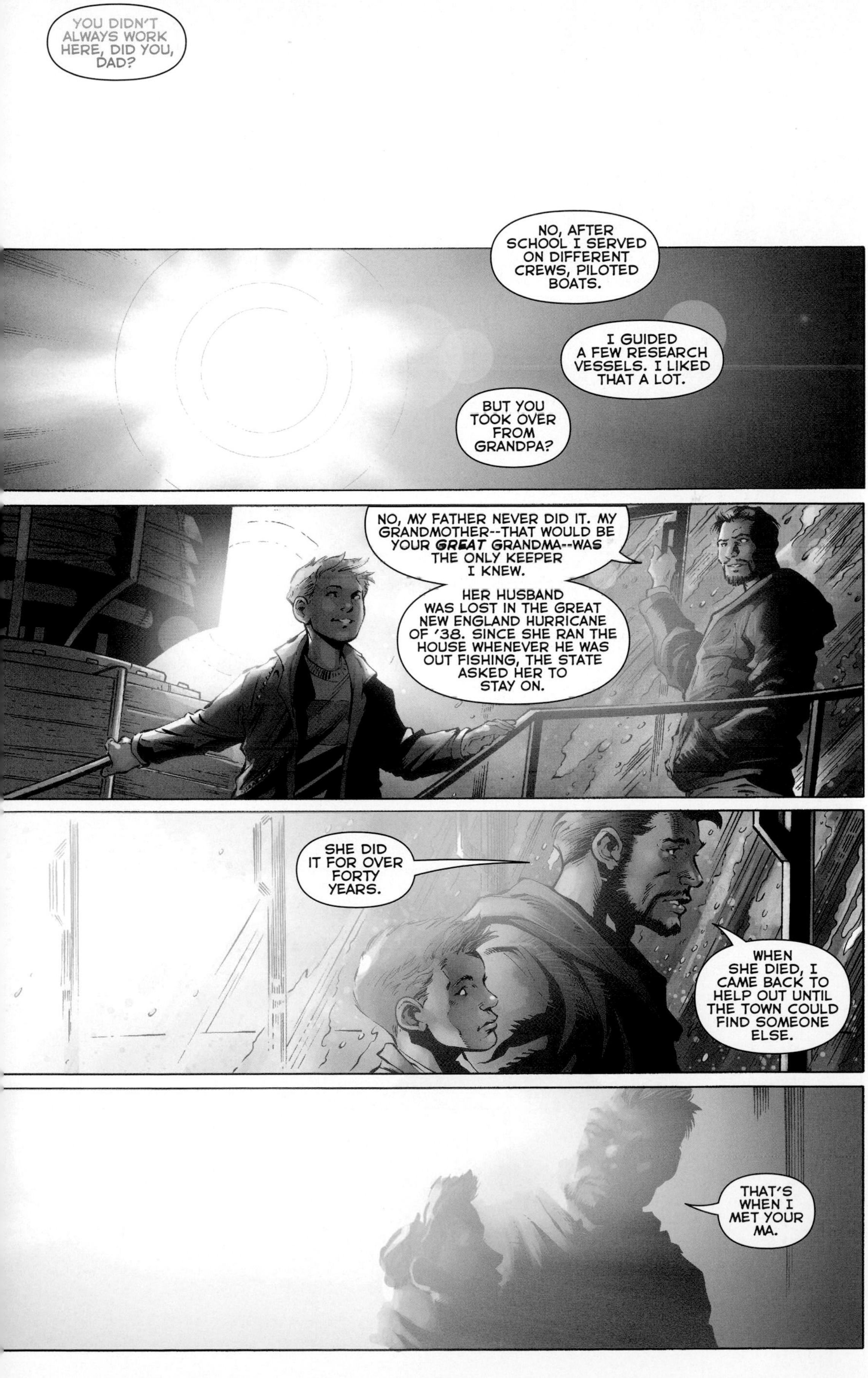
YOU DIDN'T ALWAYS WORK HERE, DID YOU, DAD?
NO, AFTER SCHOOL I SERVED ON DIFFERENT CREWS, PILOTED BOATS.
I GUIDED A FEW RESEARCH VESSELS. I LIKED THAT A LOT.
BUT YOU TOOK OVER FROM GRANDPA?
NO, MY FATHER NEVER DID IT. MY GRANDMOTHER--THAT WOULD BE YOUR GREAT GRANDMA--WAS THE ONLY KEEPER I KNEW.
HER HUSBAND WAS LOST IN THE GREAT NEW ENGLAND HURRICANE OF '38. SINCE SHE RAN THE HOUSE WHENEVER HE WAS OUT FISHING, THE STATE ASKED HER TO STAY ON.
SHE DID IT FOR OVER FORTY YEARS.
WHEN SHE DIED, I CAME BACK TO HELP OUT UNTIL THE TOWN COULD FIND SOMEONE ELSE.
THAT'S WHEN I MET YOUR MA.

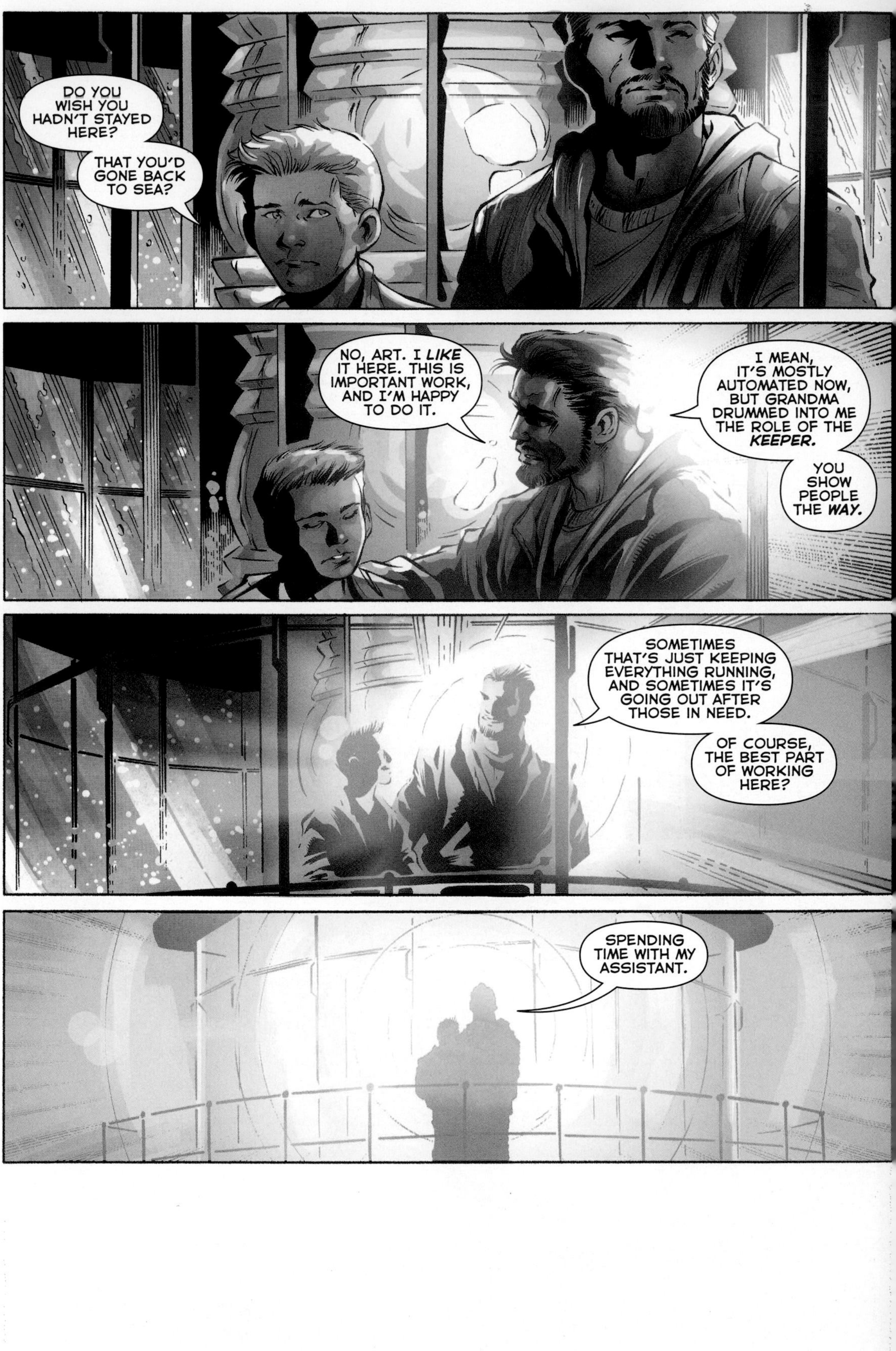
DO YOU WISH YOU HADN'T STAYED HERE?
THAT YOU'D GONE BACK TO SEA?
NO, ART. I *LIKE* IT HERE. THIS IS IMPORTANT WORK, AND I'M HAPPY TO DO IT.
I MEAN, IT'S MOSTLY AUTOMATED NOW, BUT GRANDMA DRUMMED INTO ME THE ROLE OF THE *KEEPER.*
YOU SHOW PEOPLE THE *WAY.*
SOMETIMES THAT'S JUST KEEPING EVERYTHING RUNNING, AND SOMETIMES IT'S GOING OUT AFTER THOSE IN NEED.
OF COURSE, THE BEST PART OF WORKING HERE?
SPENDING TIME WITH MY ASSISTANT.

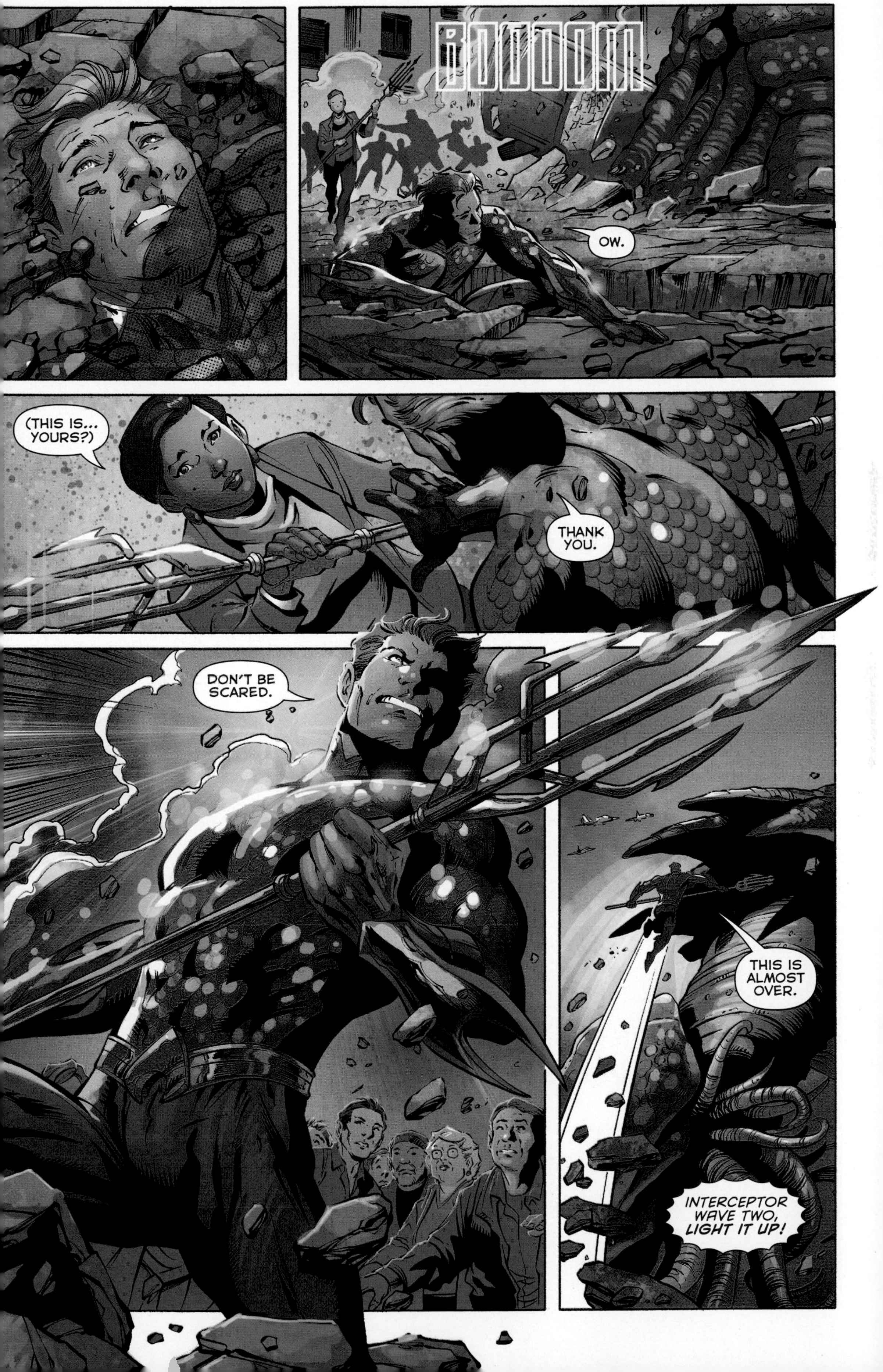
BOOOOM
OW.
(THIS IS... YOURS?)
THANK YOU.
DON'T BE SCARED.
THIS IS ALMOST OVER.
INTERCEPTOR WAVE TWO, *LIGHT IT UP!*

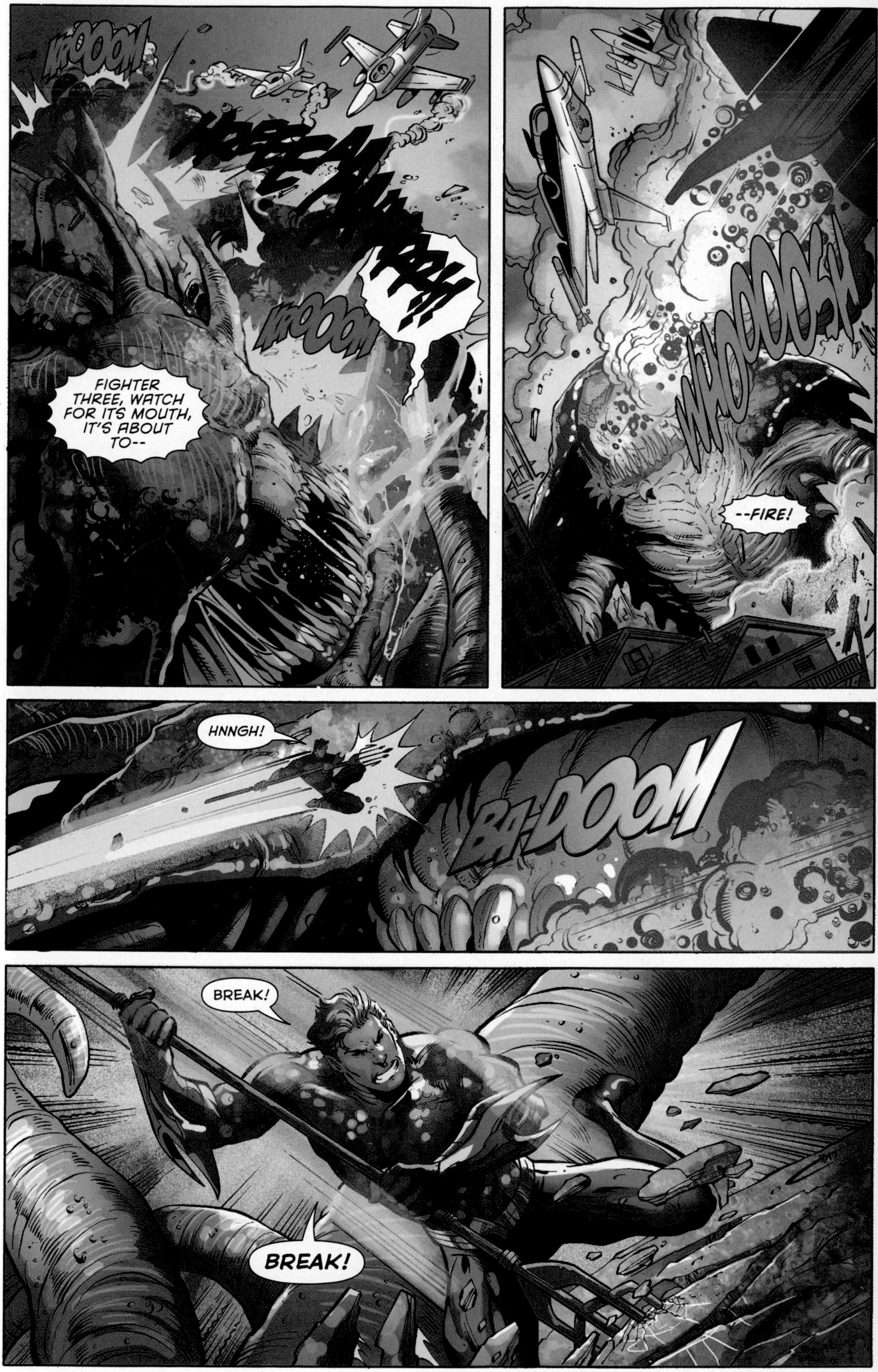
FIGHTER THREE, WATCH FOR ITS MOUTH, IT'S ABOUT TO--
--FIRE!
HNNGH!
BA-DOOM
BREAK!
BREAK!

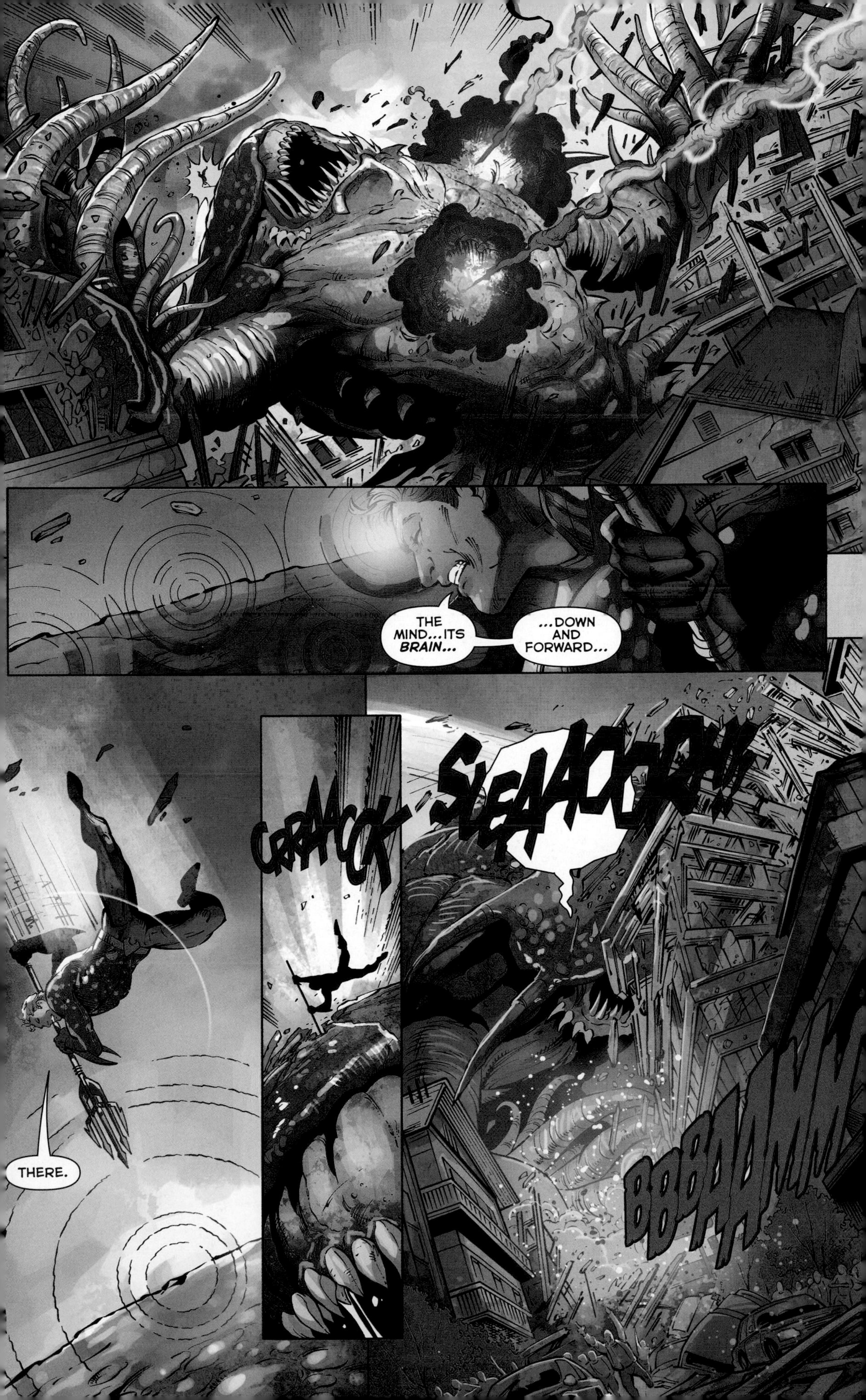
THE MIND...ITS BRAIN...
...DOWN AND FORWARD...
THERE.
CRRAACK
SLEAAOOOH!!
BBBAAMM

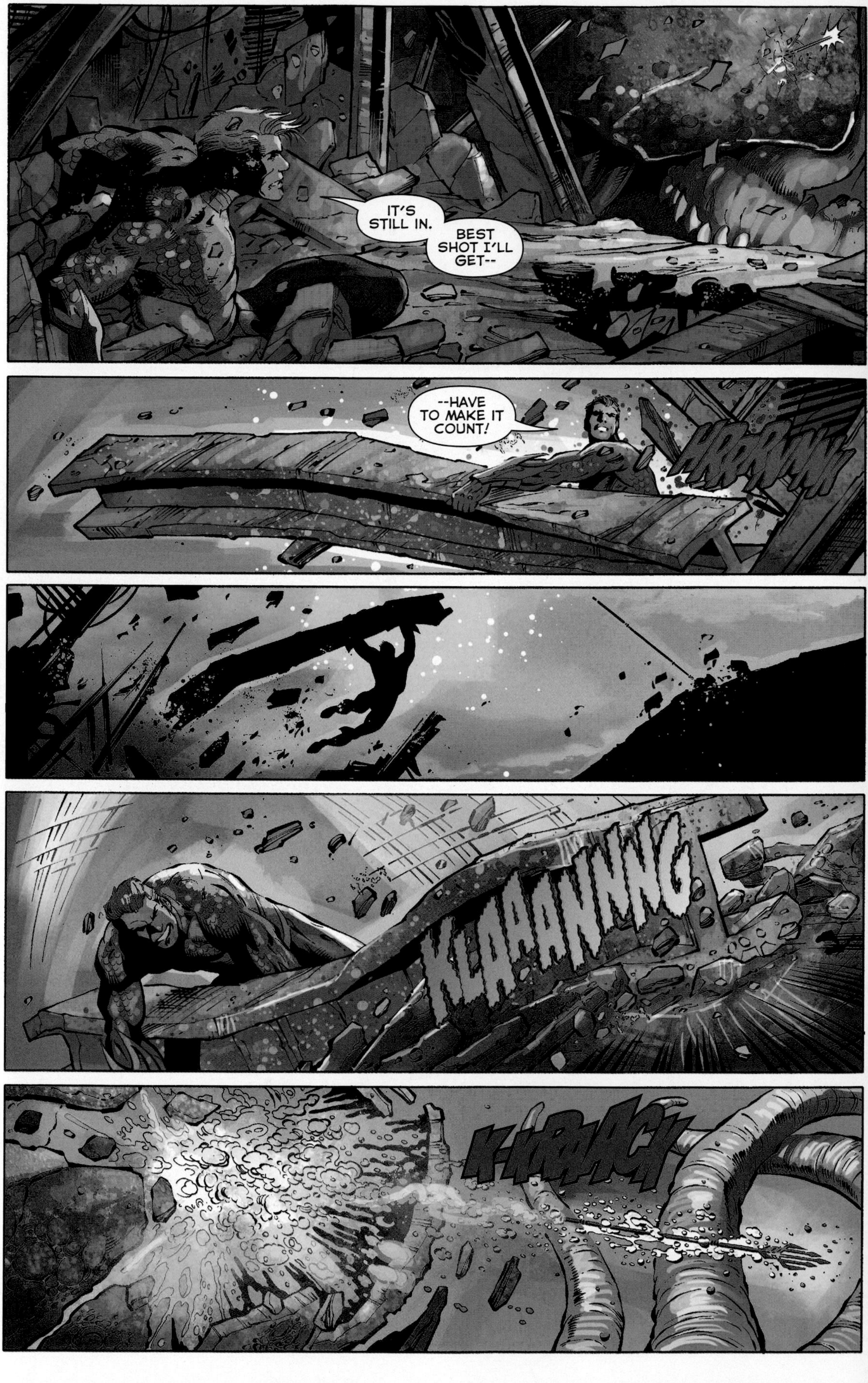
IT'S STILL IN.
BEST SHOT I'LL GET--
--HAVE TO MAKE IT COUNT!
KLAAANNNG
K-KRAACK

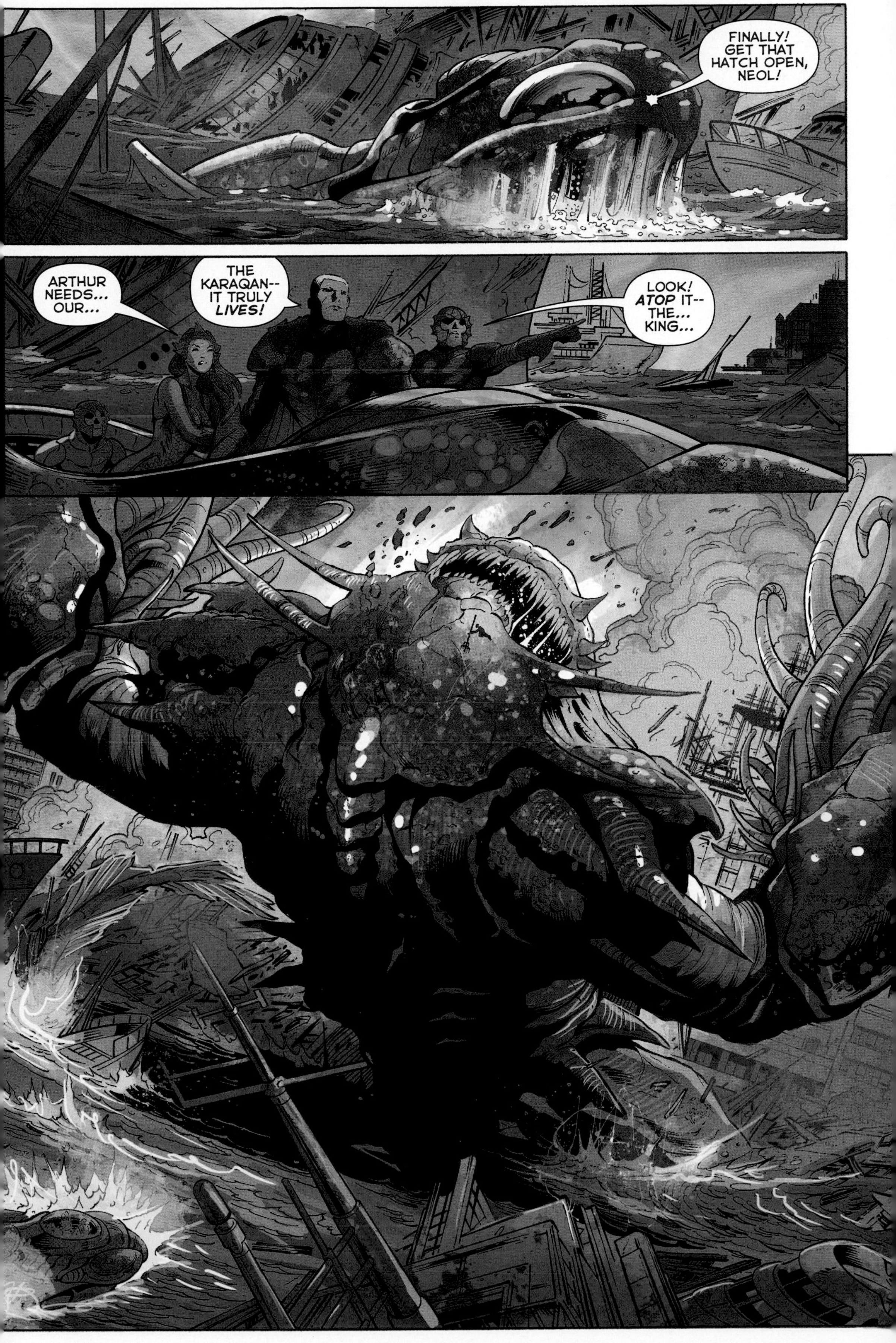
FINALLY! GET THAT HATCH OPEN, NEOL!
ARTHUR NEEDS... OUR...
THE KARAQAN-- IT TRULY LIVES!
LOOK! ATOP IT-- THE... KING...

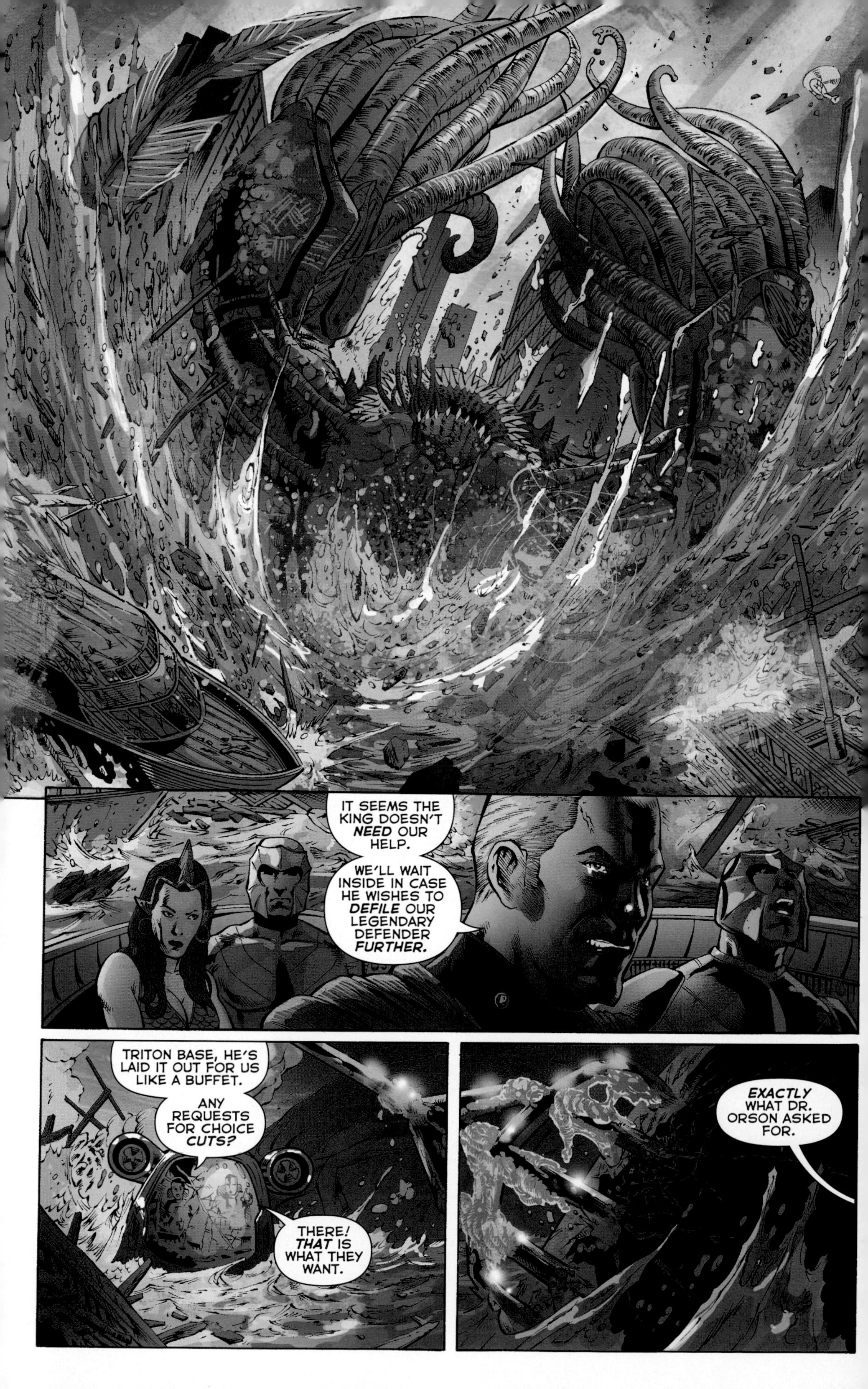
IT SEEMS THE KING DOESN'T NEED OUR HELP.
WE'LL WAIT INSIDE IN CASE HE WISHES TO DEFILE OUR LEGENDARY DEFENDER FURTHER.
TRITON BASE, HE'S LAID IT OUT FOR US LIKE A BUFFET.
ANY REQUESTS FOR CHOICE CUTS?
THERE! THAT IS WHAT THEY WANT.
EXACTLY WHAT DR. ORSON ASKED FOR.

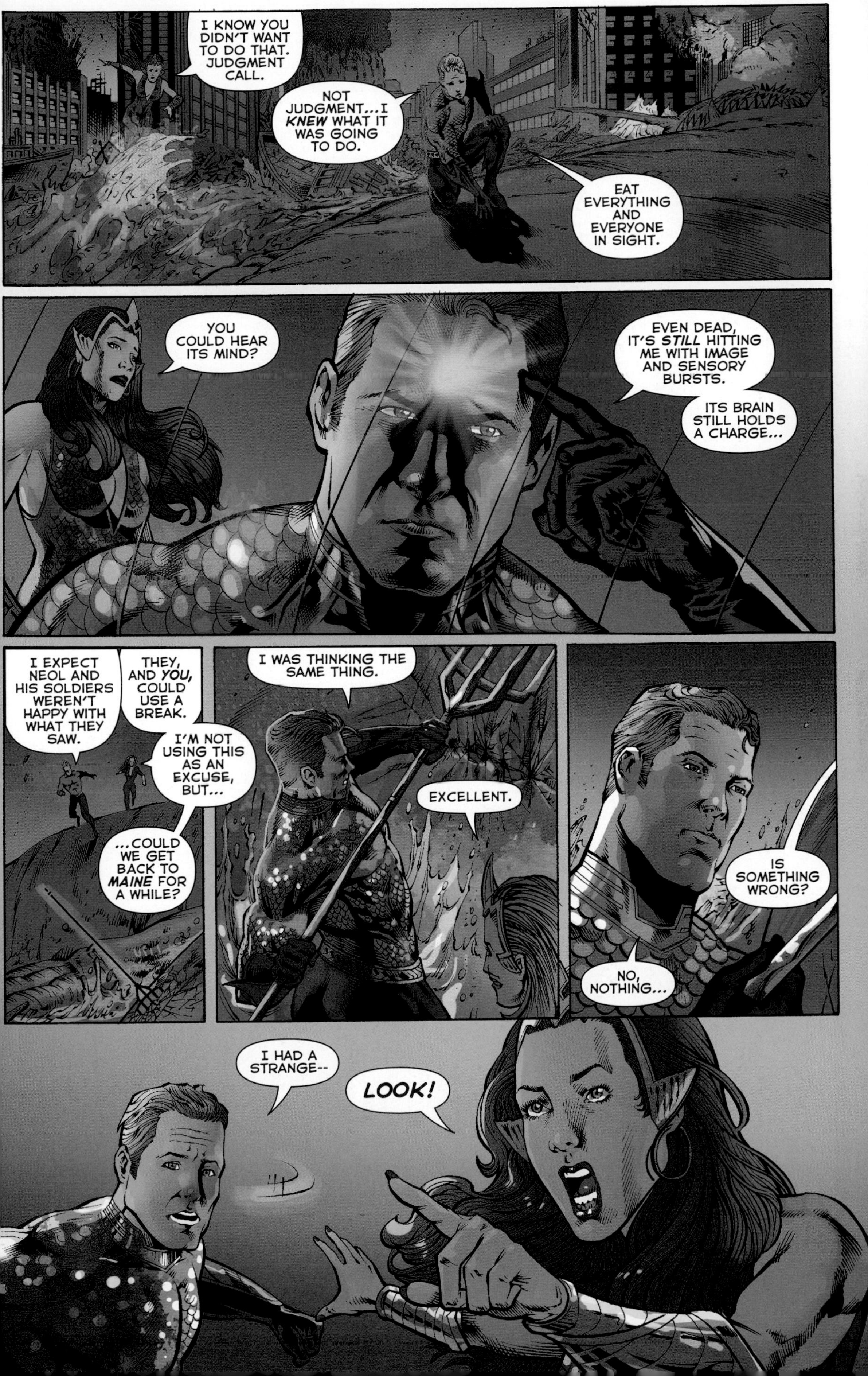
I KNOW YOU DIDN'T WANT TO DO THAT. JUDGMENT CALL.
NOT JUDGMENT...I *KNEW* WHAT IT WAS GOING TO DO.
EAT EVERYTHING AND EVERYONE IN SIGHT.
YOU COULD HEAR ITS MIND?
EVEN DEAD, IT'S *STILL* HITTING ME WITH IMAGE AND SENSORY BURSTS.
ITS BRAIN STILL HOLDS A CHARGE...
I EXPECT NEOL AND HIS SOLDIERS WEREN'T HAPPY WITH WHAT THEY SAW.
THEY, AND *YOU*, COULD USE A BREAK.
I'M NOT USING THIS AS AN EXCUSE, BUT...
...COULD WE GET BACK TO *MAINE* FOR A WHILE?
I WAS THINKING THE SAME THING.
EXCELLENT.
IS SOMETHING WRONG?
NO, NOTHING...
I HAD A STRANGE--
LOOK!

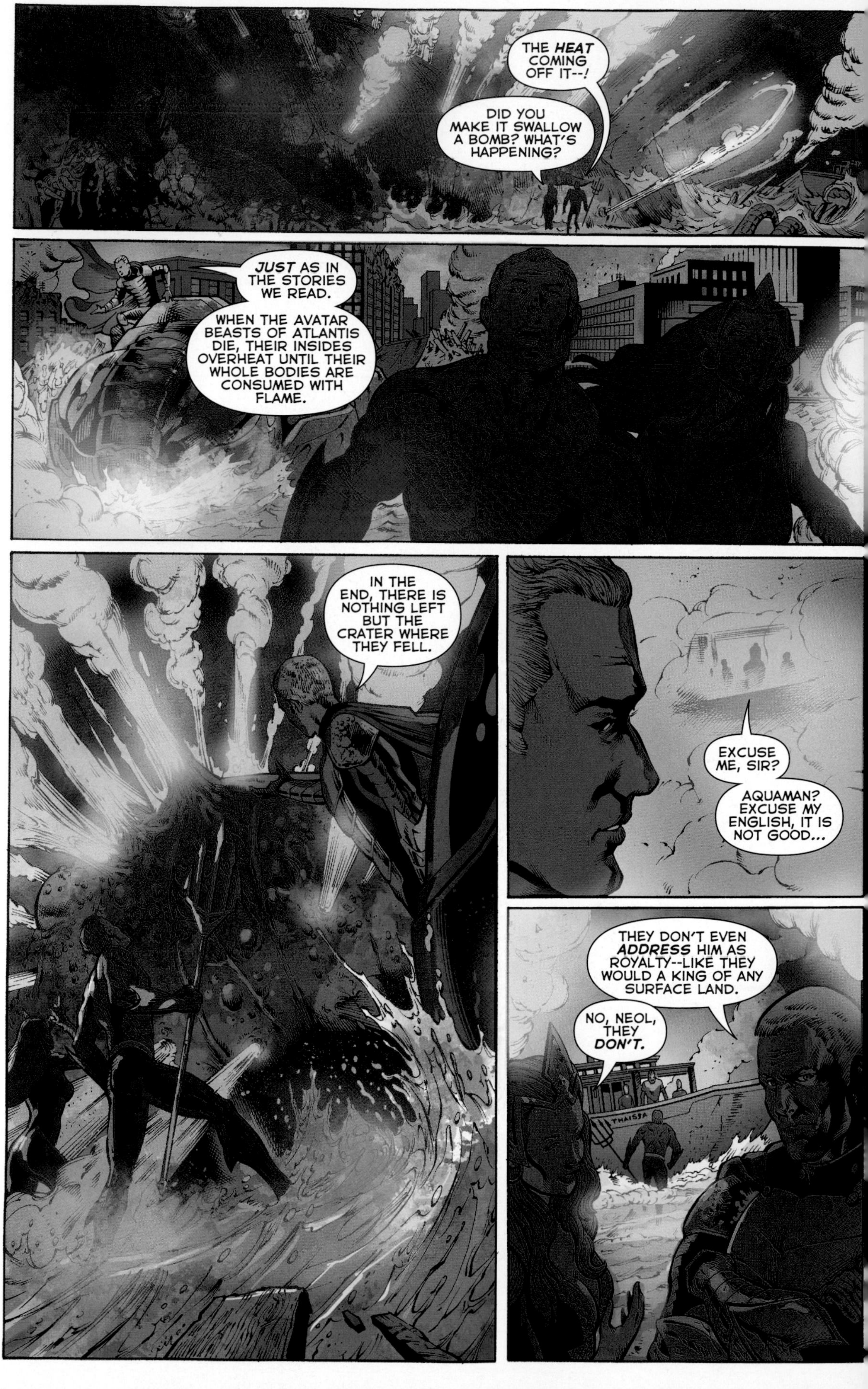
THE HEAT COMING OFF IT--!
DID YOU MAKE IT SWALLOW A BOMB? WHAT'S HAPPENING?
JUST AS IN THE STORIES WE READ.
WHEN THE AVATAR BEASTS OF ATLANTIS DIE, THEIR INSIDES OVERHEAT UNTIL THEIR WHOLE BODIES ARE CONSUMED WITH FLAME.
IN THE END, THERE IS NOTHING LEFT BUT THE CRATER WHERE THEY FELL.
EXCUSE ME, SIR?
AQUAMAN? EXCUSE MY ENGLISH, IT IS NOT GOOD...
THEY DON'T EVEN ADDRESS HIM AS ROYALTY--LIKE THEY WOULD A KING OF ANY SURFACE LAND.
NO, NEOL, THEY DON'T.
THAISSA

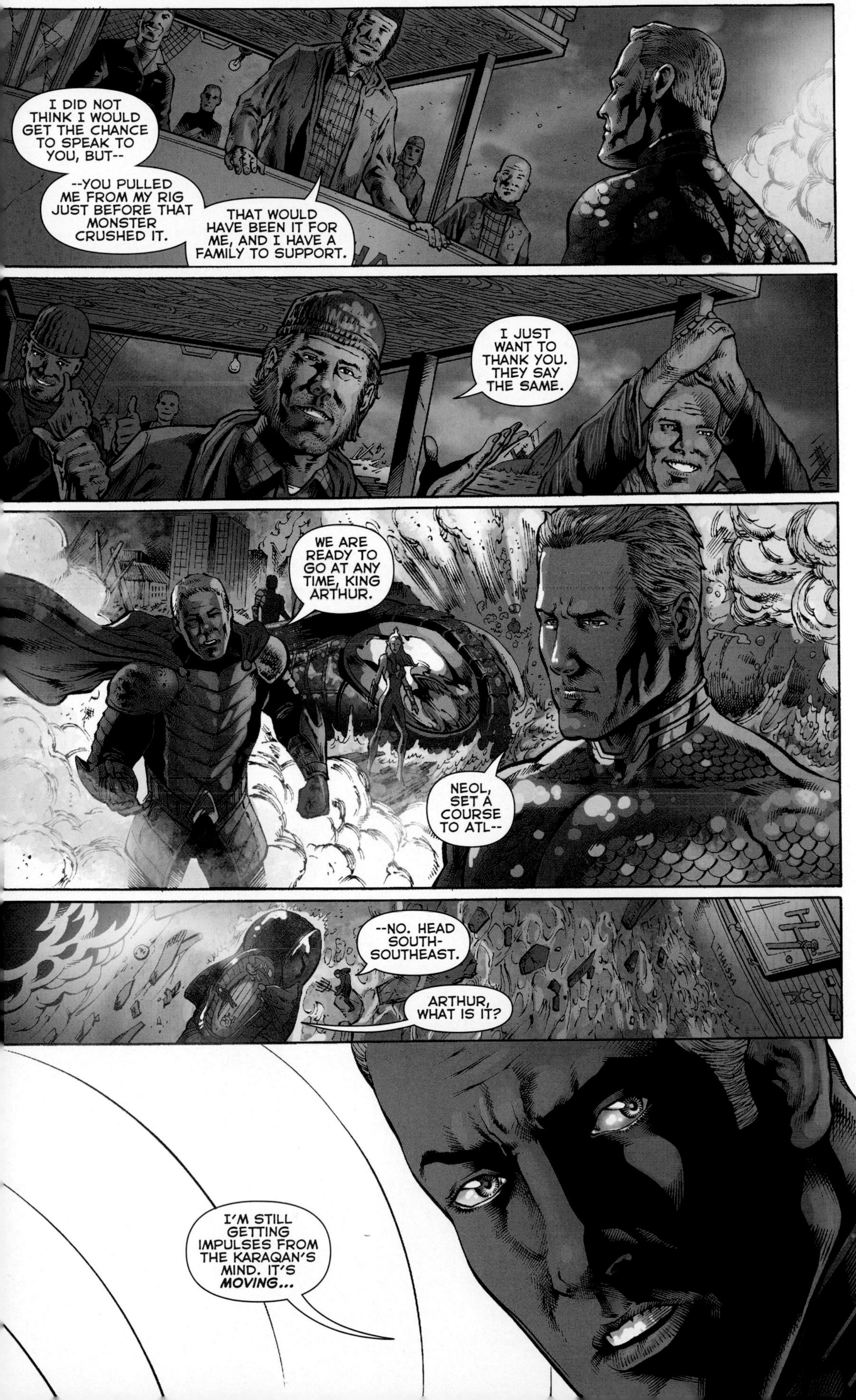
I DID NOT THINK I WOULD GET THE CHANCE TO SPEAK TO YOU, BUT--
--YOU PULLED ME FROM MY RIG JUST BEFORE THAT MONSTER CRUSHED IT.
THAT WOULD HAVE BEEN IT FOR ME, AND I HAVE A FAMILY TO SUPPORT.
I JUST WANT TO THANK YOU. THEY SAY THE SAME.
WE ARE READY TO GO AT ANY TIME, KING ARTHUR.
NEOL, SET A COURSE TO ATL--
--NO. HEAD SOUTH-SOUTHEAST.
ARTHUR, WHAT IS IT?
I'M STILL GETTING IMPULSES FROM THE KARAQAN'S MIND. IT'S *MOVING...*

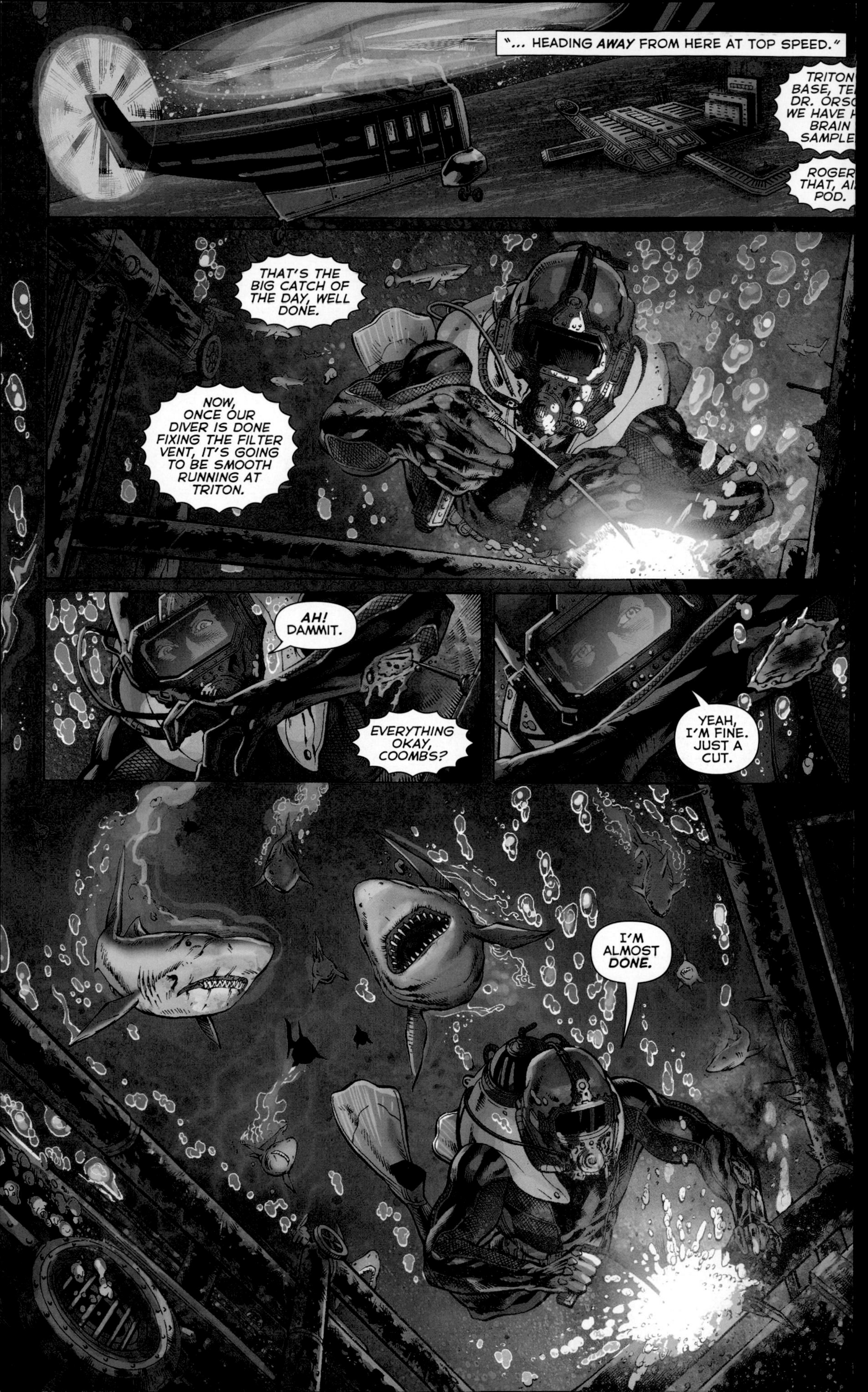
"... HEADING AWAY FROM HERE AT TOP SPEED."
TRITON BASE, TE DR. ORSO WE HAVE BRAIN SAMPLE
ROGER THAT, AI POD.
THAT'S THE BIG CATCH OF THE DAY, WELL DONE.
NOW, ONCE OUR DIVER IS DONE FIXING THE FILTER VENT, IT'S GOING TO BE SMOOTH RUNNING AT TRITON.
AH! DAMMIT.
EVERYTHING OKAY, COOMBS?
YEAH, I'M FINE. JUST A CUT.
I'M ALMOST DONE.

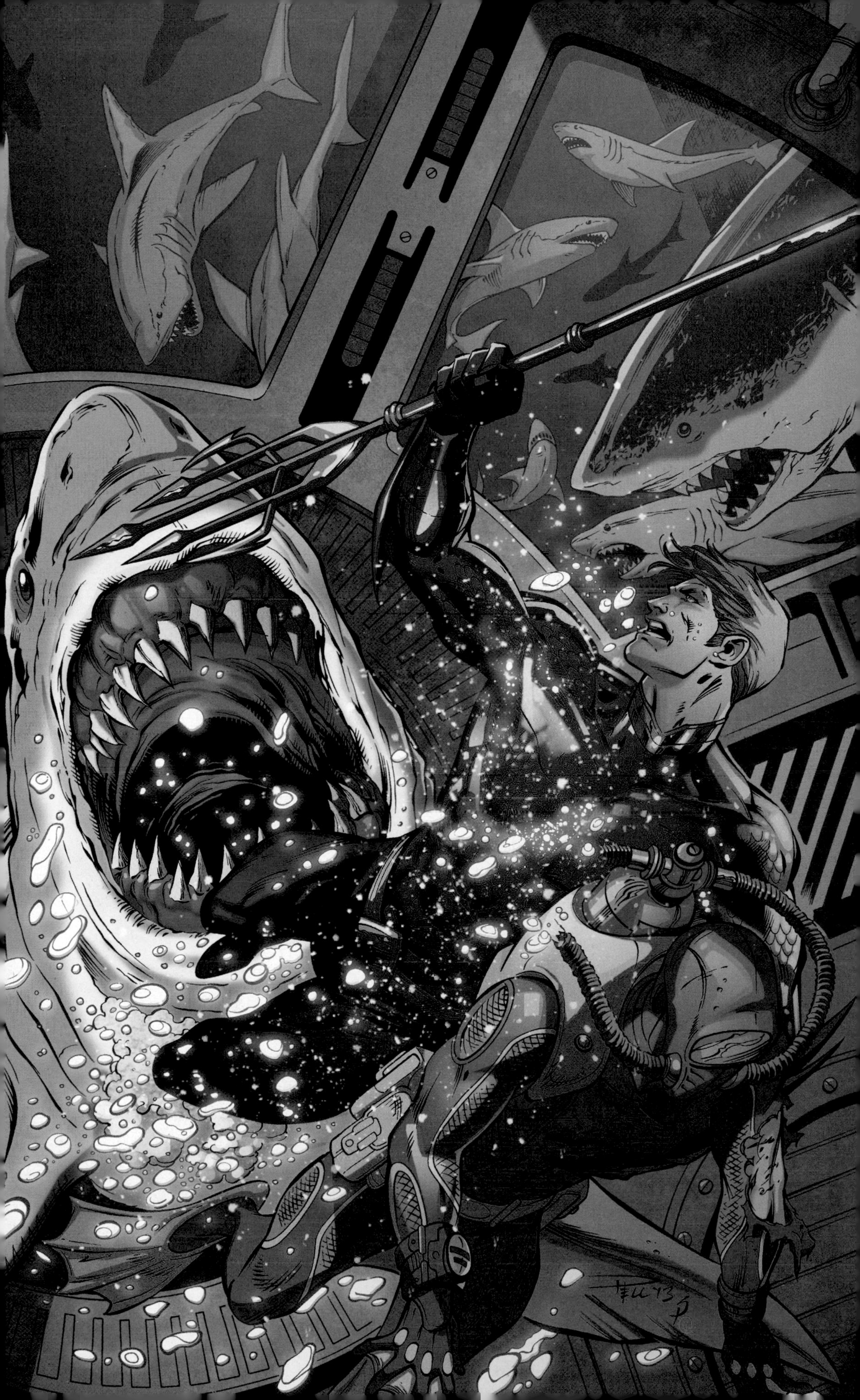

TRITON

JEFF PARKER writer PAUL PELLETIER penciller SEAN PARSONS ANDREW HENNESSY (pgs 67-68) inkers
JEROMY COX colorist DEZI SIENTY letterer cover by PAUL PELLETIER, SEAN PARSONS and WIL QUINTANA

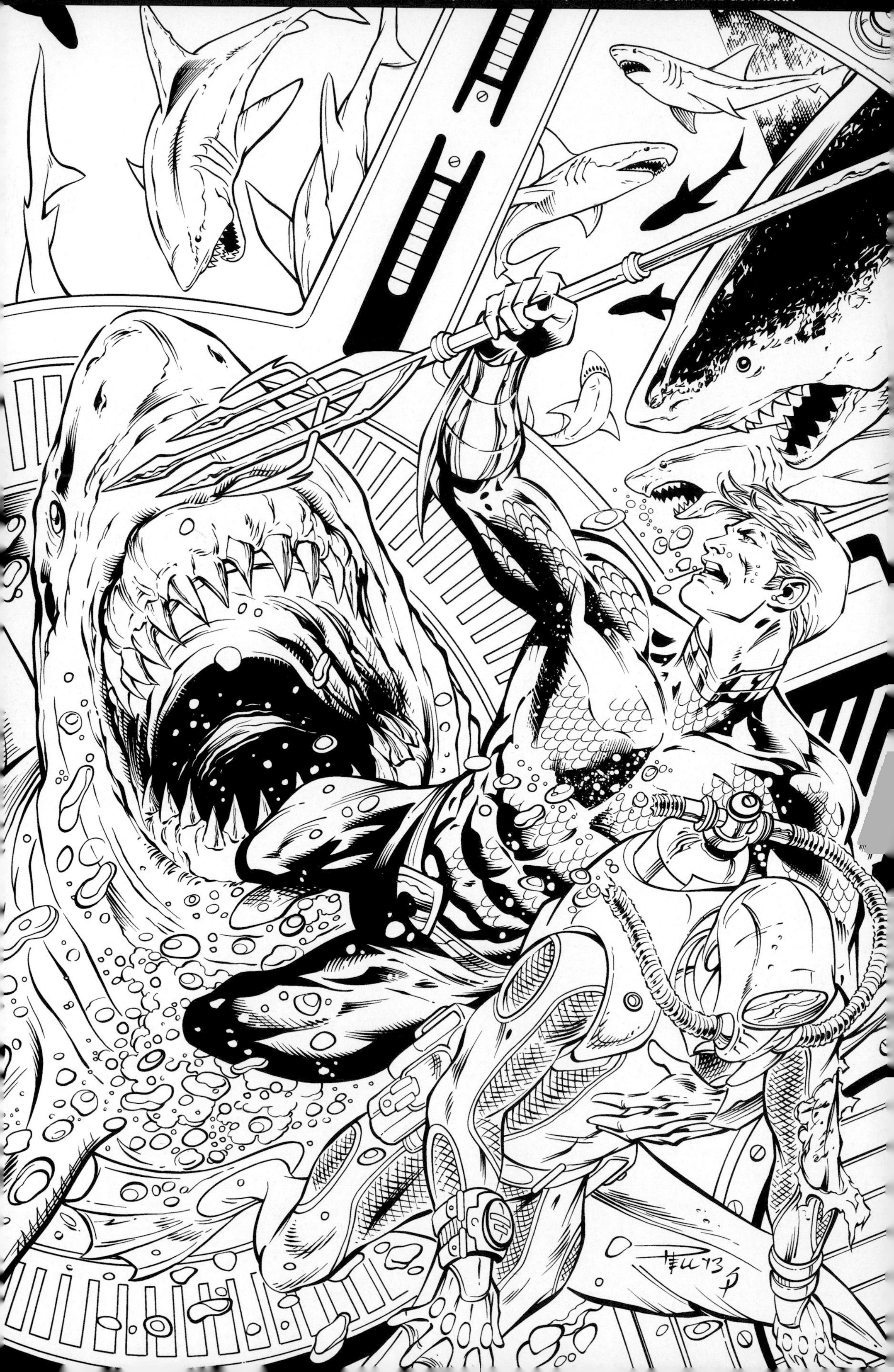

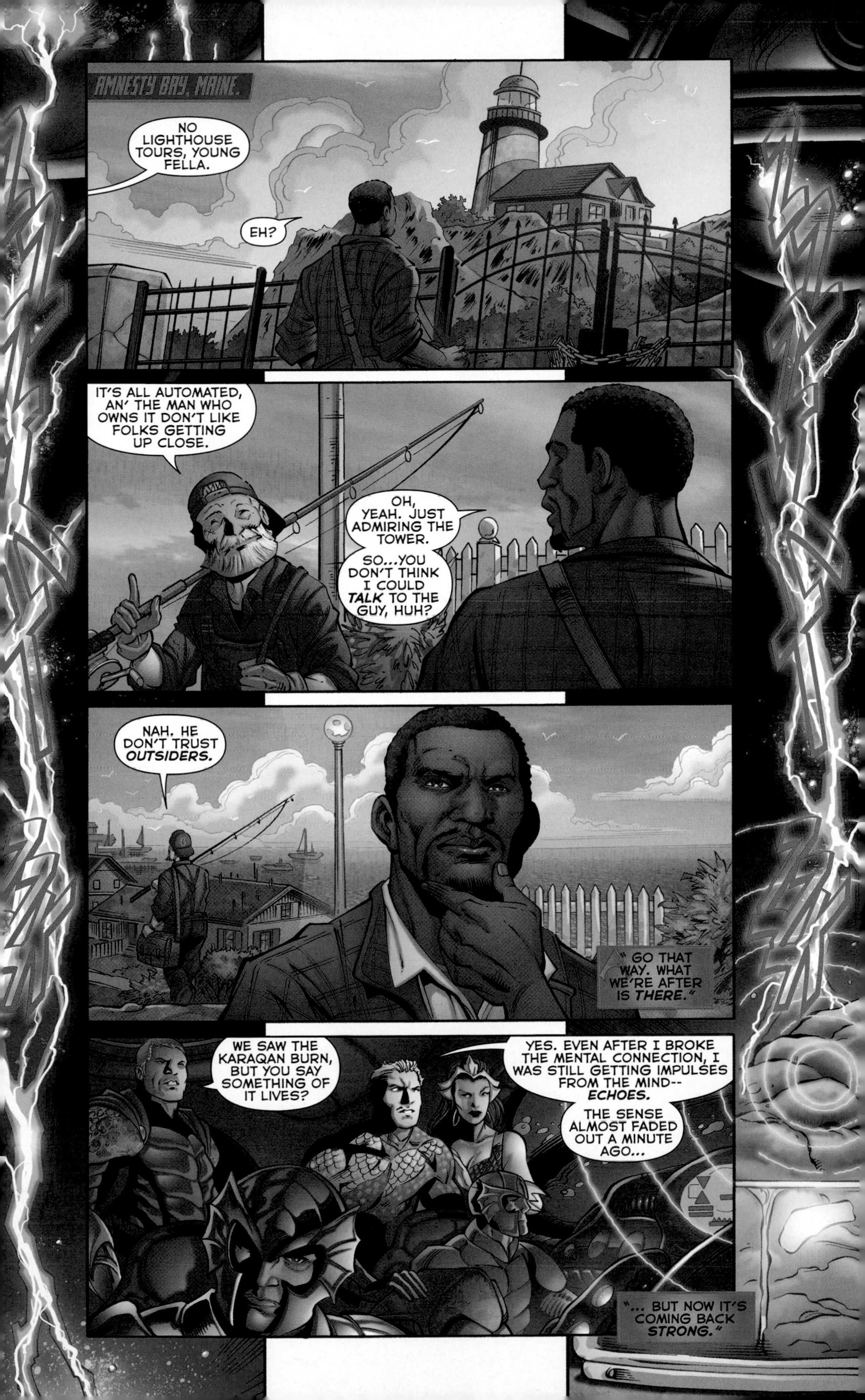
AMNESTY BAY, MAINE.
NO LIGHTHOUSE TOURS, YOUNG FELLA.
EH?
IT'S ALL AUTOMATED, AN' THE MAN WHO OWNS IT DON'T LIKE FOLKS GETTING UP CLOSE.
OH, YEAH. JUST ADMIRING THE TOWER.
SO...YOU DON'T THINK I COULD TALK TO THE GUY, HUH?
NAH. HE DON'T TRUST OUTSIDERS.
"GO THAT WAY. WHAT WE'RE AFTER IS THERE."
WE SAW THE KARAQAN BURN, BUT YOU SAY SOMETHING OF IT LIVES?
YES. EVEN AFTER I BROKE THE MENTAL CONNECTION, I WAS STILL GETTING IMPULSES FROM THE MIND-- ECHOES.
THE SENSE ALMOST FADED OUT A MINUTE AGO...
"... BUT NOW IT'S COMING BACK STRONG."

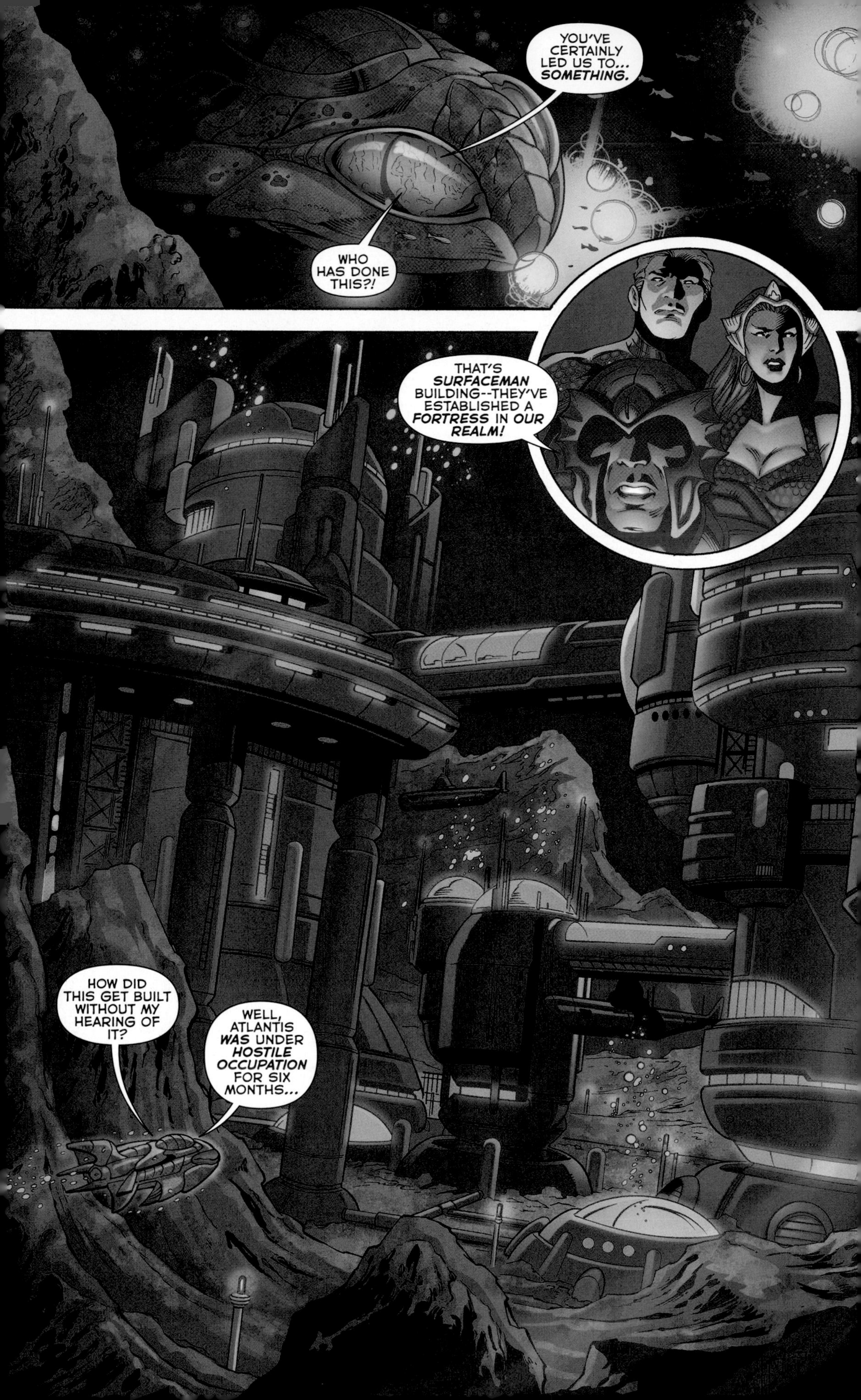

YOU'VE CERTAINLY LED US TO... SOMETHING.
WHO HAS DONE THIS?!
THAT'S SURFACEMAN BUILDING--THEY'VE ESTABLISHED A FORTRESS IN OUR REALM!
HOW DID THIS GET BUILT WITHOUT MY HEARING OF IT?
WELL, ATLANTIS WAS UNDER HOSTILE OCCUPATION FOR SIX MONTHS...

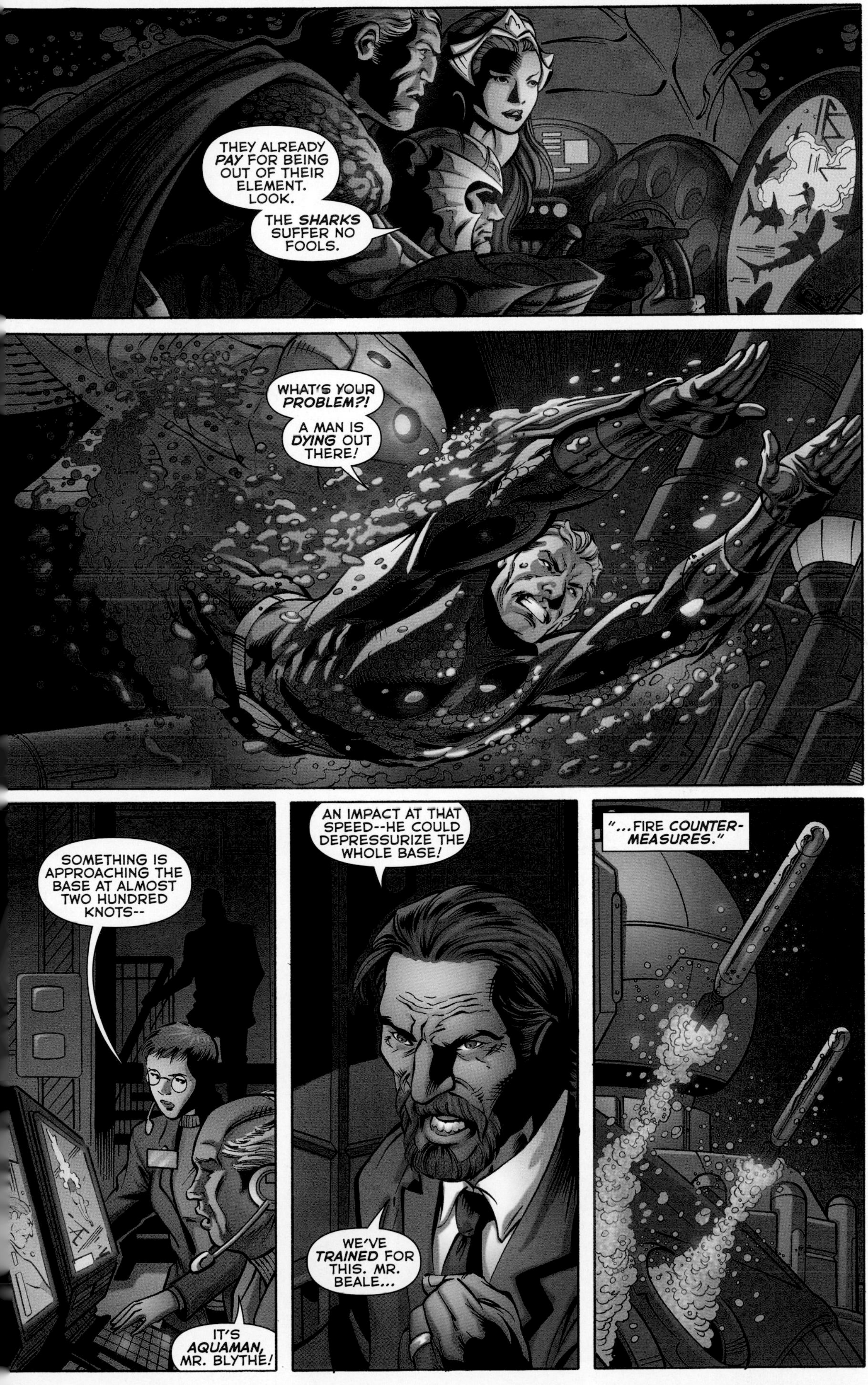
THEY ALREADY PAY FOR BEING OUT OF THEIR ELEMENT. LOOK.
THE SHARKS SUFFER NO FOOLS.
WHAT'S YOUR PROBLEM?!
A MAN IS DYING OUT THERE!
SOMETHING IS APPROACHING THE BASE AT ALMOST TWO HUNDRED KNOTS--
IT'S AQUAMAN, MR. BLYTHE!
AN IMPACT AT THAT SPEED--HE COULD DEPRESSURIZE THE WHOLE BASE!
WE'VE TRAINED FOR THIS. MR. BEALE...
"...FIRE COUNTER-MEASURES."

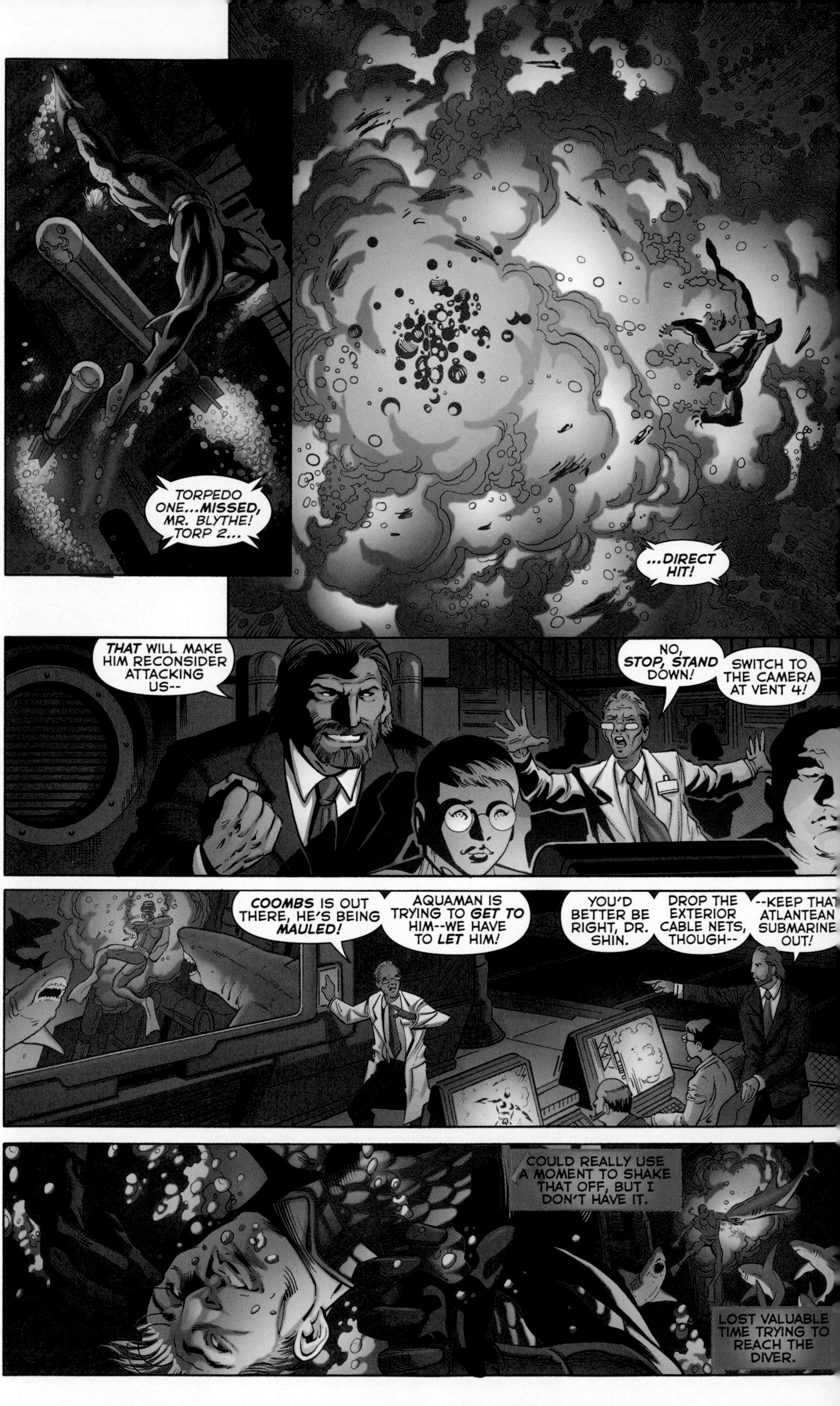

TORPEDO ONE...MISSED, MR. BLYTHE! TORP 2...
...DIRECT HIT!
THAT WILL MAKE HIM RECONSIDER ATTACKING US--
NO, STOP, STAND DOWN!
SWITCH TO THE CAMERA AT VENT 4!
COOMBS IS OUT THERE, HE'S BEING MAULED!
AQUAMAN IS TRYING TO GET TO HIM--WE HAVE TO LET HIM!
YOU'D BETTER BE RIGHT, DR. SHIN.
DROP THE EXTERIOR CABLE NETS, THOUGH--
--KEEP THAT ATLANTEAN SUBMARINE OUT!
COULD REALLY USE A MOMENT TO SHAKE THAT OFF, BUT I DON'T HAVE IT.
LOST VALUABLE TIME TRYING TO REACH THE DIVER.

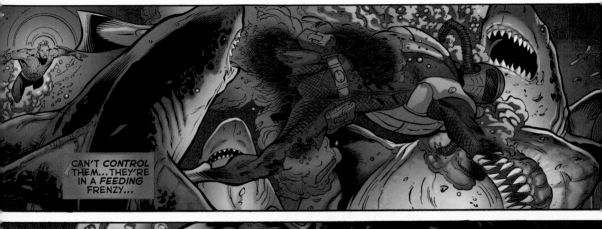

CAN'T *CONTROL* THEM...THEY'RE IN A *FEEDING* FRENZY...

I'M JUST IN A *FRENZY.*

NOT LIKELY HE'LL MAKE IT.

THIS BASE BETTER HAVE A MEDICAL BAY--AND NO MORE *TORPEDOES.*

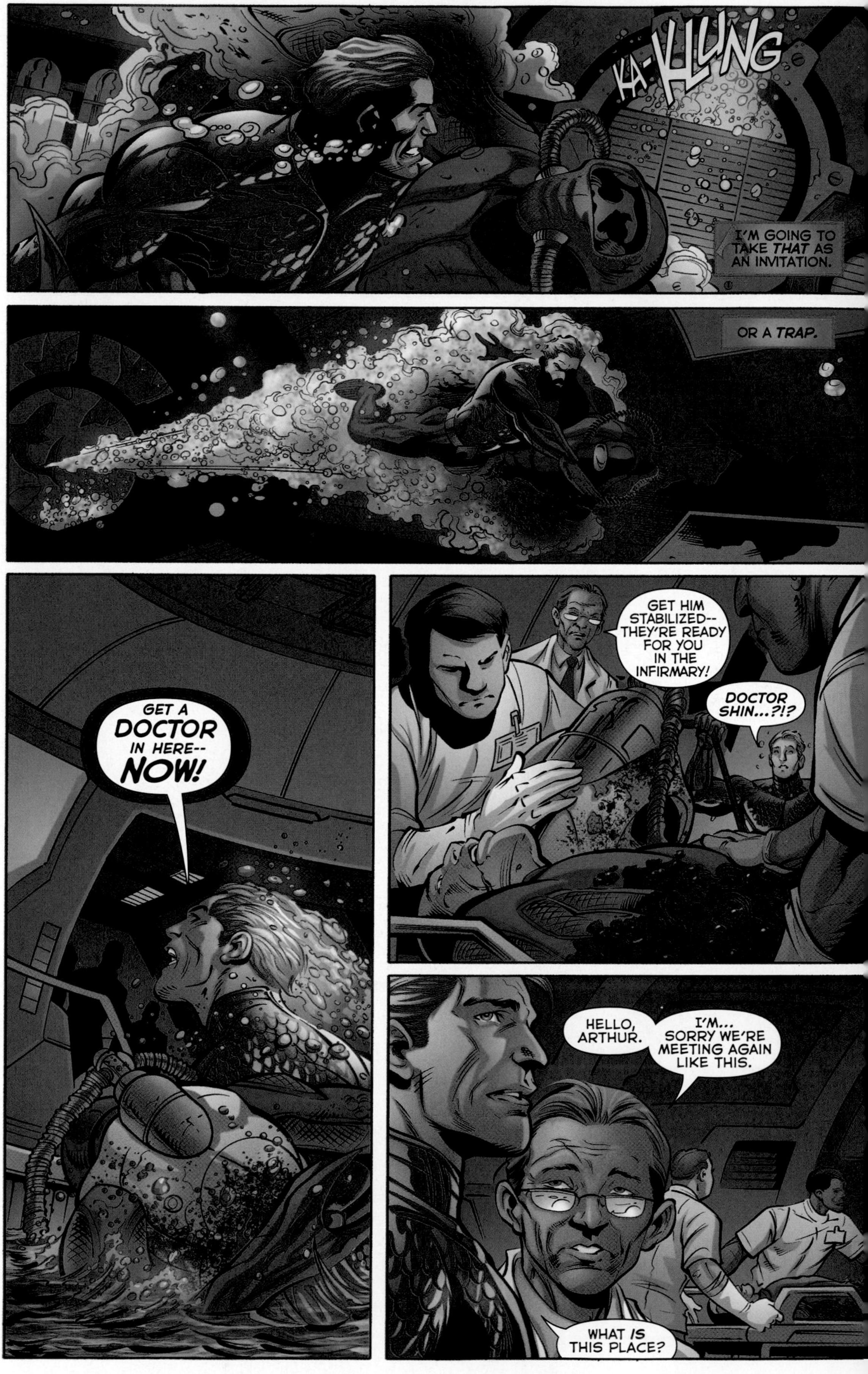
KA-KLUNG
I'M GOING TO TAKE THAT AS AN INVITATION.
OR A TRAP.
GET A DOCTOR IN HERE-- NOW!
GET HIM STABILIZED-- THEY'RE READY FOR YOU IN THE INFIRMARY!
DOCTOR SHIN...?!?
HELLO, ARTHUR.
I'M... SORRY WE'RE MEETING AGAIN LIKE THIS.
WHAT IS THIS PLACE?

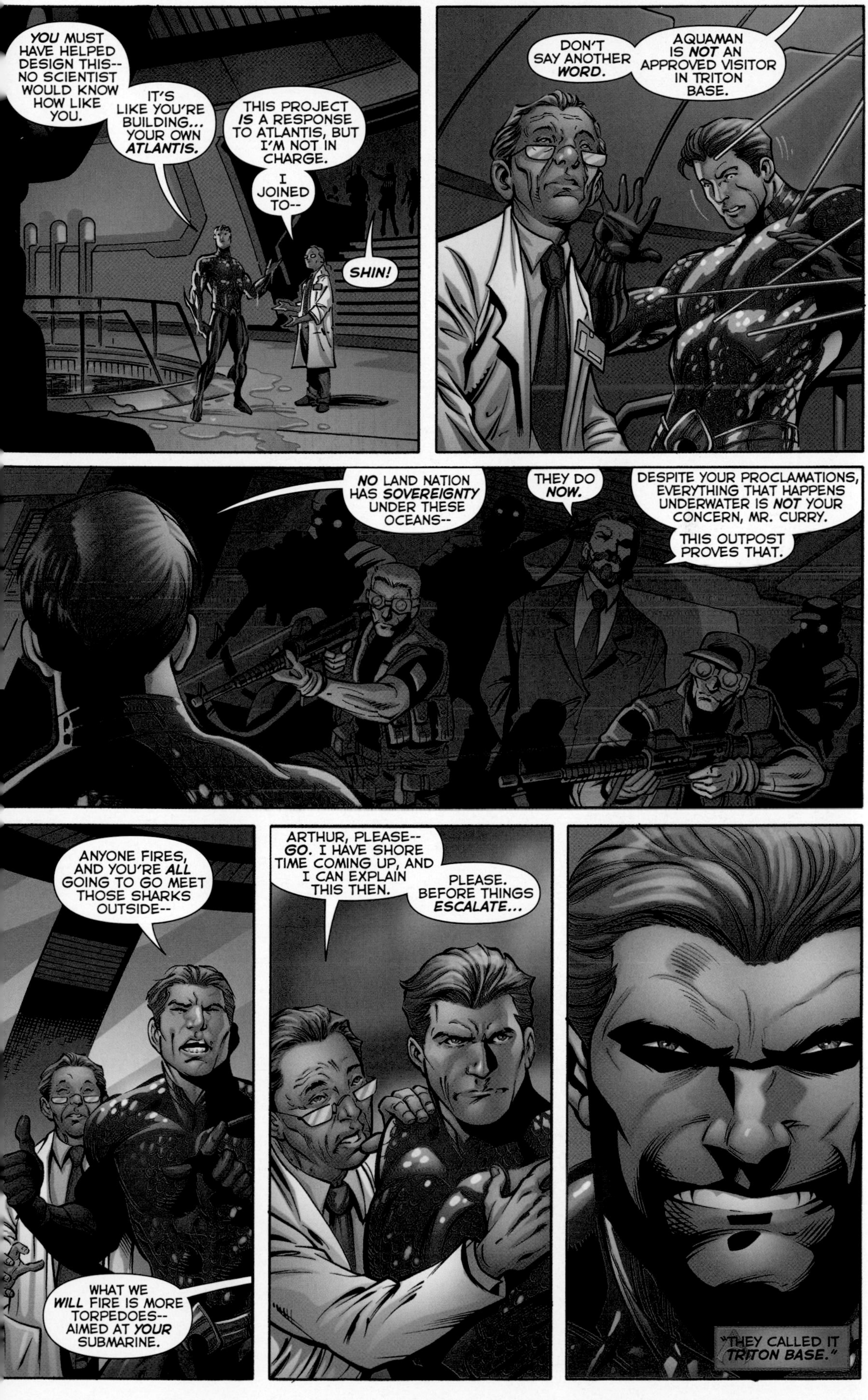

YOU MUST HAVE HELPED DESIGN THIS-- NO SCIENTIST WOULD KNOW HOW LIKE YOU.
IT'S LIKE YOU'RE BUILDING... YOUR OWN ATLANTIS.
THIS PROJECT IS A RESPONSE TO ATLANTIS, BUT I'M NOT IN CHARGE.
I JOINED TO--
SHIN!
DON'T SAY ANOTHER WORD.
AQUAMAN IS NOT AN APPROVED VISITOR IN TRITON BASE.
NO LAND NATION HAS SOVEREIGNTY UNDER THESE OCEANS--
THEY DO NOW.
DESPITE YOUR PROCLAMATIONS, EVERYTHING THAT HAPPENS UNDERWATER IS NOT YOUR CONCERN, MR. CURRY.
THIS OUTPOST PROVES THAT.
ANYONE FIRES, AND YOU'RE ALL GOING TO GO MEET THOSE SHARKS OUTSIDE--
WHAT WE WILL FIRE IS MORE TORPEDOES-- AIMED AT YOUR SUBMARINE.
ARTHUR, PLEASE-- GO. I HAVE SHORE TIME COMING UP, AND I CAN EXPLAIN THIS THEN.
PLEASE. BEFORE THINGS ESCALATE...
"THEY CALLED IT TRITON BASE."

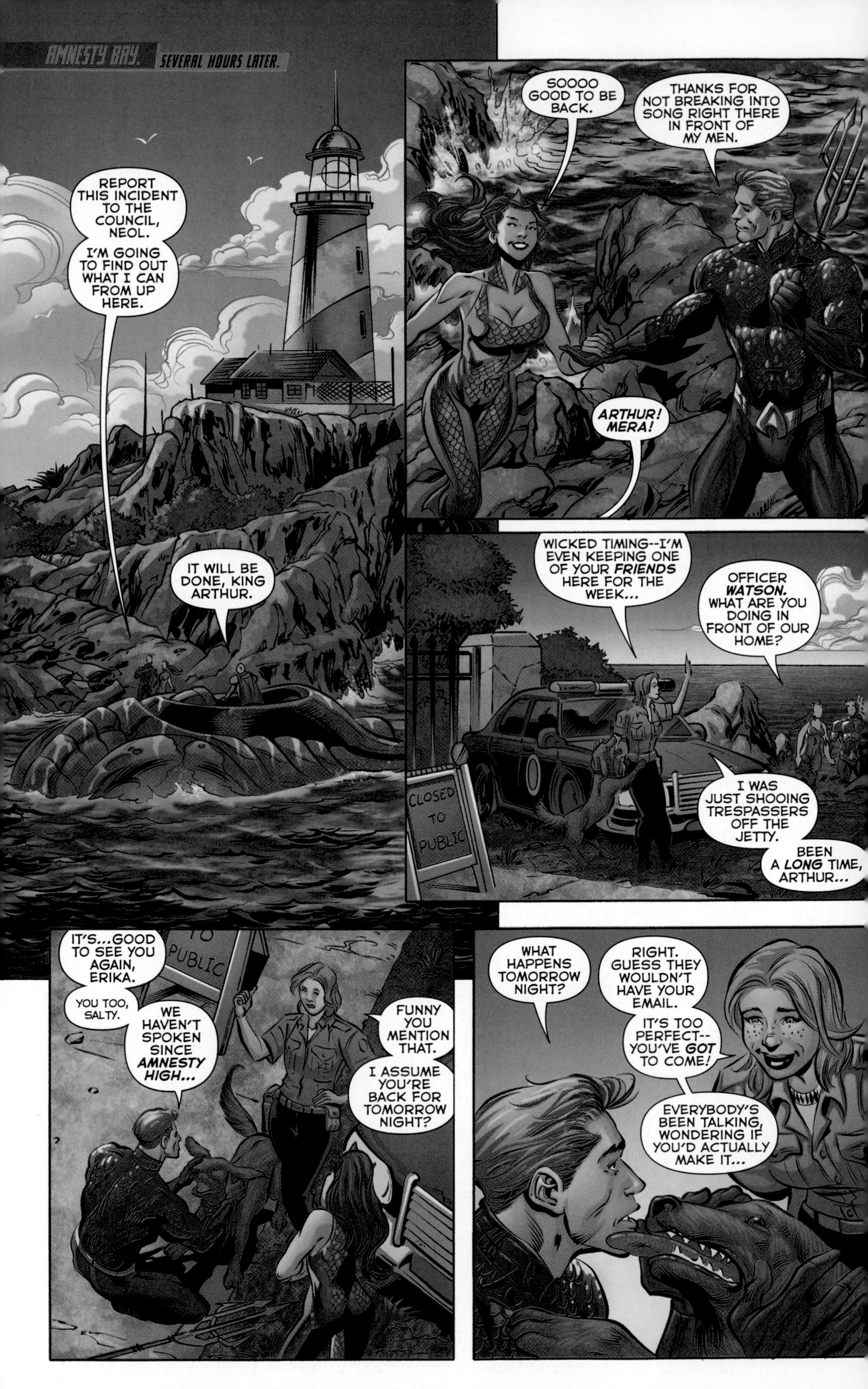

AMNESTY BAY.
SEVERAL HOURS LATER.
REPORT THIS INCIDENT TO THE COUNCIL, NEOL.
I'M GOING TO FIND OUT WHAT I CAN FROM UP HERE.
IT WILL BE DONE, KING ARTHUR.
SOOOO GOOD TO BE BACK.
THANKS FOR NOT BREAKING INTO SONG RIGHT THERE IN FRONT OF MY MEN.
ARTHUR! MERA!
WICKED TIMING--I'M EVEN KEEPING ONE OF YOUR FRIENDS HERE FOR THE WEEK...
OFFICER WATSON. WHAT ARE YOU DOING IN FRONT OF OUR HOME?
CLOSED TO PUBLIC
I WAS JUST SHOOING TRESPASSERS OFF THE JETTY.
BEEN A LONG TIME, ARTHUR...
IT'S...GOOD TO SEE YOU AGAIN, ERIKA.
YOU TOO, SALTY.
WE HAVEN'T SPOKEN SINCE AMNESTY HIGH...
FUNNY YOU MENTION THAT.
I ASSUME YOU'RE BACK FOR TOMORROW NIGHT?
WHAT HAPPENS TOMORROW NIGHT?
RIGHT. GUESS THEY WOULDN'T HAVE YOUR EMAIL.
IT'S TOO PERFECT-- YOU'VE GOT TO COME!
EVERYBODY'S BEEN TALKING, WONDERING IF YOU'D ACTUALLY MAKE IT...

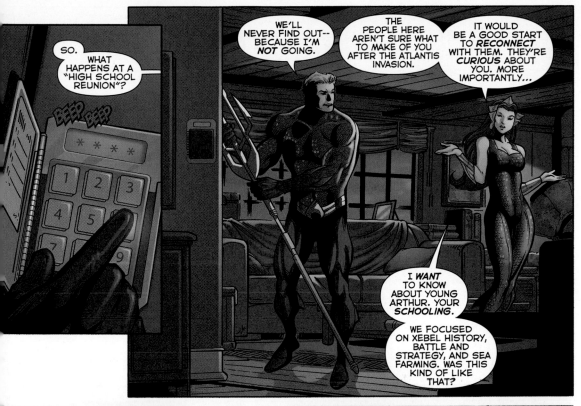

SO. WHAT HAPPENS AT A "HIGH SCHOOL REUNION"?

BEEP BEEP

WE'LL NEVER FIND OUT-- BECAUSE I'M *NOT* GOING.

THE PEOPLE HERE AREN'T SURE WHAT TO MAKE OF YOU AFTER THE ATLANTIS INVASION.

IT WOULD BE A GOOD START TO *RECONNECT* WITH THEM. THEY'RE *CURIOUS* ABOUT YOU. MORE IMPORTANTLY...

I *WANT* TO KNOW ABOUT YOUNG ARTHUR. YOUR *SCHOOLING.*

WE FOCUSED ON XEBEL HISTORY, BATTLE AND STRATEGY, AND SEA FARMING. WAS THIS KIND OF LIKE THAT?

HA. WELL, WE DID HAVE HISTORY. CHEMISTRY, ENGLISH...

BUT YOU ALREADY SPOKE ENGLISH.

IT'S *LITERATURE* REALLY, THEY JUST CALL IT THAT.

TOOK SOME ELECTIVES, LIKE WOOD SHOP...

BUT I *LEFT* PRETTY ABRUPTLY WHEN MY FATHER DIED, AND THE WORLD FOUND OUT WHAT I WAS.

AND EVEN *BEFORE* THAT... KIDS DIDN'T *WARM UP* TO ME FOR WHATEVER REASON.

LET'S START WITH WHATEVER YOU'RE *LEAVING OUT.*

WHAT HAPPENED?

I WAS THIRTEEN.

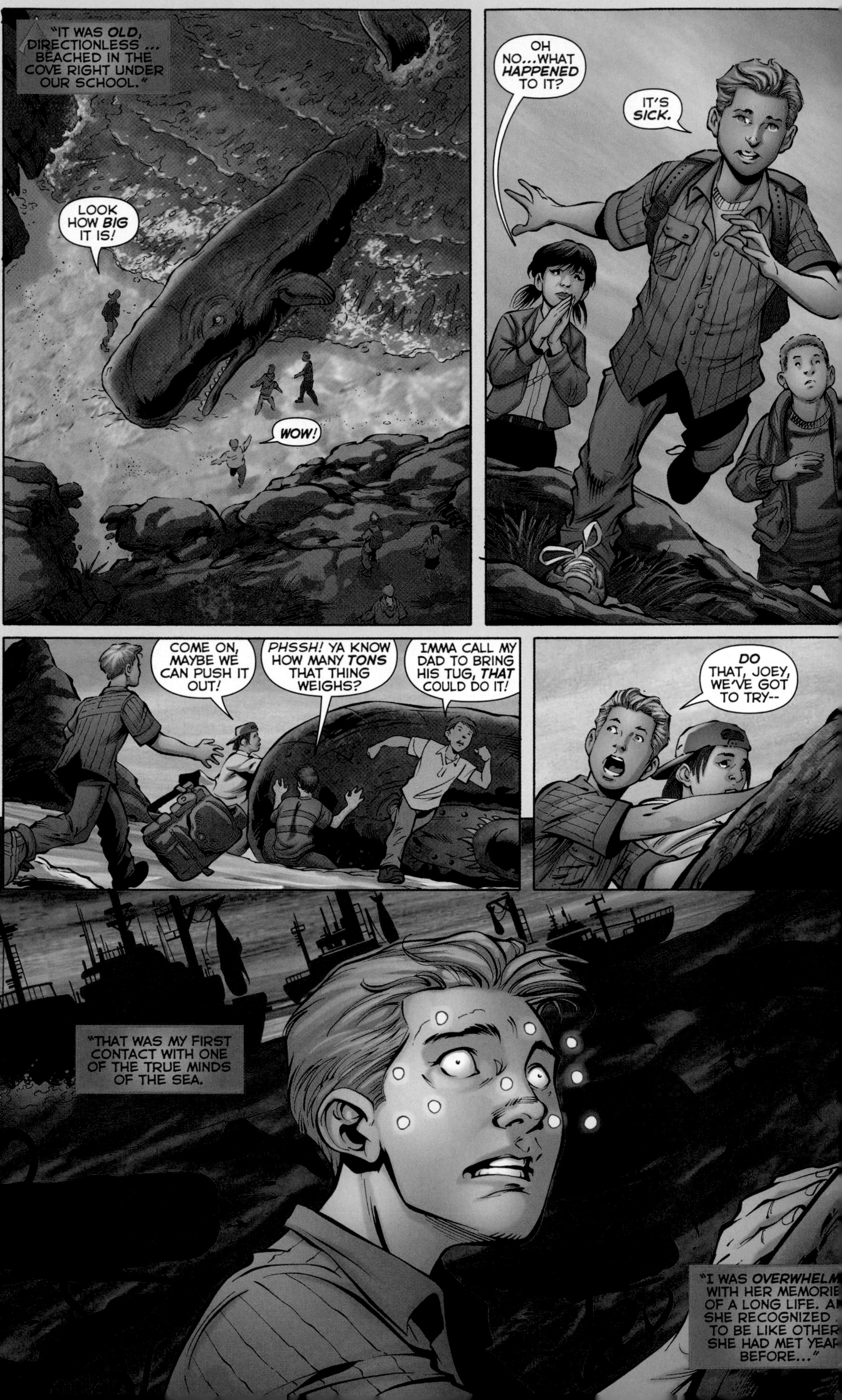
"IT WAS OLD, DIRECTIONLESS ... BEACHED IN THE COVE RIGHT UNDER OUR SCHOOL."
LOOK HOW BIG IT IS!
WOW!
OH NO...WHAT HAPPENED TO IT?
IT'S SICK.
COME ON, MAYBE WE CAN PUSH IT OUT!
PHSSH! YA KNOW HOW MANY TONS THAT THING WEIGHS?
IMMA CALL MY DAD TO BRING HIS TUG, THAT COULD DO IT!
DO THAT, JOEY, WE'VE GOT TO TRY--
"THAT WAS MY FIRST CONTACT WITH ONE OF THE TRUE MINDS OF THE SEA.
"I WAS OVERWHELM WITH HER MEMORIE OF A LONG LIFE. A SHE RECOGNIZED TO BE LIKE OTHER SHE HAD MET YEAR BEFORE..."

"AND THEN... PAIN."

AH!

STOP IT, SPENCE, IT'S STILL ALIVE!

MAYBE SOMEBODY IN A *SUB* WILL SEE IT THEN!

GET AWAY!

"IT WAS RIGHT AT THE TIME MY *STRENGTH* STARTED KICKING IN...I WASN'T USED TO IT. JUST REACTING."

"HE WAS IN A *COMA* FOR WEEKS. HE NEVER CAME BACK TO SCHOOL.

"THE KIDS MOSTLY *AVOIDED* ME AFTER THAT. I COULD NEVER SHAKE THAT DAY."

THANKS FOR TELLING ME THAT.

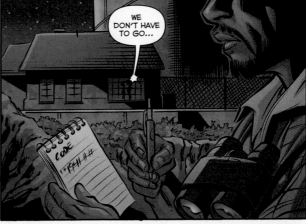

WE DON'T HAVE TO GO...

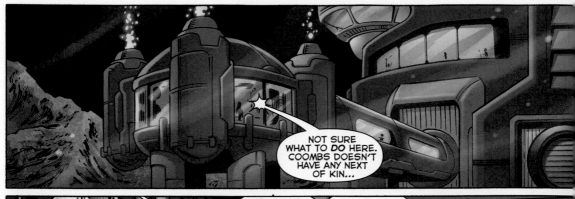

NOT SURE WHAT TO *DO* HERE. COOMBS DOESN'T HAVE ANY NEXT OF KIN...

HE DIDN'T LEAVE ANY LIVING WILL THAT WOULD COVER A VEGETATIVE STATE.

BUT HE CAN'T *SURVIVE* OFF LIFE SUPPORT--TOO MUCH BRAIN LOSS.

AND EVEN IF HE *DID*...

I DON'T NEED THIS DILEMMA RIGHT NOW.

MR. BLYTHE, IF I MAY...

AS THIS IS AN *EXTREME* CASE OF A PATIENT WITH *NOTHING* TO LOSE...

...I WOULD LIKE TO TRY SOME *EXPERIMENTAL* MEASURES. AS YOU KNOW, I'VE GLEANED MUCH FROM MY STUDIES OF SEA LIFE...

THEN TAKE HIM BACK TO YOUR LAB, DR. ORSON. IT'S CERTAINLY THE ONLY HOPE HE HAS.

IF NOTHING ELSE, MAYBE SOME USEFUL DEVELOPMENT WILL COME OF IT.

THANK YOU, SIR!

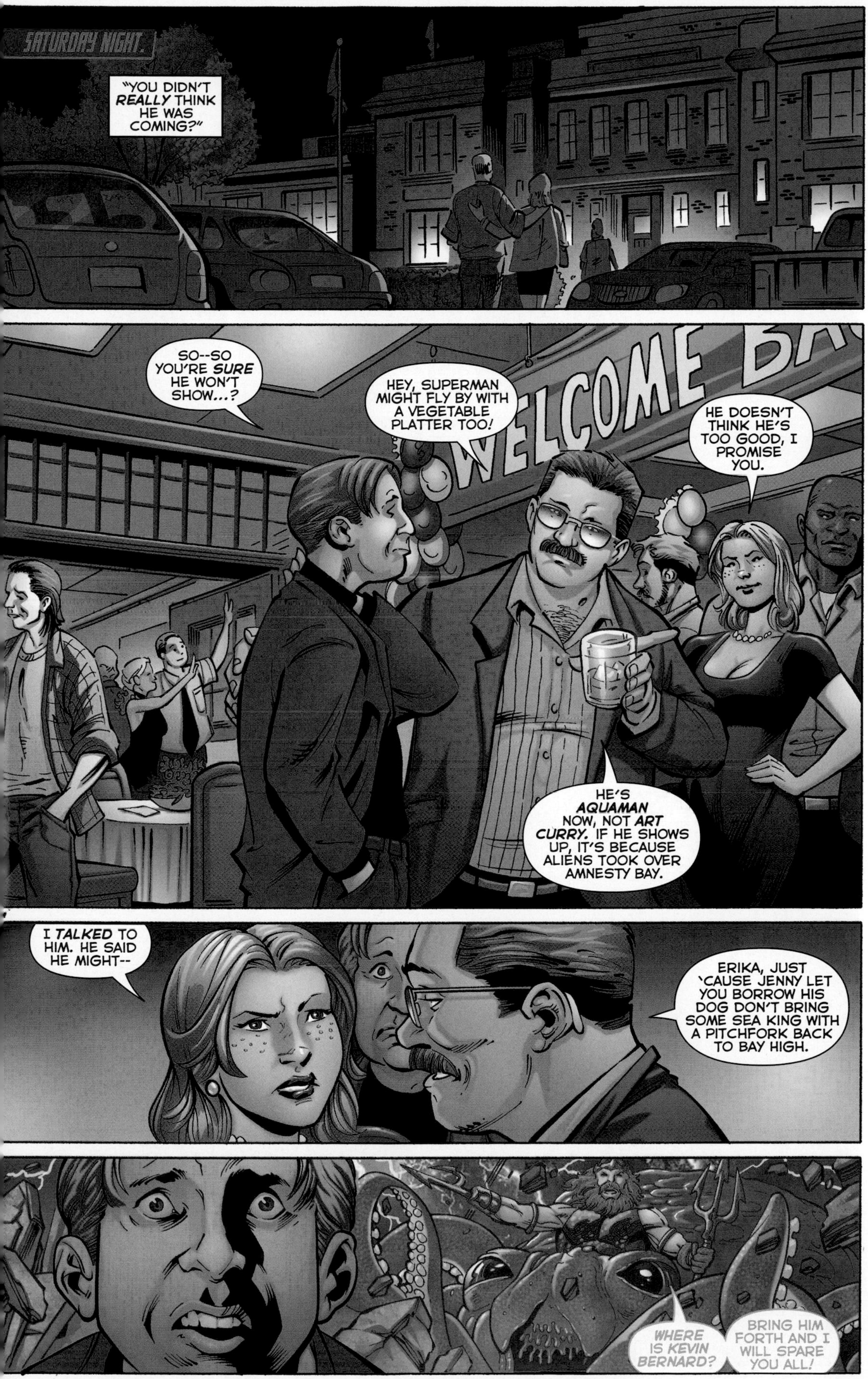
SATURDAY NIGHT.
"YOU DIDN'T REALLY THINK HE WAS COMING?"
SO--SO YOU'RE SURE HE WON'T SHOW...?
HEY, SUPERMAN MIGHT FLY BY WITH A VEGETABLE PLATTER TOO!
WELCOME BA
HE DOESN'T THINK HE'S TOO GOOD, I PROMISE YOU.
HE'S AQUAMAN NOW, NOT ART CURRY. IF HE SHOWS UP, IT'S BECAUSE ALIENS TOOK OVER AMNESTY BAY.
I TALKED TO HIM. HE SAID HE MIGHT--
ERIKA, JUST 'CAUSE JENNY LET YOU BORROW HIS DOG DON'T BRING SOME SEA KING WITH A PITCHFORK BACK TO BAY HIGH.
WHERE IS KEVIN BERNARD?
BRING HIM FORTH AND I WILL SPARE YOU ALL!

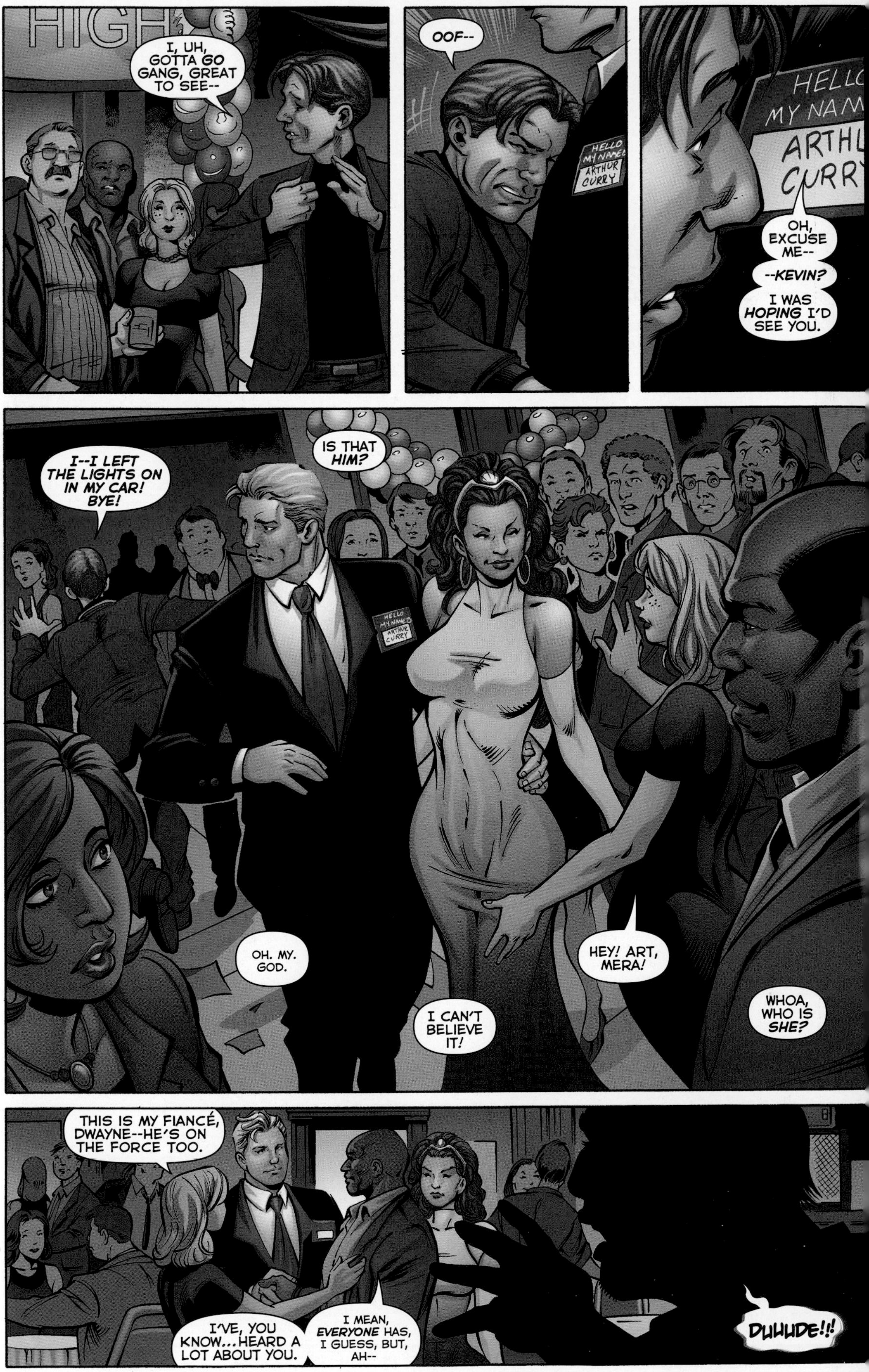
HIGH
I, UH, GOTTA GO GANG, GREAT TO SEE--
OOF--
HELLO MY NAME IS ARTHUR CURRY
OH, EXCUSE ME--
--KEVIN?
I WAS HOPING I'D SEE YOU.
I--I LEFT THE LIGHTS ON IN MY CAR! BYE!
IS THAT HIM?
OH. MY. GOD.
I CAN'T BELIEVE IT!
HEY! ART, MERA!
WHOA, WHO IS SHE?
THIS IS MY FIANCÉ, DWAYNE--HE'S ON THE FORCE TOO.
I'VE, YOU KNOW...HEARD A LOT ABOUT YOU.
I MEAN, EVERYONE HAS, I GUESS, BUT, AH--
DUUUDE!!!

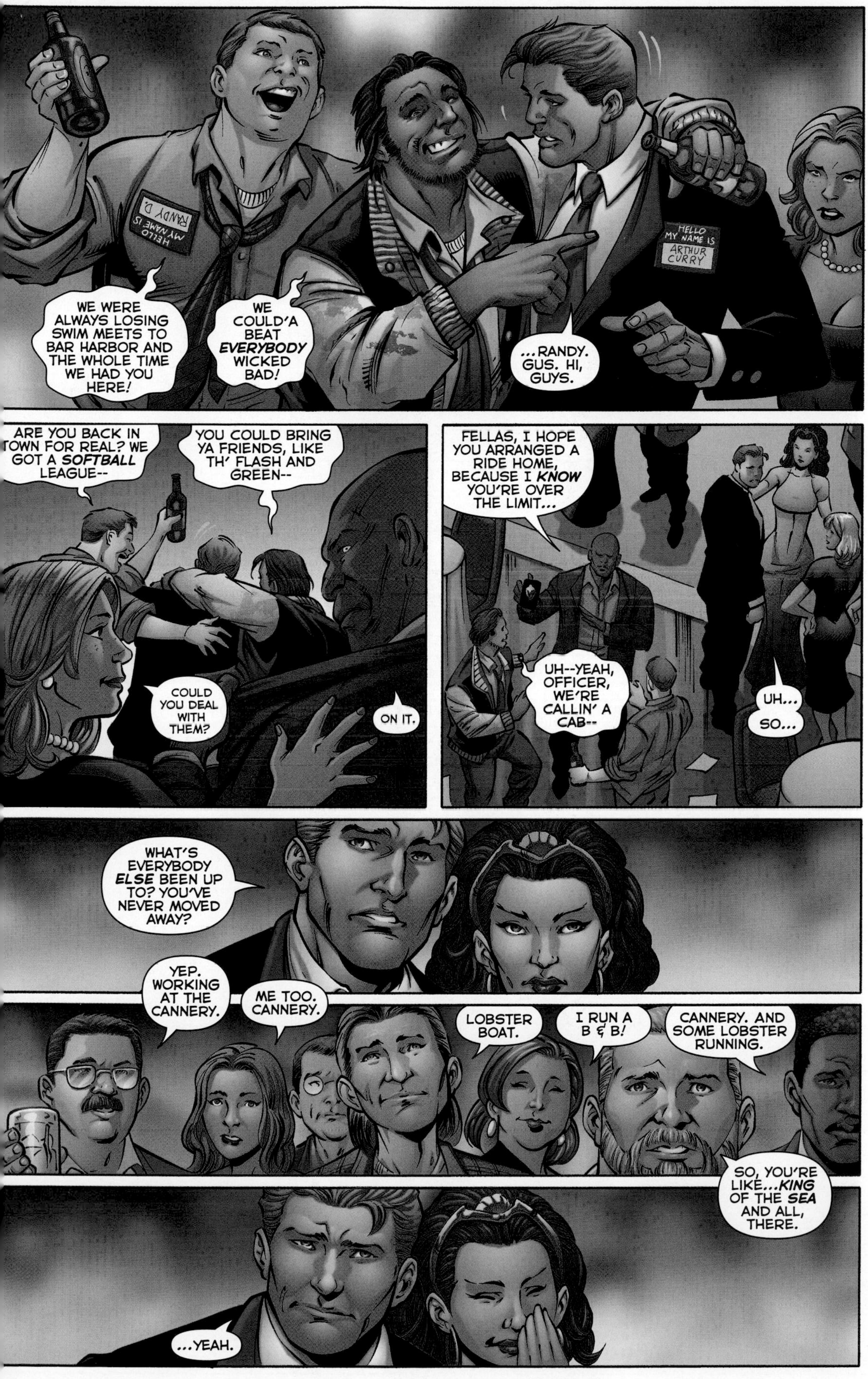
HELLO MY NAME IS RANDY D.
HELLO MY NAME IS ARTHUR CURRY
WE WERE ALWAYS LOSING SWIM MEETS TO BAR HARBOR AND THE WHOLE TIME WE HAD YOU HERE!
WE COULD'A BEAT EVERYBODY WICKED BAD!
...RANDY. GUS. HI, GUYS.
ARE YOU BACK IN TOWN FOR REAL? WE GOT A SOFTBALL LEAGUE--
YOU COULD BRING YA FRIENDS, LIKE TH' FLASH AND GREEN--
COULD YOU DEAL WITH THEM?
ON IT.
FELLAS, I HOPE YOU ARRANGED A RIDE HOME, BECAUSE I KNOW YOU'RE OVER THE LIMIT...
UH--YEAH, OFFICER, WE'RE CALLIN' A CAB--
UH... SO...
WHAT'S EVERYBODY ELSE BEEN UP TO? YOU'VE NEVER MOVED AWAY?
YEP. WORKING AT THE CANNERY.
ME TOO. CANNERY.
LOBSTER BOAT.
I RUN A B & B!
CANNERY. AND SOME LOBSTER RUNNING.
SO, YOU'RE LIKE...KING OF THE SEA AND ALL, THERE.
...YEAH.

DANNY! HOW HAVE *YOU* BEEN?

GREAT. *NOW*, I MEAN.

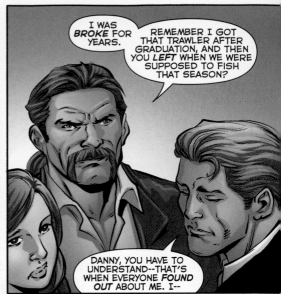

I WAS *BROKE* FOR YEARS.

REMEMBER I GOT THAT TRAWLER AFTER GRADUATION, AND THEN YOU *LEFT* WHEN WE WERE SUPPOSED TO FISH THAT SEASON?

DANNY, YOU HAVE TO UNDERSTAND--THAT'S WHEN EVERYONE *FOUND OUT* ABOUT ME. I--

HELL, I DIDN'T CARE, I KNEW SOMETHING WAS UP WITH YOU SINCE WE WERE *KIDS*.

WHAT *IS* IT WITH YOUR WATER PEOPLE, BY THE WAY--ARE THEY GOING TO FLOOD HALF THE U.S. AGAIN? I THOUGHT THEY DO WHAT *YOU* TELL THEM!

THEY DO *NOW*. I DON'T BLAME ANYONE FOR BEING WORRIED ABOUT THAT, BUT I PROMISE YOU.

THAT PROBLEM IS *OVER*.

YEAH.

I'VE HEARD YOUR PROMISES BEFORE.

HEY, DON'T SWEAT IT, ART.

LISTEN, SOME OF US COMPARED *NOTES* OVER THE YEARS.

AND...WE GOTTA *ASK* IN CASE WE DON'T GET THE CHANCE AGAIN...

ME FIRST, ART. PLEASE.

DON'T KNOW IF YOU REMEMBER ME, OR SOPHOMORE YEAR. I'M MIKE TILLMAN.

ME AND SOME OF THE GUYS WENT OUT ON MY DAD'S BOAT WITHOUT CHECKING THE STORM WARNINGS, AND RAN OUT OF GAS.

WE TOOK ON A LOT OF WATER AND WERE ONE MORE WAVE AWAY FROM BEING SWAMPED... *MILES* OFFSHORE.

EVERYBODY WAS CLINGING TO ANYTHING THEY COULD, SCREAMING AND PRAYING.

THEN I SAW THE LINE, BEING *PULLED*. BY *WHAT*, I DIDN'T KNOW. EVERYBODY ELSE THOUGHT WE DRIFTED BACK INTO THE BAY.

THAT WAS *YOU*, WASN'T IT?

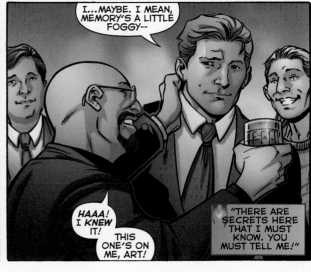

I...MAYBE. I MEAN, MEMORY'S A LITTLE FOGGY--

HAAA! I *KNEW* IT!

THIS ONE'S ON ME, ART!

"THERE ARE SECRETS HERE THAT I MUST KNOW. YOU MUST TELL ME!"

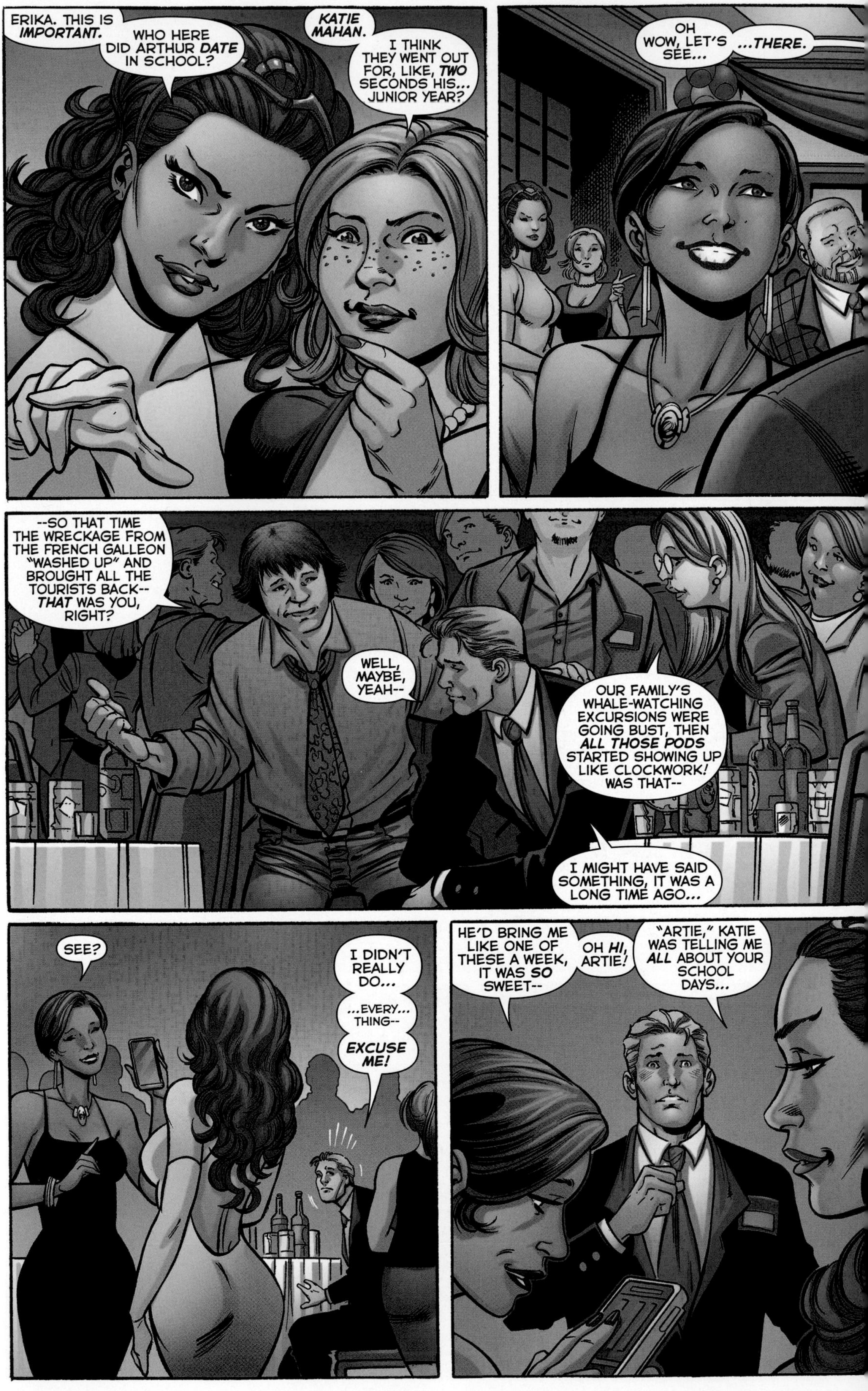
ERIKA. THIS IS *IMPORTANT.*
WHO HERE DID ARTHUR *DATE* IN SCHOOL?
KATIE MAHAN.
I THINK THEY WENT OUT FOR, LIKE, *TWO* SECONDS HIS... JUNIOR YEAR?
OH WOW, LET'S SEE...
...THERE.
--SO THAT TIME THE WRECKAGE FROM THE FRENCH GALLEON "WASHED UP" AND BROUGHT ALL THE TOURISTS BACK-- *THAT* WAS YOU, RIGHT?
WELL, MAYBE, YEAH--
OUR FAMILY'S WHALE-WATCHING EXCURSIONS WERE GOING BUST, THEN *ALL THOSE PODS* STARTED SHOWING UP LIKE CLOCKWORK! WAS THAT--
I MIGHT HAVE SAID SOMETHING, IT WAS A LONG TIME AGO...
SEE?
I DIDN'T REALLY DO...
...EVERY... THING--
EXCUSE ME!
HE'D BRING ME LIKE ONE OF THESE A WEEK, IT WAS *SO* SWEET--
OH *HI,* ARTIE!
"ARTIE," KATIE WAS TELLING ME *ALL* ABOUT YOUR SCHOOL DAYS...

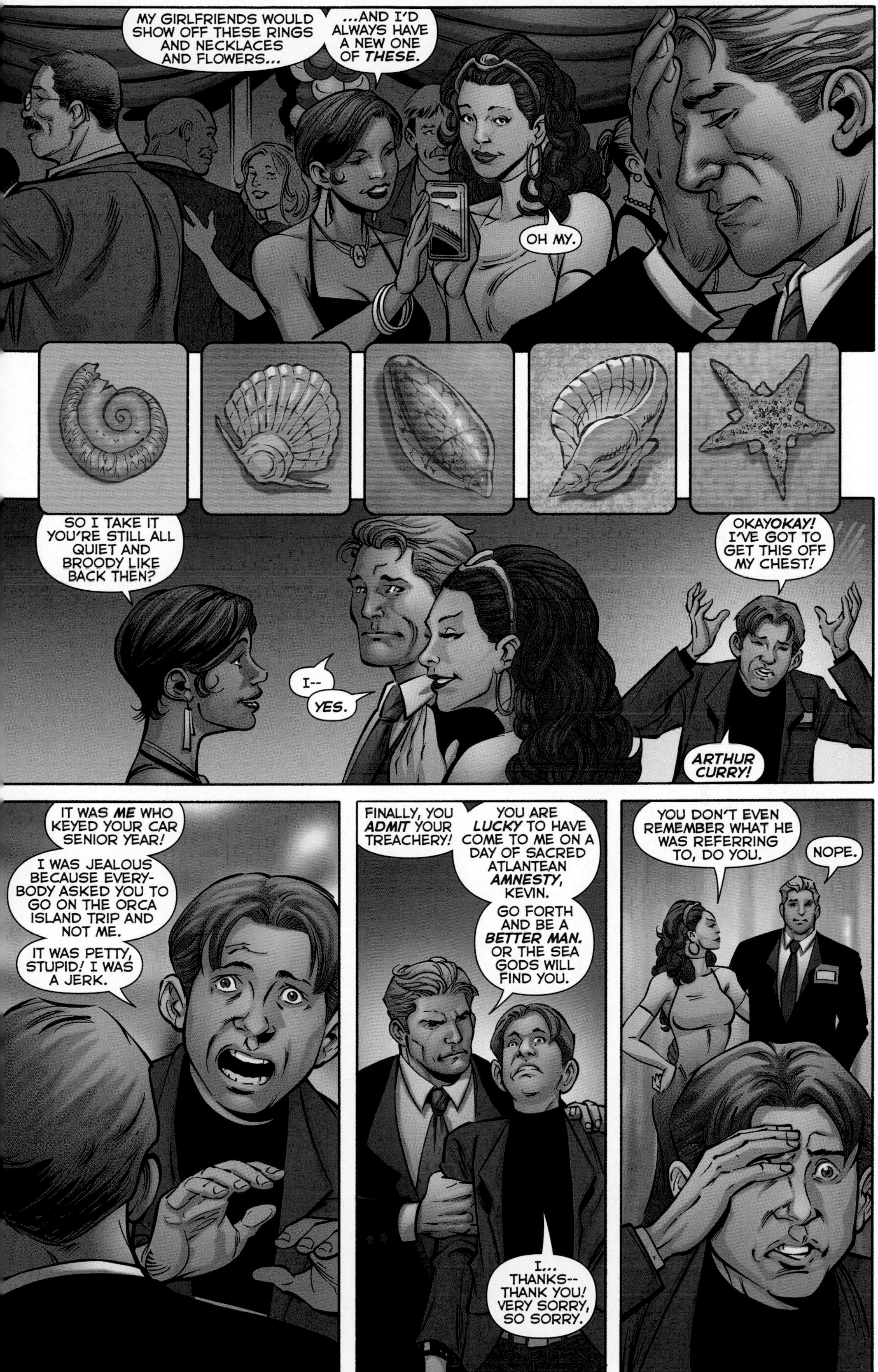
MY GIRLFRIENDS WOULD SHOW OFF THESE RINGS AND NECKLACES AND FLOWERS...
...AND I'D ALWAYS HAVE A NEW ONE OF *THESE.*
OH MY.
SO I TAKE IT YOU'RE STILL ALL QUIET AND BROODY LIKE BACK THEN?
I--
YES.
OKAY*OKAY!* I'VE GOT TO GET THIS OFF MY CHEST!
ARTHUR CURRY!
IT WAS *ME* WHO KEYED YOUR CAR SENIOR YEAR!
I WAS JEALOUS BECAUSE EVERYBODY ASKED YOU TO GO ON THE ORCA ISLAND TRIP AND NOT ME.
IT WAS PETTY, STUPID! I WAS A JERK.
FINALLY, YOU *ADMIT* YOUR TREACHERY!
YOU ARE *LUCKY* TO HAVE COME TO ME ON A DAY OF SACRED ATLANTEAN *AMNESTY,* KEVIN.
GO FORTH AND BE A *BETTER MAN.* OR THE SEA GODS WILL FIND YOU.
I... THANKS-- THANK YOU! VERY SORRY, SO SORRY.
YOU DON'T EVEN REMEMBER WHAT HE WAS REFERRING TO, DO YOU.
NOPE.

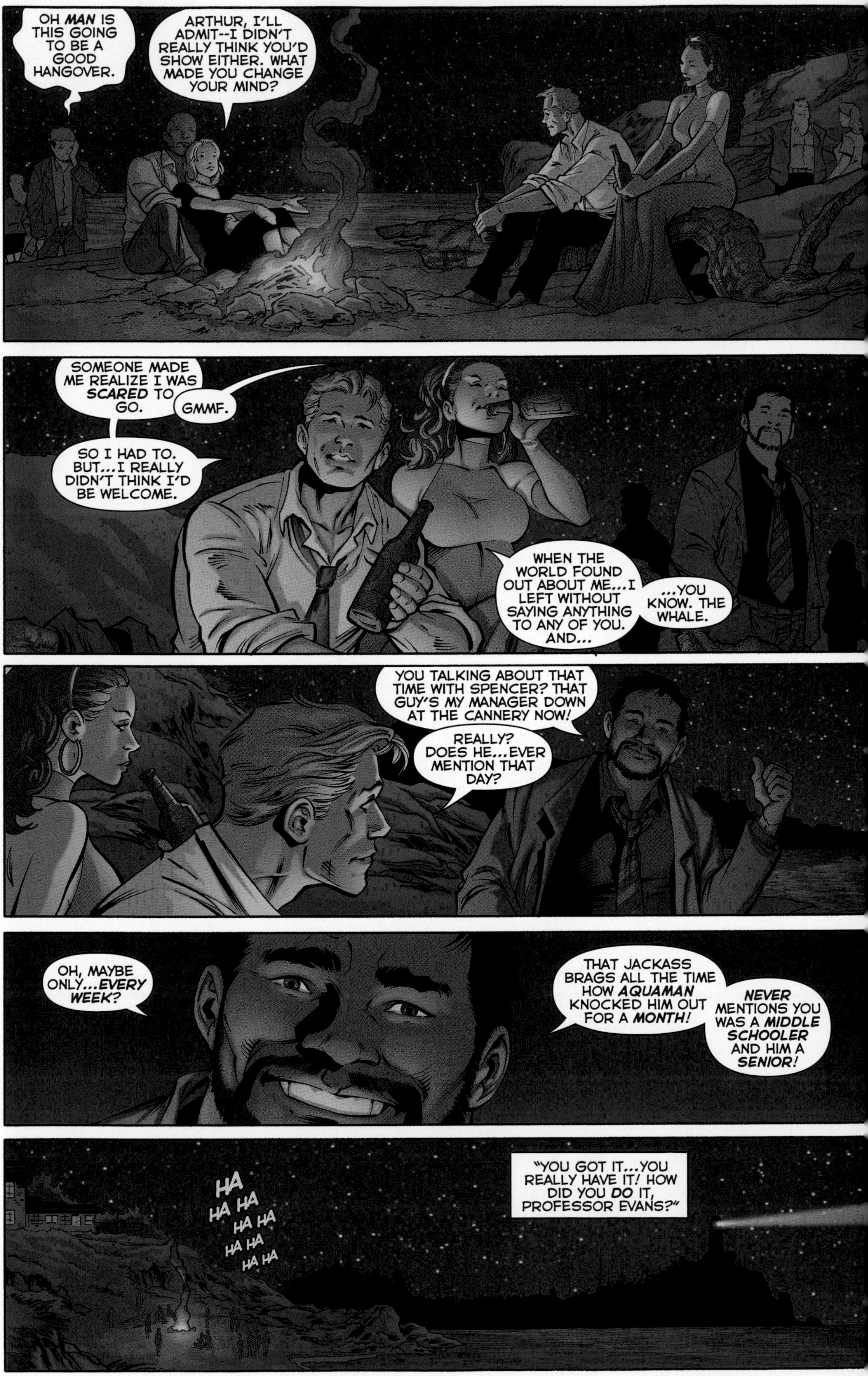
OH MAN IS THIS GOING TO BE A GOOD HANGOVER.
ARTHUR, I'LL ADMIT--I DIDN'T REALLY THINK YOU'D SHOW EITHER. WHAT MADE YOU CHANGE YOUR MIND?
SOMEONE MADE ME REALIZE I WAS SCARED TO GO.
GMMF.
SO I HAD TO. BUT... I REALLY DIDN'T THINK I'D BE WELCOME.
WHEN THE WORLD FOUND OUT ABOUT ME... I LEFT WITHOUT SAYING ANYTHING TO ANY OF YOU. AND...
...YOU KNOW. THE WHALE.
YOU TALKING ABOUT THAT TIME WITH SPENCER? THAT GUY'S MY MANAGER DOWN AT THE CANNERY NOW!
REALLY? DOES HE... EVER MENTION THAT DAY?
OH, MAYBE ONLY... EVERY WEEK?
THAT JACKASS BRAGS ALL THE TIME HOW AQUAMAN KNOCKED HIM OUT FOR A MONTH!
NEVER MENTIONS YOU WAS A MIDDLE SCHOOLER AND HIM A SENIOR!
HA HA HA HA HA HA HA HA HA
"YOU GOT IT... YOU REALLY HAVE IT! HOW DID YOU DO IT, PROFESSOR EVANS?"

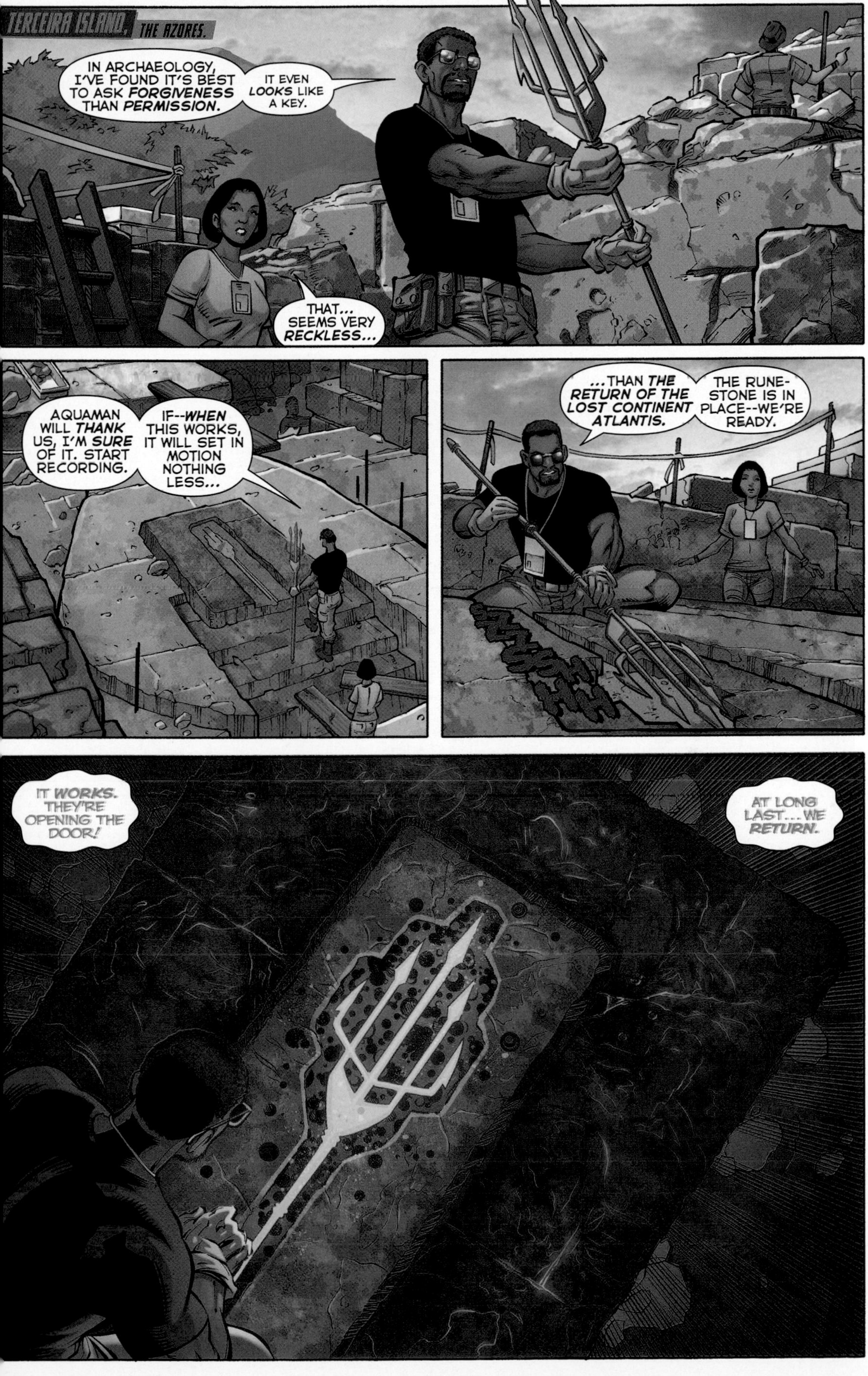
TERCEIRA ISLAND, THE AZORES.
IN ARCHAEOLOGY, I'VE FOUND IT'S BEST TO ASK FORGIVENESS THAN PERMISSION.
IT EVEN LOOKS LIKE A KEY.
THAT... SEEMS VERY RECKLESS...
AQUAMAN WILL THANK US, I'M SURE OF IT. START RECORDING.
IF--WHEN THIS WORKS, IT WILL SET IN MOTION NOTHING LESS...
...THAN THE RETURN OF THE LOST CONTINENT ATLANTIS.
THE RUNE-STONE IS IN PLACE--WE'RE READY.
IT WORKS. THEY'RE OPENING THE DOOR!
AT LONG LAST... WE RETURN.

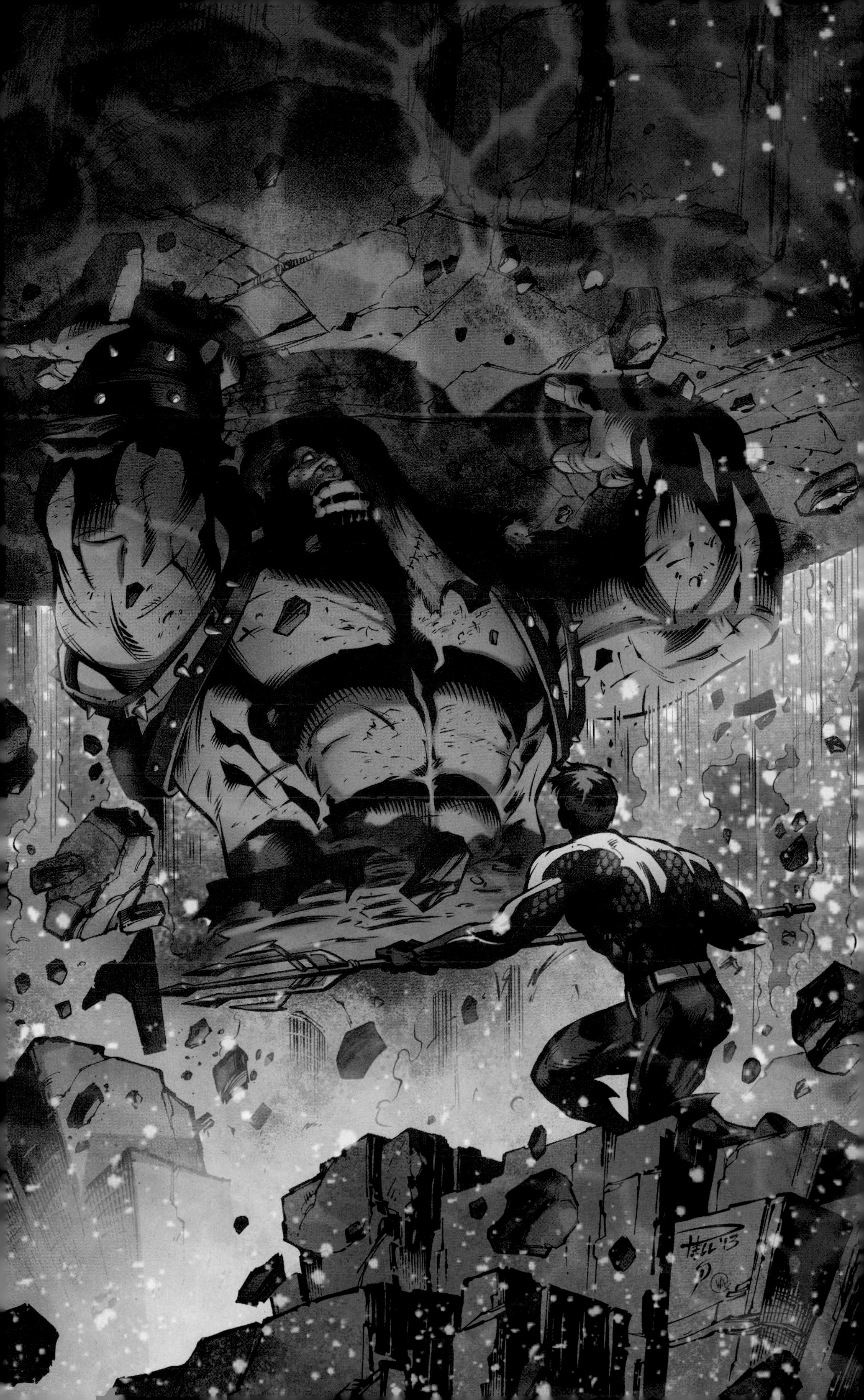

OLYMPIAN

JEFF PARKER writer **PAUL PELLETIER** penciller **SEAN PARSONS NORM RAPMUND** (pg 94) inkers
RAIN BEREDO colorist **DEZI SIENTY** letterer cover by **PAUL PELLETIER, SEAN PARSONS** and **WIL QUINTANA**

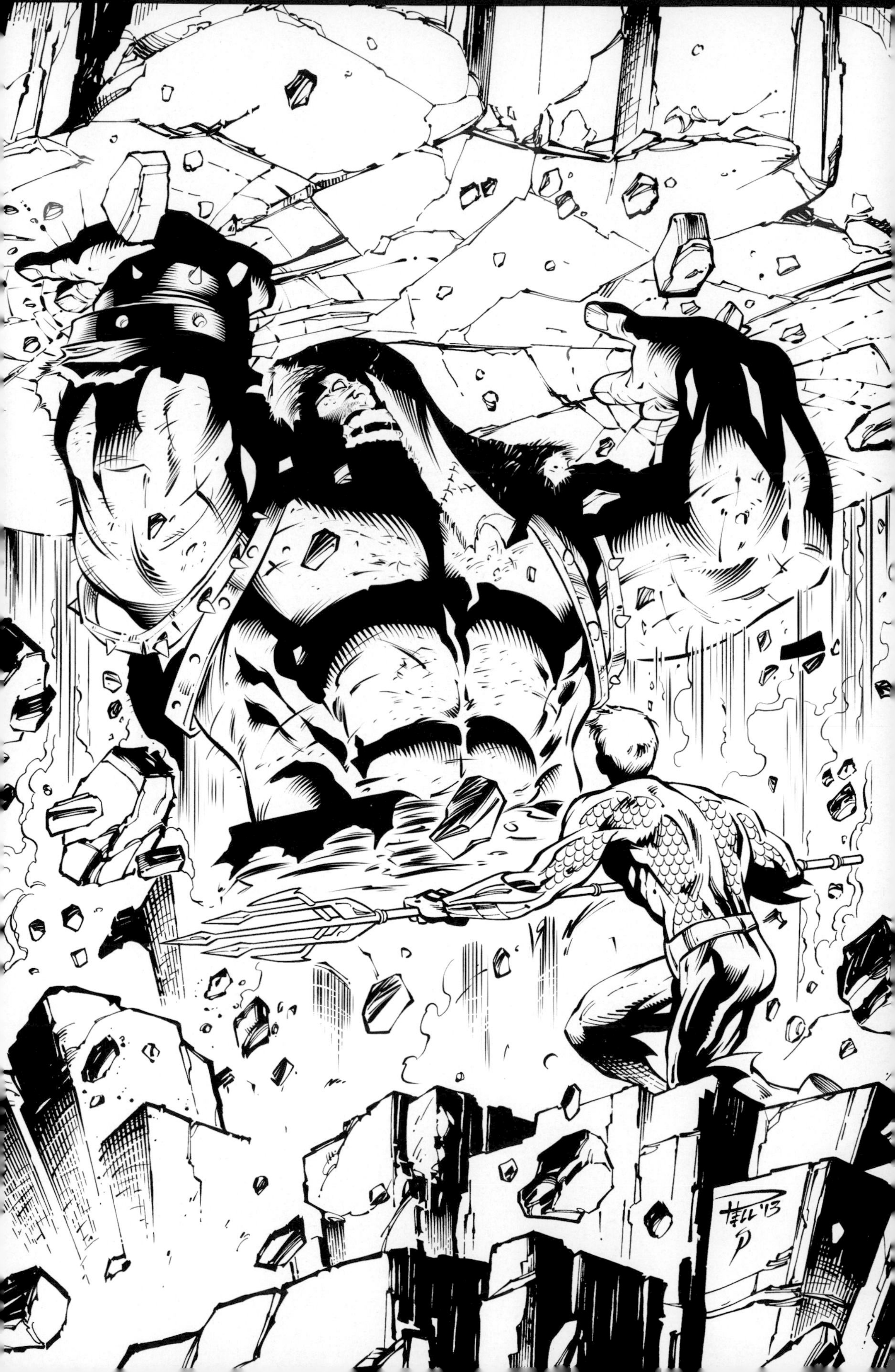

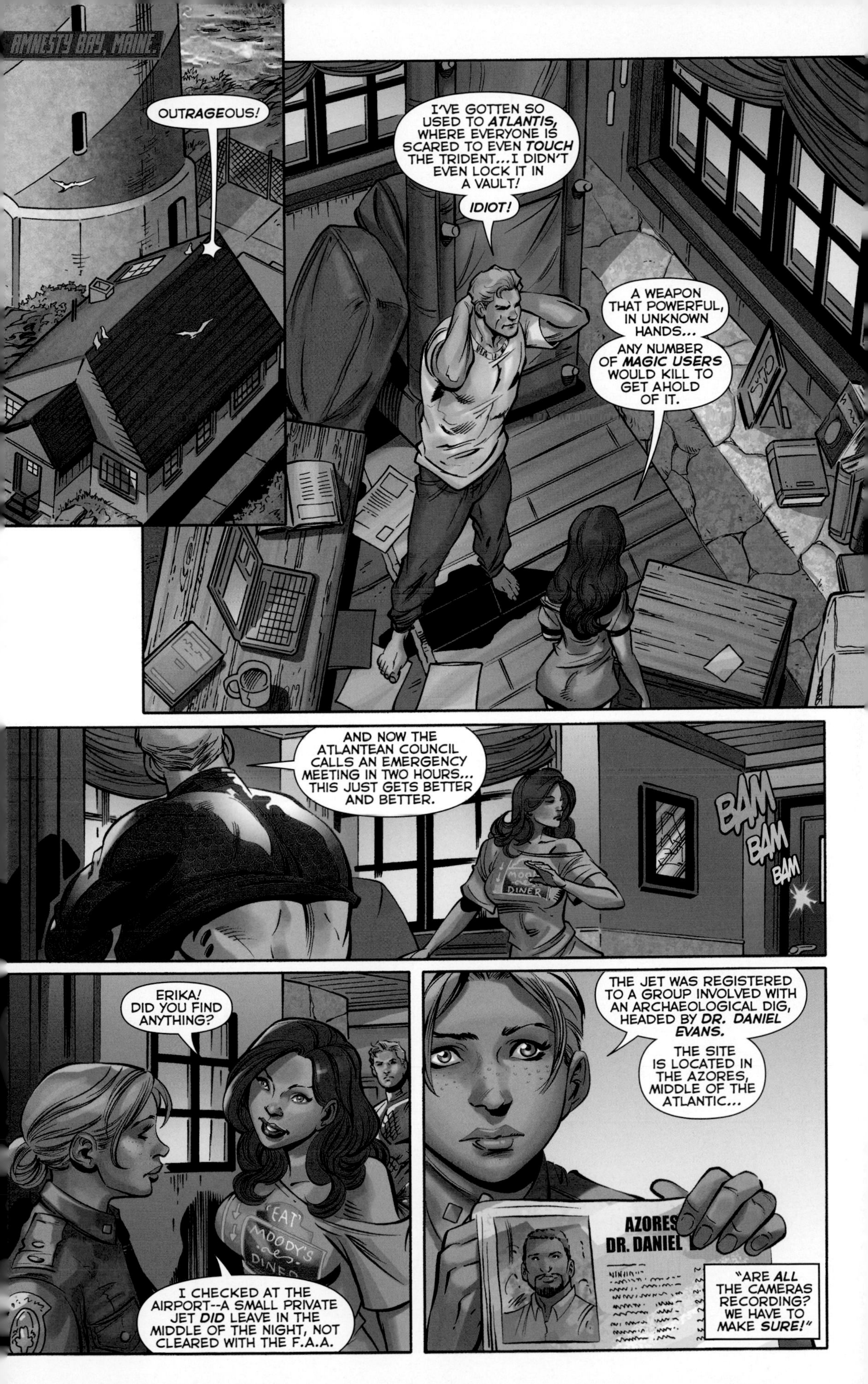
AMNESTY BAY, MAINE.
OUTRAGEOUS!
I'VE GOTTEN SO USED TO ATLANTIS, WHERE EVERYONE IS SCARED TO EVEN TOUCH THE TRIDENT...I DIDN'T EVEN LOCK IT IN A VAULT!
IDIOT!
A WEAPON THAT POWERFUL, IN UNKNOWN HANDS...
ANY NUMBER OF MAGIC USERS WOULD KILL TO GET AHOLD OF IT.
AND NOW THE ATLANTEAN COUNCIL CALLS AN EMERGENCY MEETING IN TWO HOURS... THIS JUST GETS BETTER AND BETTER.
BAM
BAM
BAM
ERIKA! DID YOU FIND ANYTHING?
I CHECKED AT THE AIRPORT--A SMALL PRIVATE JET DID LEAVE IN THE MIDDLE OF THE NIGHT, NOT CLEARED WITH THE F.A.A.
THE JET WAS REGISTERED TO A GROUP INVOLVED WITH AN ARCHAEOLOGICAL DIG, HEADED BY DR. DANIEL EVANS.
THE SITE IS LOCATED IN THE AZORES, MIDDLE OF THE ATLANTIC...
AZORES
DR. DANIEL
"ARE ALL THE CAMERAS RECORDING? WE HAVE TO MAKE SURE!"

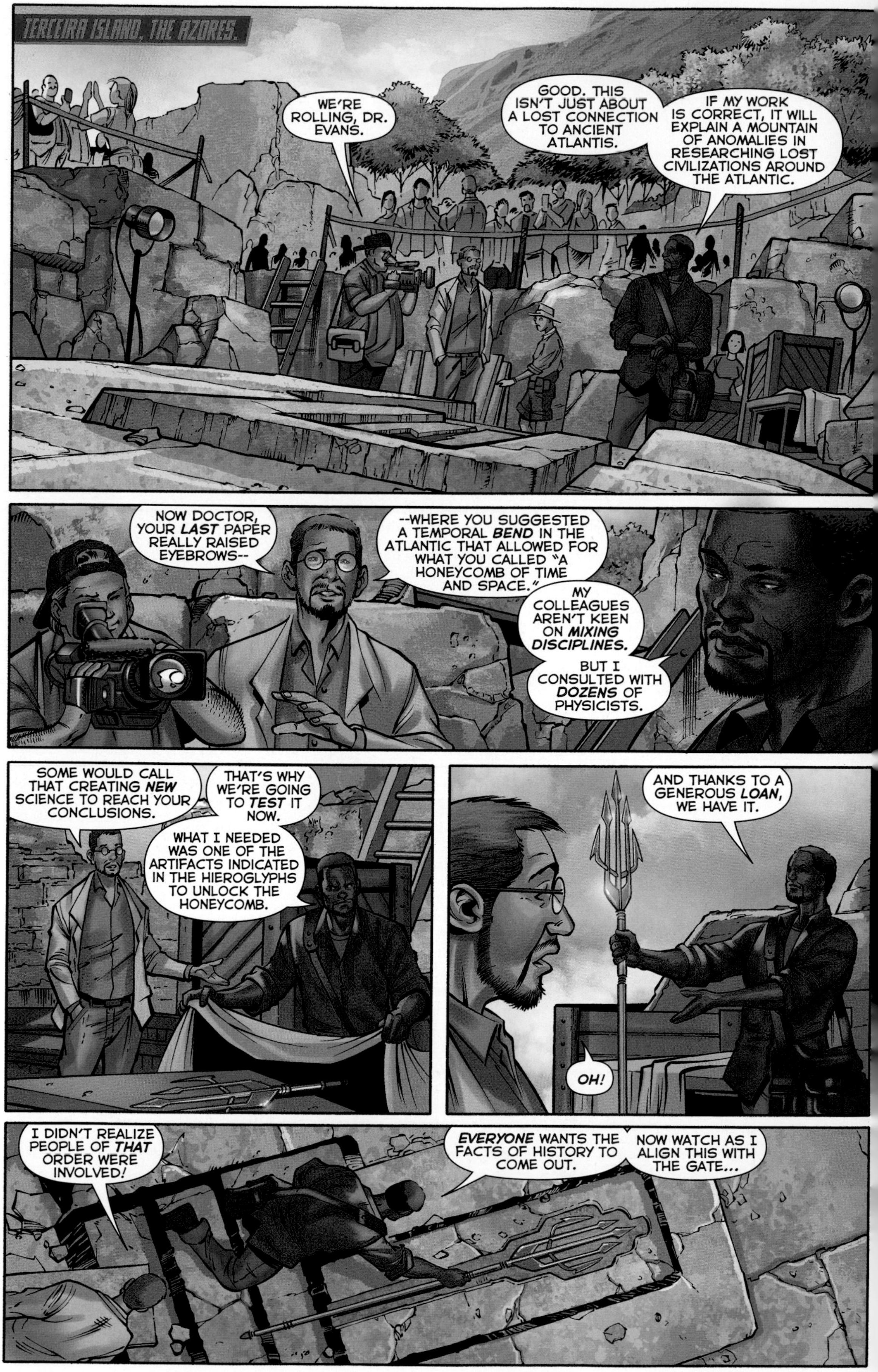
TERCEIRA ISLAND, THE AZORES.
WE'RE ROLLING, DR. EVANS.
GOOD. THIS ISN'T JUST ABOUT A LOST CONNECTION TO ANCIENT ATLANTIS.
IF MY WORK IS CORRECT, IT WILL EXPLAIN A MOUNTAIN OF ANOMALIES IN RESEARCHING LOST CIVILIZATIONS AROUND THE ATLANTIC.
NOW DOCTOR, YOUR LAST PAPER REALLY RAISED EYEBROWS--
--WHERE YOU SUGGESTED A TEMPORAL BEND IN THE ATLANTIC THAT ALLOWED FOR WHAT YOU CALLED "A HONEYCOMB OF TIME AND SPACE."
MY COLLEAGUES AREN'T KEEN ON MIXING DISCIPLINES.
BUT I CONSULTED WITH DOZENS OF PHYSICISTS.
SOME WOULD CALL THAT CREATING NEW SCIENCE TO REACH YOUR CONCLUSIONS.
THAT'S WHY WE'RE GOING TO TEST IT NOW.
WHAT I NEEDED WAS ONE OF THE ARTIFACTS INDICATED IN THE HIEROGLYPHS TO UNLOCK THE HONEYCOMB.
AND THANKS TO A GENEROUS LOAN, WE HAVE IT.
OH!
I DIDN'T REALIZE PEOPLE OF THAT ORDER WERE INVOLVED!
EVERYONE WANTS THE FACTS OF HISTORY TO COME OUT.
NOW WATCH AS I ALIGN THIS WITH THE GATE...

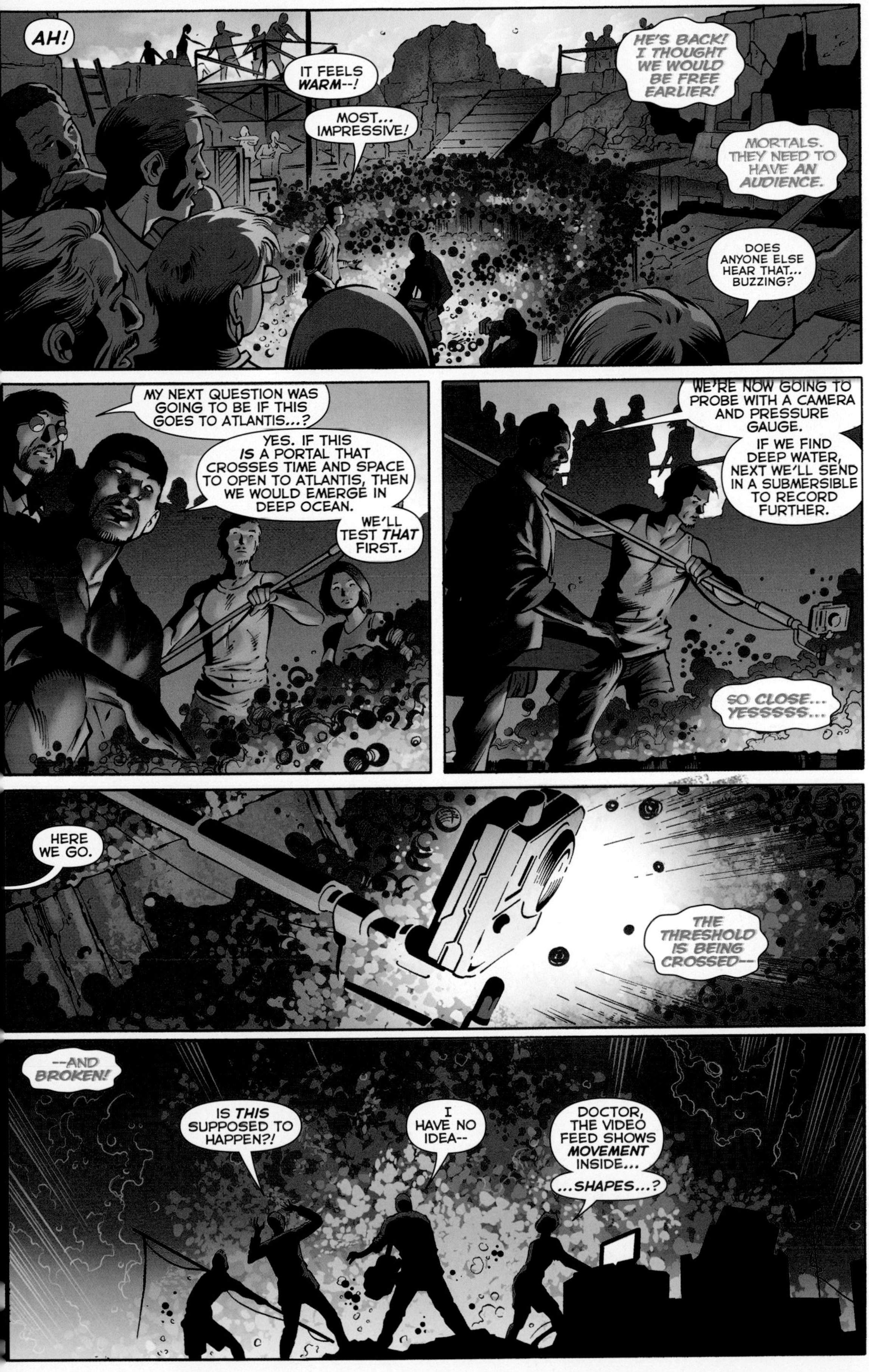
AH!
IT FEELS WARM--!
MOST... IMPRESSIVE!
HE'S BACK! I THOUGHT WE WOULD BE FREE EARLIER!
MORTALS. THEY NEED TO HAVE AN AUDIENCE.
DOES ANYONE ELSE HEAR THAT... BUZZING?
MY NEXT QUESTION WAS GOING TO BE IF THIS GOES TO ATLANTIS...?
YES. IF THIS IS A PORTAL THAT CROSSES TIME AND SPACE TO OPEN TO ATLANTIS, THEN WE WOULD EMERGE IN DEEP OCEAN.
WE'LL TEST THAT FIRST.
WE'RE NOW GOING TO PROBE WITH A CAMERA AND PRESSURE GAUGE.
IF WE FIND DEEP WATER, NEXT WE'LL SEND IN A SUBMERSIBLE TO RECORD FURTHER.
SO CLOSE... YESSSSS...
HERE WE GO.
THE THRESHOLD IS BEING CROSSED--
--AND BROKEN!
IS THIS SUPPOSED TO HAPPEN?!
I HAVE NO IDEA--
DOCTOR, THE VIDEO FEED SHOWS MOVEMENT INSIDE...
...SHAPES...?

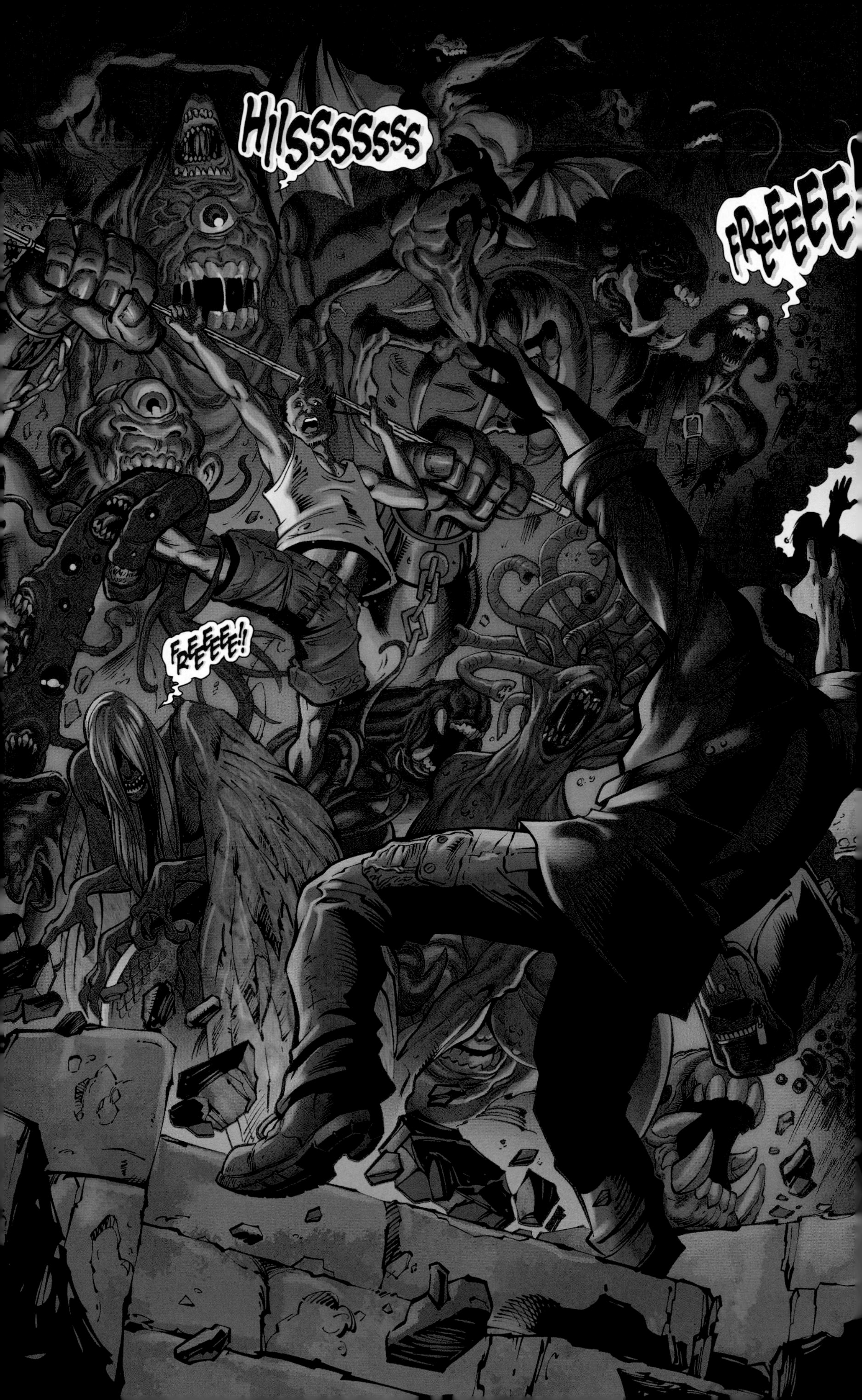
HISSSSSSS
FREEEEE
FREEEEEEEE!!

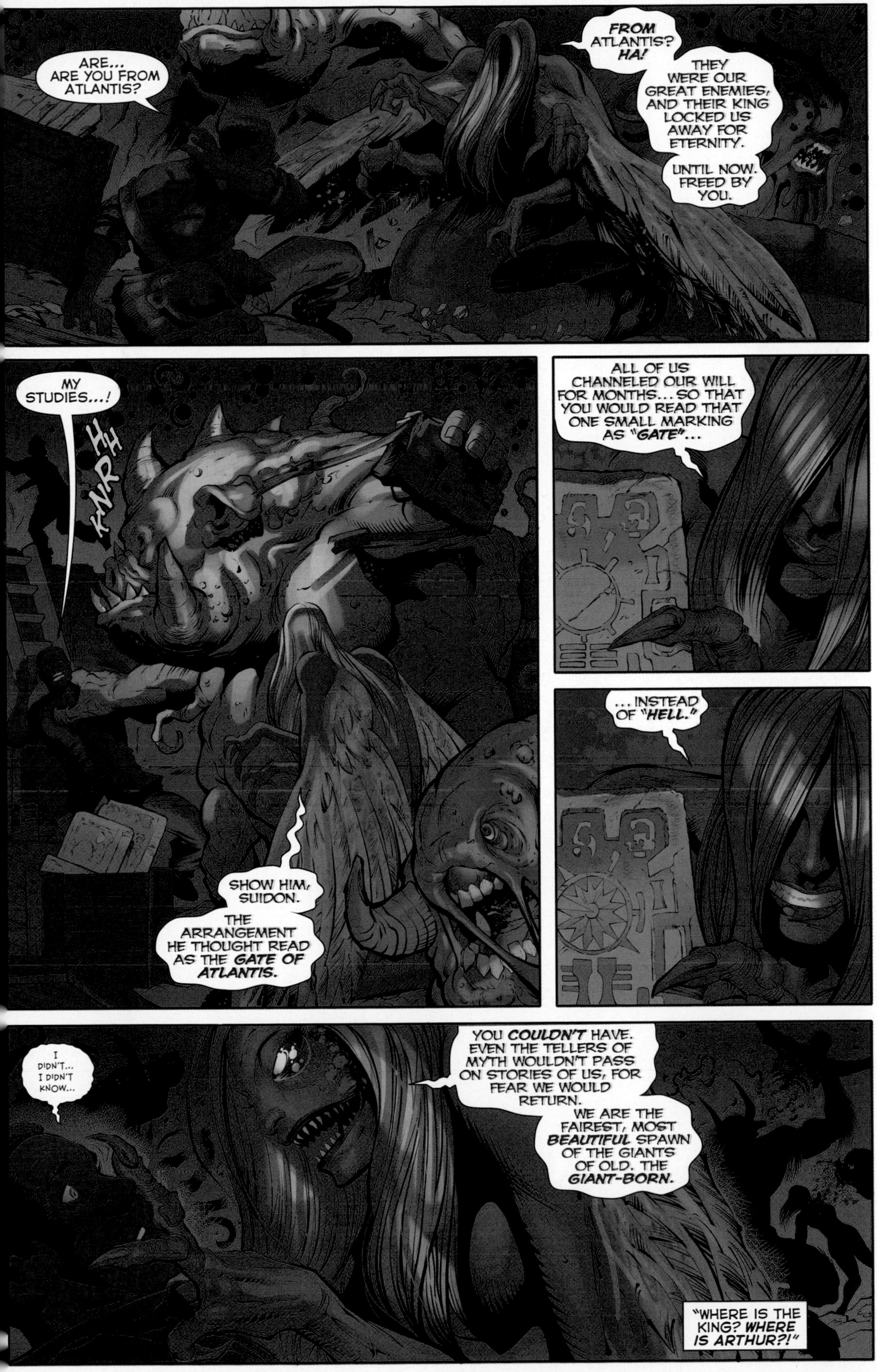
ARE... ARE YOU FROM ATLANTIS?
FROM ATLANTIS? HA!
THEY WERE OUR GREAT ENEMIES, AND THEIR KING LOCKED US AWAY FOR ETERNITY.
UNTIL NOW. FREED BY YOU.
MY STUDIES...!
HHKNRR
SHOW HIM, SUIDON.
THE ARRANGEMENT HE THOUGHT READ AS THE GATE OF ATLANTIS.
ALL OF US CHANNELED OUR WILL FOR MONTHS... SO THAT YOU WOULD READ THAT ONE SMALL MARKING AS "GATE"...
...INSTEAD OF "HELL."
I DIDN'T... I DIDN'T KNOW...
YOU COULDN'T HAVE. EVEN THE TELLERS OF MYTH WOULDN'T PASS ON STORIES OF US, FOR FEAR WE WOULD RETURN.
WE ARE THE FAIREST, MOST BEAUTIFUL SPAWN OF THE GIANTS OF OLD. THE GIANT-BORN.
"WHERE IS THE KING? WHERE IS ARTHUR?!"

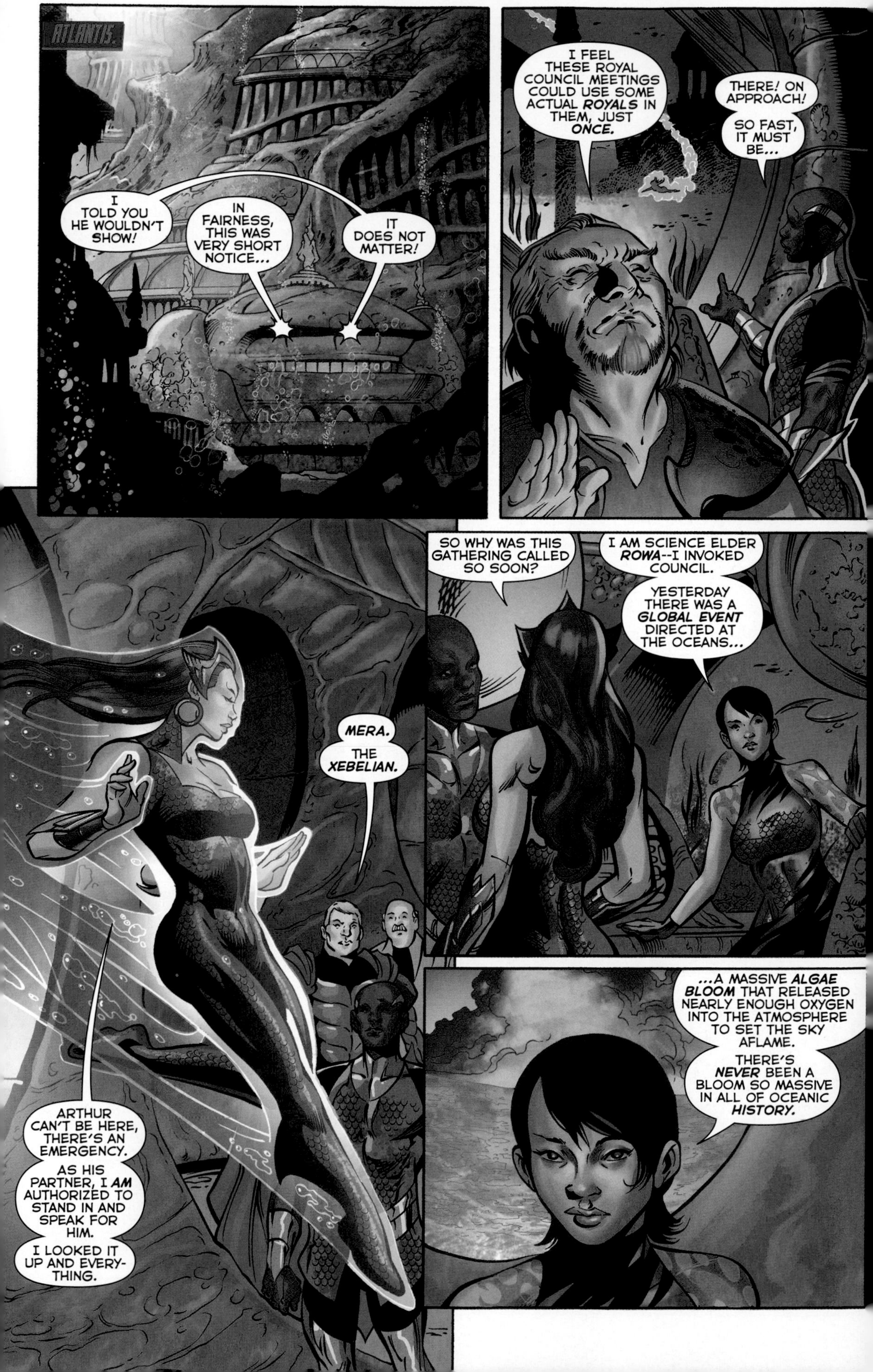
ATLANTIS.
I TOLD YOU HE WOULDN'T SHOW!
IN FAIRNESS, THIS WAS VERY SHORT NOTICE...
IT DOES NOT MATTER!
I FEEL THESE ROYAL COUNCIL MEETINGS COULD USE SOME ACTUAL ROYALS IN THEM, JUST ONCE.
THERE! ON APPROACH!
SO FAST, IT MUST BE...
MERA.
THE XEBELIAN.
ARTHUR CAN'T BE HERE, THERE'S AN EMERGENCY.
AS HIS PARTNER, I AM AUTHORIZED TO STAND IN AND SPEAK FOR HIM.
I LOOKED IT UP AND EVERY-THING.
SO WHY WAS THIS GATHERING CALLED SO SOON?
I AM SCIENCE ELDER ROWA--I INVOKED COUNCIL.
YESTERDAY THERE WAS A GLOBAL EVENT DIRECTED AT THE OCEANS...
...A MASSIVE ALGAE BLOOM THAT RELEASED NEARLY ENOUGH OXYGEN INTO THE ATMOSPHERE TO SET THE SKY AFLAME.
THERE'S NEVER BEEN A BLOOM SO MASSIVE IN ALL OF OCEANIC HISTORY.

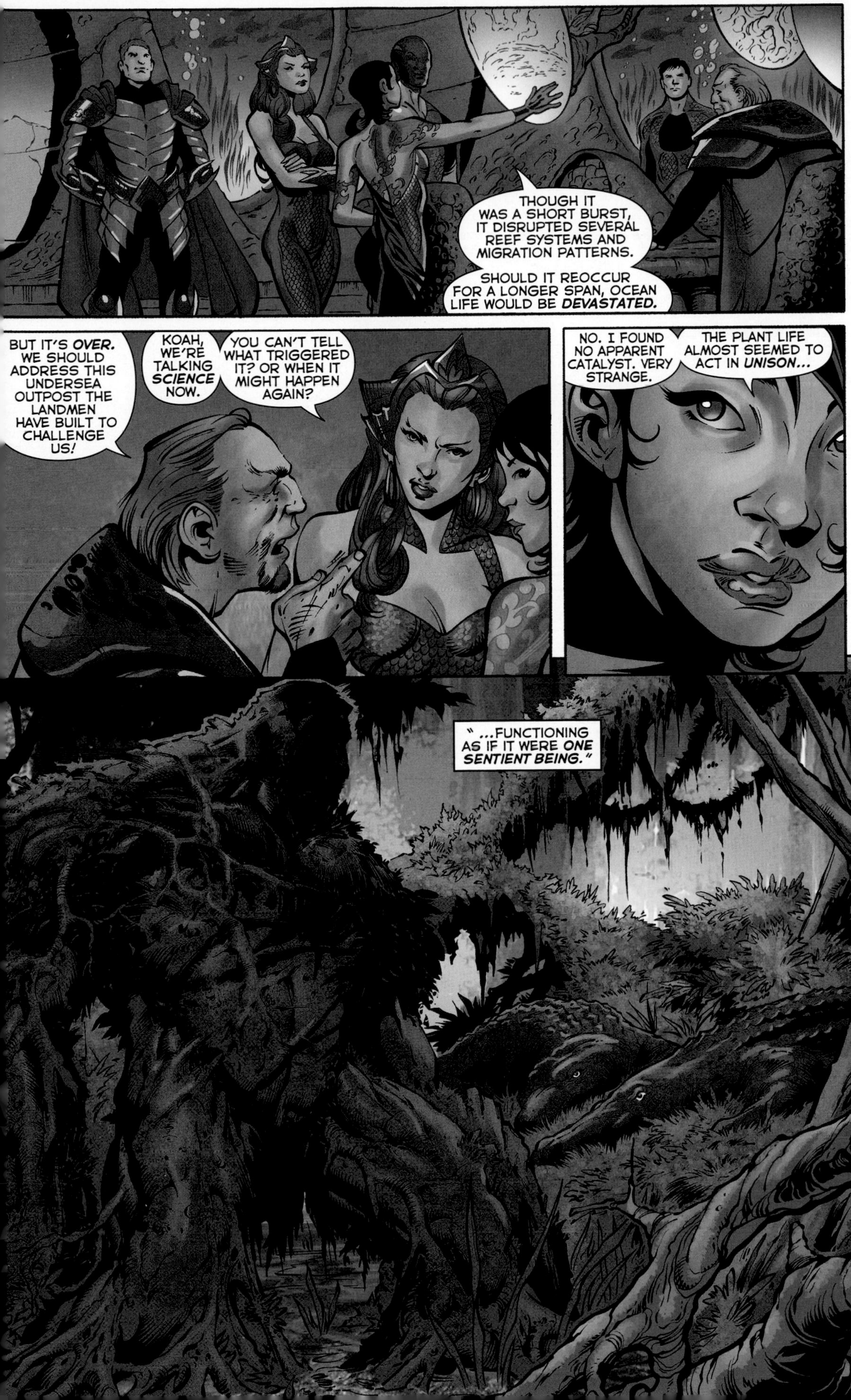

THOUGH IT WAS A SHORT BURST, IT DISRUPTED SEVERAL REEF SYSTEMS AND MIGRATION PATTERNS.
SHOULD IT REOCCUR FOR A LONGER SPAN, OCEAN LIFE WOULD BE *DEVASTATED.*
BUT IT'S *OVER.* WE SHOULD ADDRESS THIS UNDERSEA OUTPOST THE LANDMEN HAVE BUILT TO CHALLENGE US!
KOAH, WE'RE TALKING *SCIENCE* NOW.
YOU CAN'T TELL WHAT TRIGGERED IT? OR WHEN IT MIGHT HAPPEN AGAIN?
NO. I FOUND NO APPARENT CATALYST. VERY STRANGE.
THE PLANT LIFE ALMOST SEEMED TO ACT IN *UNISON...*
"...FUNCTIONING AS IF IT WERE *ONE SENTIENT BEING.*"

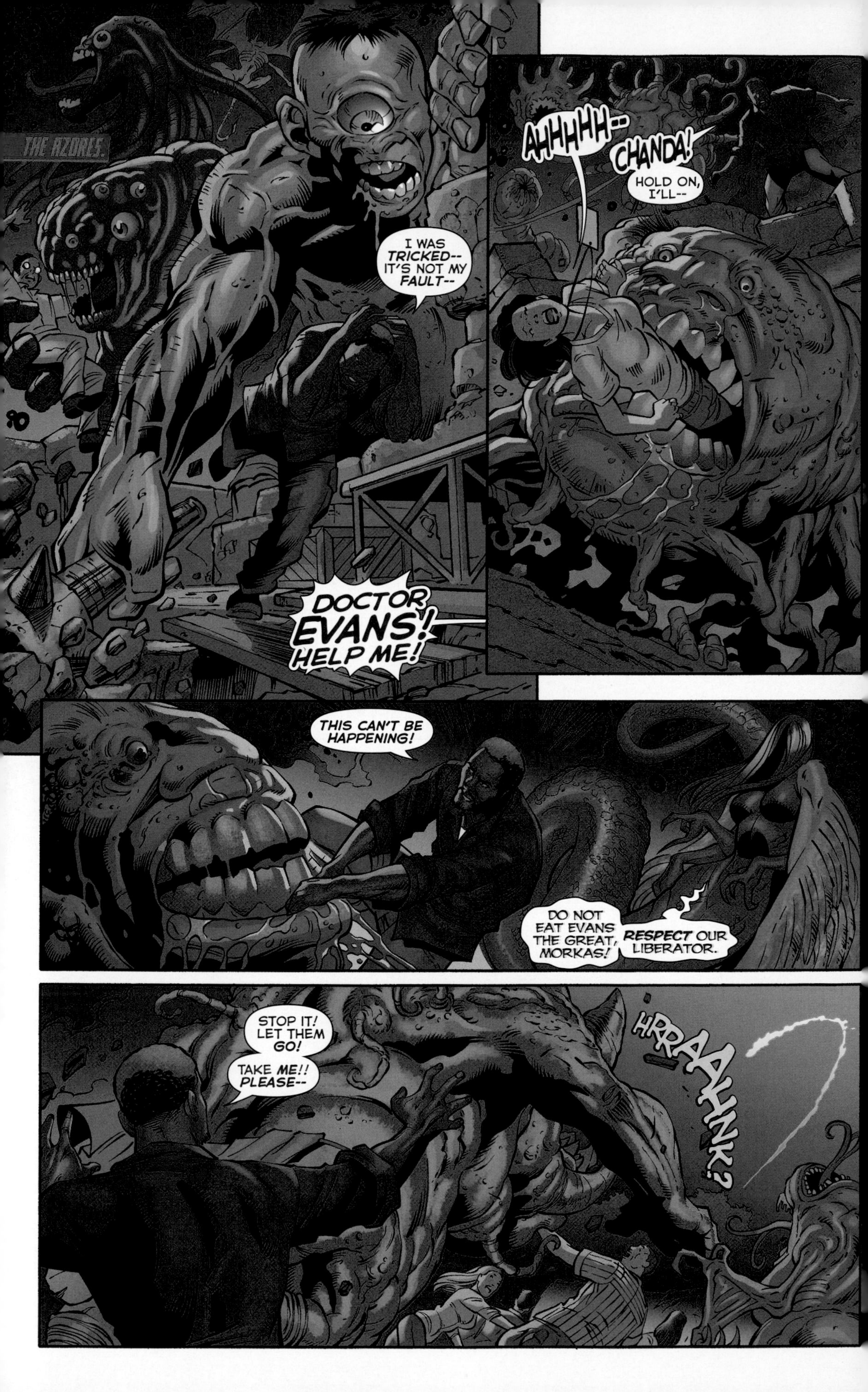
THE AZORES.
I WAS TRICKED-- IT'S NOT MY FAULT--
DOCTOR EVANS! HELP ME!
AHHHHH--
CHANDA!
HOLD ON, I'LL--
THIS CAN'T BE HAPPENING!
DO NOT EAT EVANS THE GREAT, MORKAS!
RESPECT OUR LIBERATOR.
STOP IT! LET THEM GO!
TAKE ME!! PLEASE--
HRRAAHNK?

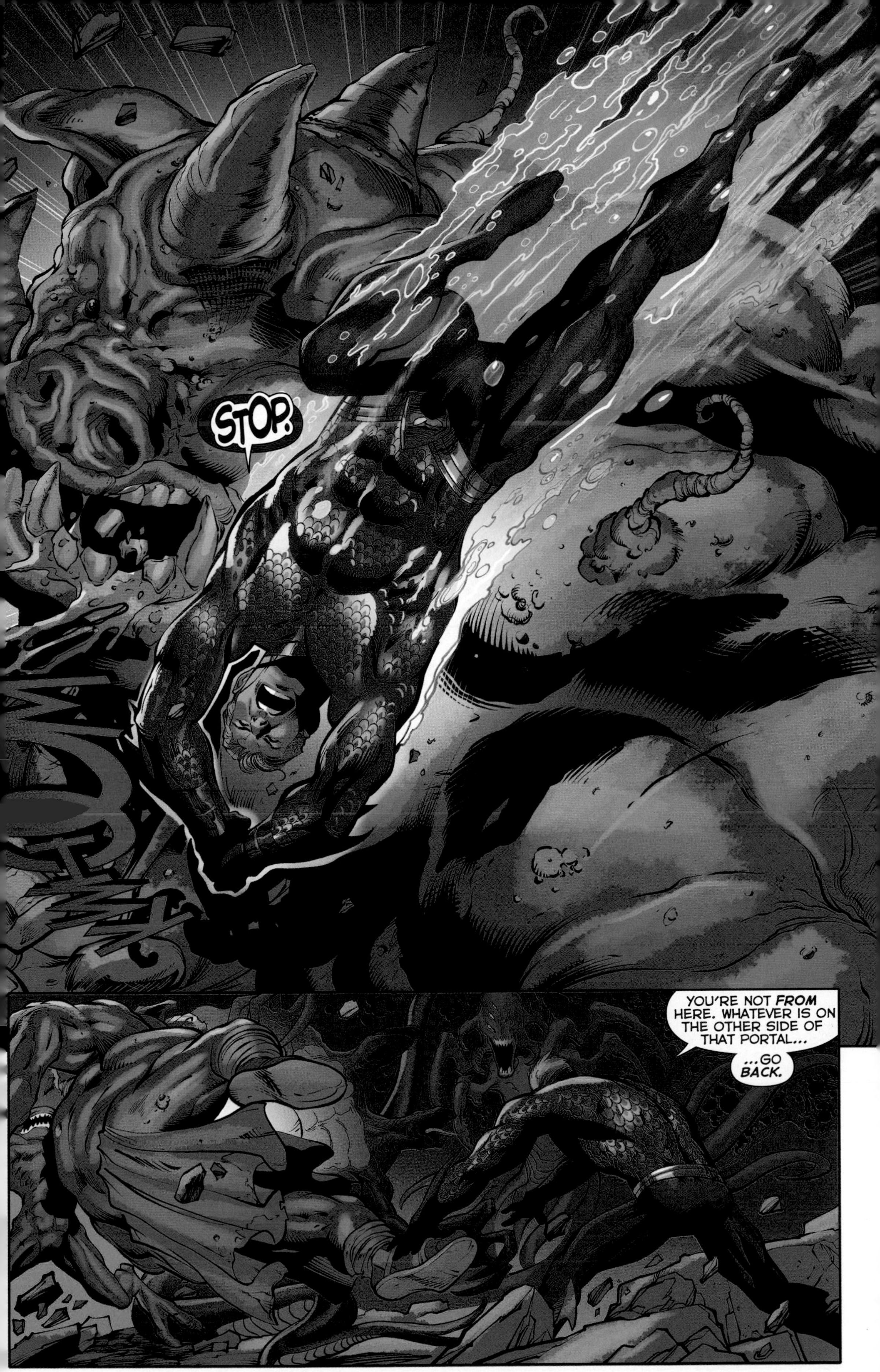
STOP.
YOU'RE NOT *FROM* HERE. WHATEVER IS ON THE OTHER SIDE OF THAT PORTAL...
...GO *BACK.*

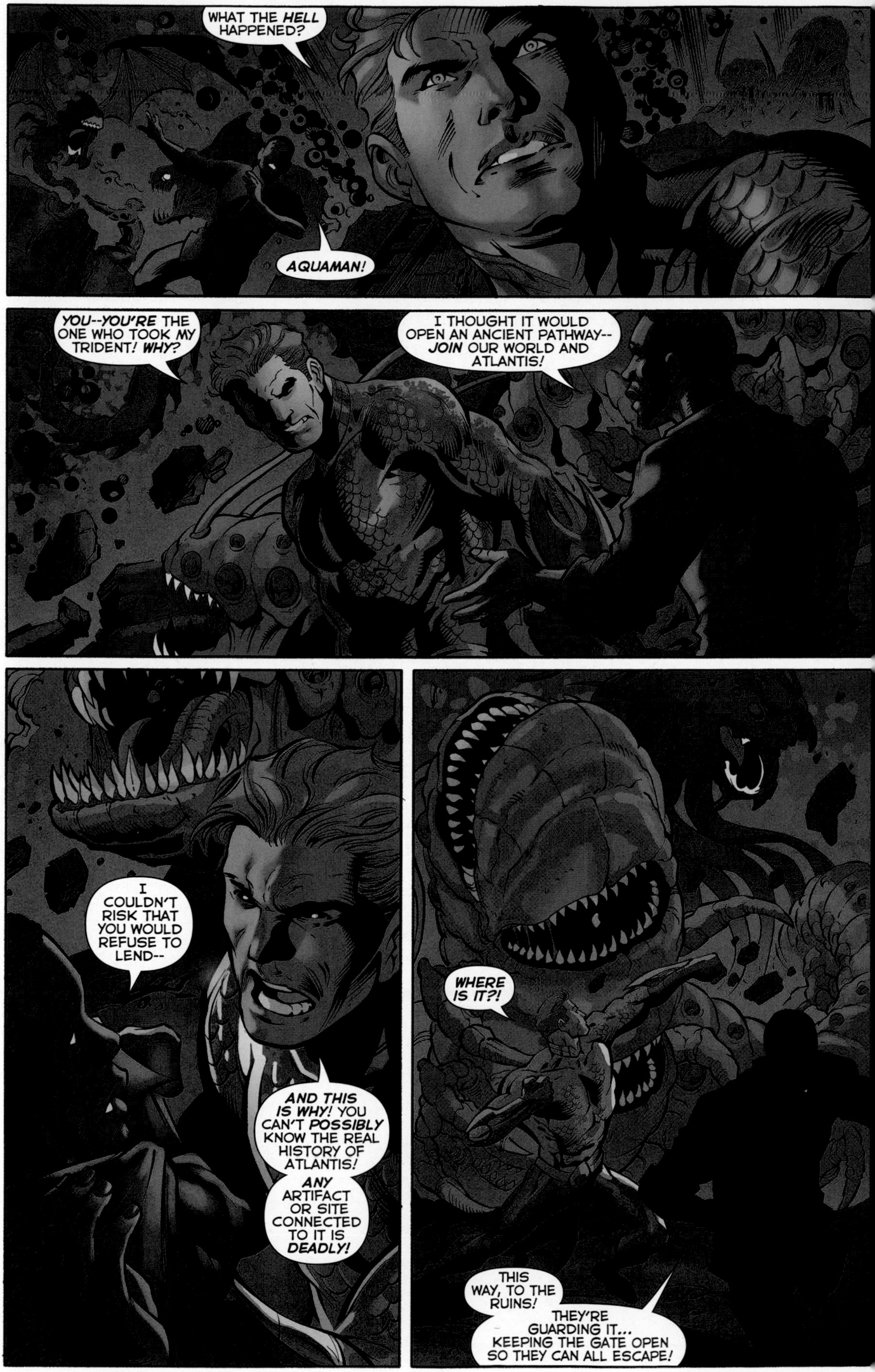
WHAT THE HELL HAPPENED?
AQUAMAN!
YOU--YOU'RE THE ONE WHO TOOK MY TRIDENT! WHY?
I THOUGHT IT WOULD OPEN AN ANCIENT PATHWAY-- JOIN OUR WORLD AND ATLANTIS!
I COULDN'T RISK THAT YOU WOULD REFUSE TO LEND--
AND THIS IS WHY! YOU CAN'T POSSIBLY KNOW THE REAL HISTORY OF ATLANTIS!
ANY ARTIFACT OR SITE CONNECTED TO IT IS DEADLY!
WHERE IS IT?!
THIS WAY, TO THE RUINS!
THEY'RE GUARDING IT... KEEPING THE GATE OPEN SO THEY CAN ALL ESCAPE!

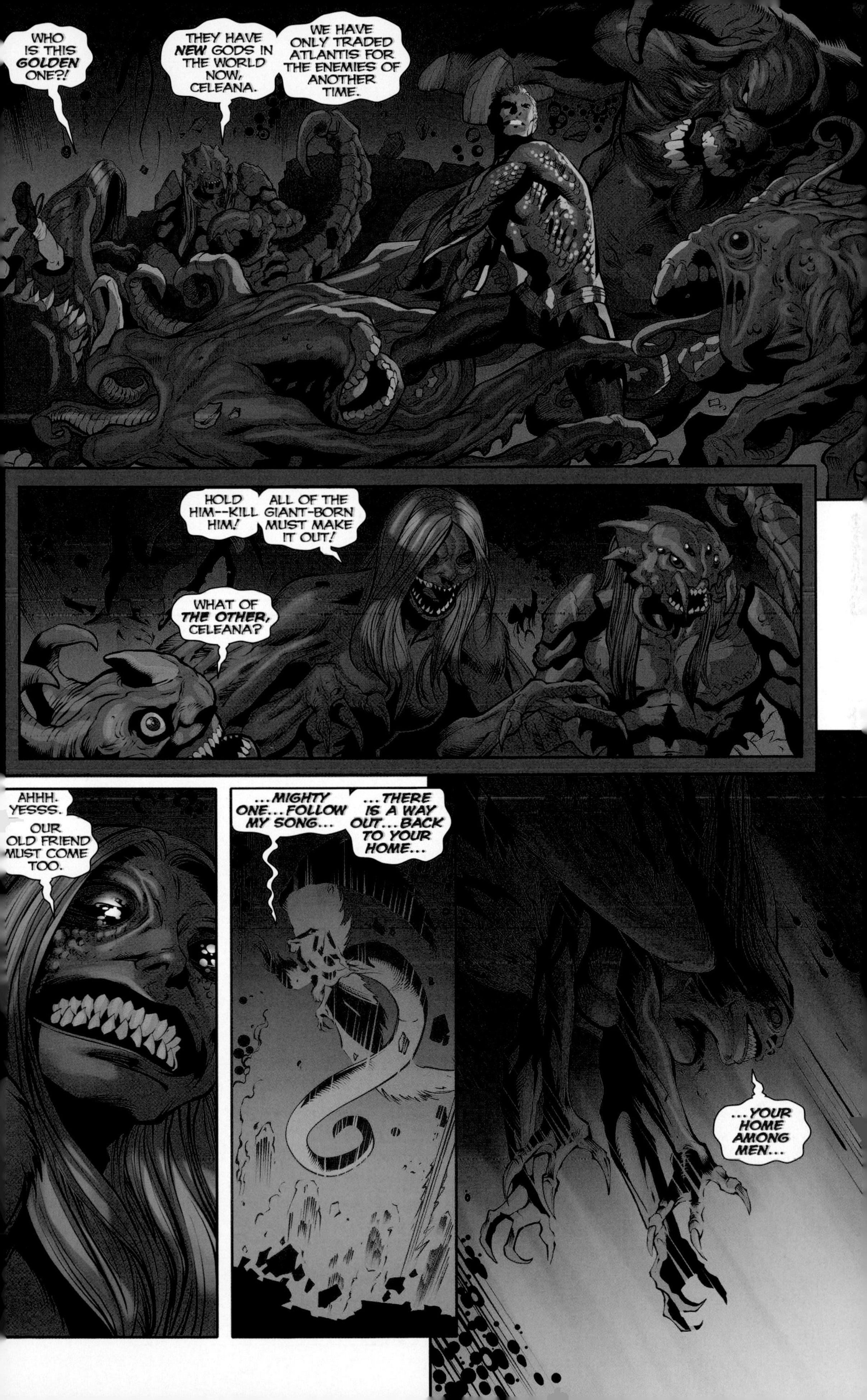
WHO IS THIS GOLDEN ONE?!
THEY HAVE NEW GODS IN THE WORLD NOW, CELEANA.
WE HAVE ONLY TRADED ATLANTIS FOR THE ENEMIES OF ANOTHER TIME.
HOLD HIM--KILL HIM!
ALL OF THE GIANT-BORN MUST MAKE IT OUT!
WHAT OF THE OTHER, CELEANA?
AHHH. YESSS. OUR OLD FRIEND MUST COME TOO.
...MIGHTY ONE...FOLLOW MY SONG...
...THERE IS A WAY OUT...BACK TO YOUR HOME...
...YOUR HOME AMONG MEN...

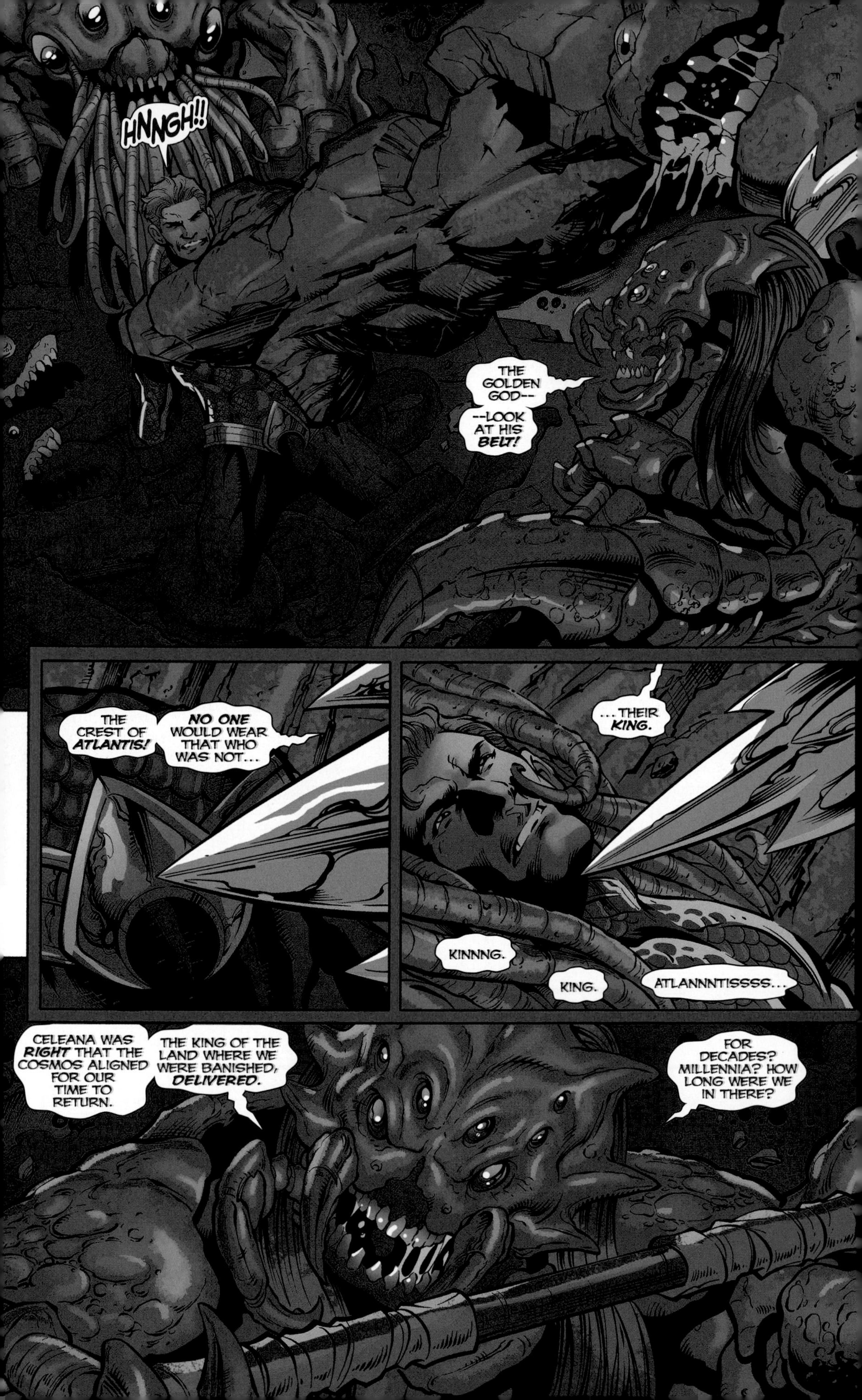
HNNGH!!
THE GOLDEN GOD--
--LOOK AT HIS BELT!
THE CREST OF ATLANTIS!
NO ONE WOULD WEAR THAT WHO WAS NOT...
...THEIR KING.
KINNNG.
KING.
ATLANNNTISSSS...
CELEANA WAS RIGHT THAT THE COSMOS ALIGNED FOR OUR TIME TO RETURN.
THE KING OF THE LAND WHERE WE WERE BANISHED, DELIVERED.
FOR DECADES? MILLENNIA? HOW LONG WERE WE IN THERE?

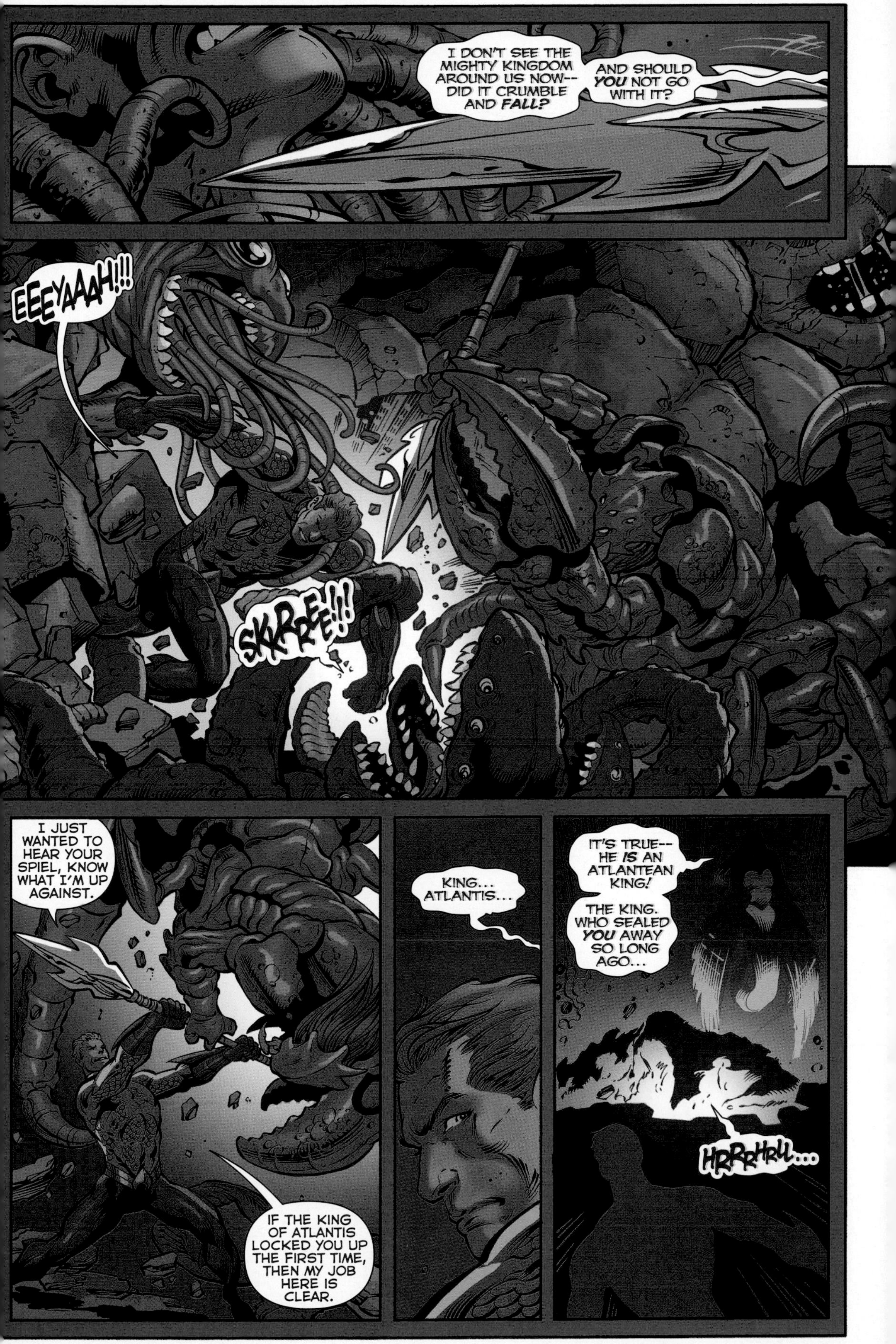
I DON'T SEE THE MIGHTY KINGDOM AROUND US NOW-- DID IT CRUMBLE AND *FALL?*
AND SHOULD *YOU* NOT GO WITH IT?
EEEYAAAH!!!
SKKRREE!!!
I JUST WANTED TO HEAR YOUR SPIEL, KNOW WHAT I'M UP AGAINST.
IF THE KING OF ATLANTIS LOCKED YOU UP THE FIRST TIME, THEN MY JOB HERE IS CLEAR.
KING... ATLANTIS...
IT'S TRUE-- HE *IS* AN ATLANTEAN KING!
THE KING. WHO SEALED *YOU* AWAY SO LONG AGO...
HRRRHRLL...

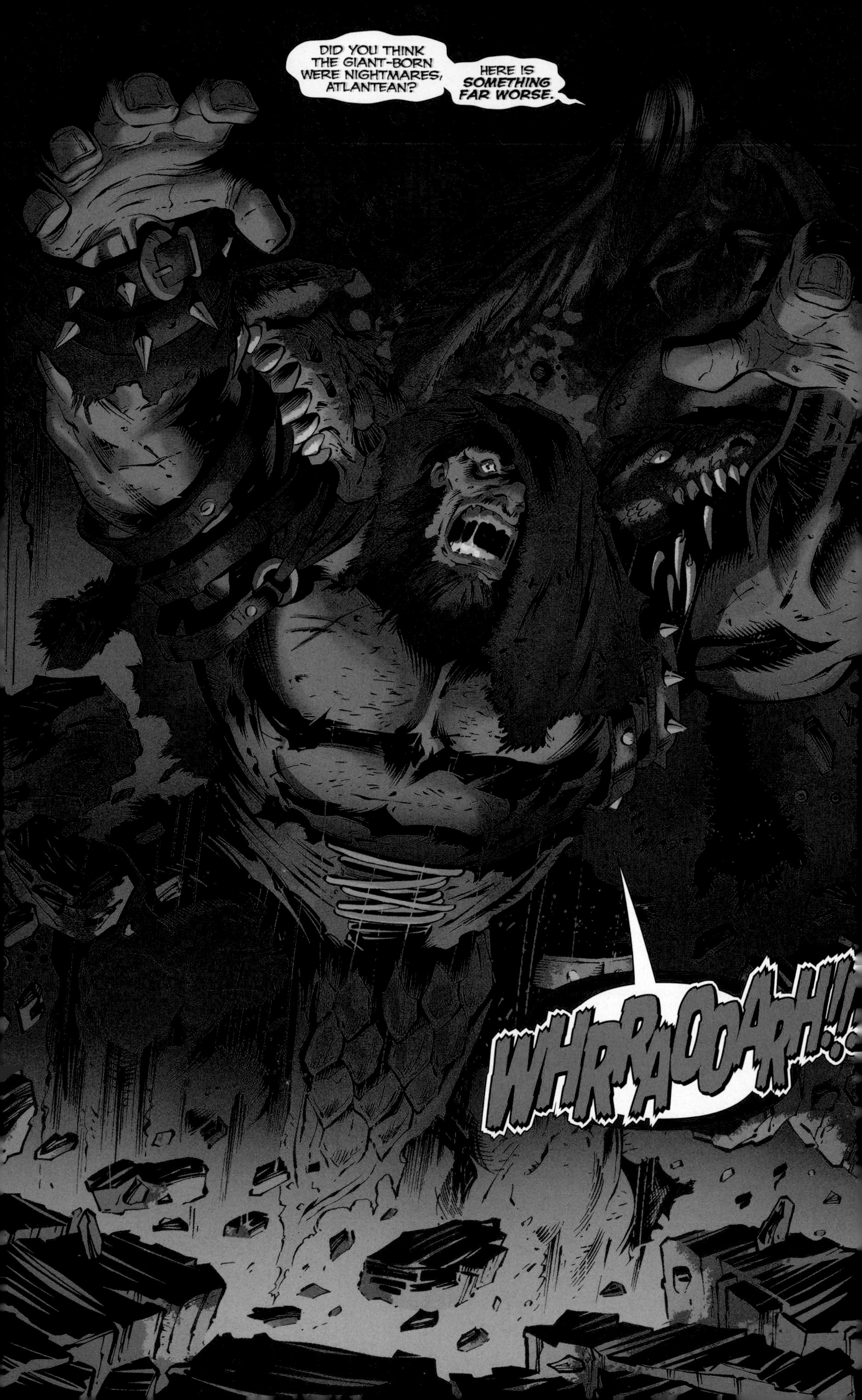
DID YOU THINK THE GIANT-BORN WERE NIGHTMARES, ATLANTEAN?
HERE IS SOMETHING FAR WORSE.
WHRRAOOARH!!

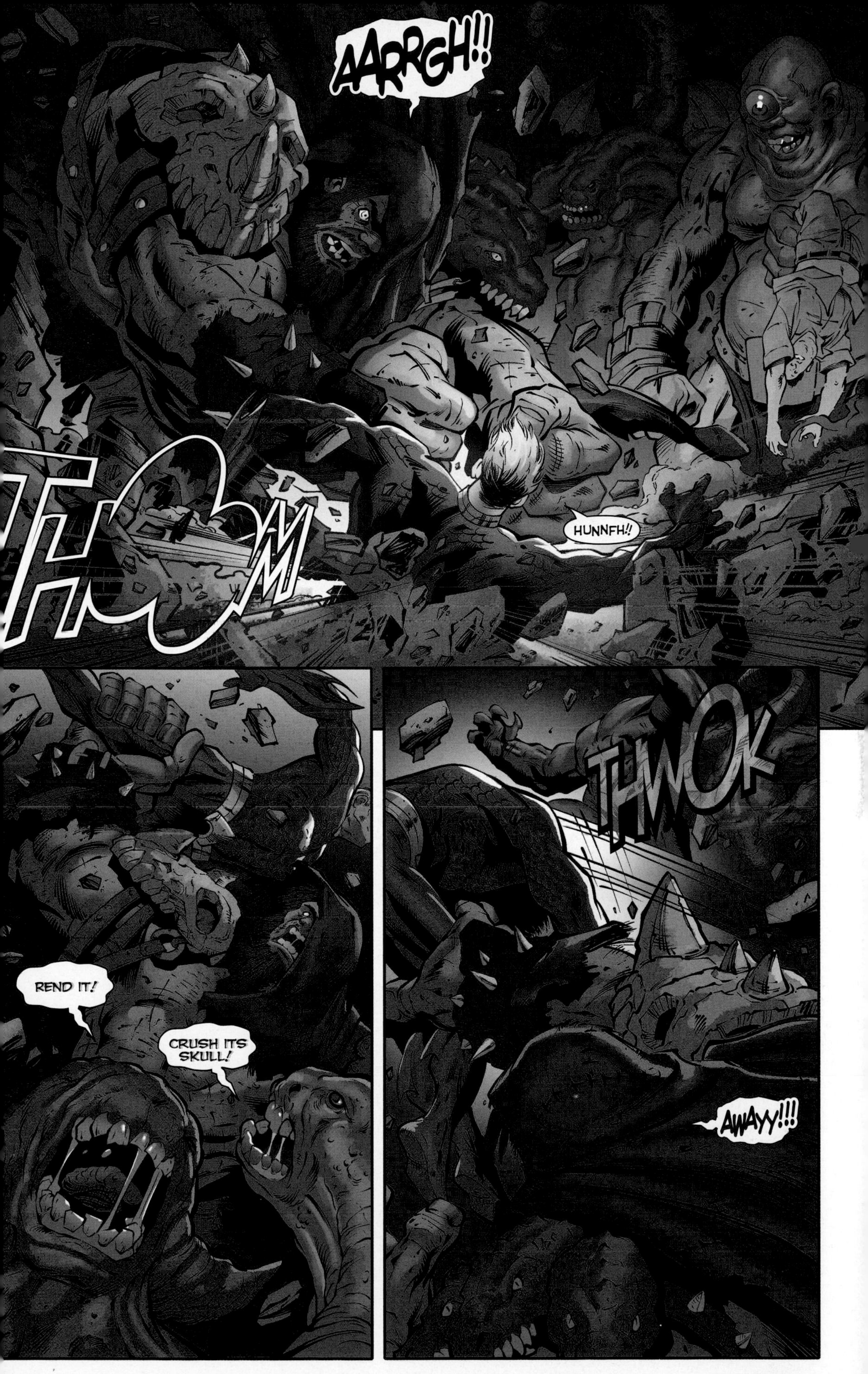
AARRGH!!
THOOM
HUNNFH!!
REND IT!
CRUSH ITS SKULL!
THWOK
AWAYY!!!

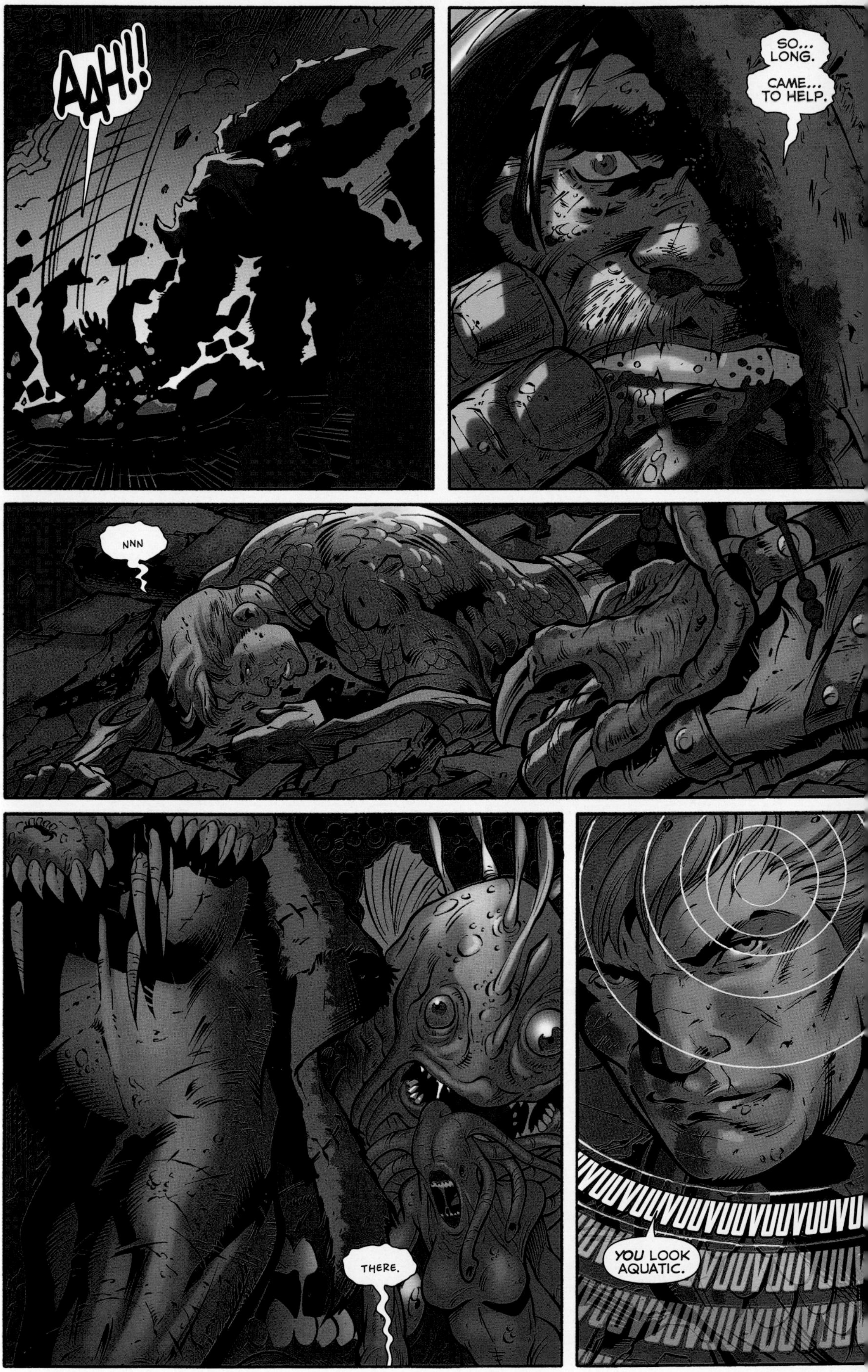
AAH!!
SO... LONG.
CAME... TO HELP.
NNN
THERE.
VUUVUUVUUVUUVUUVU
YOU LOOK AQUATIC.

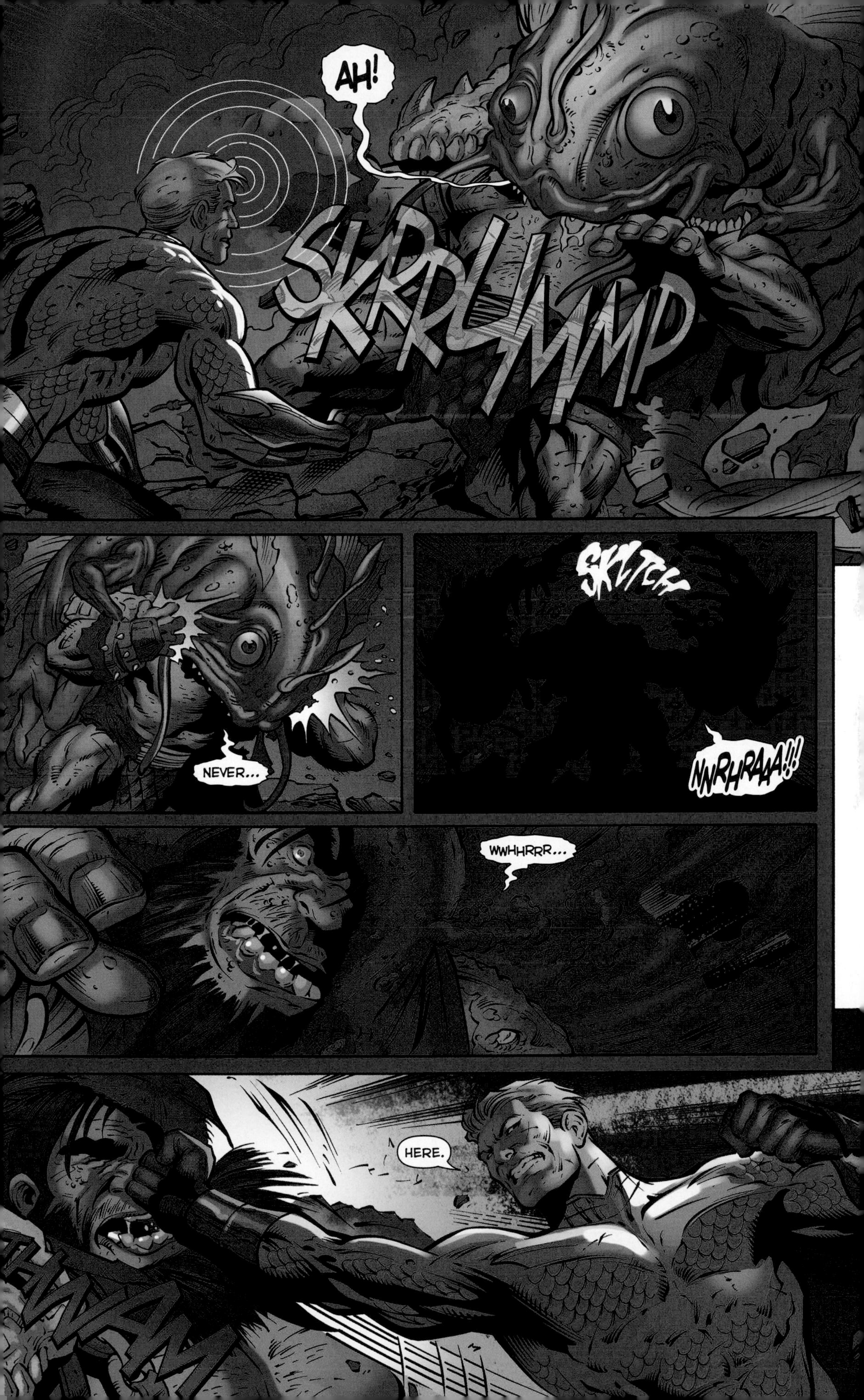
AH!
NEVER...
NNRHRAAA!!!
WWHHRRR...
HERE.

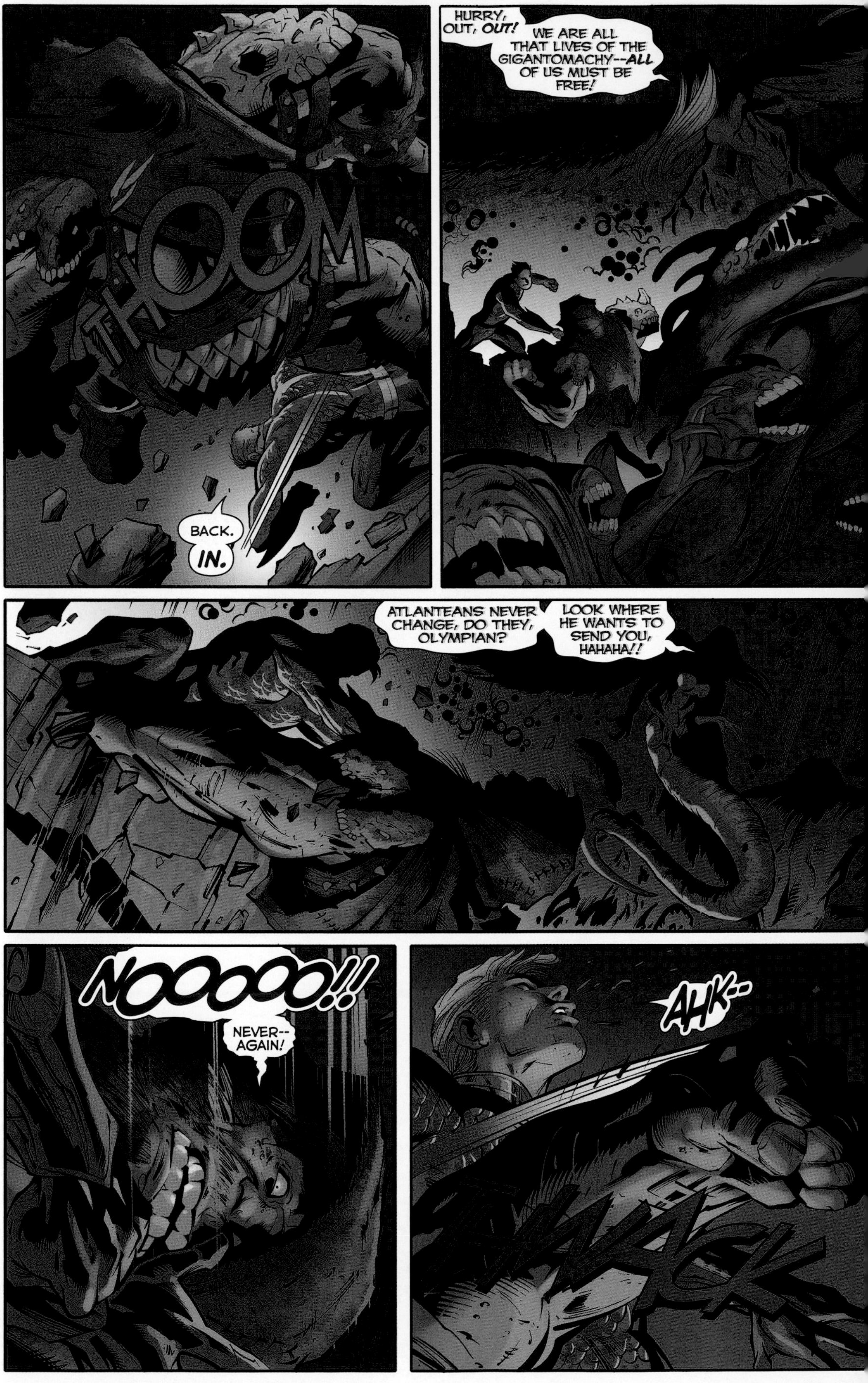
THOOM
BACK. IN.
HURRY, OUT, OUT!
WE ARE ALL THAT LIVES OF THE GIGANTOMACHY--ALL OF US MUST BE FREE!
ATLANTEANS NEVER CHANGE, DO THEY, OLYMPIAN?
LOOK WHERE HE WANTS TO SEND YOU, HAHAHA!!
NOOOOO!!
NEVER-- AGAIN!
AHK--

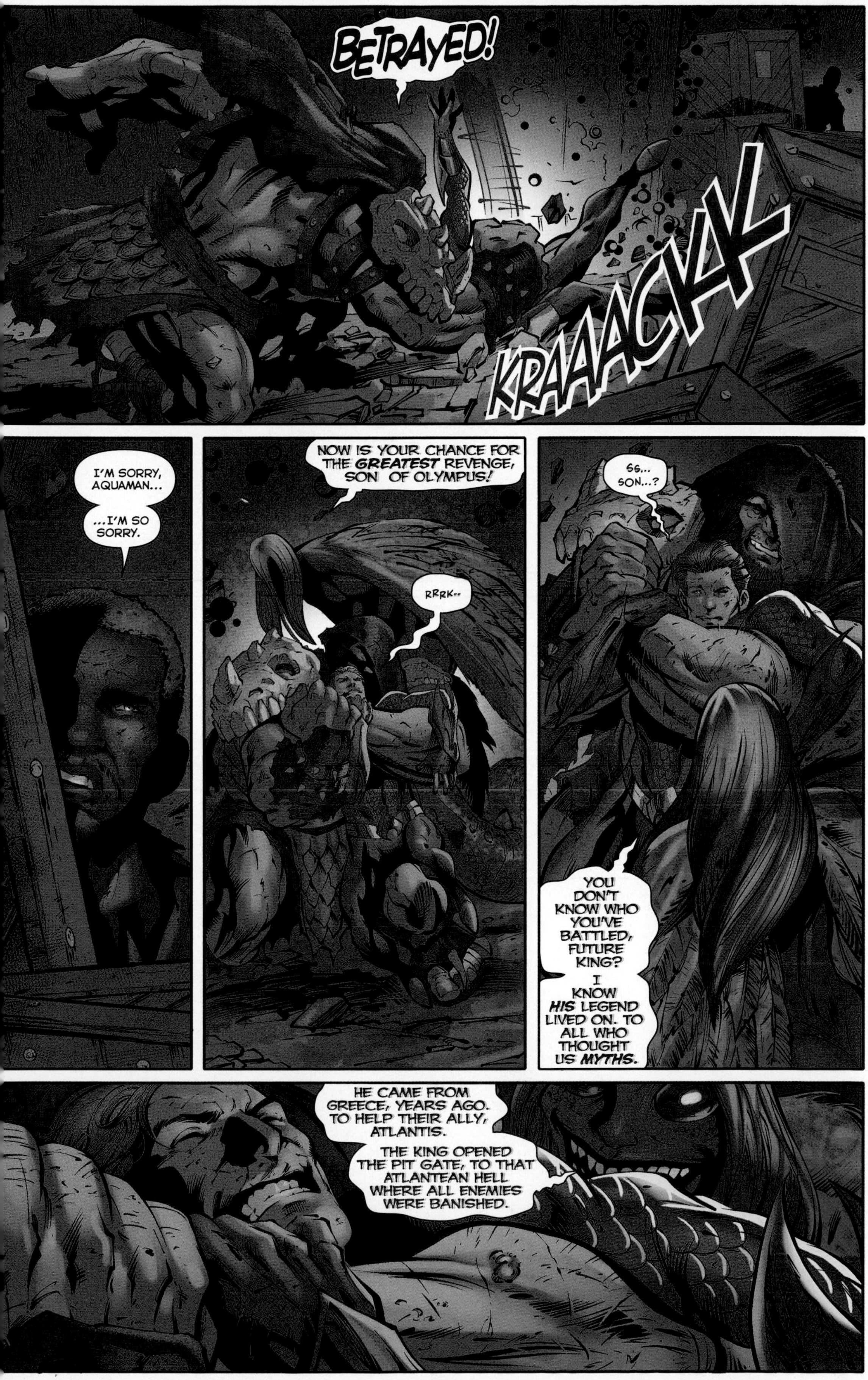
BETRAYED!
KRAAACKK
I'M SORRY, AQUAMAN...
...I'M SO SORRY.
NOW IS YOUR CHANCE FOR THE GREATEST REVENGE, SON OF OLYMPUS!
RRRK--
SS... SON...?
YOU DON'T KNOW WHO YOU'VE BATTLED, FUTURE KING?
I KNOW HIS LEGEND LIVED ON. TO ALL WHO THOUGHT US MYTHS.
HE CAME FROM GREECE, YEARS AGO. TO HELP THEIR ALLY, ATLANTIS.
THE KING OPENED THE PIT GATE, TO THAT ATLANTEAN HELL WHERE ALL ENEMIES WERE BANISHED.

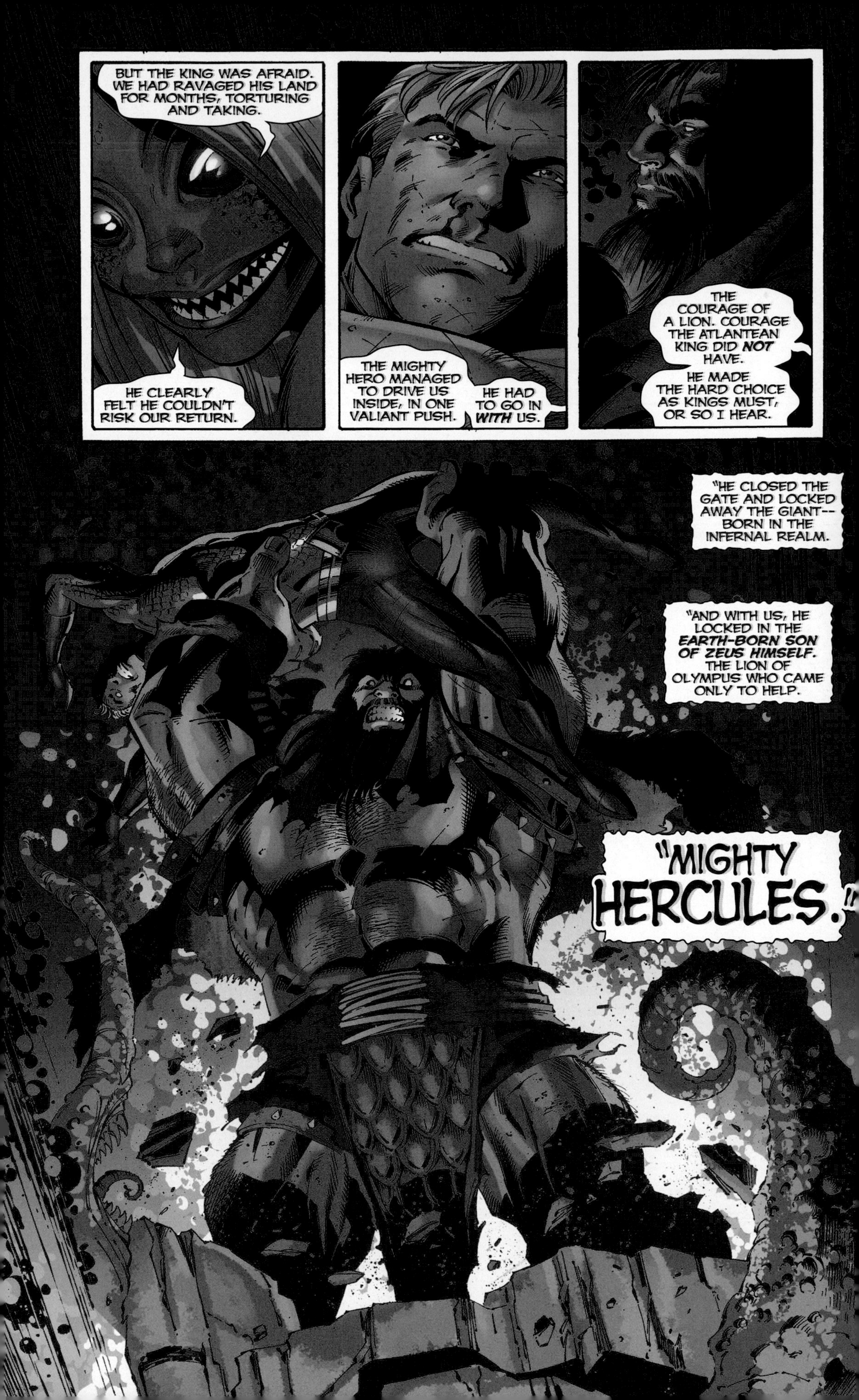
BUT THE KING WAS AFRAID. WE HAD RAVAGED HIS LAND FOR MONTHS, TORTURING AND TAKING.
HE CLEARLY FELT HE COULDN'T RISK OUR RETURN.
THE MIGHTY HERO MANAGED TO DRIVE US INSIDE, IN ONE VALIANT PUSH.
HE HAD TO GO IN **WITH** US.
THE COURAGE OF A LION. COURAGE THE ATLANTEAN KING DID **NOT** HAVE.
HE MADE THE HARD CHOICE AS KINGS MUST, OR SO I HEAR.
"HE CLOSED THE GATE AND LOCKED AWAY THE GIANT-- BORN IN THE INFERNAL REALM.
"AND WITH US, HE LOCKED IN THE ***EARTH-BORN SON OF ZEUS HIMSELF.*** THE LION OF OLYMPUS WHO CAME ONLY TO HELP.
"MIGHTY HERCULES."

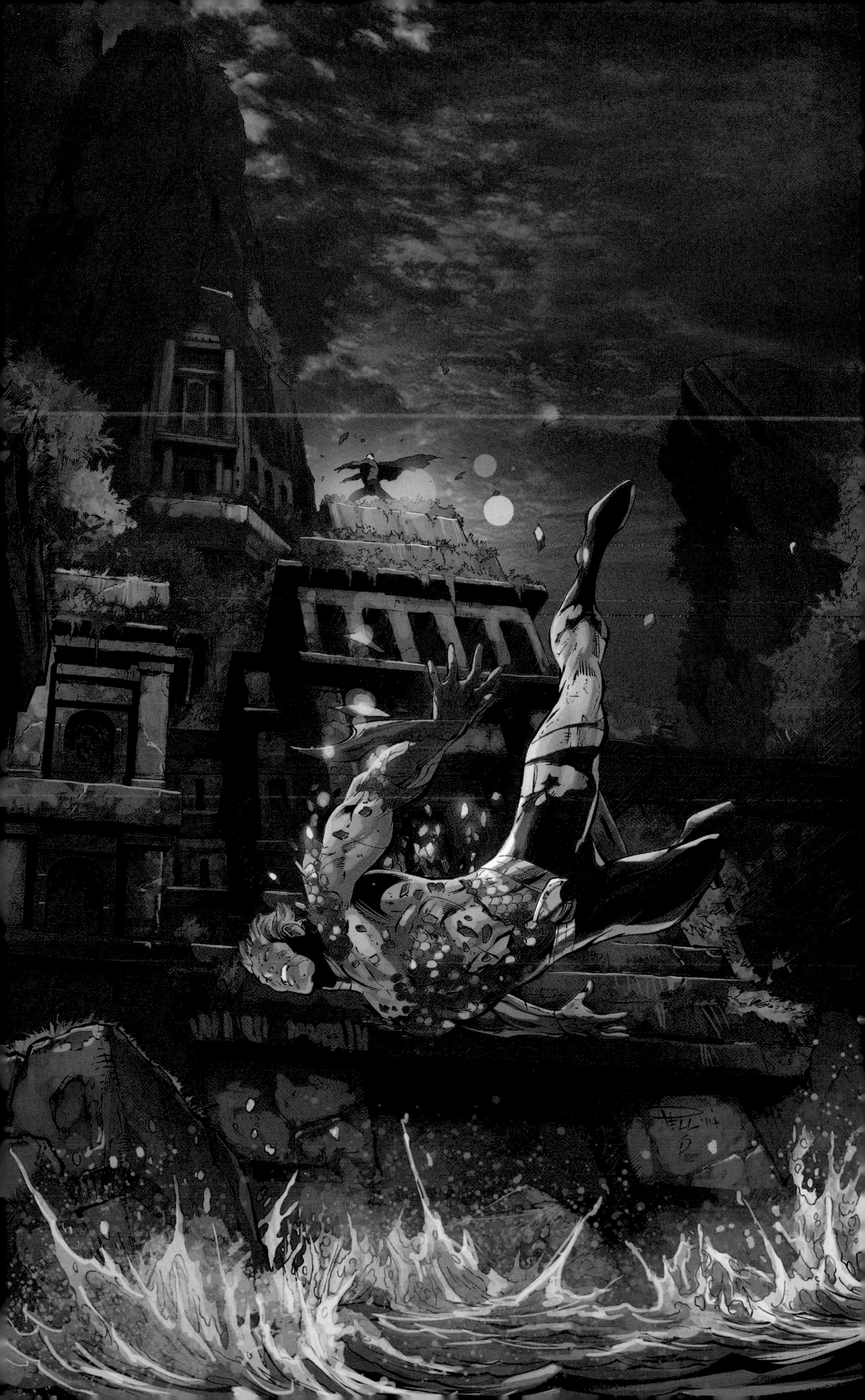

FALLEN

JEFF PARKER writer **PAUL PELLETIER ALVARO MARTINEZ** (pgs 97, 104-107, 115) pencillers **SEAN PARSONS RAUL FERNANDEZ** (pgs 97, 104-107, 1
RAIN BEREDO colorist **DEZI SIENTY** letterer cover by **PAUL PELLETIER, SEAN PARSONS** and **ROD REIS**

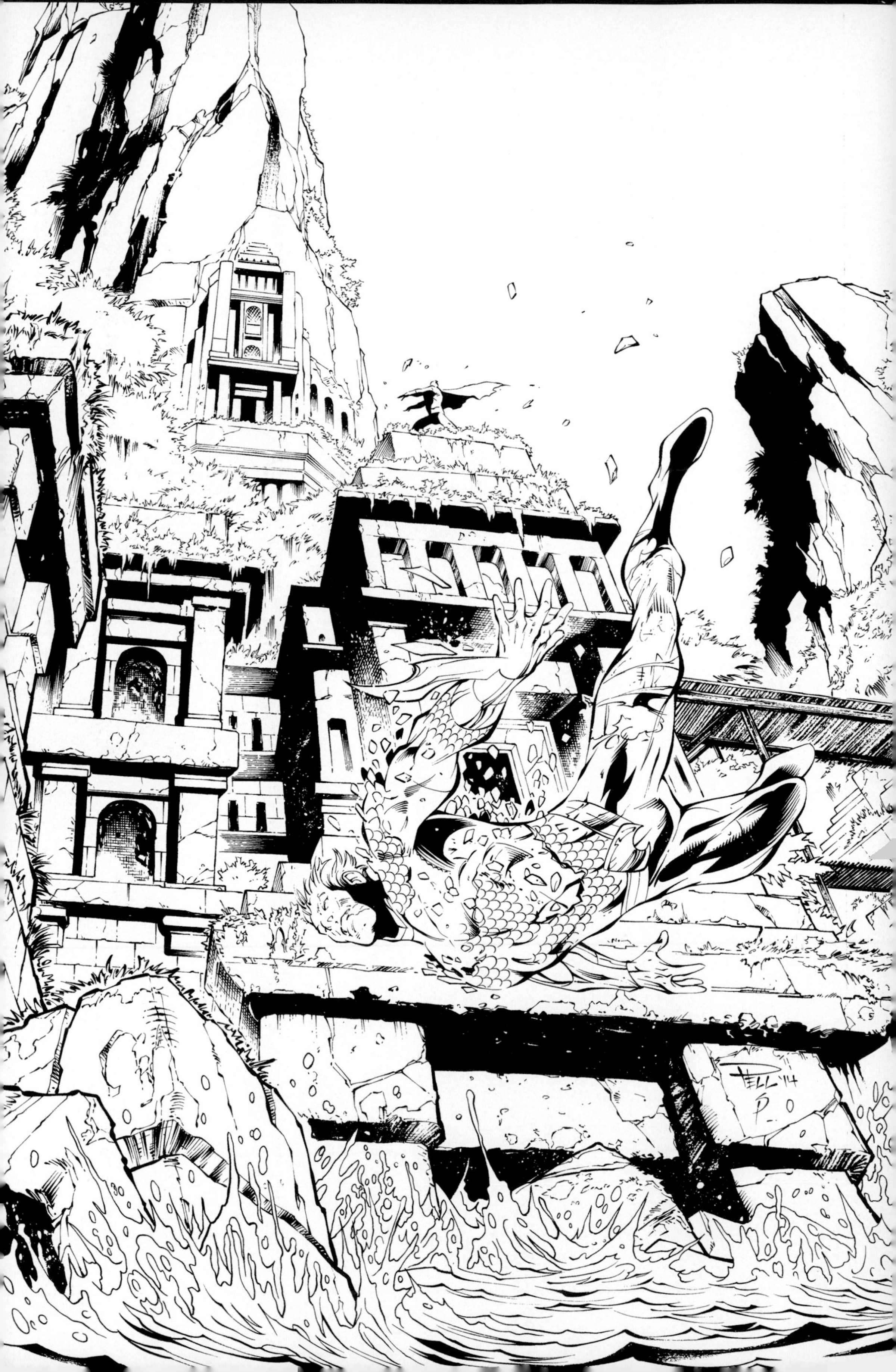

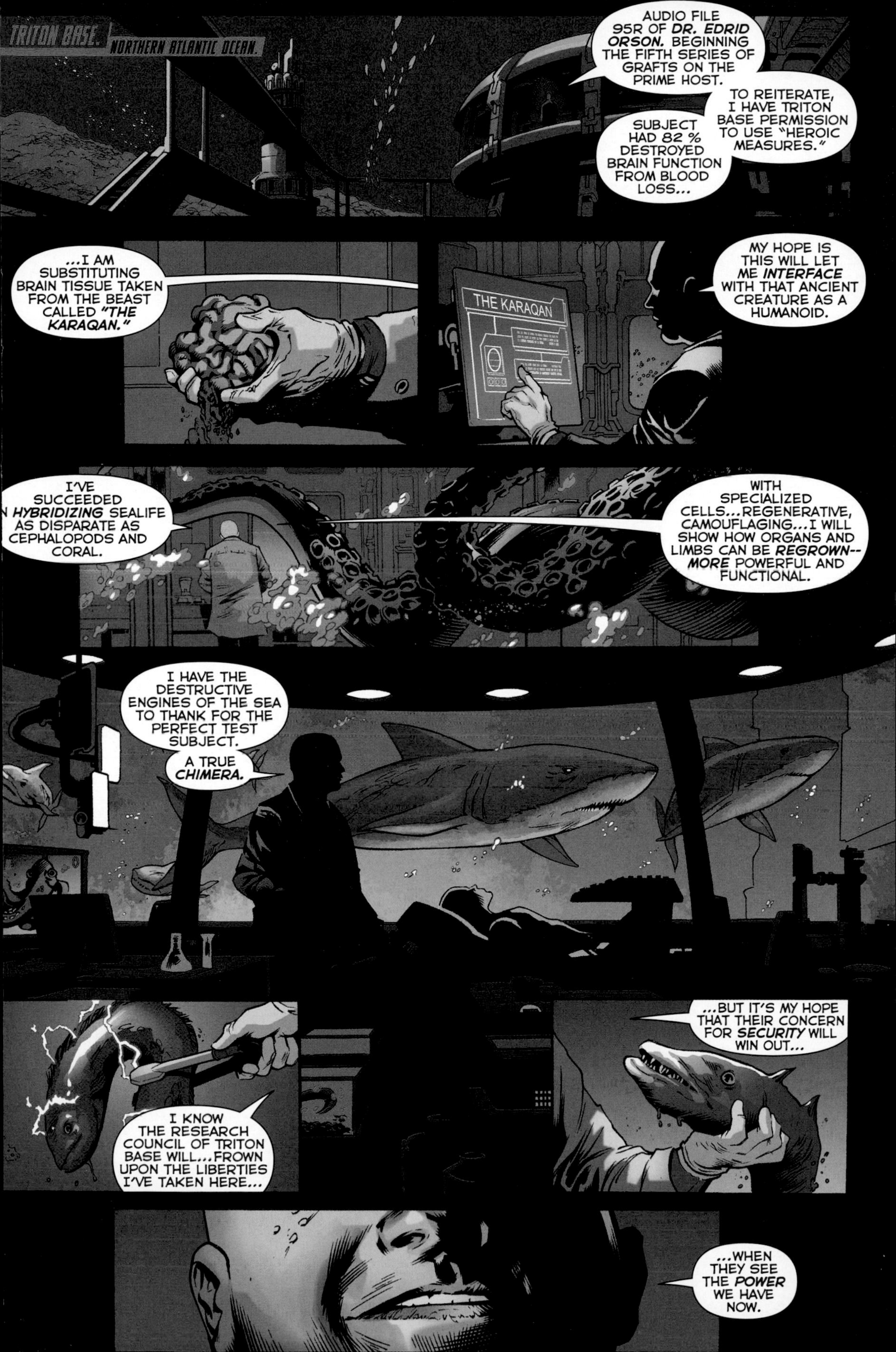
TRITON BASE.
NORTHERN ATLANTIC OCEAN.
AUDIO FILE 95R OF DR. EDRID ORSON. BEGINNING THE FIFTH SERIES OF GRAFTS ON THE PRIME HOST.
TO REITERATE, I HAVE TRITON BASE PERMISSION TO USE "HEROIC MEASURES."
SUBJECT HAD 82 % DESTROYED BRAIN FUNCTION FROM BLOOD LOSS...
...I AM SUBSTITUTING BRAIN TISSUE TAKEN FROM THE BEAST CALLED "THE KARAQAN."
THE KARAQAN
MY HOPE IS THIS WILL LET ME INTERFACE WITH THAT ANCIENT CREATURE AS A HUMANOID.
I'VE SUCCEEDED N HYBRIDIZING SEALIFE AS DISPARATE AS CEPHALOPODS AND CORAL.
WITH SPECIALIZED CELLS...REGENERATIVE, CAMOUFLAGING...I WILL SHOW HOW ORGANS AND LIMBS CAN BE REGROWN--MORE POWERFUL AND FUNCTIONAL.
I HAVE THE DESTRUCTIVE ENGINES OF THE SEA TO THANK FOR THE PERFECT TEST SUBJECT.
A TRUE CHIMERA.
I KNOW THE RESEARCH COUNCIL OF TRITON BASE WILL...FROWN UPON THE LIBERTIES I'VE TAKEN HERE...
...BUT IT'S MY HOPE THAT THEIR CONCERN FOR SECURITY WILL WIN OUT...
...WHEN THEY SEE THE POWER WE HAVE NOW.

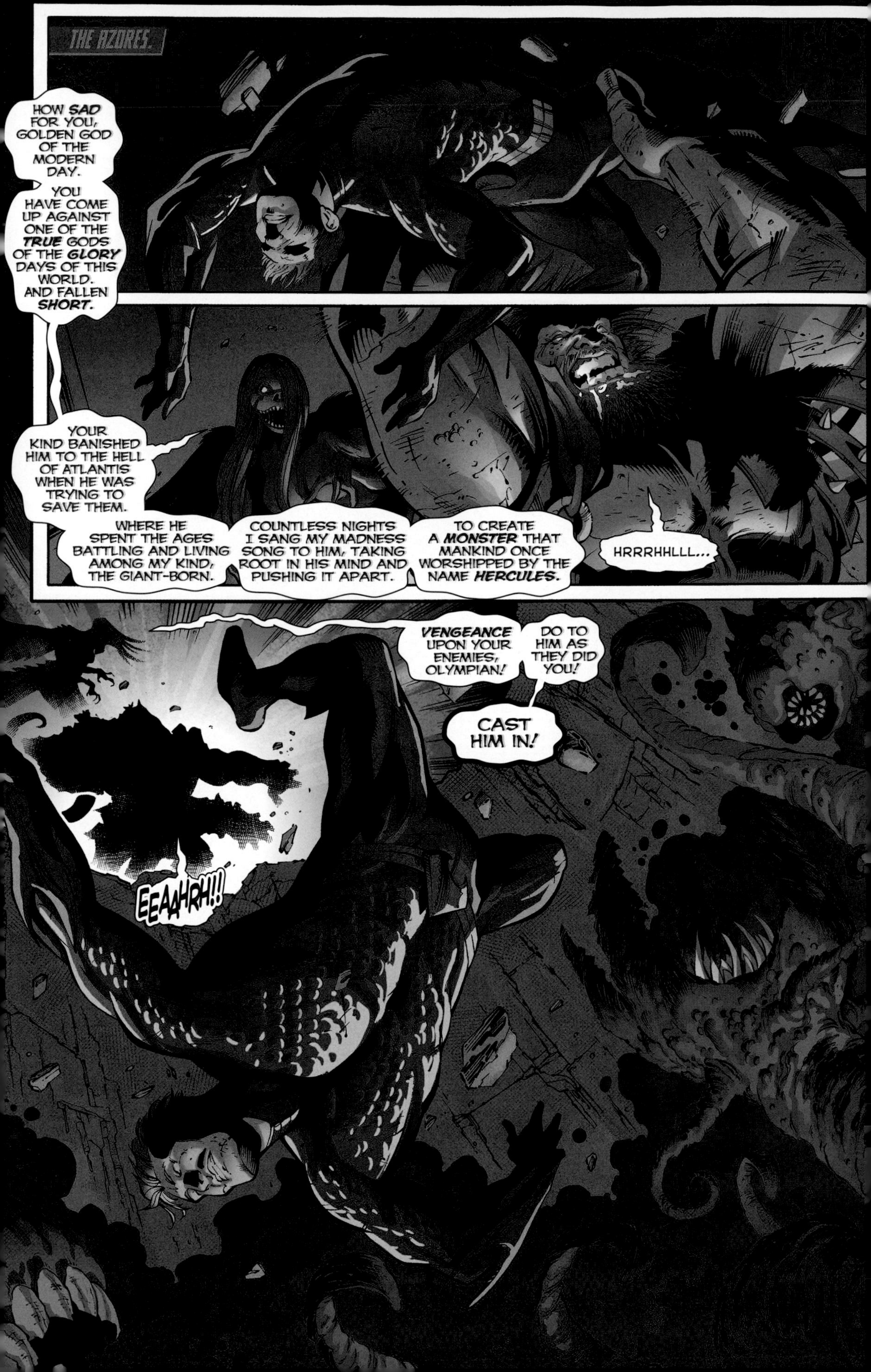
THE AZORES.
HOW SAD FOR YOU, GOLDEN GOD OF THE MODERN DAY.
YOU HAVE COME UP AGAINST ONE OF THE TRUE GODS OF THE GLORY DAYS OF THIS WORLD. AND FALLEN SHORT.
YOUR KIND BANISHED HIM TO THE HELL OF ATLANTIS WHEN HE WAS TRYING TO SAVE THEM.
WHERE HE SPENT THE AGES BATTLING AND LIVING AMONG MY KIND, THE GIANT-BORN.
COUNTLESS NIGHTS I SANG MY MADNESS SONG TO HIM, TAKING ROOT IN HIS MIND AND PUSHING IT APART.
TO CREATE A MONSTER THAT MANKIND ONCE WORSHIPPED BY THE NAME HERCULES.
HRRRHHLLL...
VENGEANCE UPON YOUR ENEMIES, OLYMPIAN!
DO TO HIM AS THEY DID YOU!
CAST HIM IN!
EEAAHRH!!

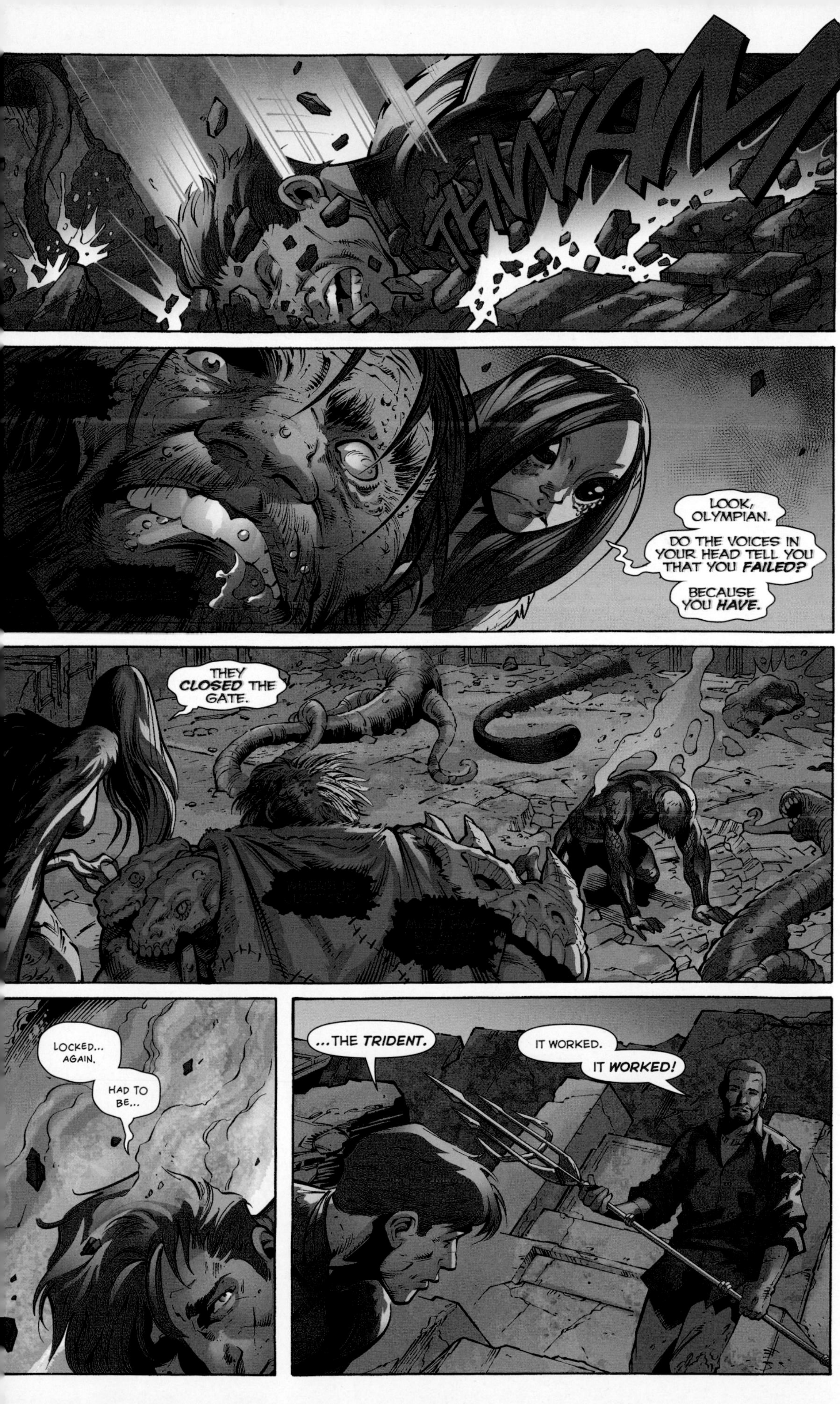
THWAM
LOOK, OLYMPIAN.
DO THE VOICES IN YOUR HEAD TELL YOU THAT YOU *FAILED?*
BECAUSE YOU *HAVE.*
THEY *CLOSED* THE GATE.
LOCKED... AGAIN.
HAD TO BE...
...THE *TRIDENT.*
IT WORKED.
IT *WORKED!*

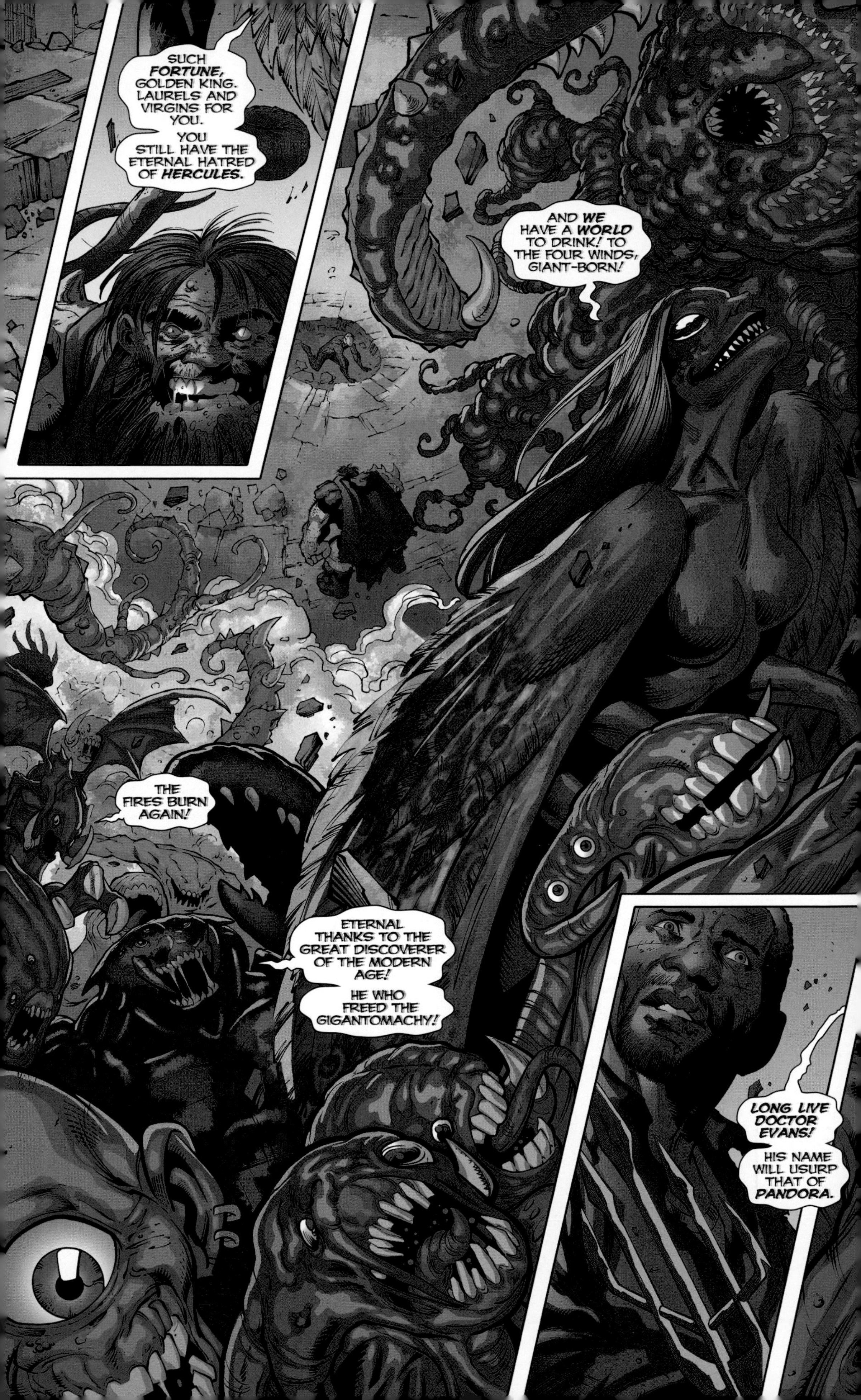
SUCH FORTUNE, GOLDEN KING. LAURELS AND VIRGINS FOR YOU.
YOU STILL HAVE THE ETERNAL HATRED OF HERCULES.
AND WE HAVE A WORLD TO DRINK! TO THE FOUR WINDS, GIANT-BORN!
THE FIRES BURN AGAIN!
ETERNAL THANKS TO THE GREAT DISCOVERER OF THE MODERN AGE!
HE WHO FREED THE GIGANTOMACHY!
LONG LIVE DOCTOR EVANS!
HIS NAME WILL USURP THAT OF PANDORA.

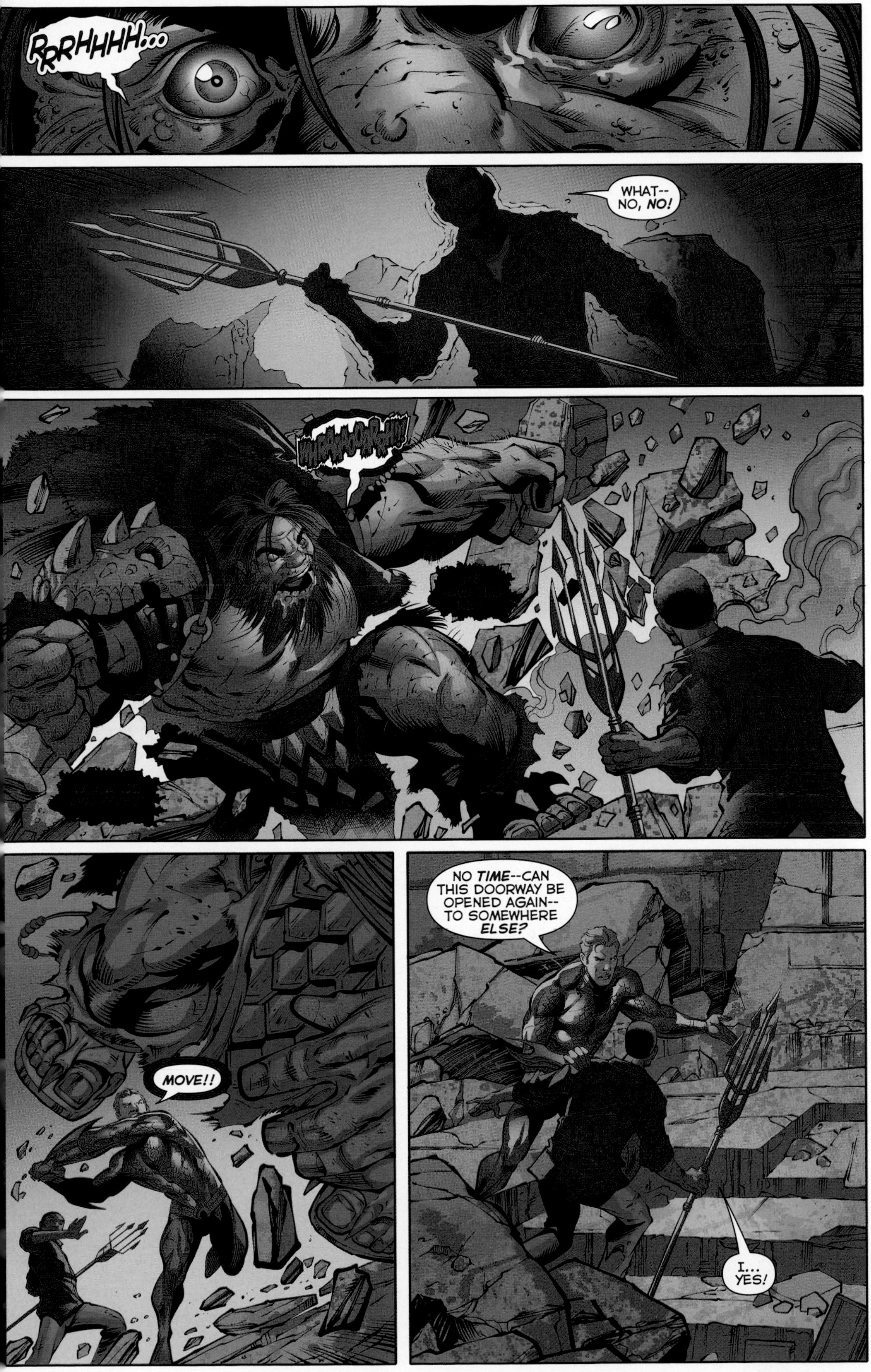
RRRHHHH...
WHAT-- NO, NO!
WHRAAAOARRH!!
MOVE!!
NO TIME--CAN THIS DOORWAY BE OPENED AGAIN-- TO SOMEWHERE ELSE?
I... YES!

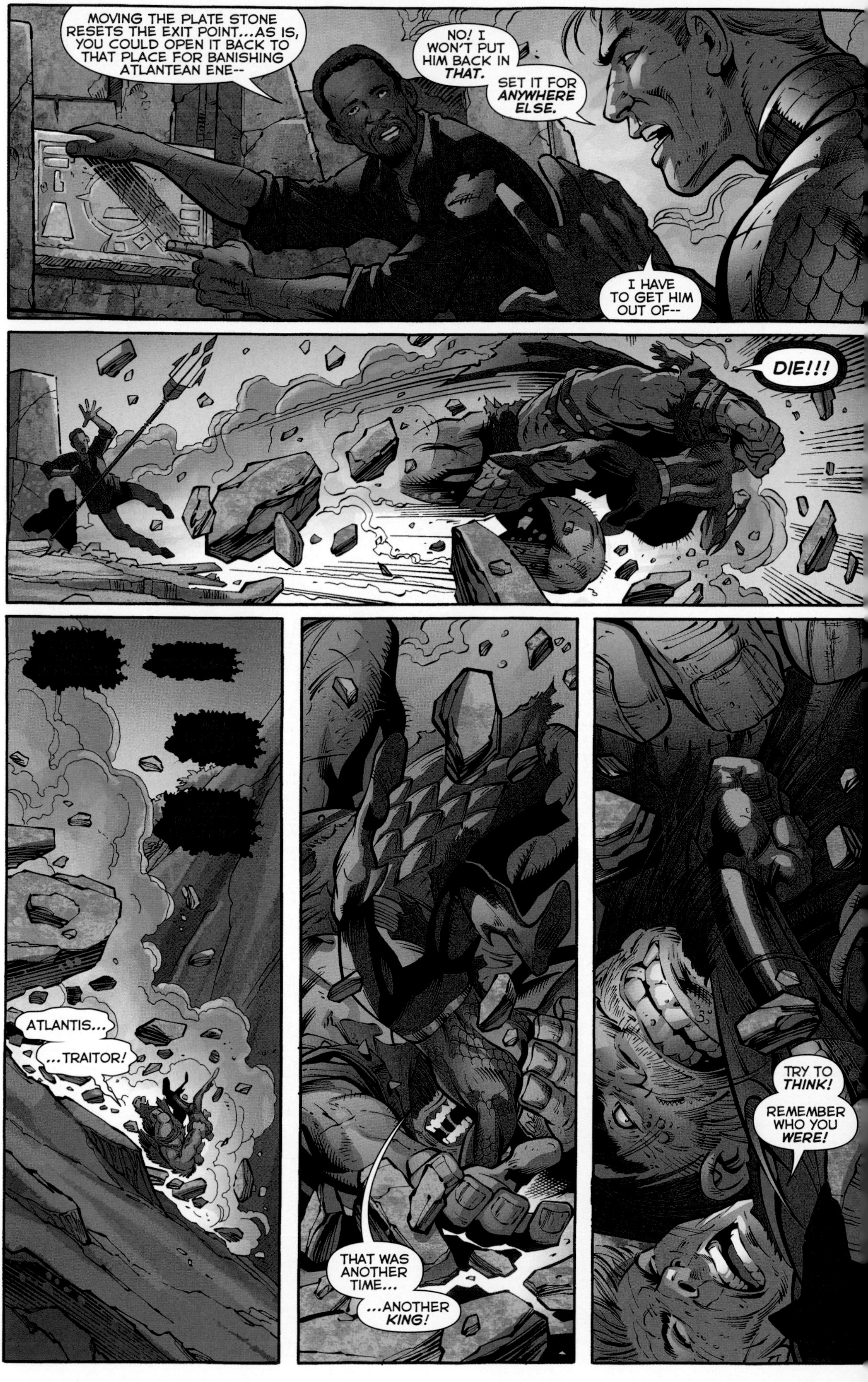
MOVING THE PLATE STONE RESETS THE EXIT POINT...AS IS, YOU COULD OPEN IT BACK TO THAT PLACE FOR BANISHING ATLANTEAN ENE--
NO! I WON'T PUT HIM BACK IN *THAT.*
SET IT FOR *ANYWHERE ELSE.*
I HAVE TO GET HIM OUT OF--
DIE!!!
ATLANTIS...
...TRAITOR!
THAT WAS ANOTHER TIME...
...ANOTHER *KING!*
TRY TO *THINK!*
REMEMBER WHO YOU *WERE!*

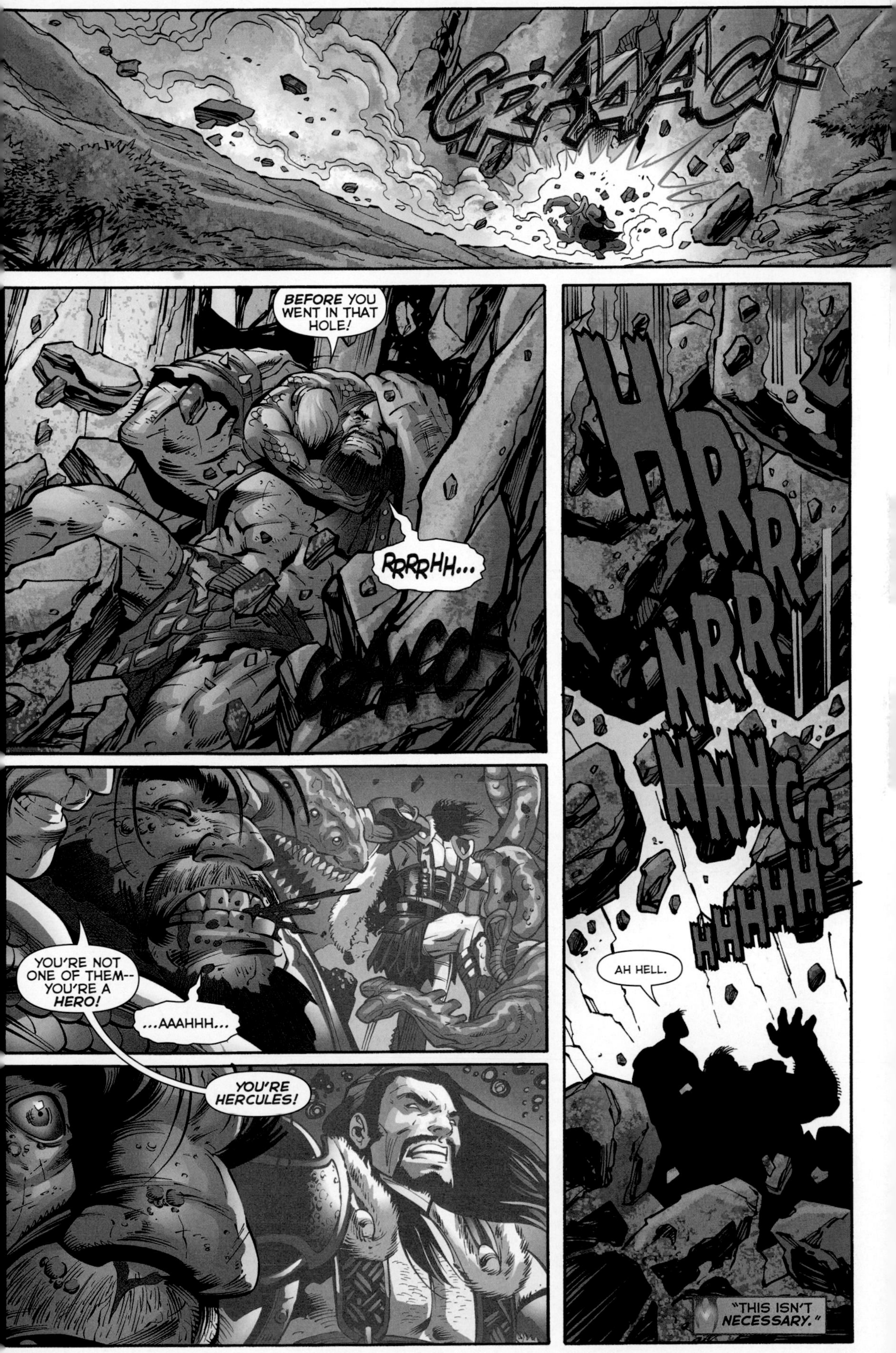
CRAAACK
BEFORE YOU WENT IN THAT HOLE!
RRRRHH...
CRAACK
YOU'RE NOT ONE OF THEM-- YOU'RE A HERO!
...AAAHHH...
YOU'RE HERCULES!
HRRRNRRNNNGGHHHHH
AH HELL.
"THIS ISN'T NECESSARY."

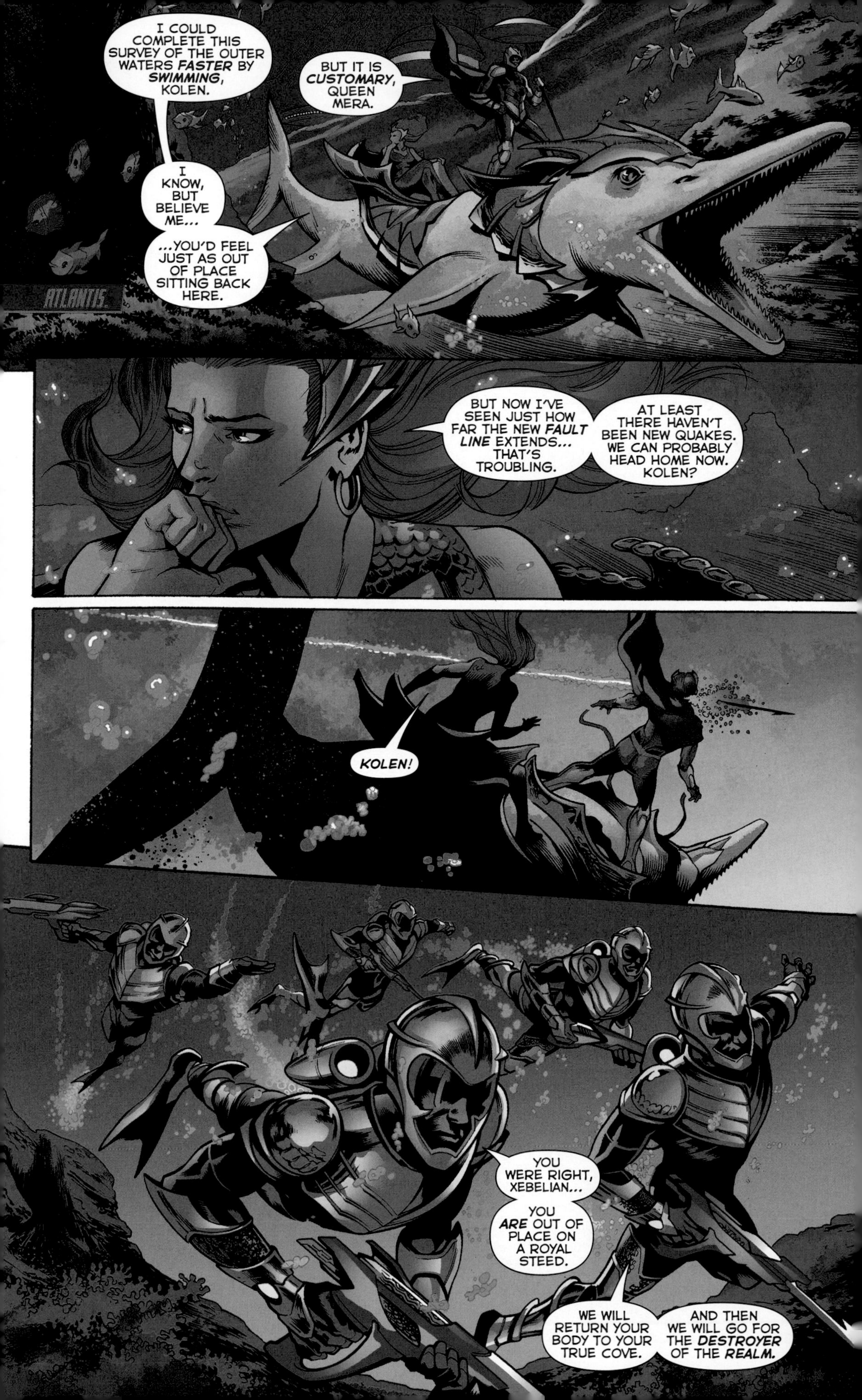
ATLANTIS.
I COULD COMPLETE THIS SURVEY OF THE OUTER WATERS FASTER BY SWIMMING, KOLEN.
BUT IT IS CUSTOMARY, QUEEN MERA.
I KNOW, BUT BELIEVE ME...
...YOU'D FEEL JUST AS OUT OF PLACE SITTING BACK HERE.
BUT NOW I'VE SEEN JUST HOW FAR THE NEW FAULT LINE EXTENDS... THAT'S TROUBLING.
AT LEAST THERE HAVEN'T BEEN NEW QUAKES. WE CAN PROBABLY HEAD HOME NOW. KOLEN?
KOLEN!
YOU WERE RIGHT, XEBELIAN...
YOU ARE OUT OF PLACE ON A ROYAL STEED.
WE WILL RETURN YOUR BODY TO YOUR TRUE COVE.
AND THEN WE WILL GO FOR THE DESTROYER OF THE REALM.

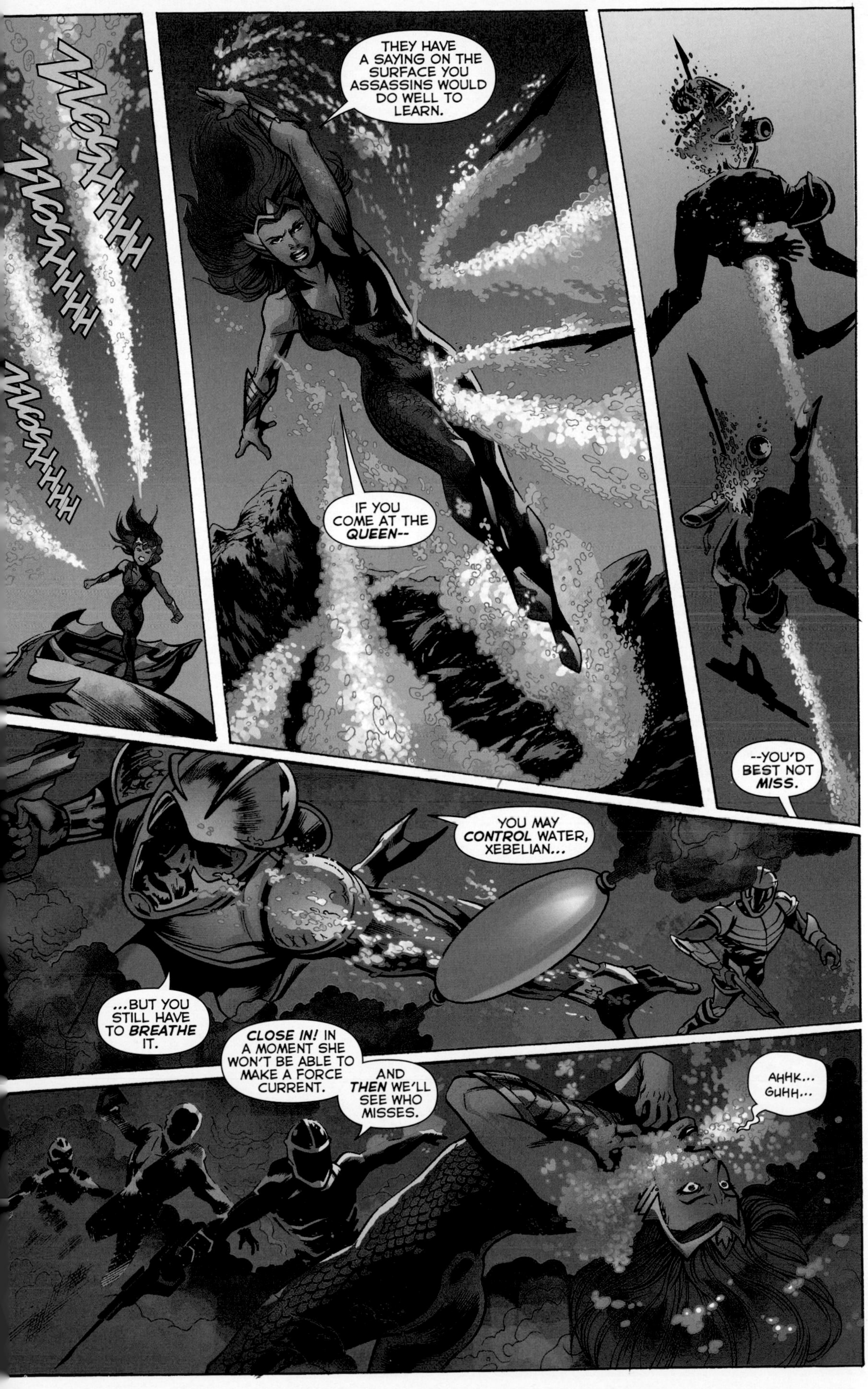
WHOOSHHHH
WHOOSHHHH
WHOOSHHHH
THEY HAVE A SAYING ON THE SURFACE YOU ASSASSINS WOULD DO WELL TO LEARN.
IF YOU COME AT THE QUEEN--
--YOU'D BEST NOT MISS.
YOU MAY CONTROL WATER, XEBELIAN...
...BUT YOU STILL HAVE TO BREATHE IT.
CLOSE IN! IN A MOMENT SHE WON'T BE ABLE TO MAKE A FORCE CURRENT.
AND THEN WE'LL SEE WHO MISSES.
AHHK... GUHH...

THE HONOR FALLS TO ME.
FOR *TRUE* ATLANTEANS.
HHHNNH!!
HK-AAAHH--
IT WENT THAT WAY, FLANK LEFT DOWN!
GASSP-- AHH--
--WHO--
WHERE IS SHE?
SOMETHING *TOOK* HER--
IT'S ON APPROACH-- READY YOUR WEAPON--!
VSSSSHHHHHH
ZSSSSSSSSHHHHH

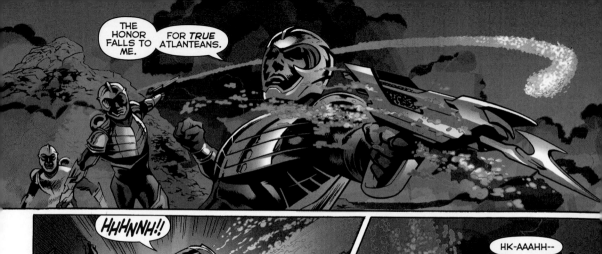

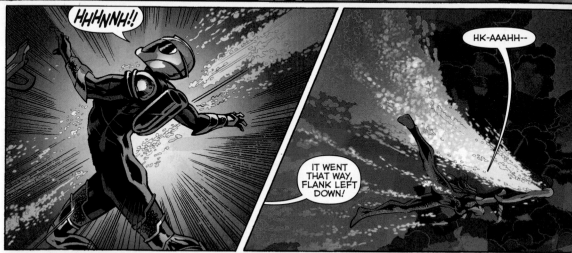

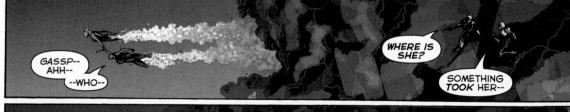

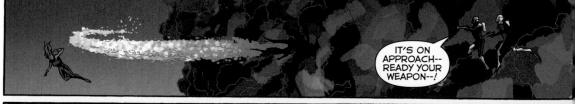

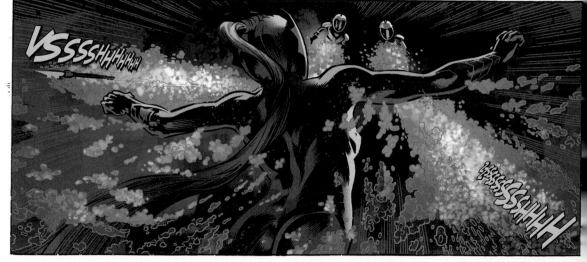

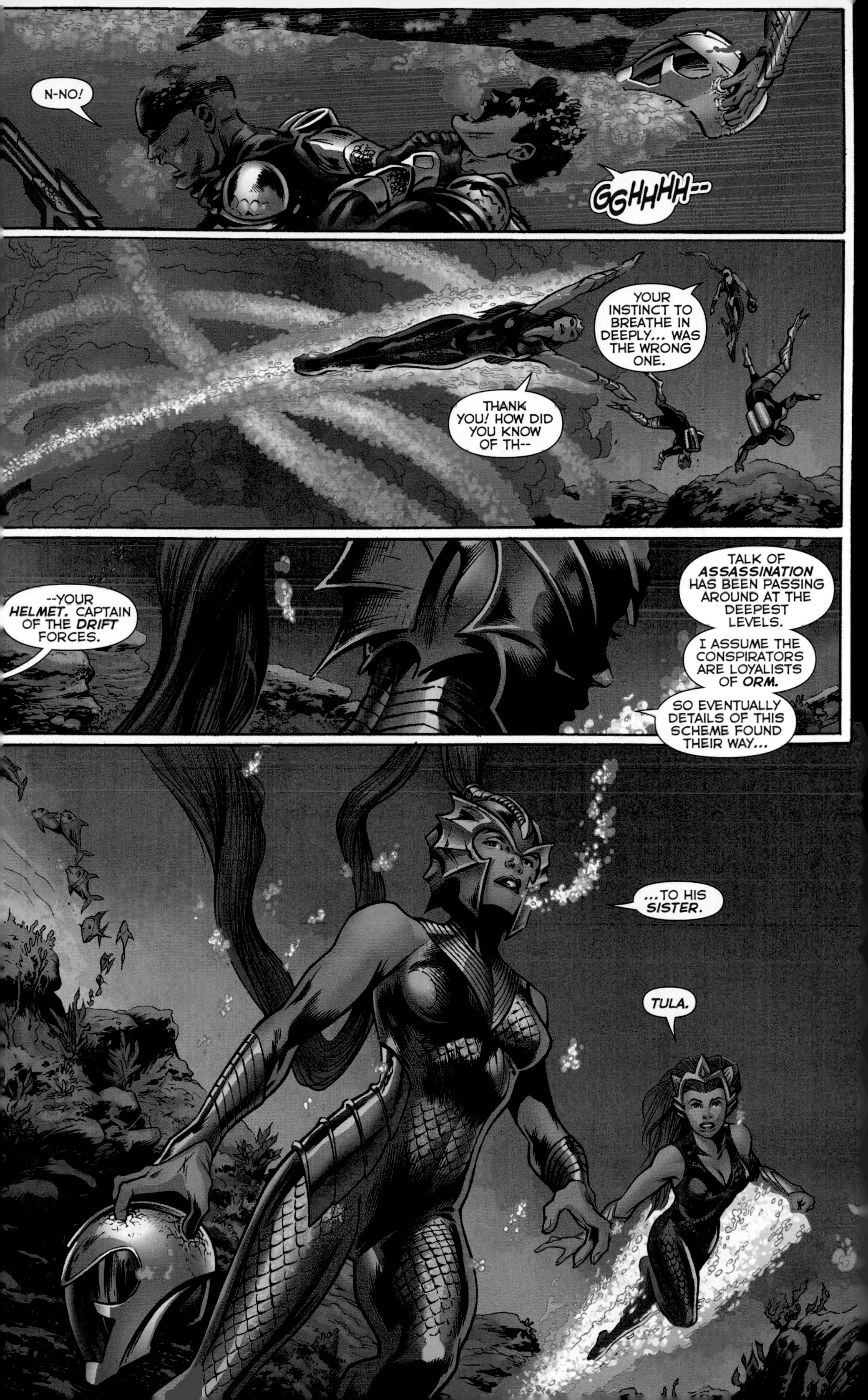
N-NO!
GGHHHH--
YOUR INSTINCT TO BREATHE IN DEEPLY... WAS THE WRONG ONE.
THANK YOU! HOW DID YOU KNOW OF TH--
--YOUR *HELMET.* CAPTAIN OF THE *DRIFT* FORCES.
TALK OF *ASSASSINATION* HAS BEEN PASSING AROUND AT THE DEEPEST LEVELS.
I ASSUME THE CONSPIRATORS ARE LOYALISTS OF *ORM.*
SO EVENTUALLY DETAILS OF THIS SCHEME FOUND THEIR WAY...
...TO HIS *SISTER.*
TULA.

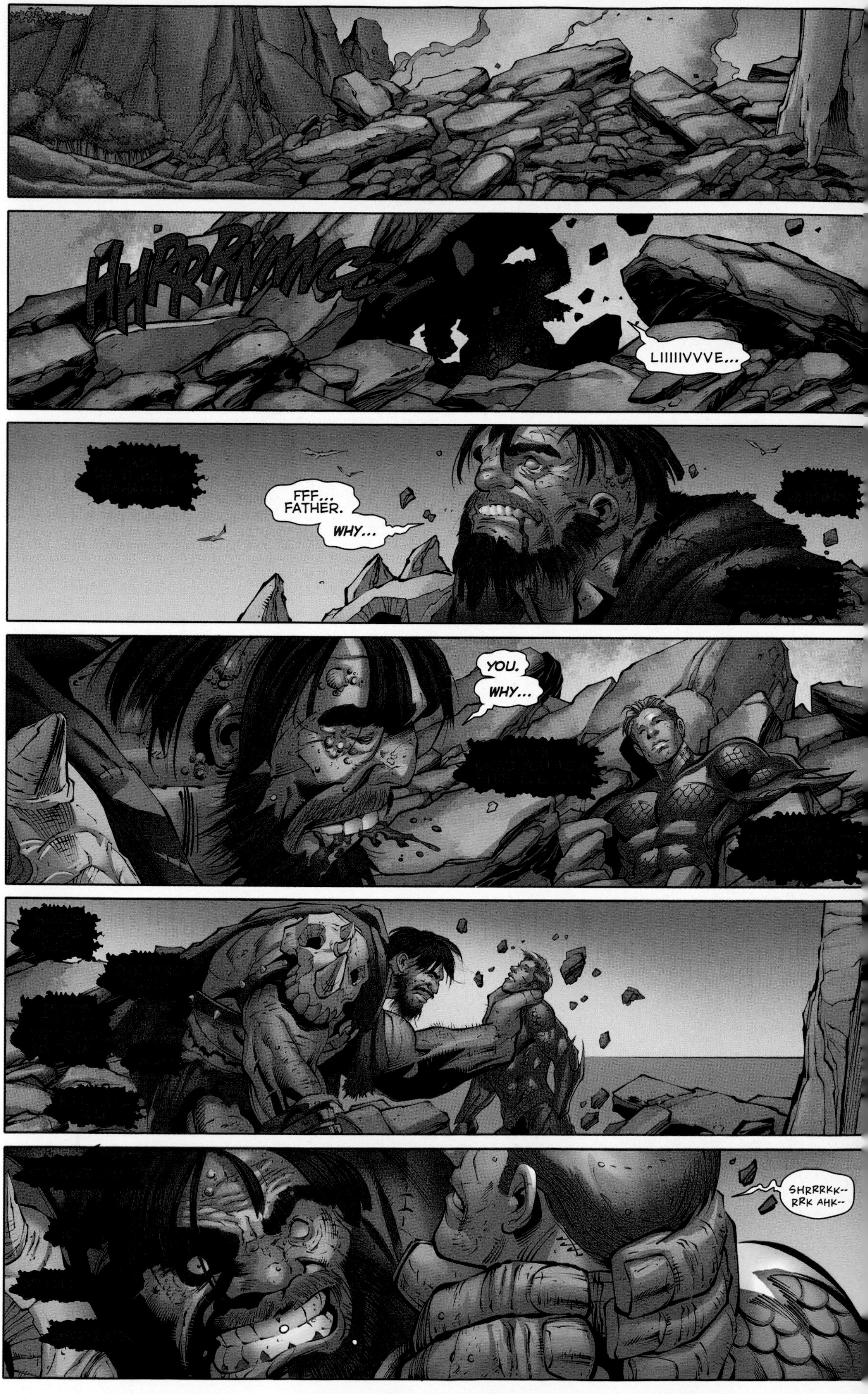
HHRRRNNNGGH
LIIIIIVVVE...
[redacted]
FFF... FATHER.
WHY...
[redacted]
[redacted]
YOU.
WHY...
[redacted]
[redacted]
[redacted]
[redacted]
SHRRRKK-- RRK AHK--

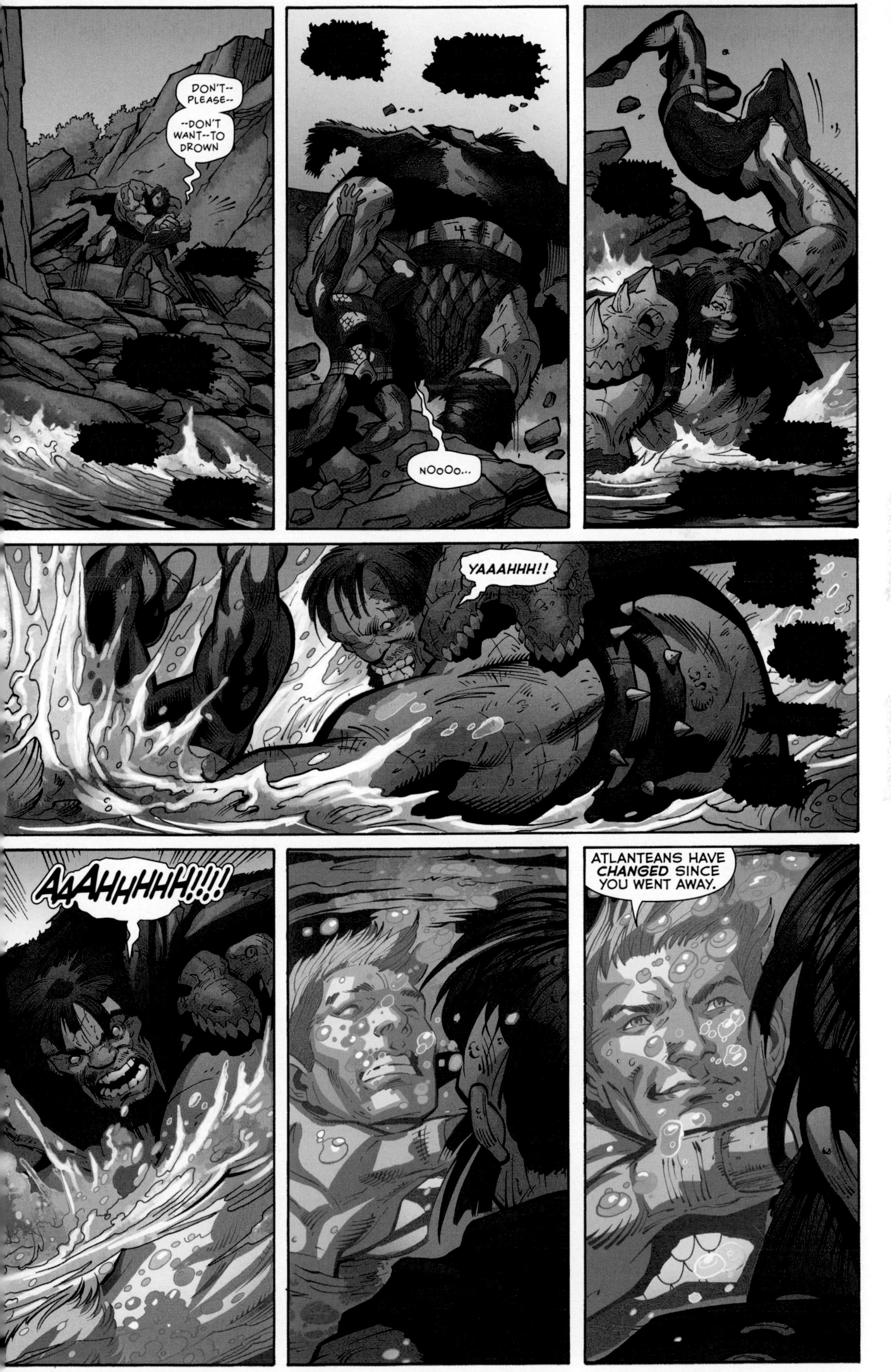
DON'T--
PLEASE--
--DON'T WANT--TO DROWN
[redacted]
[redacted]
[redacted]
[redacted]
[redacted]
[redacted]
NOOOO...
[redacted]
[redacted]
YAAAHHH!!
[redacted]
[redacted]
[redacted]
[redacted]
AAAHHHHH!!!!
ATLANTEANS HAVE CHANGED SINCE YOU WENT AWAY.

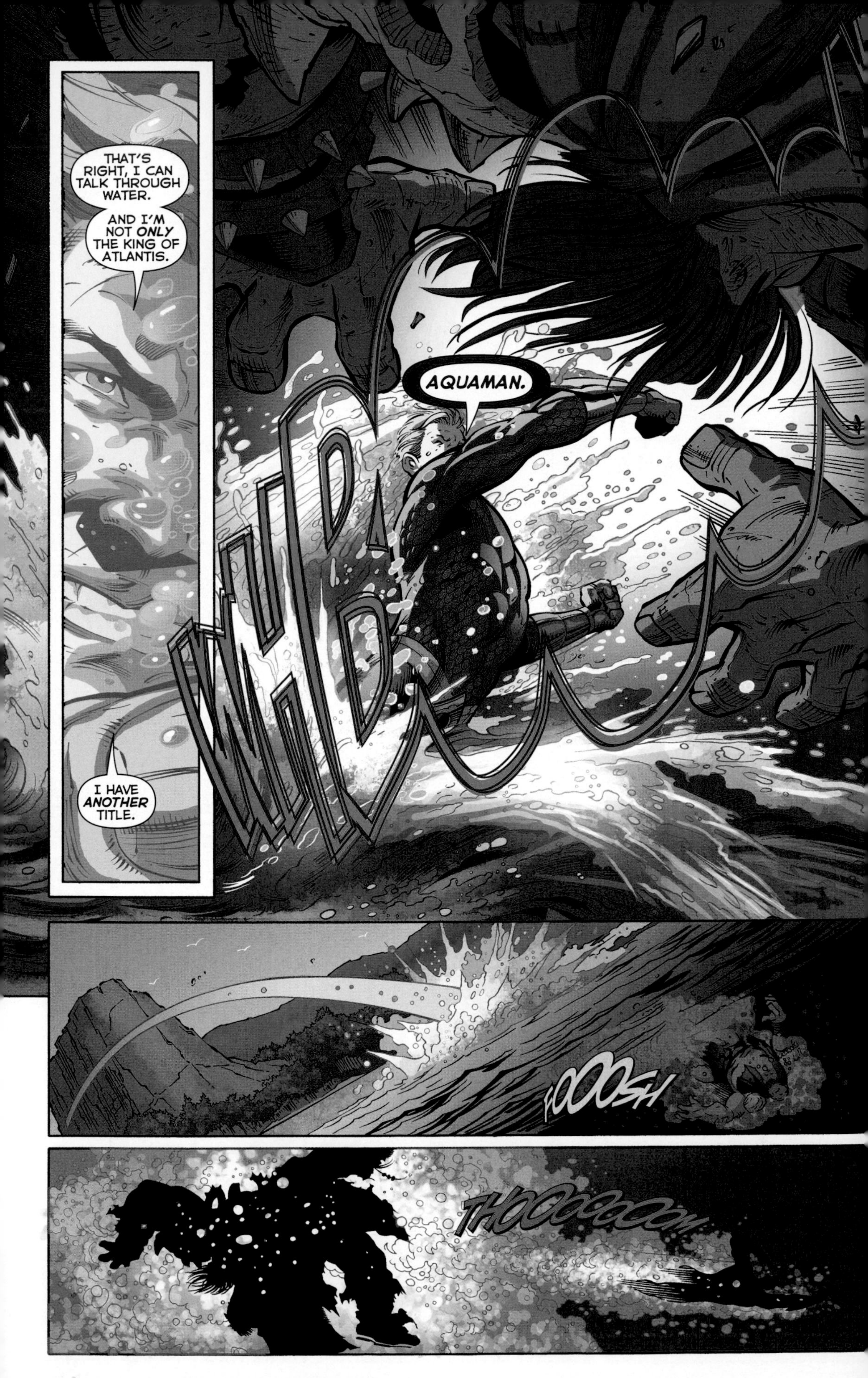
THAT'S RIGHT, I CAN TALK THROUGH WATER.
AND I'M NOT *ONLY* THE KING OF ATLANTIS.
I HAVE *ANOTHER* TITLE.
AQUAMAN.
FOOOSH
THOOOOOOOM

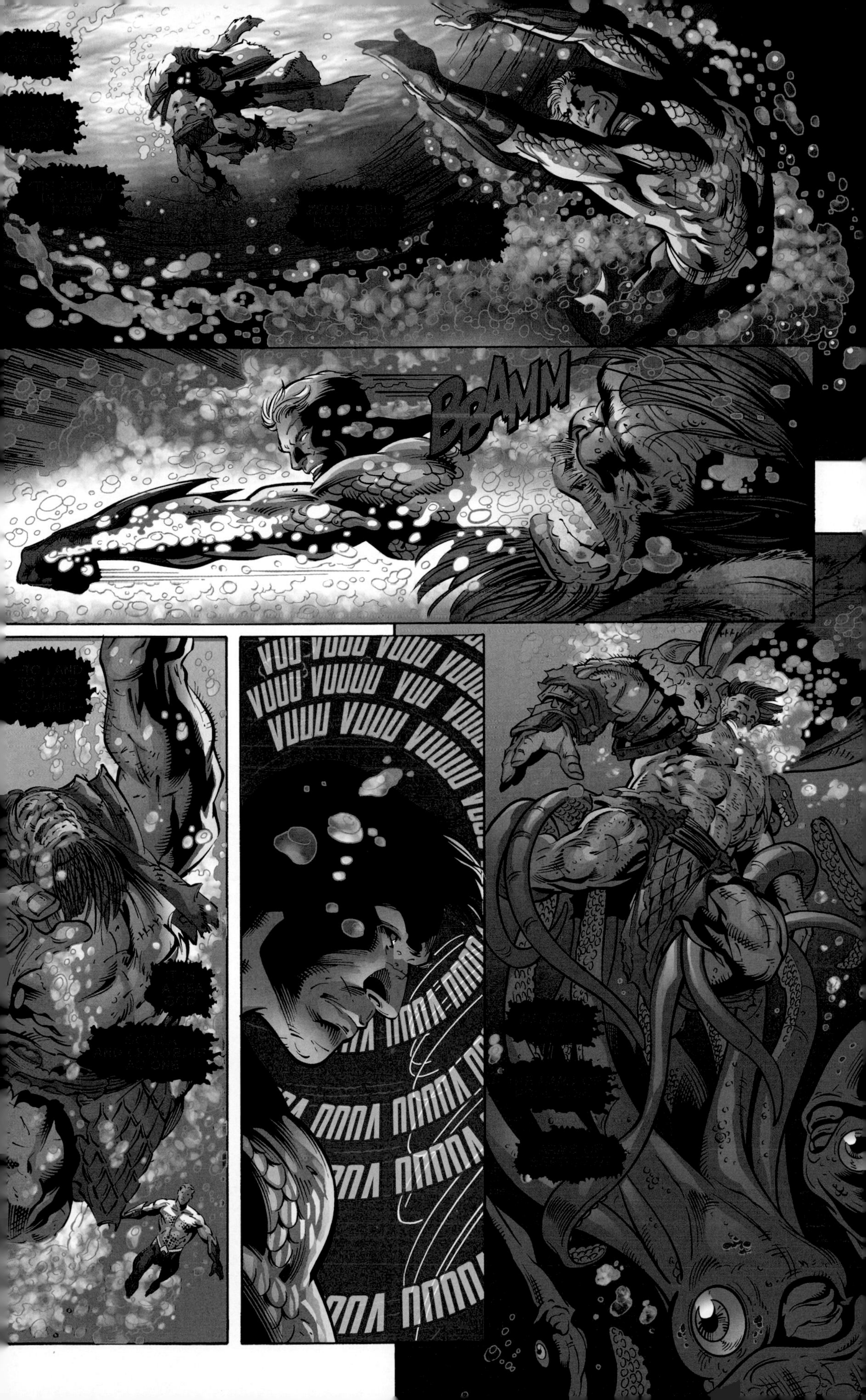
[redacted]
BBAMM
[redacted]

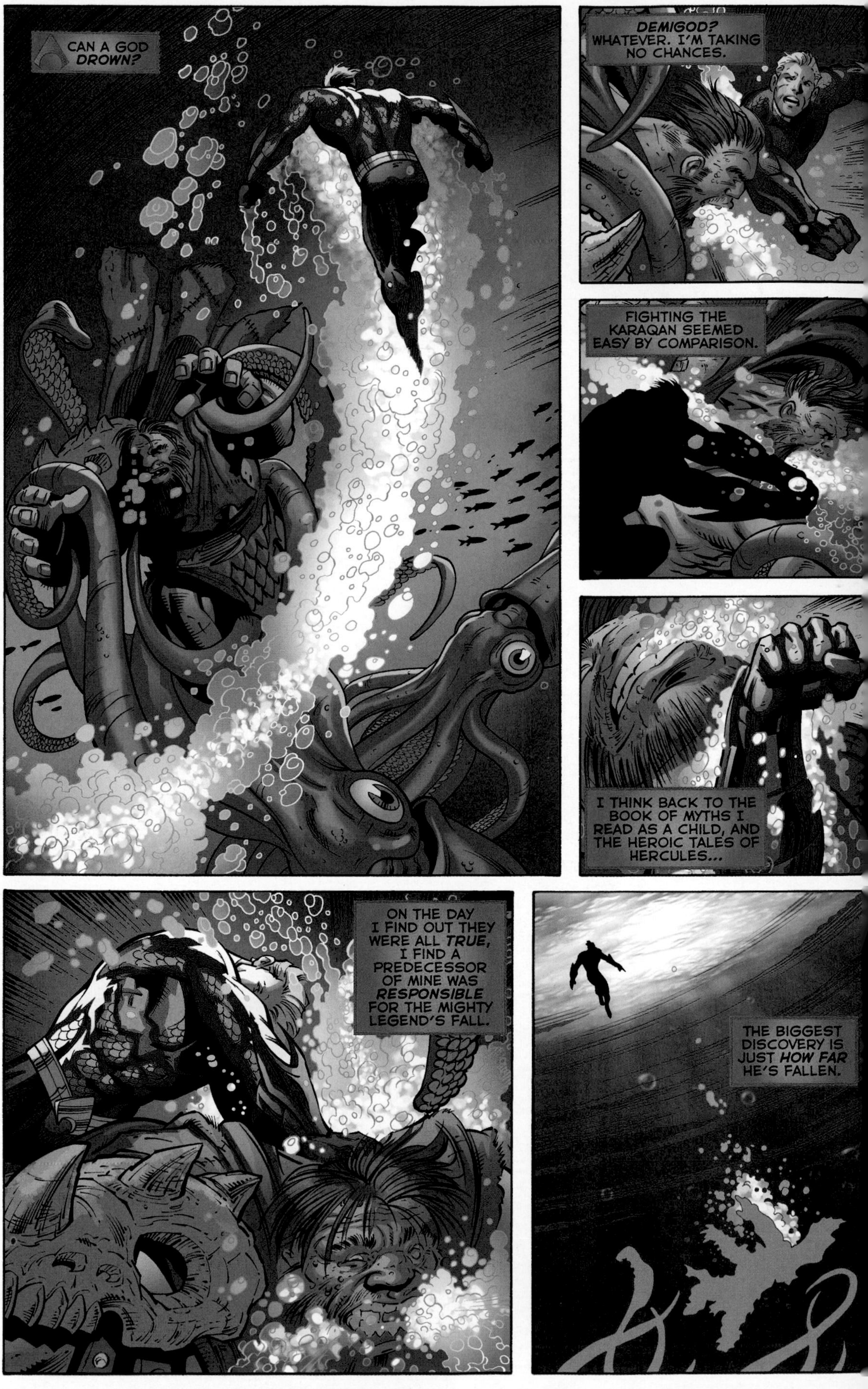
CAN A GOD *DROWN?*
DEMIGOD? WHATEVER. I'M TAKING NO CHANCES.
FIGHTING THE KARAQAN SEEMED EASY BY COMPARISON.
I THINK BACK TO THE BOOK OF MYTHS I READ AS A CHILD, AND THE HEROIC TALES OF HERCULES...
ON THE DAY I FIND OUT THEY WERE ALL *TRUE,* I FIND A PREDECESSOR OF MINE WAS *RESPONSIBLE* FOR THE MIGHTY LEGEND'S FALL.
THE BIGGEST DISCOVERY IS JUST *HOW FAR* HE'S FALLEN.

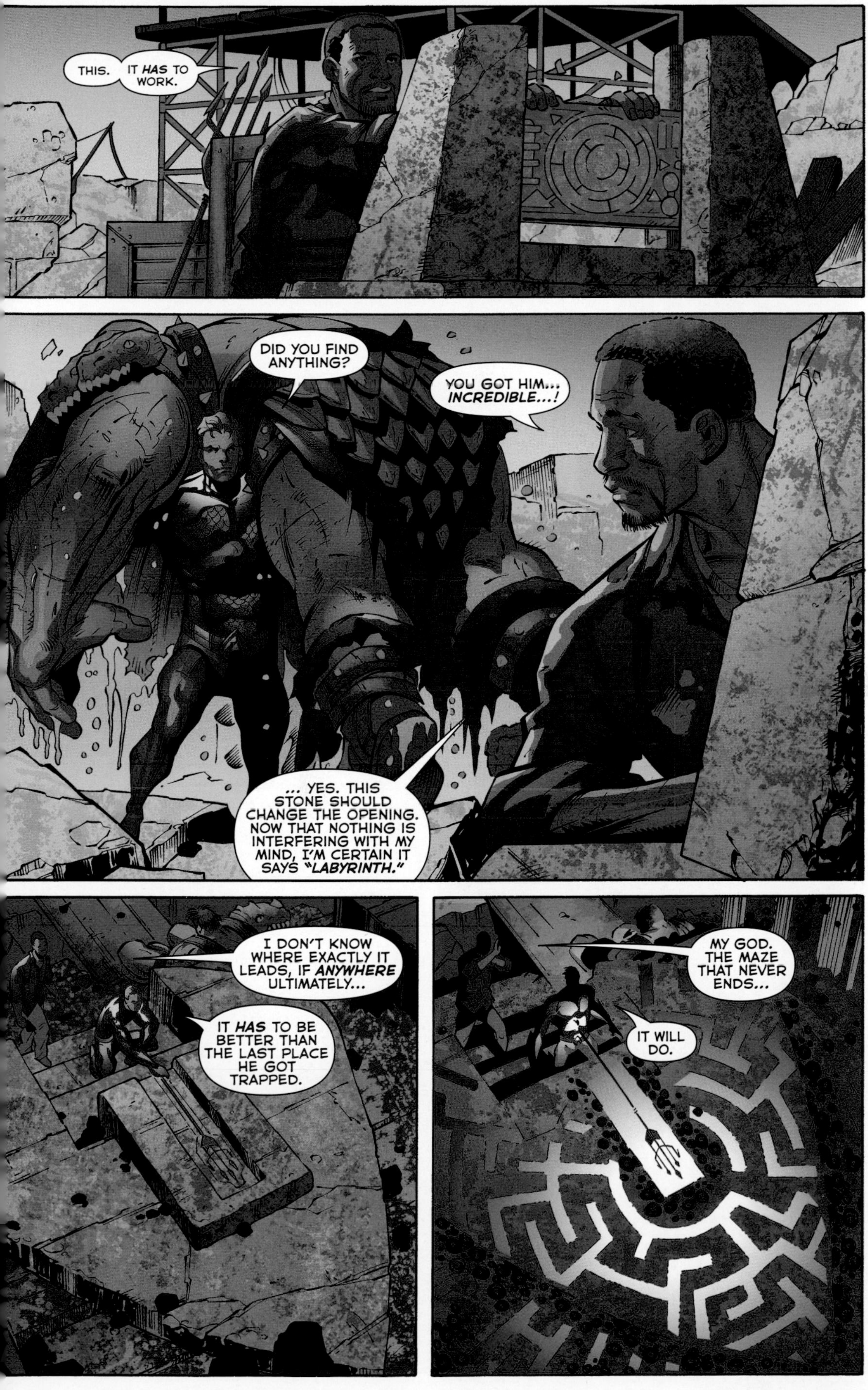
THIS. IT HAS TO WORK.
DID YOU FIND ANYTHING?
YOU GOT HIM... INCREDIBLE...!
... YES. THIS STONE SHOULD CHANGE THE OPENING. NOW THAT NOTHING IS INTERFERING WITH MY MIND, I'M CERTAIN IT SAYS "LABYRINTH."
I DON'T KNOW WHERE EXACTLY IT LEADS, IF ANYWHERE ULTIMATELY...
IT HAS TO BE BETTER THAN THE LAST PLACE HE GOT TRAPPED.
MY GOD. THE MAZE THAT NEVER ENDS...
IT WILL DO.

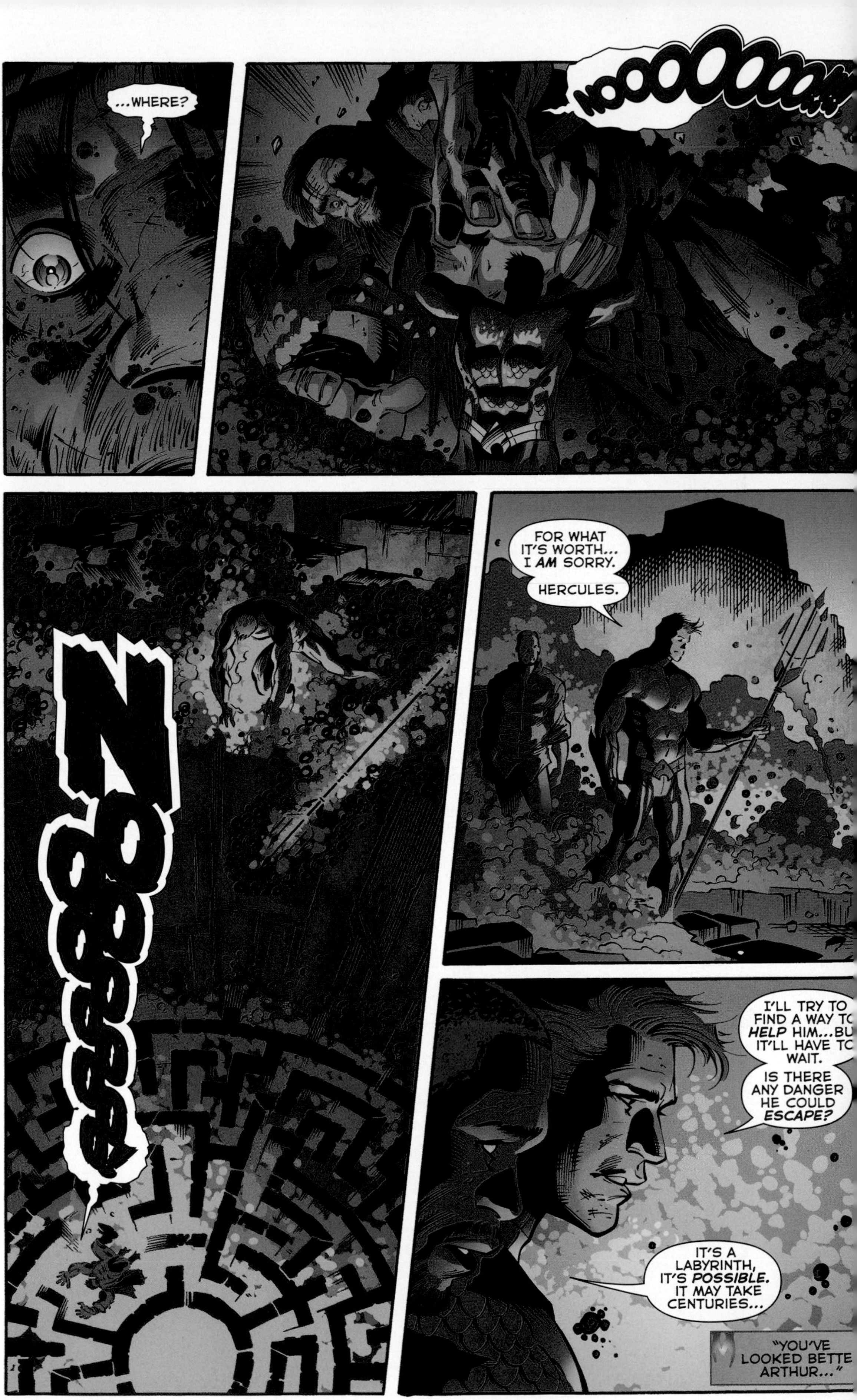
...WHERE?
FOR WHAT IT'S WORTH... I *AM* SORRY.
HERCULES.
I'LL TRY TO FIND A WAY TC *HELP* HIM...BU IT'LL HAVE TC WAIT.
IS THERE ANY DANGER HE COULD *ESCAPE?*
IT'S A LABYRINTH, IT'S *POSSIBLE.* IT MAY TAKE CENTURIES...
"YOU'VE LOOKED BETTE ARTHUR..."

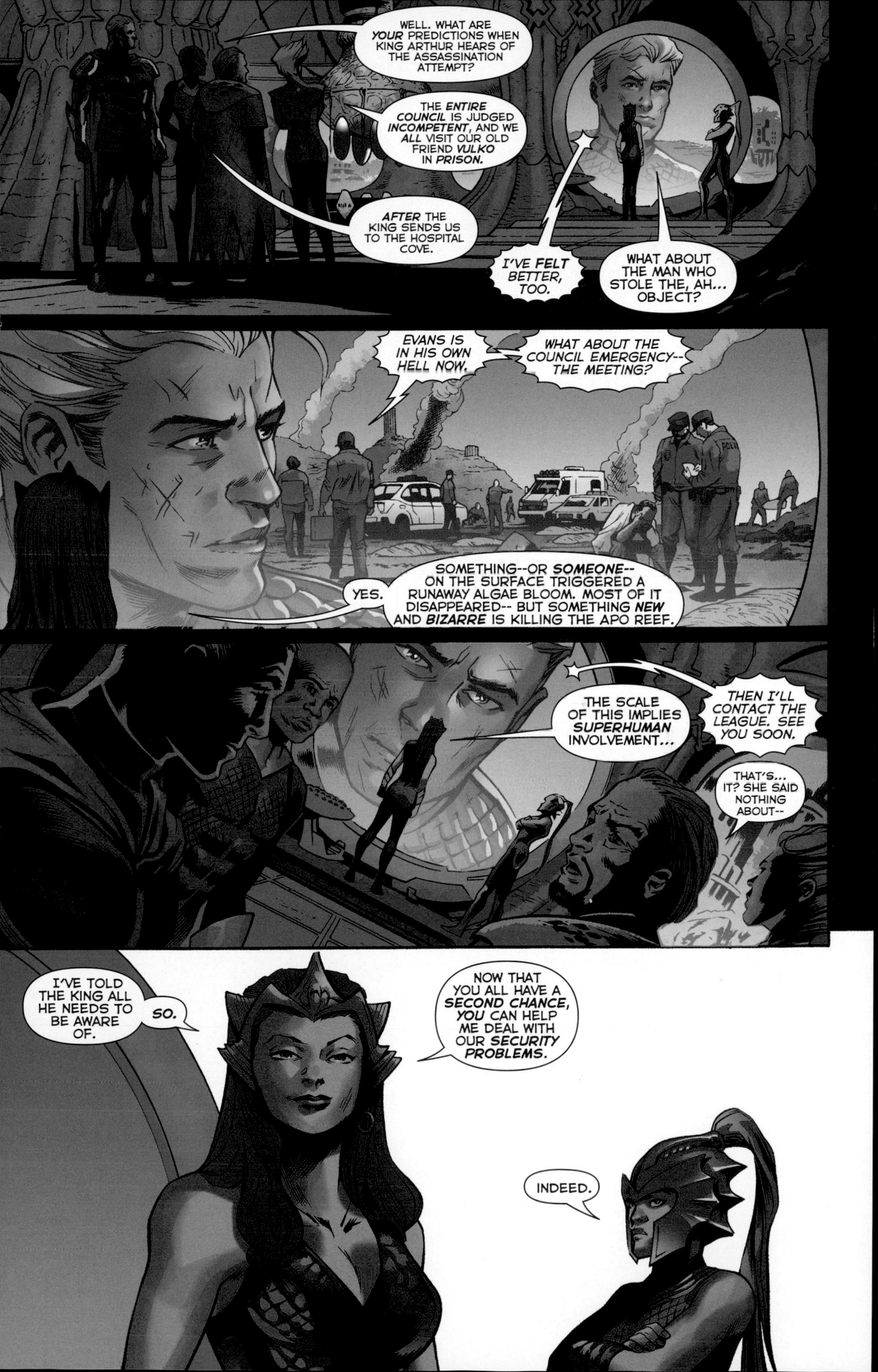
WELL. WHAT ARE YOUR PREDICTIONS WHEN KING ARTHUR HEARS OF THE ASSASSINATION ATTEMPT?
THE ENTIRE COUNCIL IS JUDGED INCOMPETENT, AND WE ALL VISIT OUR OLD FRIEND VULKO IN PRISON.
AFTER THE KING SENDS US TO THE HOSPITAL COVE.
I'VE FELT BETTER, TOO.
WHAT ABOUT THE MAN WHO STOLE THE, AH... OBJECT?
EVANS IS IN HIS OWN HELL NOW.
WHAT ABOUT THE COUNCIL EMERGENCY-- THE MEETING?
YES.
SOMETHING--OR SOMEONE-- ON THE SURFACE TRIGGERED A RUNAWAY ALGAE BLOOM. MOST OF IT DISAPPEARED-- BUT SOMETHING NEW AND BIZARRE IS KILLING THE APO REEF.
THE SCALE OF THIS IMPLIES SUPERHUMAN INVOLVEMENT...
THEN I'LL CONTACT THE LEAGUE. SEE YOU SOON.
THAT'S... IT? SHE SAID NOTHING ABOUT--
I'VE TOLD THE KING ALL HE NEEDS TO BE AWARE OF.
SO.
NOW THAT YOU ALL HAVE A SECOND CHANCE, YOU CAN HELP ME DEAL WITH OUR SECURITY PROBLEMS.
INDEED.

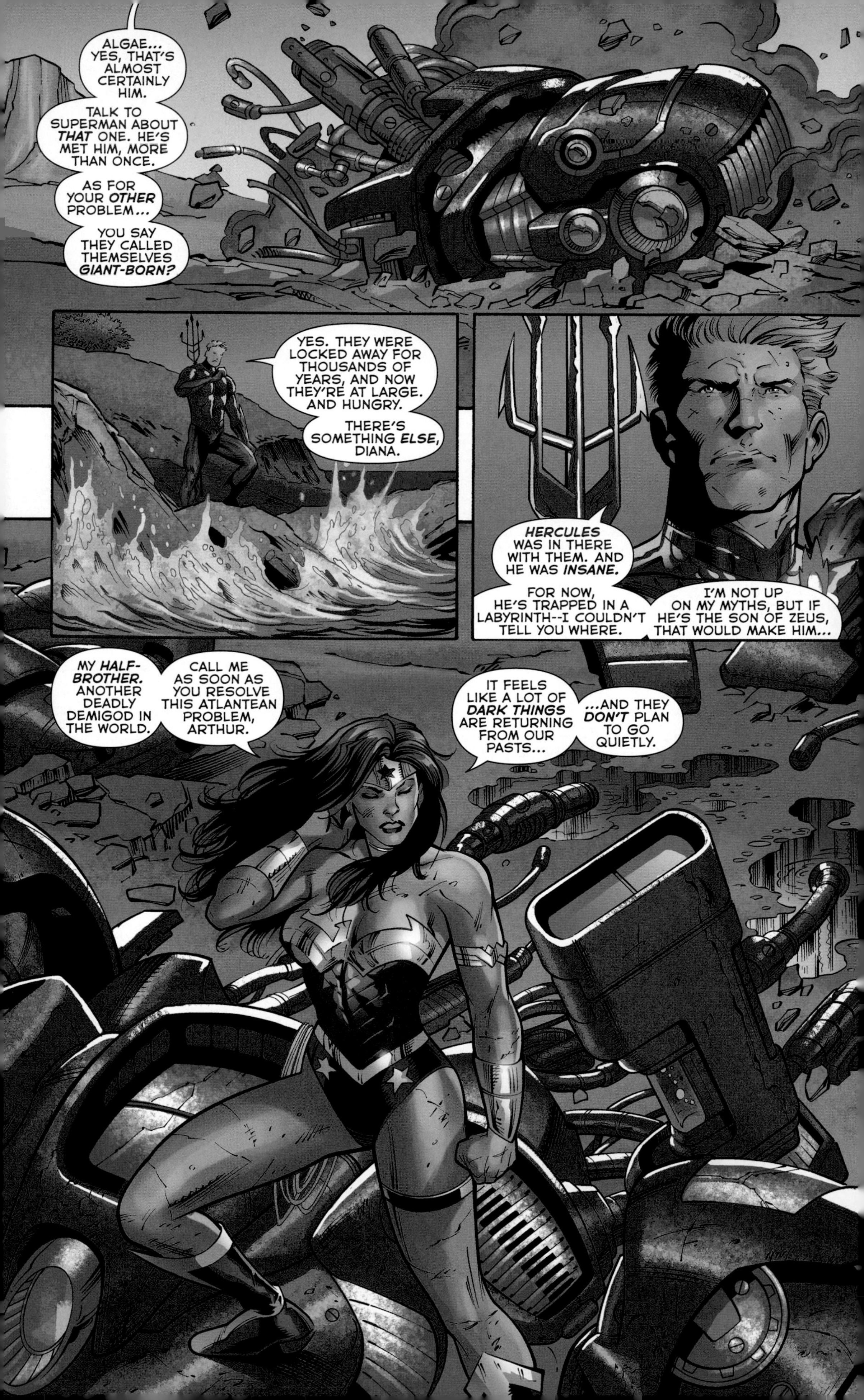
ALGAE... YES, THAT'S ALMOST CERTAINLY HIM.
TALK TO SUPERMAN ABOUT *THAT* ONE. HE'S MET HIM, MORE THAN ONCE.
AS FOR YOUR *OTHER* PROBLEM...
YOU SAY THEY CALLED THEMSELVES *GIANT-BORN?*
YES. THEY WERE LOCKED AWAY FOR THOUSANDS OF YEARS, AND NOW THEY'RE AT LARGE. AND HUNGRY.
THERE'S SOMETHING *ELSE,* DIANA.
HERCULES WAS IN THERE WITH THEM. AND HE WAS *INSANE.*
FOR NOW, HE'S TRAPPED IN A LABYRINTH--I COULDN'T TELL YOU WHERE.
I'M NOT UP ON MY MYTHS, BUT IF HE'S THE SON OF ZEUS, THAT WOULD MAKE HIM...
MY *HALF-BROTHER.* ANOTHER DEADLY DEMIGOD IN THE WORLD.
CALL ME AS SOON AS YOU RESOLVE THIS ATLANTEAN PROBLEM, ARTHUR.
IT FEELS LIKE A LOT OF *DARK THINGS* ARE RETURNING FROM OUR PASTS...
...AND THEY *DON'T* PLAN TO GO QUIETLY.

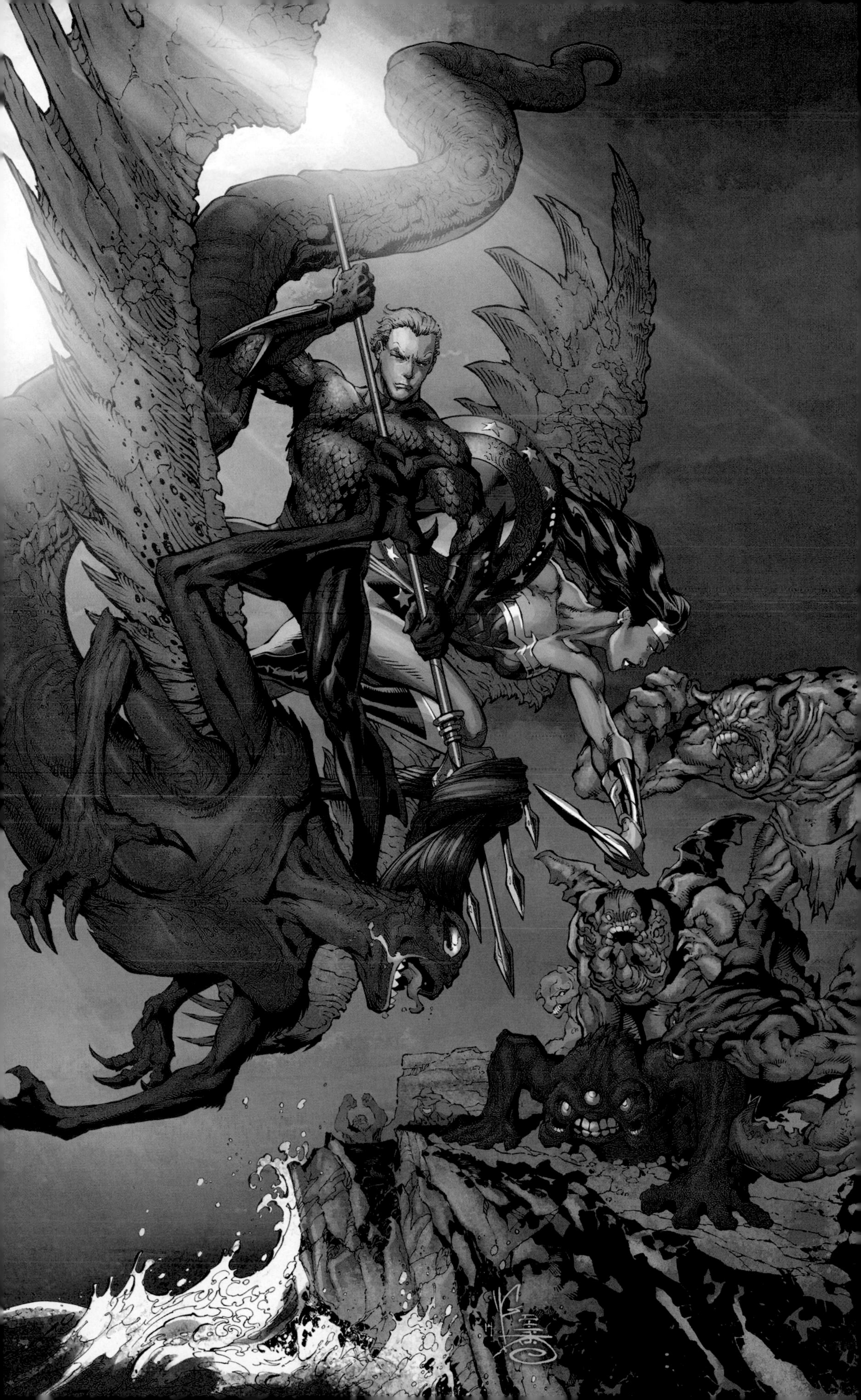

BORN OF GIANTS

JEFF PARKER writer **YVEL GUICHET ALVARO MARTINEZ** (pgs 147-156) pencillers
JASON GORDER WAYNE FAUCHER (pgs 138-146) **RAUL FERNANDEZ** (pgs 147-156) inkers **NATHAN EYRING** colorist
ROB LEIGH letterer cover by **YVEL GUICHET, DANNY MIKI** and **RAIN BEREDO**

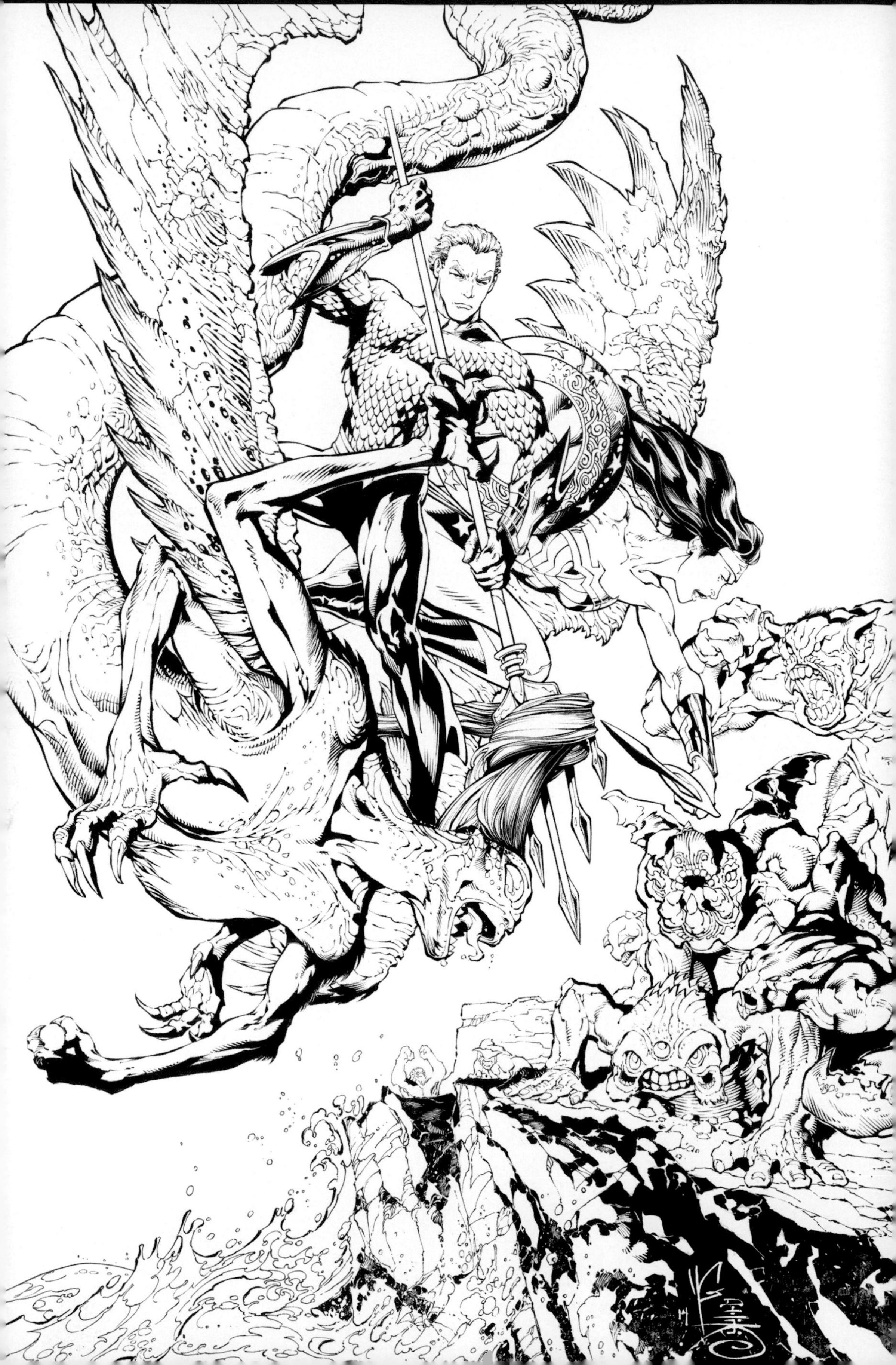

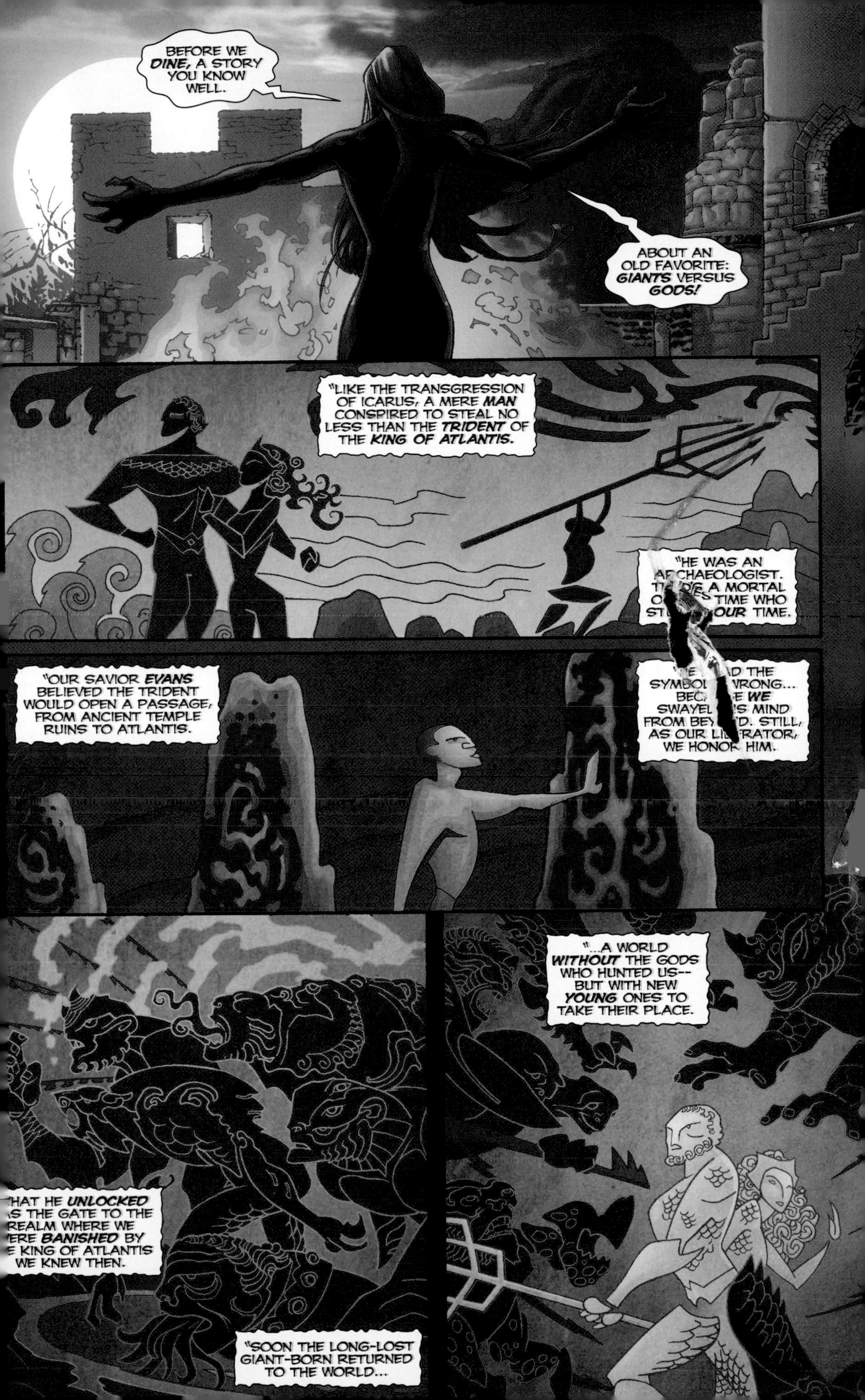
BEFORE WE DINE, A STORY YOU KNOW WELL.
ABOUT AN OLD FAVORITE: GIANTS VERSUS GODS!
"LIKE THE TRANSGRESSION OF ICARUS, A MERE MAN CONSPIRED TO STEAL NO LESS THAN THE TRIDENT OF THE KING OF ATLANTIS.
"HE WAS AN
TIME WHO
OUR TIME.
"OUR SAVIOR EVANS BELIEVED THE TRIDENT WOULD OPEN A PASSAGE, FROM ANCIENT TEMPLE RUINS TO ATLANTIS.
SWAYE
MIND
STILL,
AS OUR
WE HONOR HIM.
"...A WORLD WITHOUT THE GODS WHO HUNTED US-- BUT WITH NEW YOUNG ONES TO TAKE THEIR PLACE.
HAT HE UNLOCKED
S THE GATE TO THE
REALM WHERE WE
ERE BANISHED BY
KING OF ATLANTIS
WE KNEW THEN.
"SOON THE LONG-LOST GIANT-BORN RETURNED TO THE WORLD...

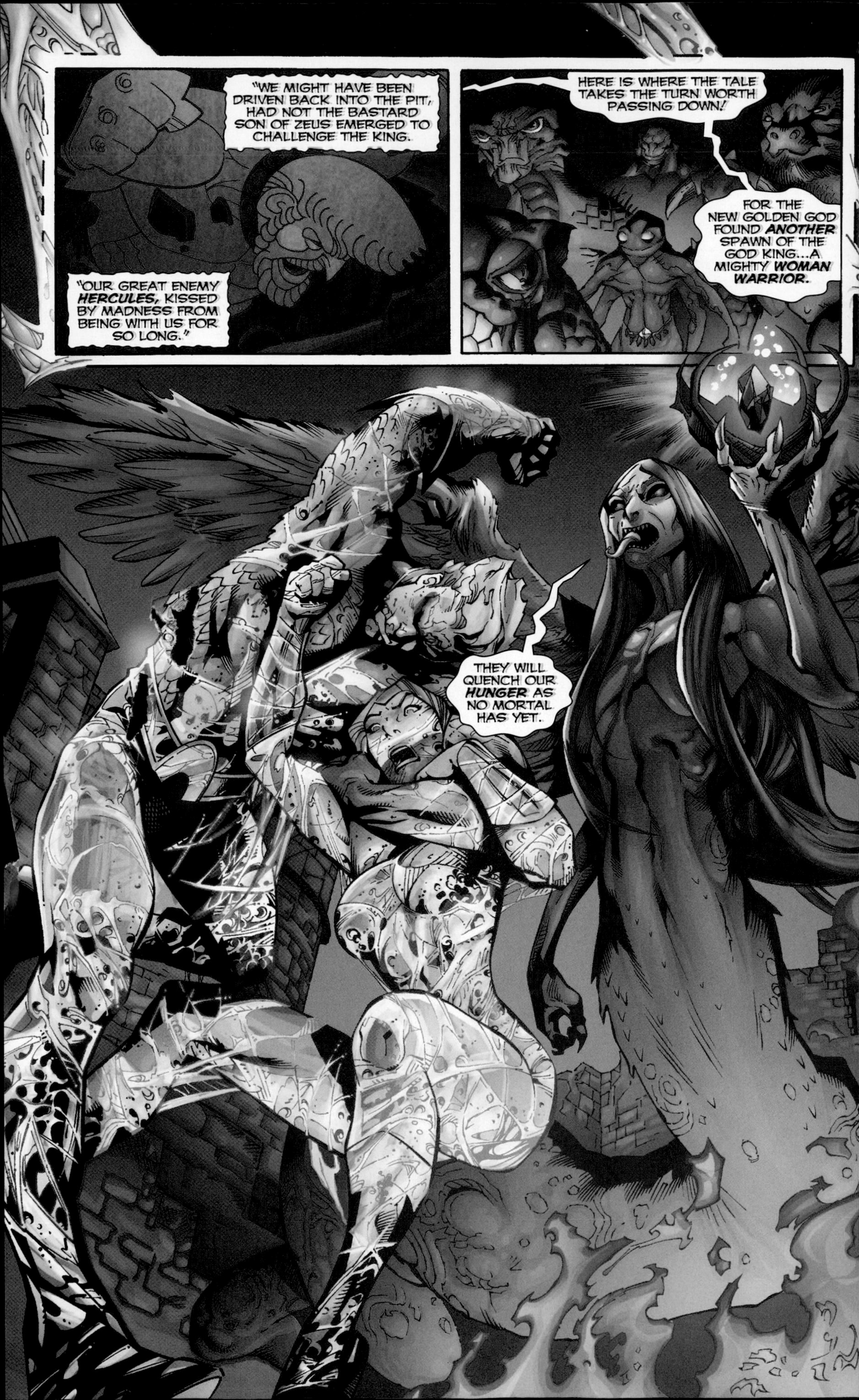
"WE MIGHT HAVE BEEN DRIVEN BACK INTO THE PIT, HAD NOT THE BASTARD SON OF ZEUS EMERGED TO CHALLENGE THE KING.
"OUR GREAT ENEMY ***HERCULES,*** KISSED BY MADNESS FROM BEING WITH US FOR SO LONG."
HERE IS WHERE THE TALE TAKES THE TURN WORTH PASSING DOWN!
FOR THE NEW GOLDEN GOD FOUND ***ANOTHER*** SPAWN OF THE GOD KING...A MIGHTY ***WOMAN WARRIOR.***
THEY WILL QUENCH OUR ***HUNGER*** AS NO MORTAL HAS YET.

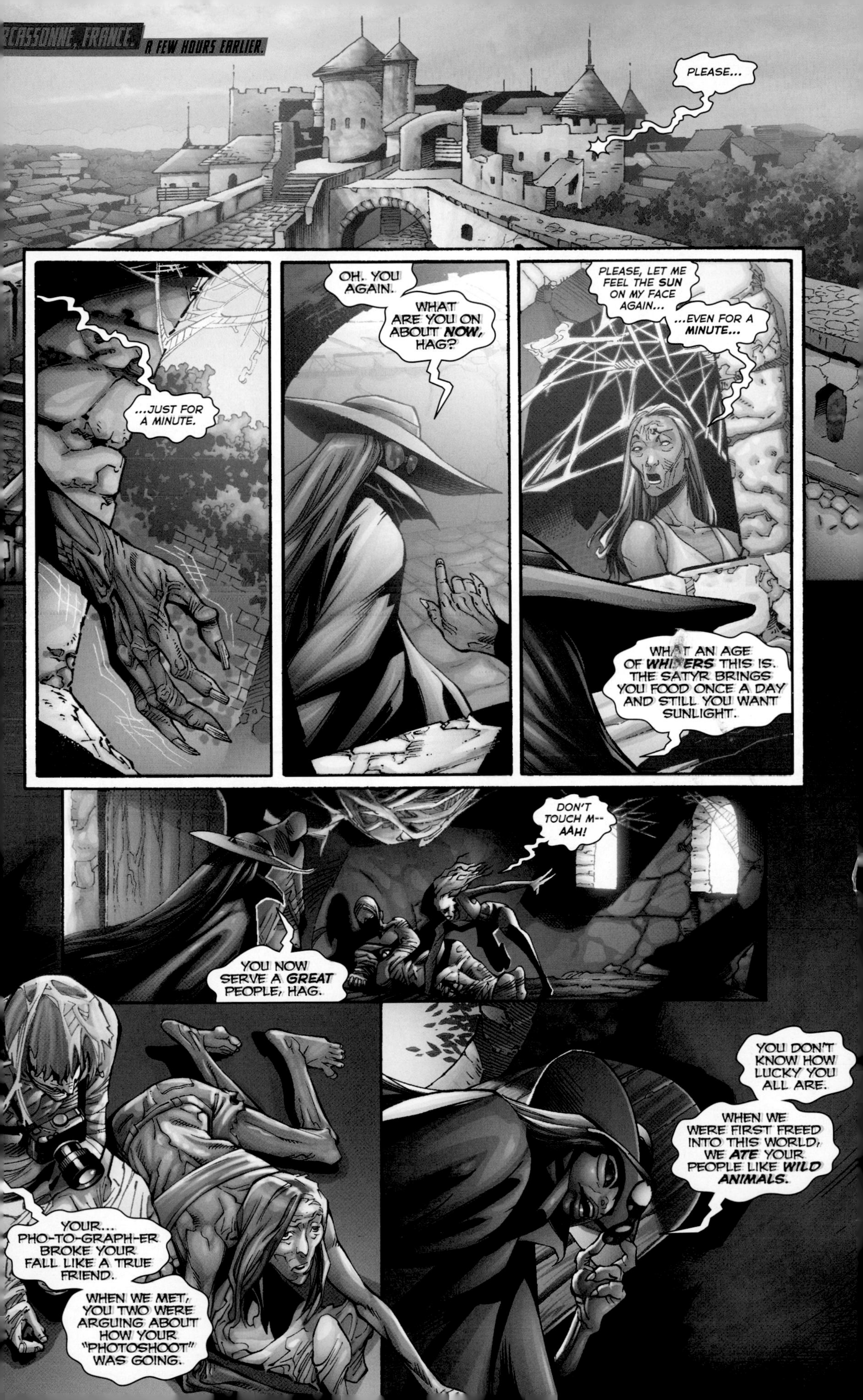
CASSONNE, FRANCE.
A FEW HOURS EARLIER.
PLEASE...
...JUST FOR A MINUTE.
OH.. YOU AGAIN.
WHAT ARE YOU ON ABOUT NOW, HAG?
PLEASE, LET ME FEEL THE SUN ON MY FACE AGAIN...
...EVEN FOR A MINUTE...
WHAT AN AGE OF WHINERS THIS IS. THE SATYR BRINGS YOU FOOD ONCE A DAY AND STILL YOU WANT SUNLIGHT..
DON'T TOUCH M-- AAH!
YOU NOW SERVE A GREAT PEOPLE, HAG.
YOUR... PHO-TO-GRAPH-ER BROKE YOUR FALL LIKE A TRUE FRIEND.
WHEN WE MET, YOU TWO WERE ARGUING ABOUT HOW YOUR "PHOTOSHOOT" WAS GOING.
YOU DON'T KNOW HOW LUCKY YOU ALL ARE.
WHEN WE WERE FIRST FREED INTO THIS WORLD, WE ATE YOUR PEOPLE LIKE WILD ANIMALS.

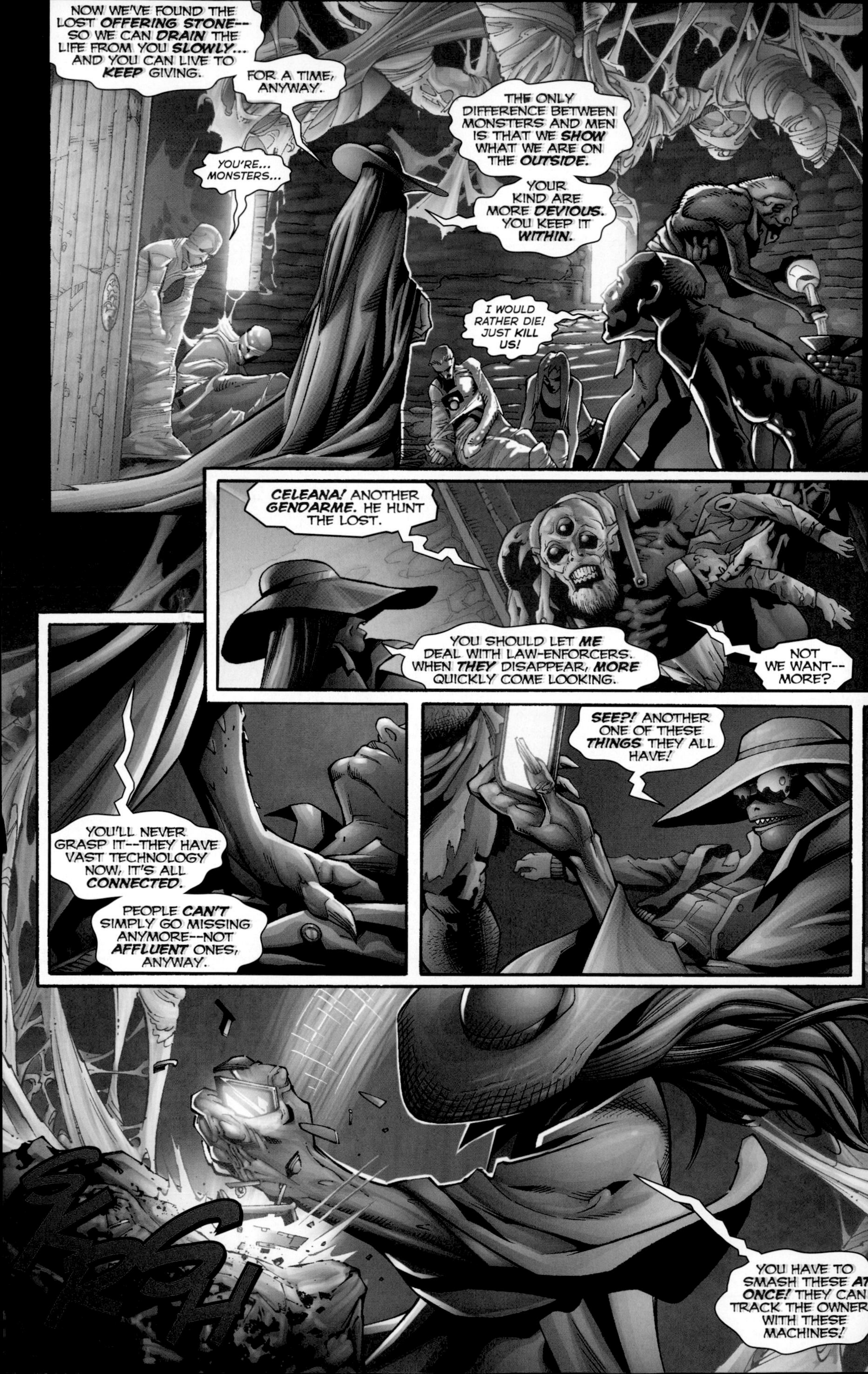
NOW WE'VE FOUND THE LOST OFFERING STONE-- SO WE CAN DRAIN THE LIFE FROM YOU SLOWLY... AND YOU CAN LIVE TO KEEP GIVING.
FOR A TIME, ANYWAY.
YOU'RE... MONSTERS...
THE ONLY DIFFERENCE BETWEEN MONSTERS AND MEN IS THAT WE SHOW WHAT WE ARE ON THE OUTSIDE.
YOUR KIND ARE MORE DEVIOUS. YOU KEEP IT WITHIN.
I WOULD RATHER DIE! JUST KILL US!
CELEANA! ANOTHER GENDARME. HE HUNT THE LOST.
YOU SHOULD LET ME DEAL WITH LAW-ENFORCERS. WHEN THEY DISAPPEAR, MORE QUICKLY COME LOOKING.
NOT WE WANT-- MORE?
YOU'LL NEVER GRASP IT--THEY HAVE VAST TECHNOLOGY NOW, IT'S ALL CONNECTED.
PEOPLE CAN'T SIMPLY GO MISSING ANYMORE--NOT AFFLUENT ONES, ANYWAY.
SEE?! ANOTHER ONE OF THESE THINGS THEY ALL HAVE!
SKRSH
YOU HAVE TO SMASH THESE AT ONCE! THEY CAN TRACK THE OWNER WITH THESE MACHINES!

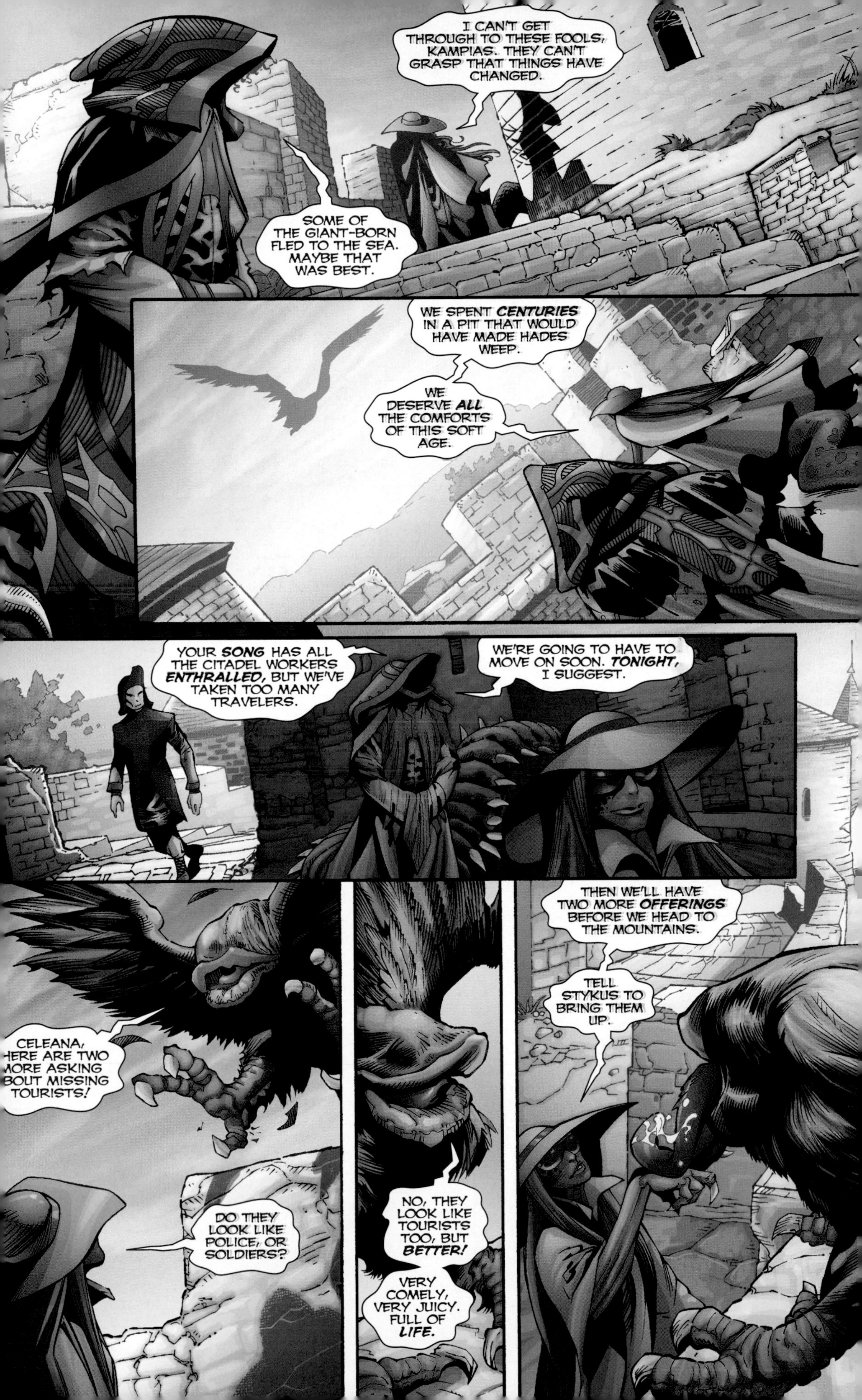
I CAN'T GET THROUGH TO THESE FOOLS, KAMPIAS. THEY CAN'T GRASP THAT THINGS HAVE CHANGED.
SOME OF THE GIANT-BORN FLED TO THE SEA. MAYBE THAT WAS BEST.
WE SPENT CENTURIES IN A PIT THAT WOULD HAVE MADE HADES WEEP.
WE DESERVE ALL THE COMFORTS OF THIS SOFT AGE.
YOUR SONG HAS ALL THE CITADEL WORKERS ENTHRALLED, BUT WE'VE TAKEN TOO MANY TRAVELERS.
WE'RE GOING TO HAVE TO MOVE ON SOON. TONIGHT, I SUGGEST.
CELEANA, HERE ARE TWO MORE ASKING BOUT MISSING TOURISTS!
DO THEY LOOK LIKE POLICE, OR SOLDIERS?
NO, THEY LOOK LIKE TOURISTS TOO, BUT BETTER!
VERY COMELY, VERY JUICY. FULL OF LIFE.
THEN WE'LL HAVE TWO MORE OFFERINGS BEFORE WE HEAD TO THE MOUNTAINS.
TELL STYKUS TO BRING THEM UP.

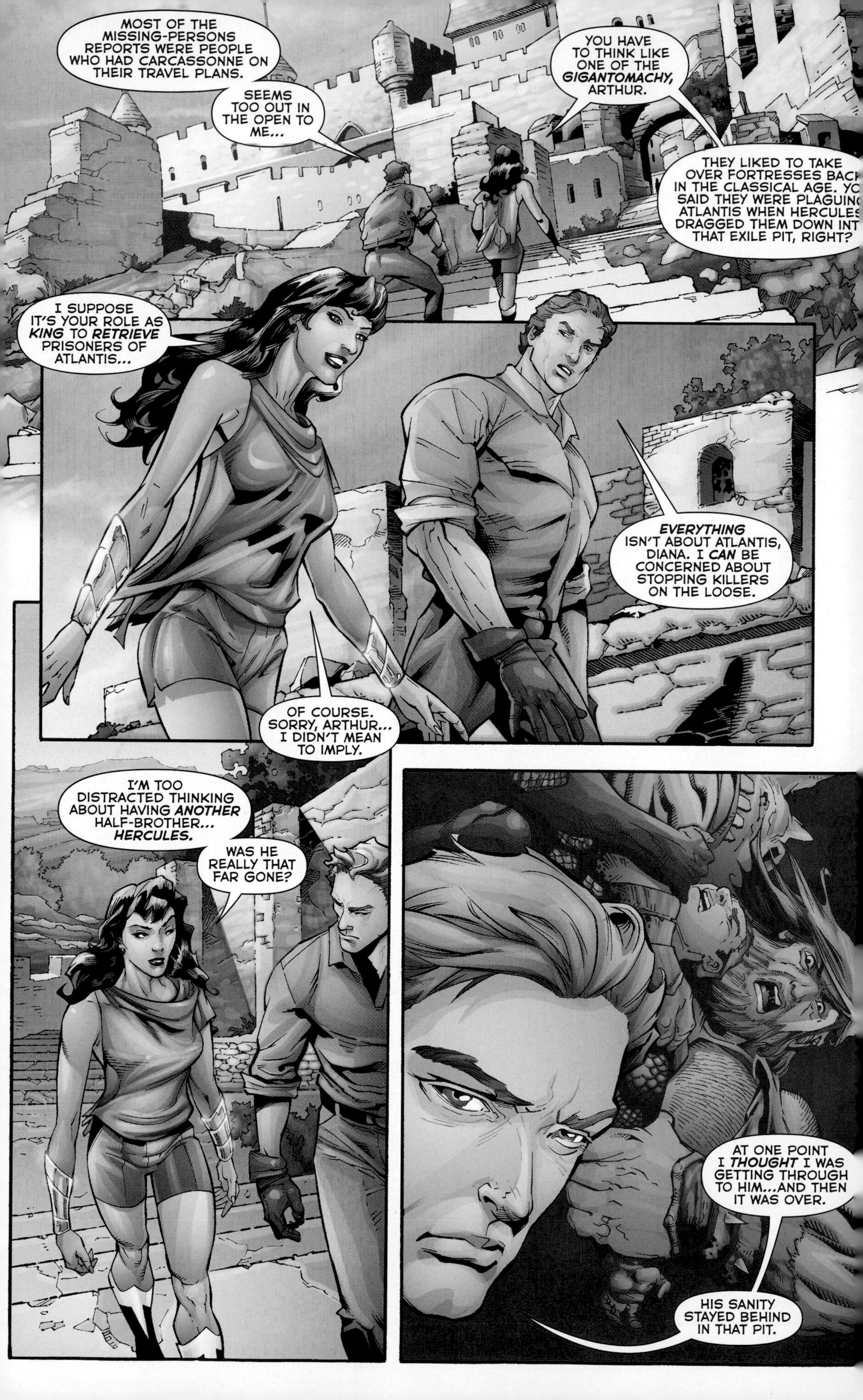
MOST OF THE MISSING-PERSONS REPORTS WERE PEOPLE WHO HAD CARCASSONNE ON THEIR TRAVEL PLANS.
SEEMS TOO OUT IN THE OPEN TO ME...
YOU HAVE TO THINK LIKE ONE OF THE GIGANTOMACHY, ARTHUR.
THEY LIKED TO TAKE OVER FORTRESSES BACK IN THE CLASSICAL AGE. YOU SAID THEY WERE PLAGUING ATLANTIS WHEN HERCULES DRAGGED THEM DOWN INTO THAT EXILE PIT, RIGHT?
I SUPPOSE IT'S YOUR ROLE AS KING TO RETRIEVE PRISONERS OF ATLANTIS...
EVERYTHING ISN'T ABOUT ATLANTIS, DIANA. I CAN BE CONCERNED ABOUT STOPPING KILLERS ON THE LOOSE.
OF COURSE. SORRY, ARTHUR... I DIDN'T MEAN TO IMPLY.
I'M TOO DISTRACTED THINKING ABOUT HAVING ANOTHER HALF-BROTHER... HERCULES.
WAS HE REALLY THAT FAR GONE?
AT ONE POINT I THOUGHT I WAS GETTING THROUGH TO HIM...AND THEN IT WAS OVER.
HIS SANITY STAYED BEHIND IN THAT PIT.

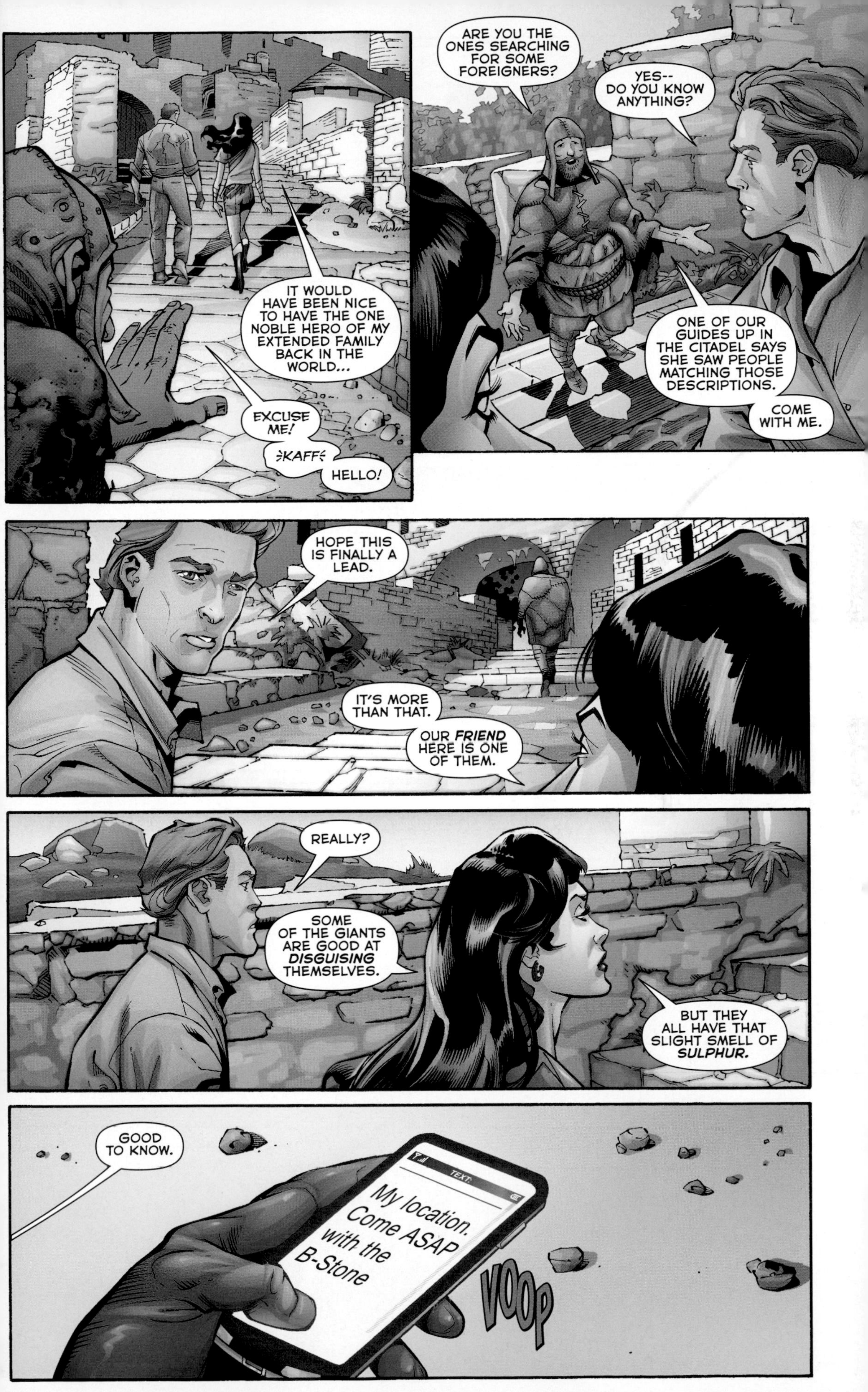
IT WOULD HAVE BEEN NICE TO HAVE THE ONE NOBLE HERO OF MY EXTENDED FAMILY BACK IN THE WORLD...
EXCUSE ME!
KAFF
HELLO!
ARE YOU THE ONES SEARCHING FOR SOME FOREIGNERS?
YES-- DO YOU KNOW ANYTHING?
ONE OF OUR GUIDES UP IN THE CITADEL SAYS SHE SAW PEOPLE MATCHING THOSE DESCRIPTIONS.
COME WITH ME.
HOPE THIS IS FINALLY A LEAD.
IT'S MORE THAN THAT.
OUR FRIEND HERE IS ONE OF THEM.
REALLY?
SOME OF THE GIANTS ARE GOOD AT DISGUISING THEMSELVES.
BUT THEY ALL HAVE THAT SLIGHT SMELL OF SULPHUR.
GOOD TO KNOW.
TEXT:
My location. Come ASAP with the B-Stone
VOOP

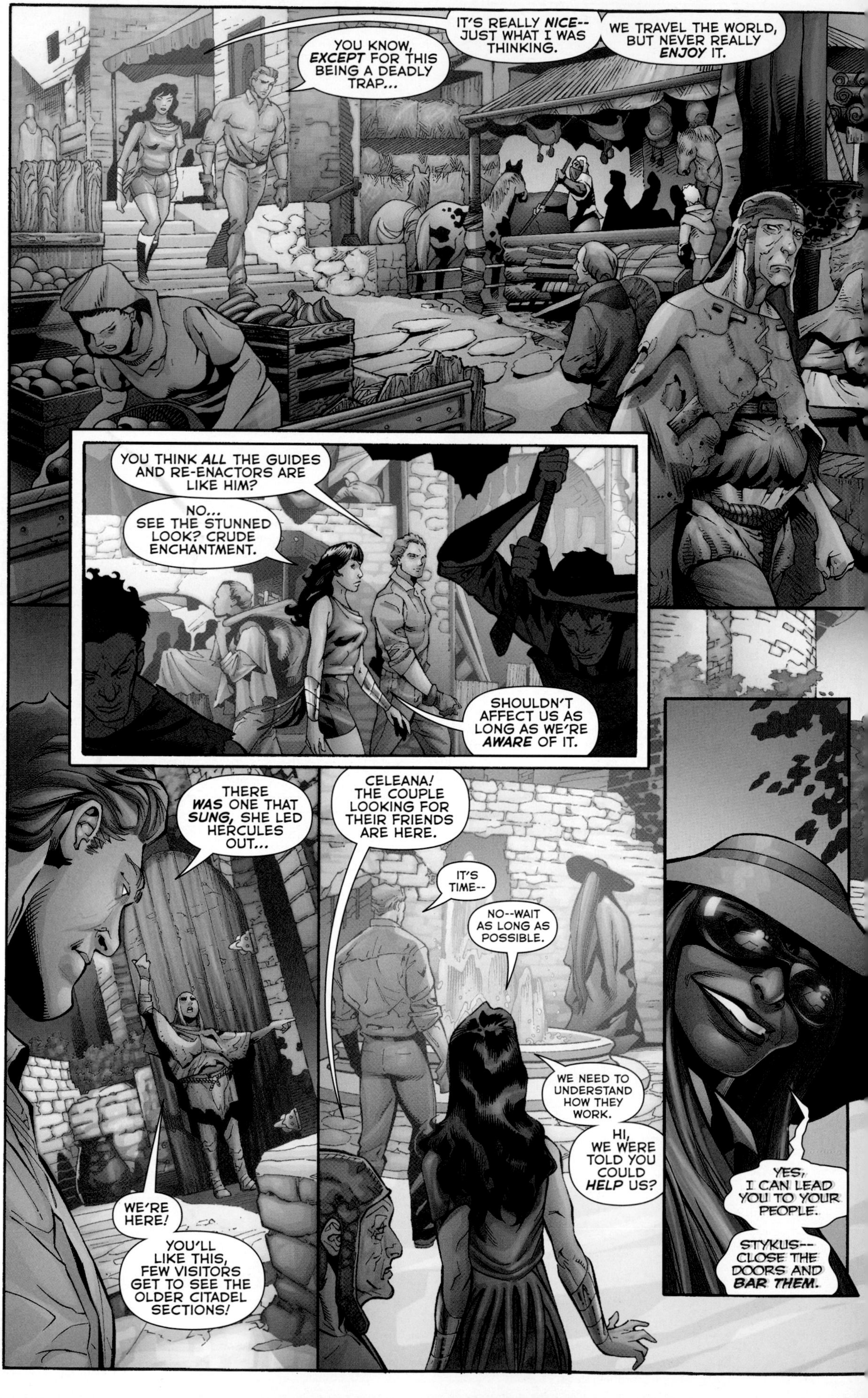
YOU KNOW, EXCEPT FOR THIS BEING A DEADLY TRAP...
IT'S REALLY NICE-- JUST WHAT I WAS THINKING.
WE TRAVEL THE WORLD, BUT NEVER REALLY ENJOY IT.
YOU THINK ALL THE GUIDES AND RE-ENACTORS ARE LIKE HIM?
NO... SEE THE STUNNED LOOK? CRUDE ENCHANTMENT.
SHOULDN'T AFFECT US AS LONG AS WE'RE AWARE OF IT.
THERE WAS ONE THAT SUNG, SHE LED HERCULES OUT...
WE'RE HERE!
YOU'LL LIKE THIS, FEW VISITORS GET TO SEE THE OLDER CITADEL SECTIONS!
CELEANA! THE COUPLE LOOKING FOR THEIR FRIENDS ARE HERE.
IT'S TIME--
NO--WAIT AS LONG AS POSSIBLE.
WE NEED TO UNDERSTAND HOW THEY WORK.
HI, WE WERE TOLD YOU COULD HELP US?
YES, I CAN LEAD YOU TO YOUR PEOPLE.
STYKUS-- CLOSE THE DOORS AND BAR THEM.

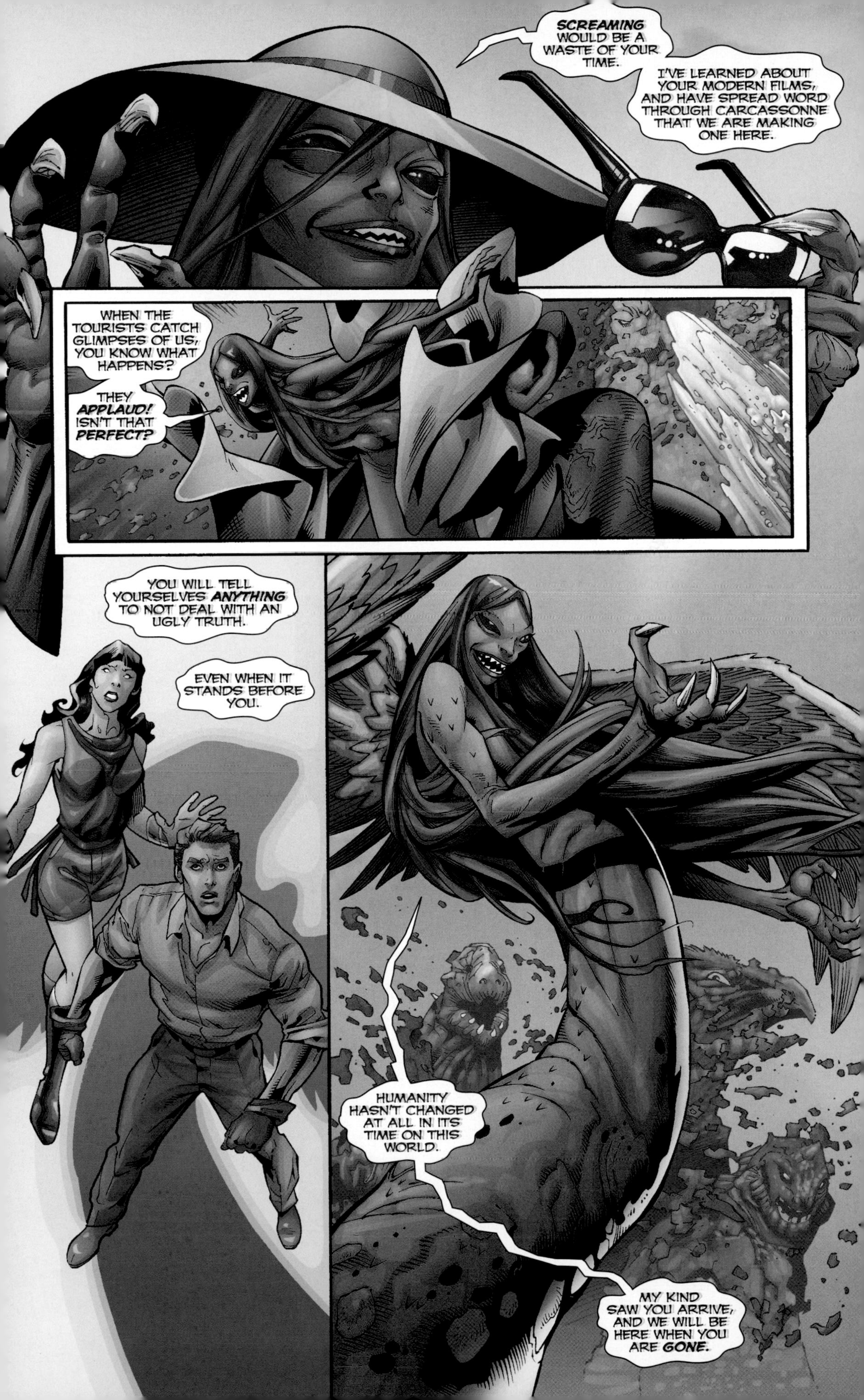
SCREAMING WOULD BE A WASTE OF YOUR TIME.
I'VE LEARNED ABOUT YOUR MODERN FILMS, AND HAVE SPREAD WORD THROUGH CARCASSONNE THAT WE ARE MAKING ONE HERE.
WHEN THE TOURISTS CATCH GLIMPSES OF US, YOU KNOW WHAT HAPPENS?
THEY APPLAUD! ISN'T THAT PERFECT?
YOU WILL TELL YOURSELVES ANYTHING TO NOT DEAL WITH AN UGLY TRUTH.
EVEN WHEN IT STANDS BEFORE YOU.
HUMANITY HASN'T CHANGED AT ALL IN ITS TIME ON THIS WORLD.
MY KIND SAW YOU ARRIVE, AND WE WILL BE HERE WHEN YOU ARE GONE.

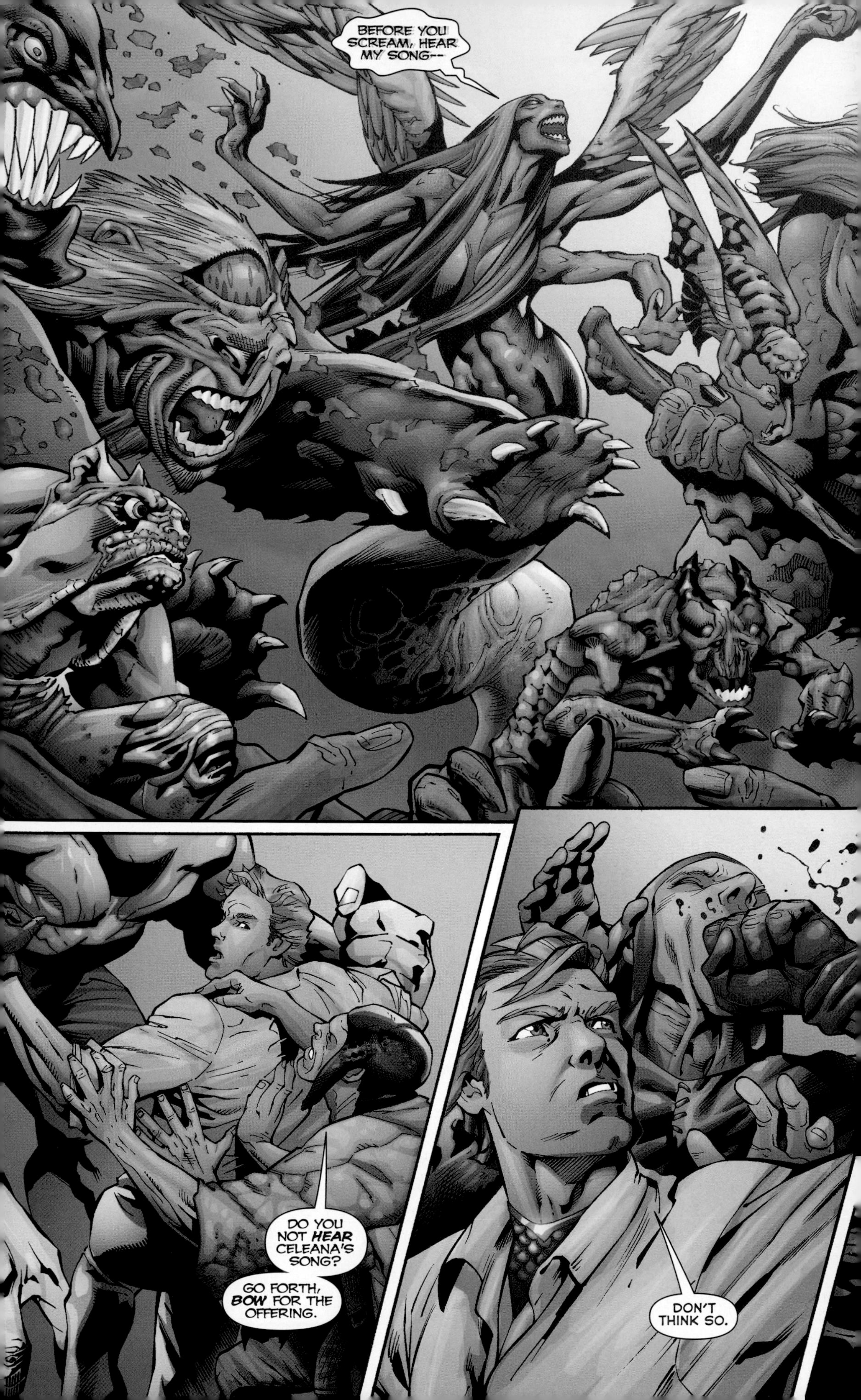
BEFORE YOU SCREAM, HEAR MY SONG--
DO YOU NOT *HEAR* CELEANA'S SONG?
GO FORTH, *BOW* FOR THE OFFERING.
DON'T THINK SO.

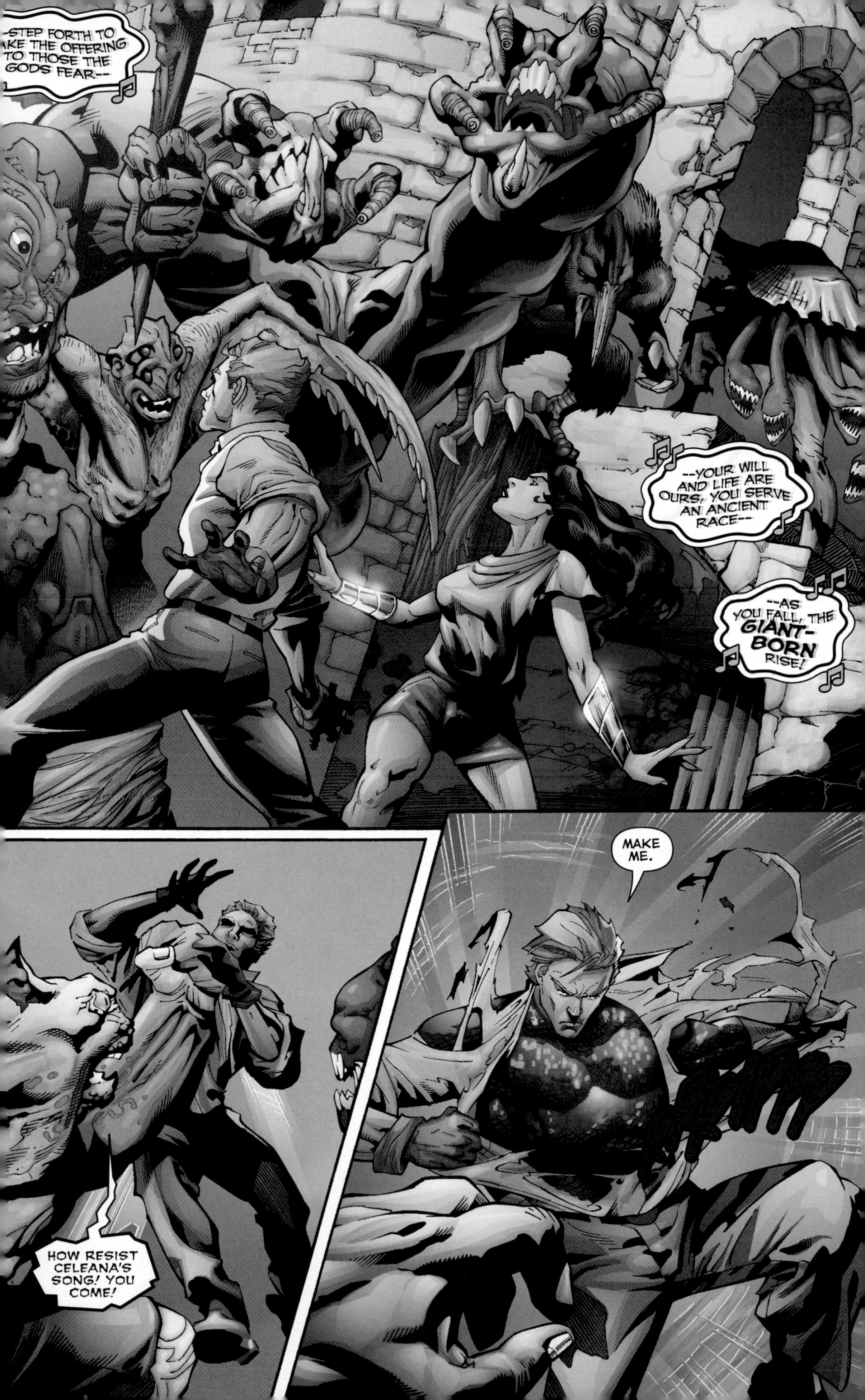

--STEP FORTH TO MAKE THE OFFERING TO THOSE THE GODS FEAR--
--YOUR WILL AND LIFE ARE OURS, YOU SERVE AN ANCIENT RACE--
--AS YOU FALL, THE GIANT-BORN RISE!
MAKE ME.
HOW RESIST CELEANA'S SONG! YOU COME!

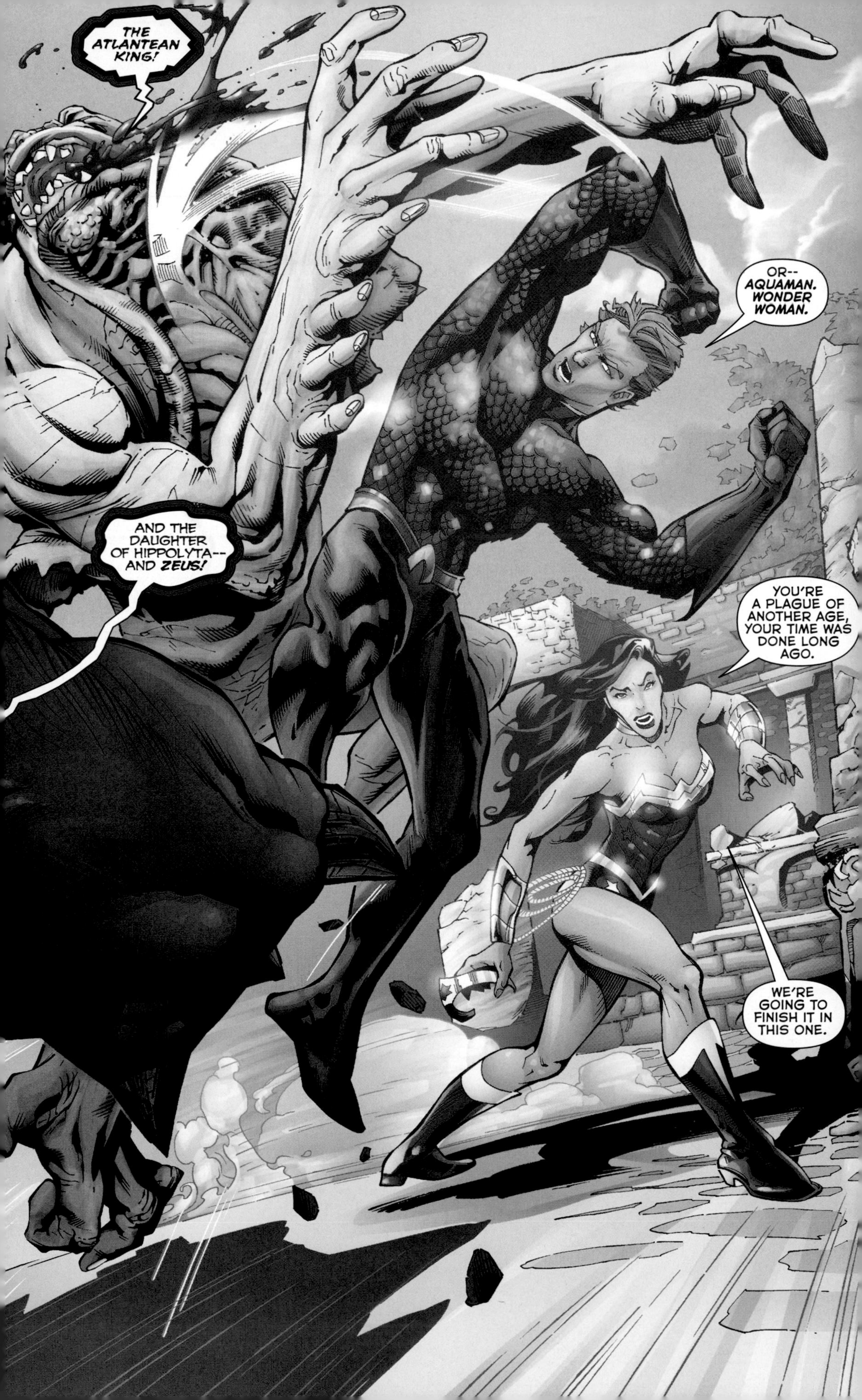
THE ATLANTEAN KING!
OR-- AQUAMAN. WONDER WOMAN.
AND THE DAUGHTER OF HIPPOLYTA-- AND ZEUS!
YOU'RE A PLAGUE OF ANOTHER AGE, YOUR TIME WAS DONE LONG AGO.
WE'RE GOING TO FINISH IT IN THIS ONE.

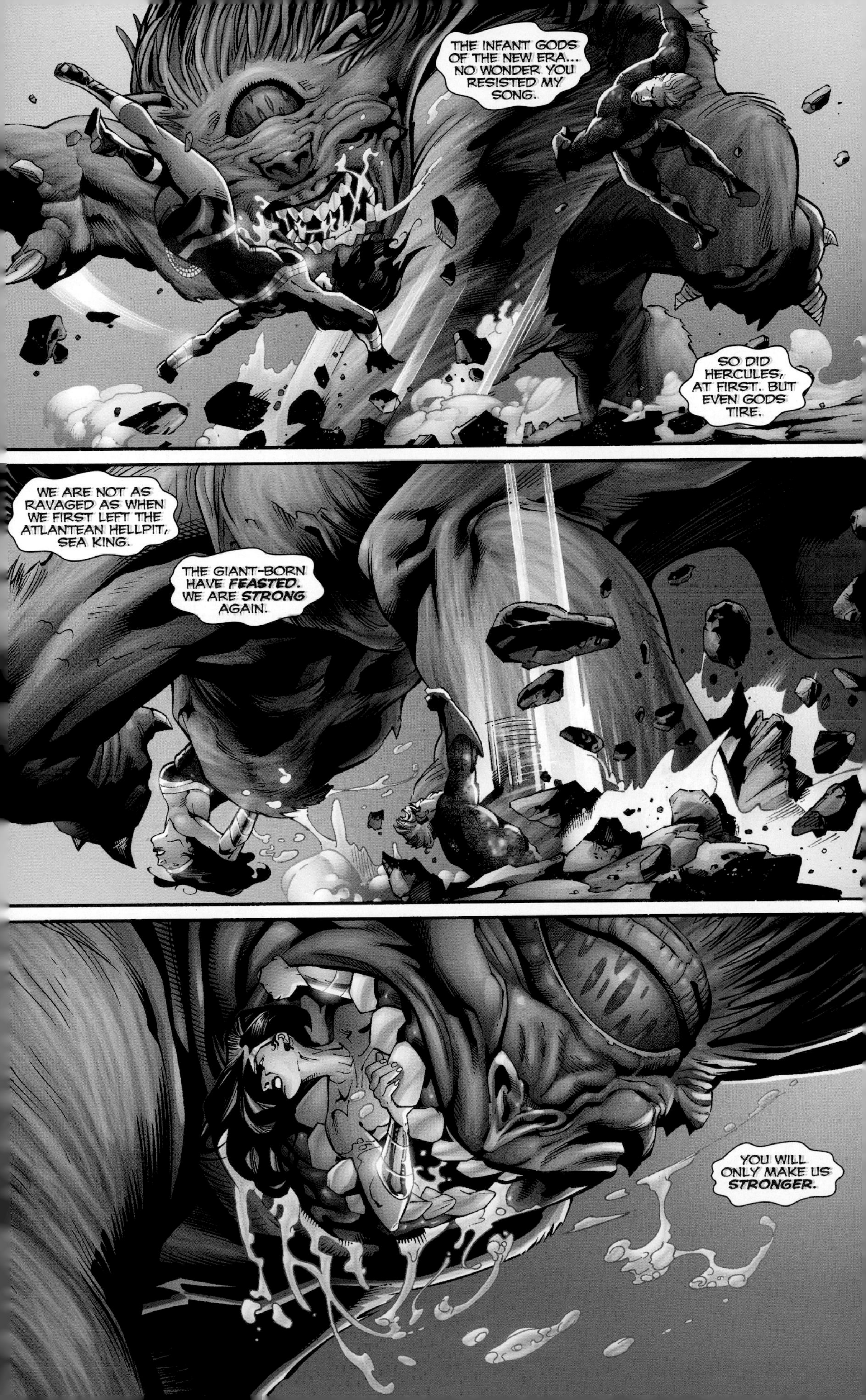
THE INFANT GODS OF THE NEW ERA... NO WONDER YOU RESISTED MY SONG.
SO DID HERCULES, AT FIRST. BUT EVEN GODS TIRE.
WE ARE NOT AS RAVAGED AS WHEN WE FIRST LEFT THE ATLANTEAN HELLPIT, SEA KING.
THE GIANT-BORN HAVE FEASTED. WE ARE STRONG AGAIN.
YOU WILL ONLY MAKE US STRONGER.

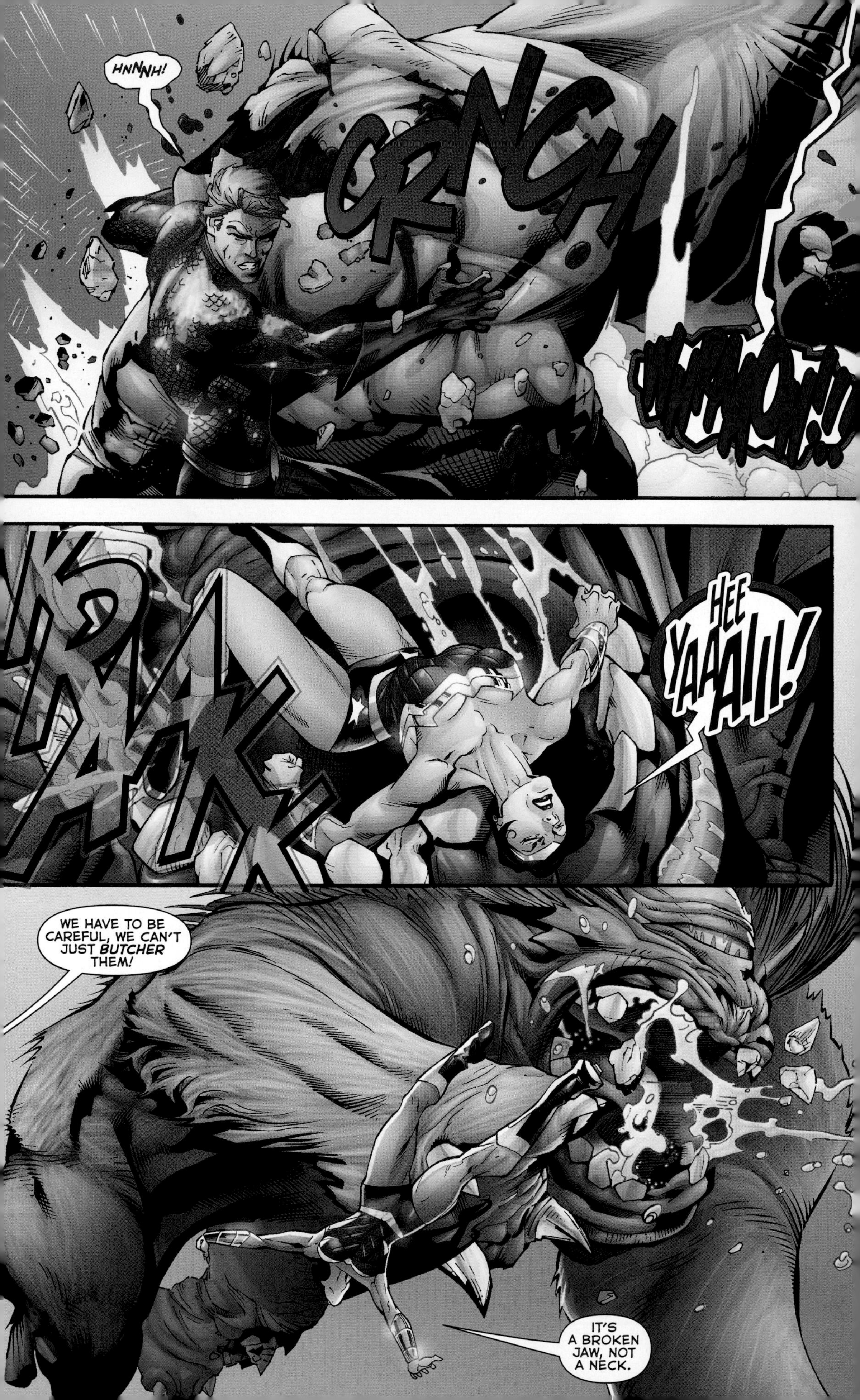
HNNNH!
CRNCH
KRAKK
HEE YAAAIII!
WE HAVE TO BE CAREFUL, WE CAN'T JUST *BUTCHER* THEM!
IT'S A BROKEN JAW, NOT A NECK.

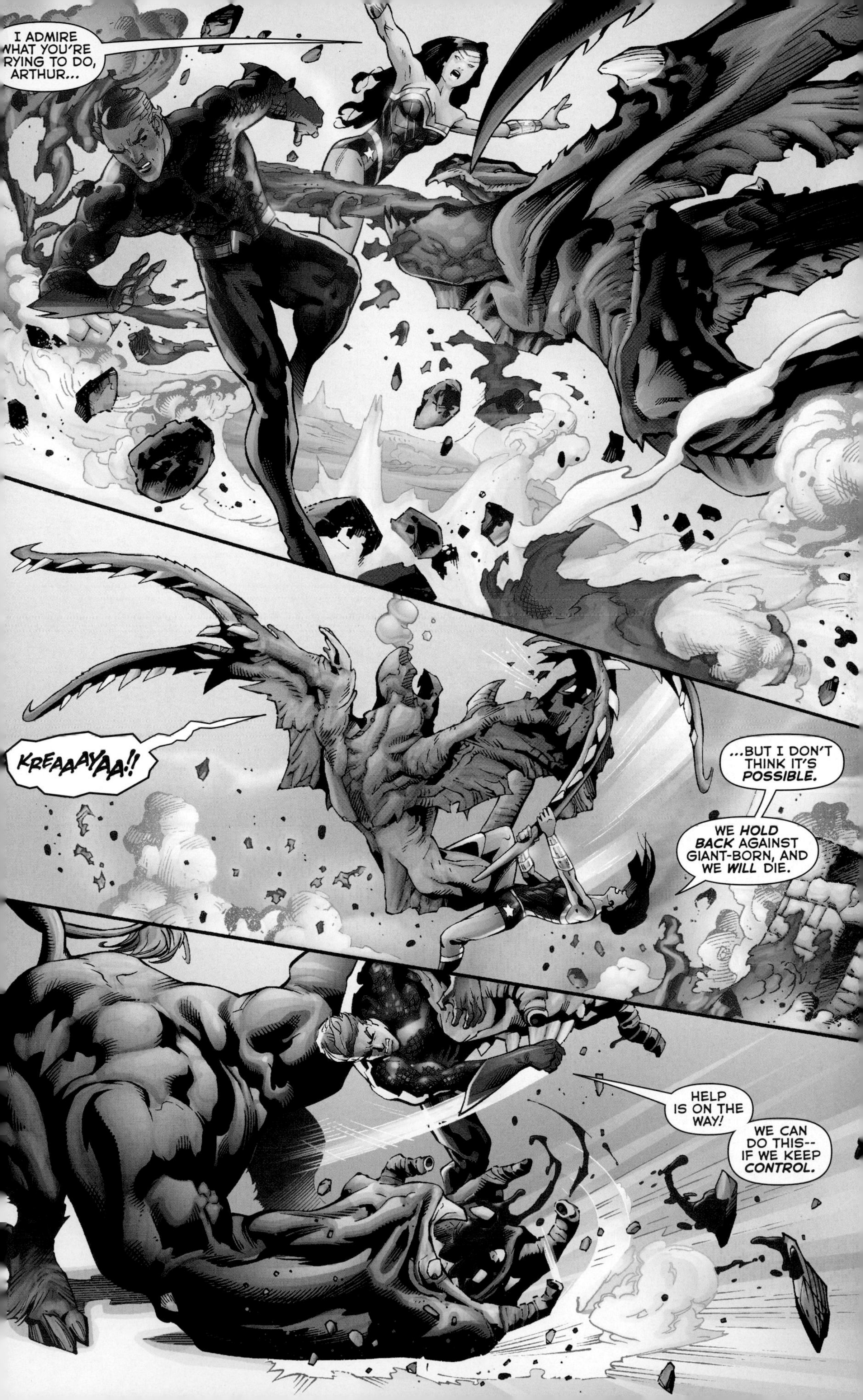
I ADMIRE WHAT YOU'RE TRYING TO DO, ARTHUR...
KREAAAYAA!!
...BUT I DON'T THINK IT'S POSSIBLE.
WE HOLD BACK AGAINST GIANT-BORN, AND WE WILL DIE.
HELP IS ON THE WAY!
WE CAN DO THIS-- IF WE KEEP CONTROL.

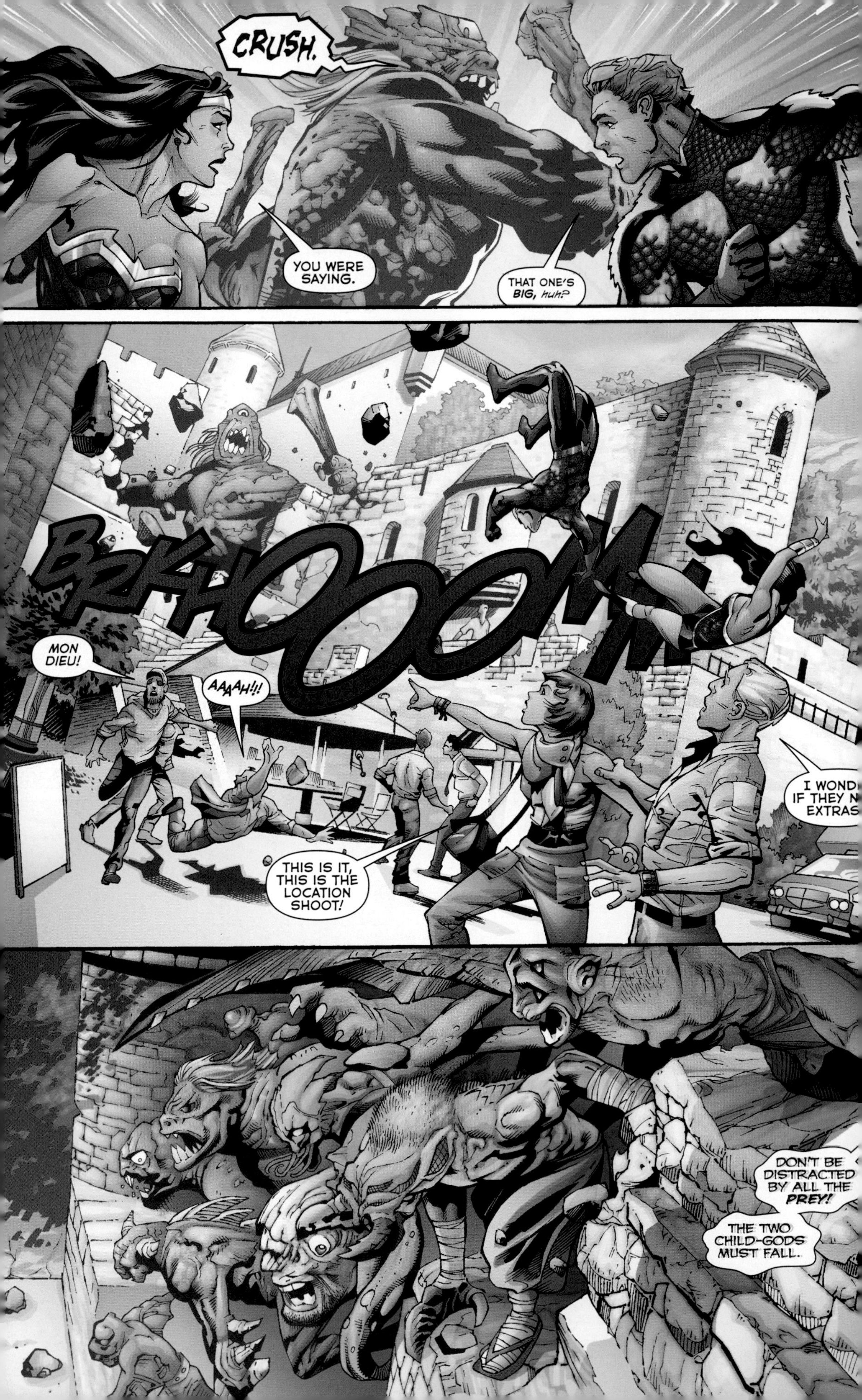
CRUSH.
YOU WERE SAYING.
THAT ONE'S *BIG*, *huh?*
BRKHOOOOM!
MON DIEU!
AAAAH!!!
THIS IS IT, THIS IS THE LOCATION SHOOT!
I WOND IF THEY N EXTRAS
DON'T BE DISTRACTED BY ALL THE *PREY!*
THE TWO CHILD-GODS MUST FALL.

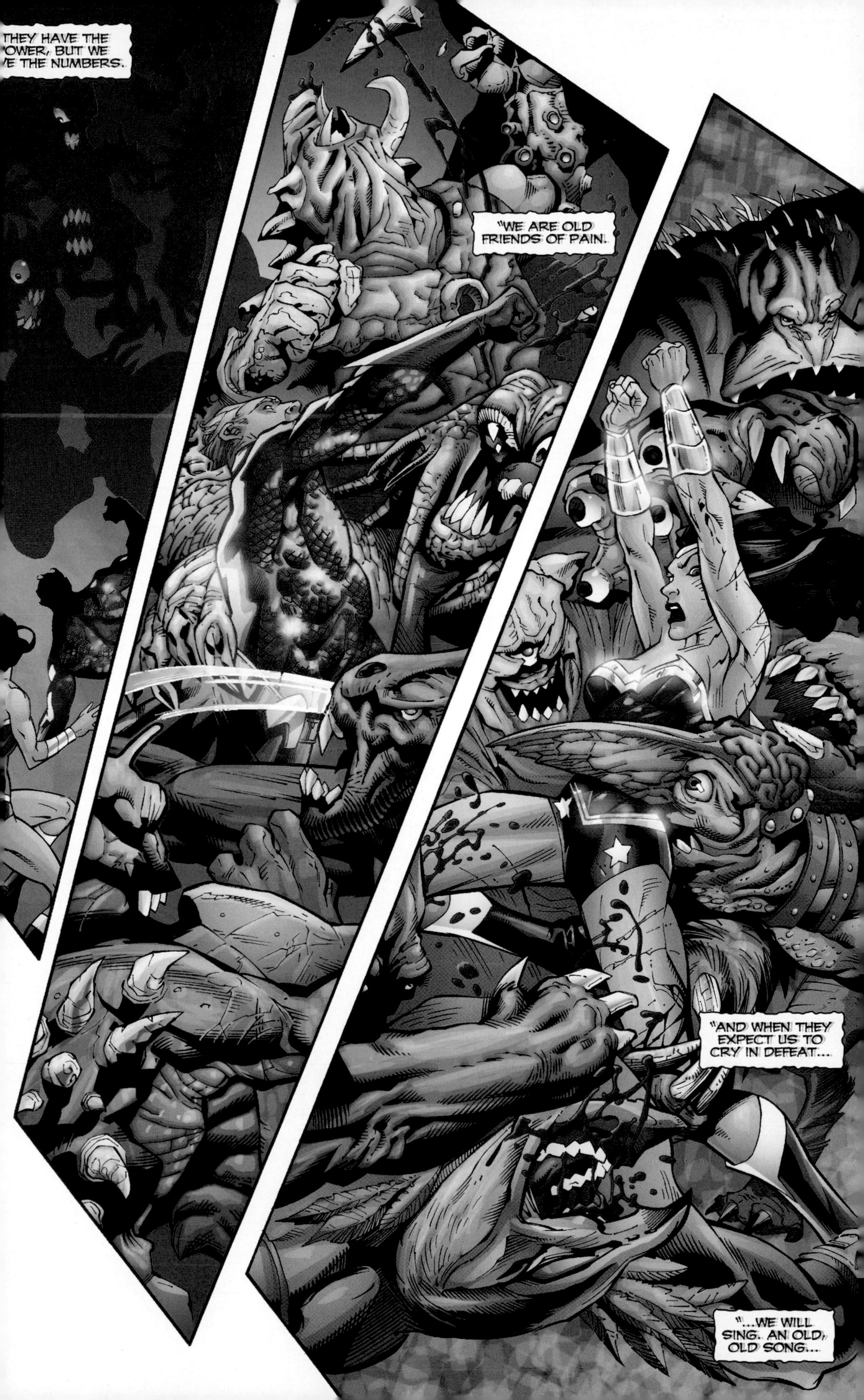
THEY HAVE THE
OWER, BUT WE
E THE NUMBERS.
"WE ARE OLD FRIENDS OF PAIN.
"AND WHEN THEY EXPECT US TO CRY IN DEFEAT...
"...WE WILL SING. AN OLD, OLD SONG...

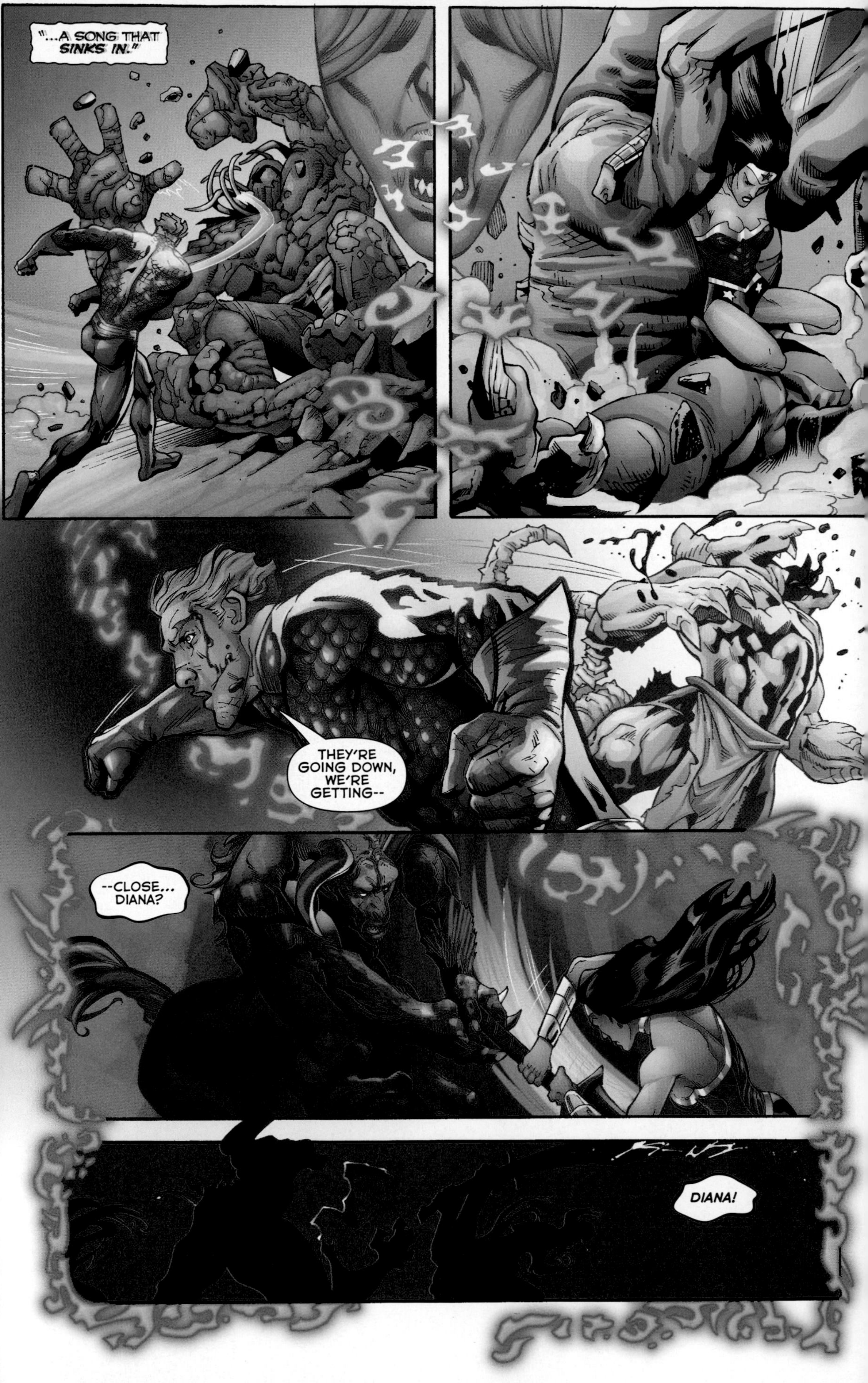
"...A SONG THAT SINKS IN."
THEY'RE GOING DOWN, WE'RE GETTING--
--CLOSE... DIANA?
DIANA!

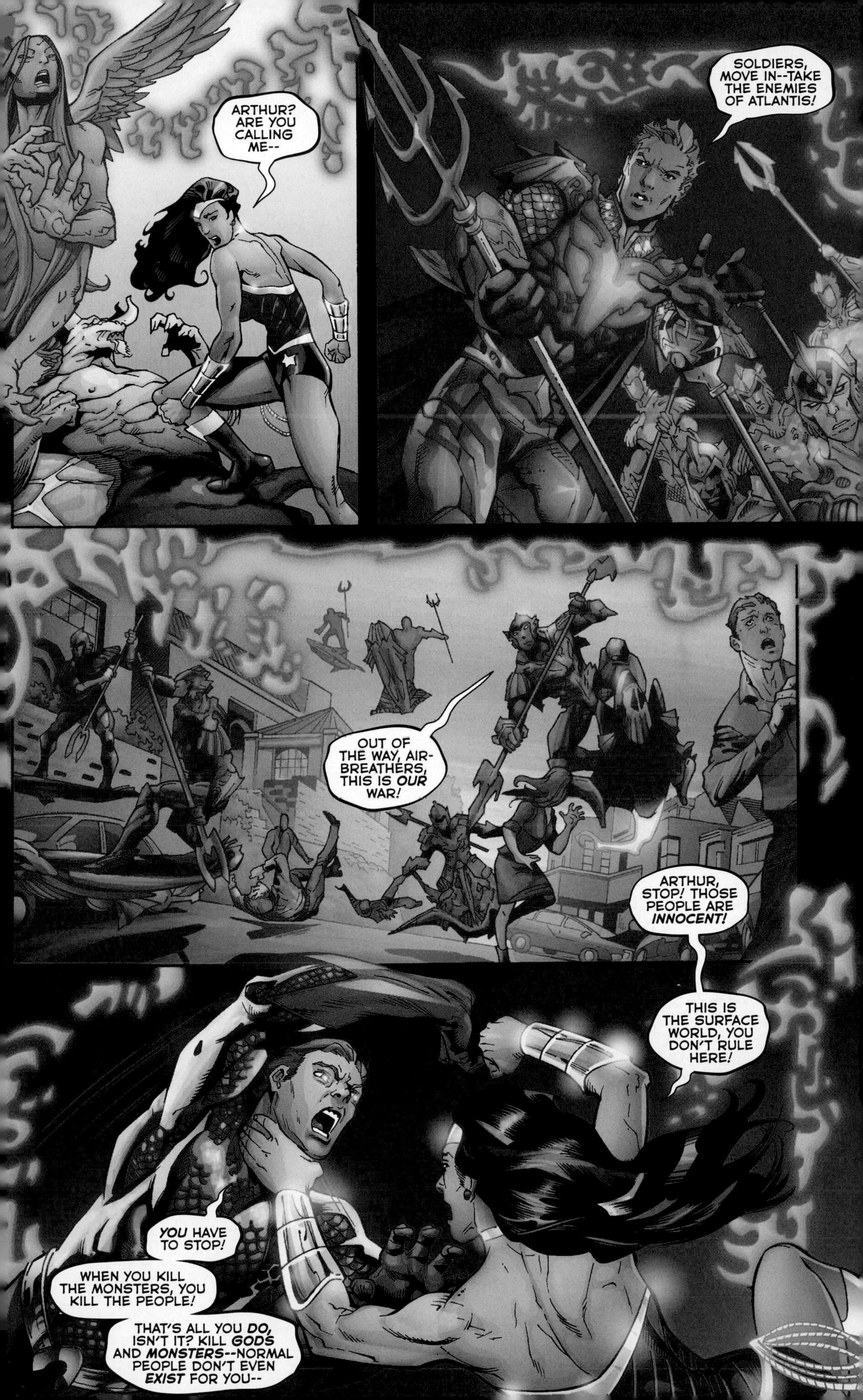
ARTHUR? ARE YOU CALLING ME--
SOLDIERS, MOVE IN--TAKE THE ENEMIES OF ATLANTIS!
OUT OF THE WAY, AIR-BREATHERS, THIS IS OUR WAR!
ARTHUR, STOP! THOSE PEOPLE ARE INNOCENT!
THIS IS THE SURFACE WORLD, YOU DON'T RULE HERE!
YOU HAVE TO STOP!
WHEN YOU KILL THE MONSTERS, YOU KILL THE PEOPLE!
THAT'S ALL YOU DO, ISN'T IT? KILL GODS AND MONSTERS--NORMAL PEOPLE DON'T EVEN EXIST FOR YOU--

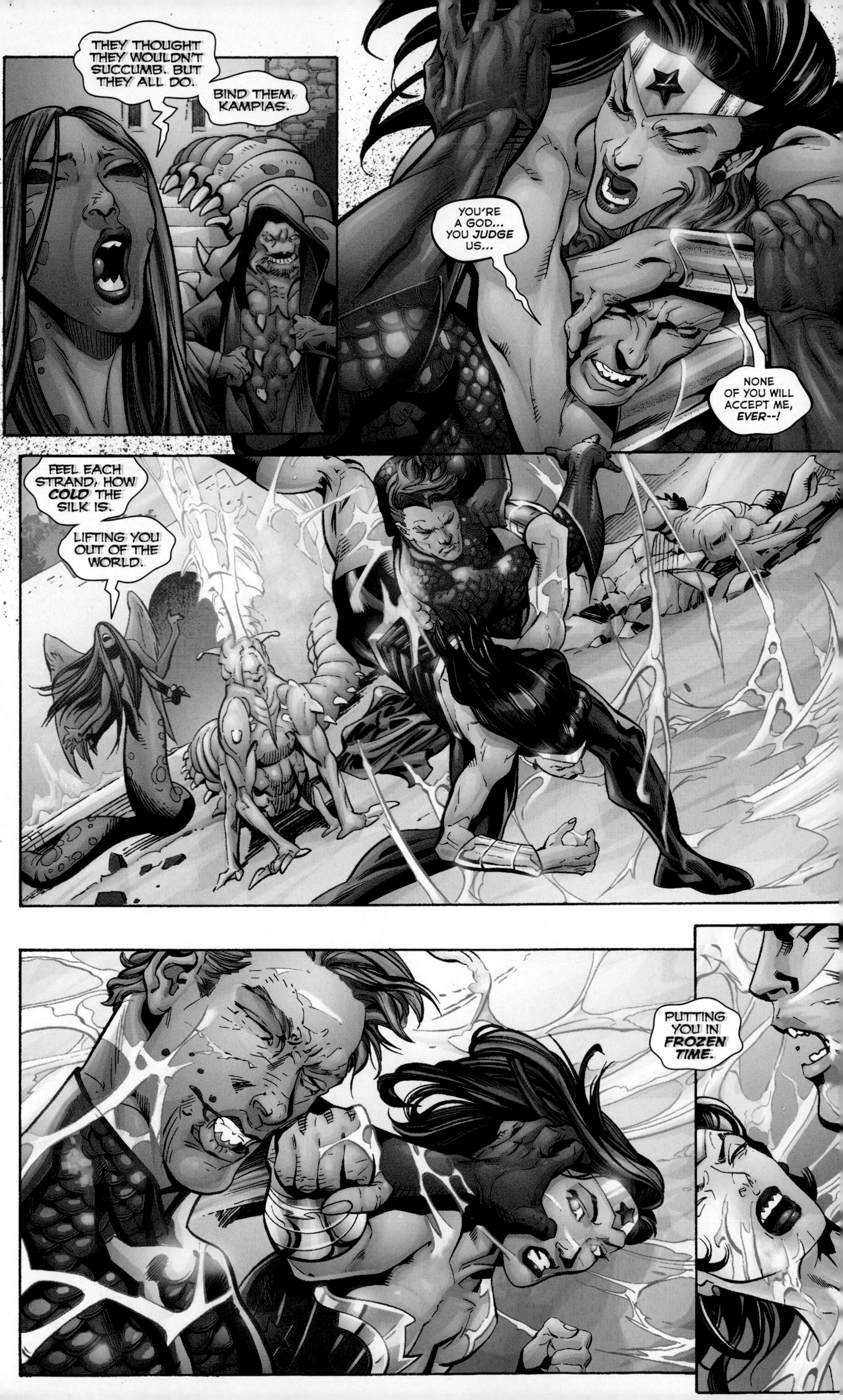
THEY THOUGHT THEY WOULDN'T SUCCUMB. BUT THEY ALL DO.
BIND THEM, KAMPIAS.
YOU'RE A GOD... YOU JUDGE US...
NONE OF YOU WILL ACCEPT ME, EVER--!
FEEL EACH STRAND, HOW COLD THE SILK IS.
LIFTING YOU OUT OF THE WORLD.
PUTTING YOU IN FROZEN TIME.

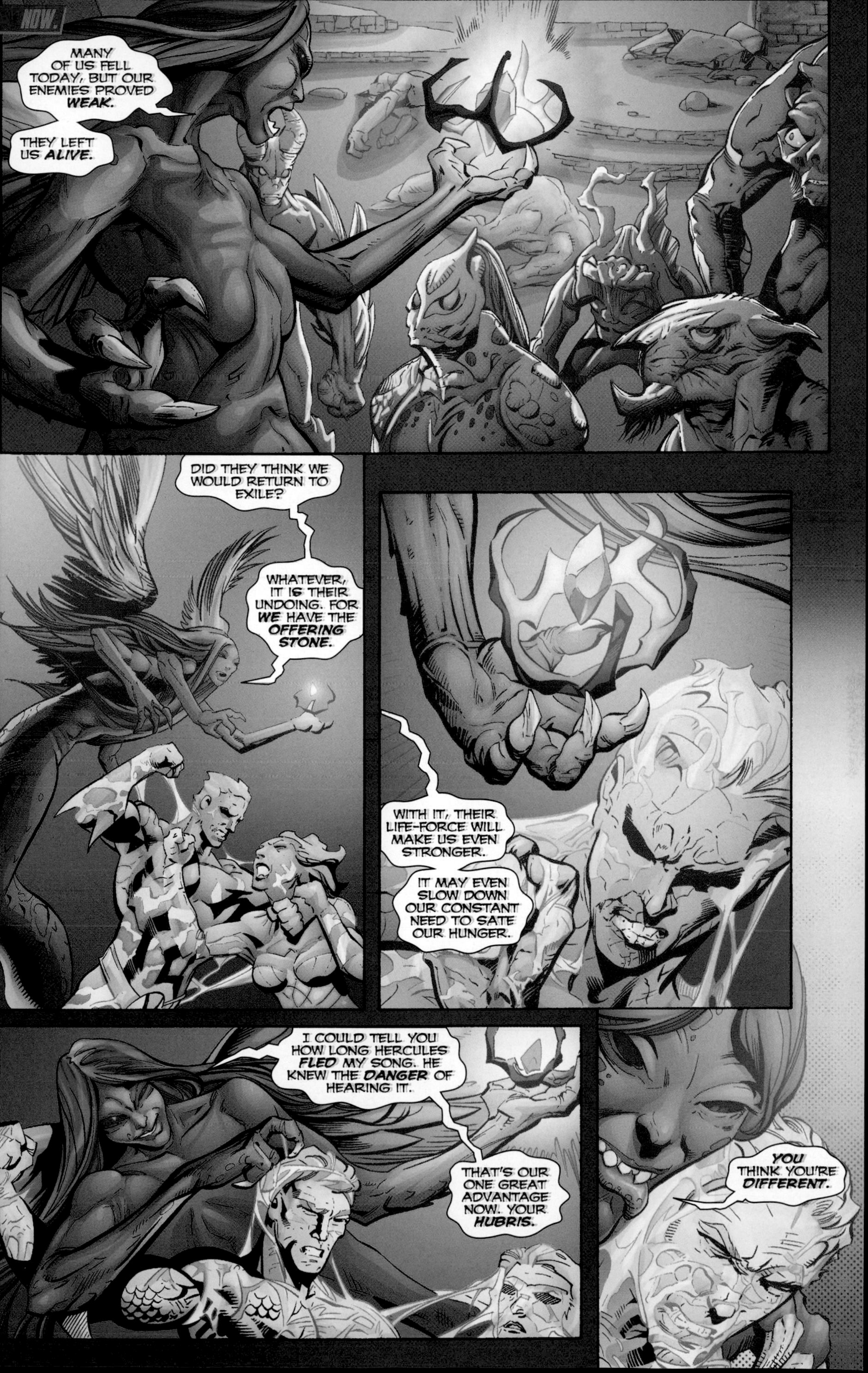
NOW.
MANY OF US FELL TODAY, BUT OUR ENEMIES PROVED WEAK.
THEY LEFT US ALIVE.
DID THEY THINK WE WOULD RETURN TO EXILE?
WHATEVER, IT IS THEIR UNDOING. FOR WE HAVE THE OFFERING STONE.
WITH IT, THEIR LIFE-FORCE WILL MAKE US EVEN STRONGER.
IT MAY EVEN SLOW DOWN OUR CONSTANT NEED TO SATE OUR HUNGER.
I COULD TELL YOU HOW LONG HERCULES FLED MY SONG. HE KNEW THE DANGER OF HEARING IT.
THAT'S OUR ONE GREAT ADVANTAGE NOW. YOUR HUBRIS.
YOU THINK YOU'RE DIFFERENT.

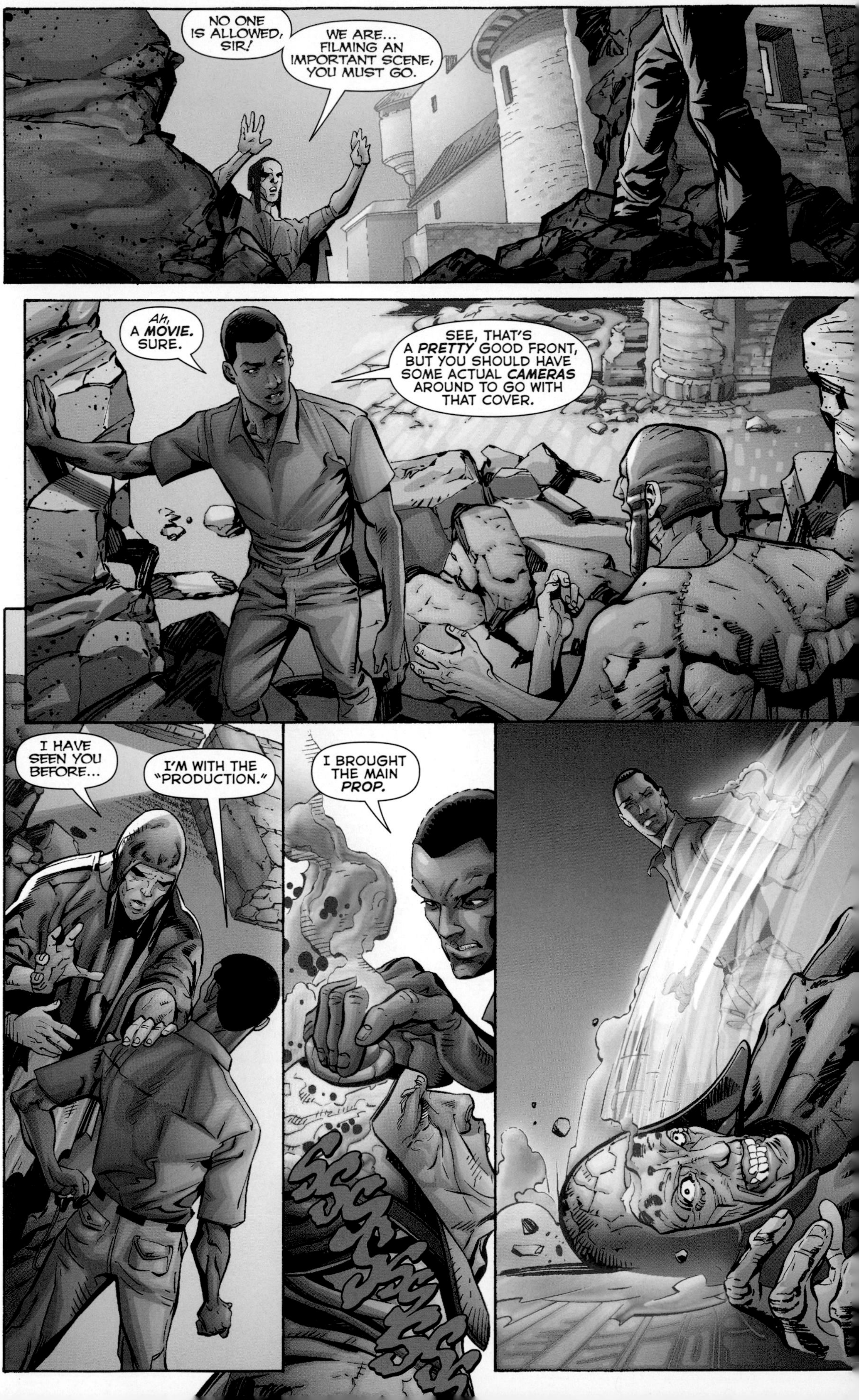
NO ONE IS ALLOWED, SIR!
WE ARE... FILMING AN IMPORTANT SCENE, YOU MUST GO.
Ah, A MOVIE. SURE.
SEE, THAT'S A PRETTY GOOD FRONT, BUT YOU SHOULD HAVE SOME ACTUAL CAMERAS AROUND TO GO WITH THAT COVER.
I HAVE SEEN YOU BEFORE...
I'M WITH THE "PRODUCTION."
I BROUGHT THE MAIN PROP.

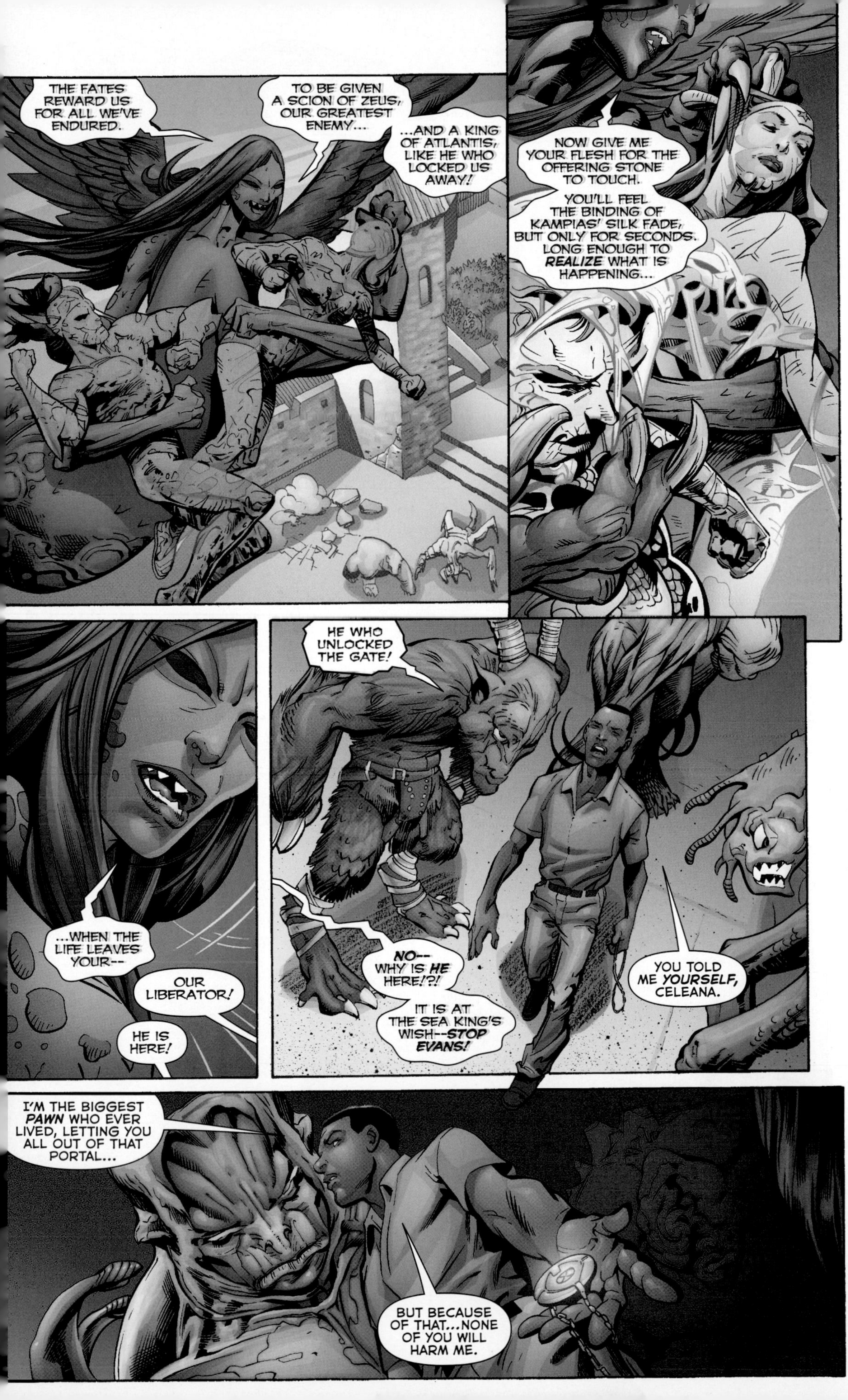
THE FATES REWARD US FOR ALL WE'VE ENDURED.
TO BE GIVEN A SCION OF ZEUS, OUR GREATEST ENEMY...
...AND A KING OF ATLANTIS, LIKE HE WHO LOCKED US AWAY!
NOW GIVE ME YOUR FLESH FOR THE OFFERING STONE TO TOUCH.
YOU'LL FEEL THE BINDING OF KAMPIAS' SILK FADE, BUT ONLY FOR SECONDS. LONG ENOUGH TO *REALIZE* WHAT IS HAPPENING...
...WHEN THE LIFE LEAVES YOUR--
OUR LIBERATOR!
HE IS HERE!
HE WHO UNLOCKED THE GATE!
NO-- WHY IS *HE* HERE!?!
IT IS AT THE SEA KING'S WISH--*STOP EVANS!*
YOU TOLD ME *YOURSELF,* CELEANA.
I'M THE BIGGEST *PAWN* WHO EVER LIVED, LETTING YOU ALL OUT OF THAT PORTAL...
BUT BECAUSE OF THAT...NONE OF YOU WILL HARM ME.

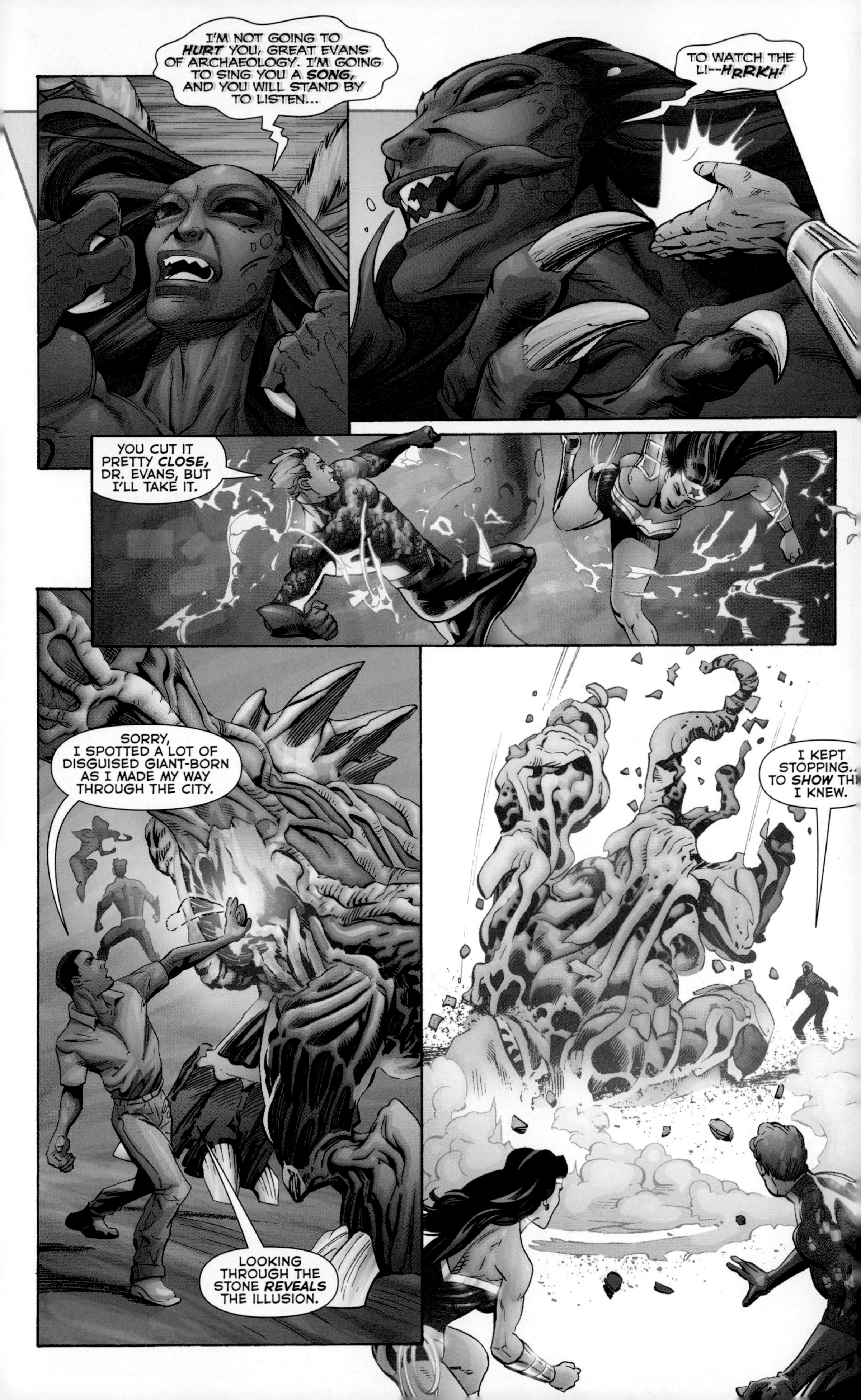
I'M NOT GOING TO HURT YOU, GREAT EVANS OF ARCHAEOLOGY. I'M GOING TO SING YOU A SONG, AND YOU WILL STAND BY TO LISTEN...
TO WATCH THE LI--HRRKH!
YOU CUT IT PRETTY CLOSE, DR. EVANS, BUT I'LL TAKE IT.
SORRY, I SPOTTED A LOT OF DISGUISED GIANT-BORN AS I MADE MY WAY THROUGH THE CITY.
LOOKING THROUGH THE STONE REVEALS THE ILLUSION.
I KEPT STOPPING.. TO SHOW TH I KNEW.

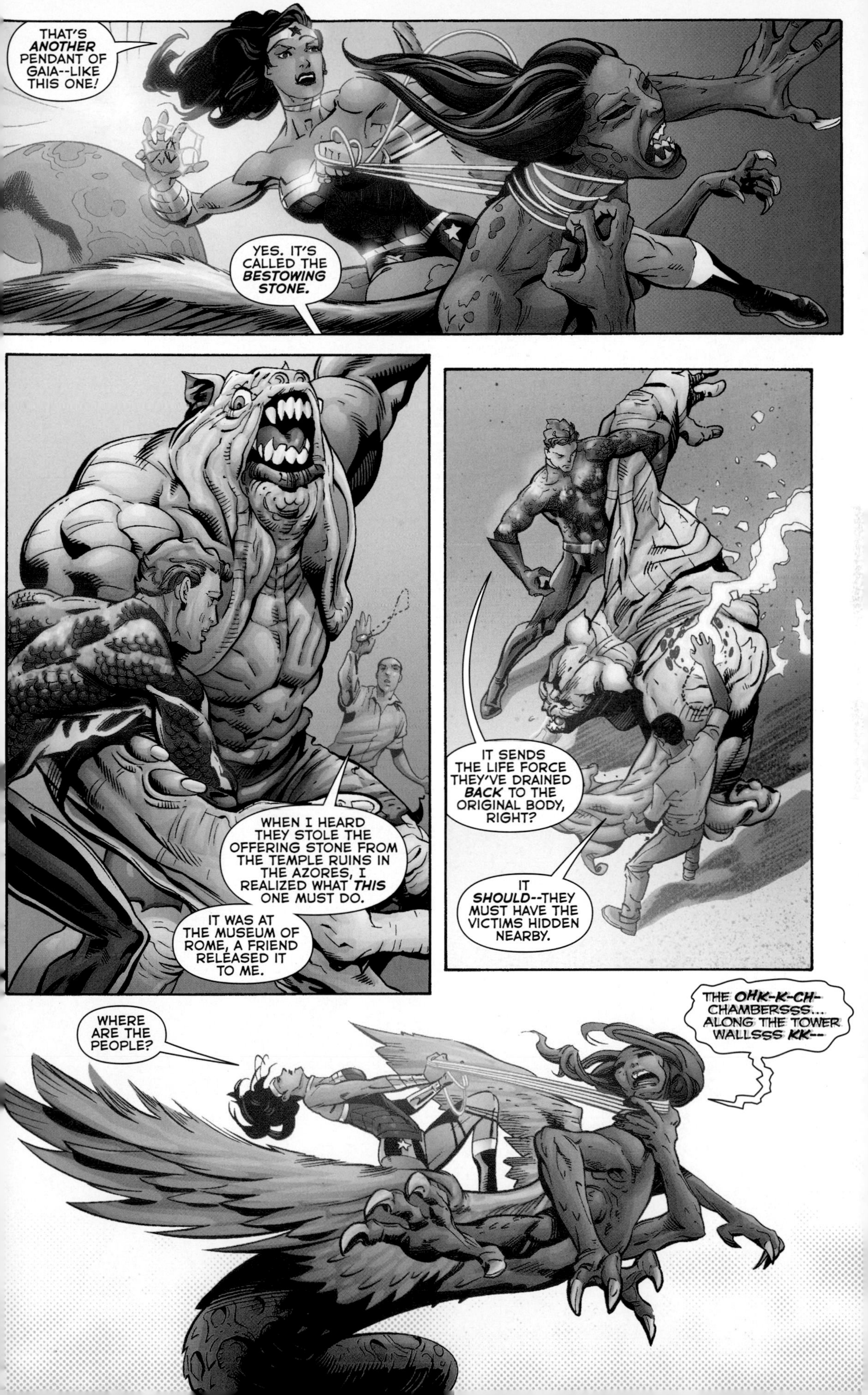
THAT'S ANOTHER PENDANT OF GAIA--LIKE THIS ONE!
YES. IT'S CALLED THE BESTOWING STONE.
WHEN I HEARD THEY STOLE THE OFFERING STONE FROM THE TEMPLE RUINS IN THE AZORES, I REALIZED WHAT THIS ONE MUST DO.
IT WAS AT THE MUSEUM OF ROME, A FRIEND RELEASED IT TO ME.
IT SENDS THE LIFE FORCE THEY'VE DRAINED BACK TO THE ORIGINAL BODY, RIGHT?
IT SHOULD--THEY MUST HAVE THE VICTIMS HIDDEN NEARBY.
WHERE ARE THE PEOPLE?
THE OHK-K-CH-CHAMBERSSS... ALONG THE TOWER WALLSSS KK--

IT WAS LIKE BEING IN HELL, I CAN'T BELIEVE IT.

I CAN'T EVEN--IT'S OVER, *IT'S OVER.*

THIS ISN'T RIGHT, SHE'S NOT AS *YOUNG* AS SHE WAS--AND MY... MY SKIN IS LOOSER...!

IT'S NOT AN EXACT PROCESS...IT'S MIRACULOUS THAT IT CAN BE REVERSED AT ALL.

VANITY. PRIDE. ARROGANCE.

MORTALS ARE THE SAME AS THEY EVER WERE.

I'VE GOTTEN TO ALL THE REST ON SITE...NOW THE LAST ONE.

NO! I BARELY TOOK ANYTHING FROM THEM!

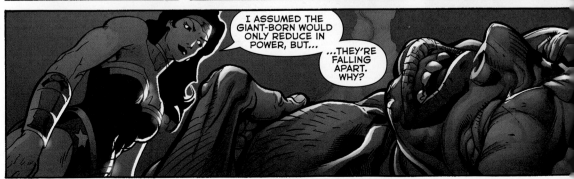

I ASSUMED THE GIANT-BORN WOULD ONLY REDUCE IN POWER, BUT...

...THEY'RE FALLING APART. WHY?

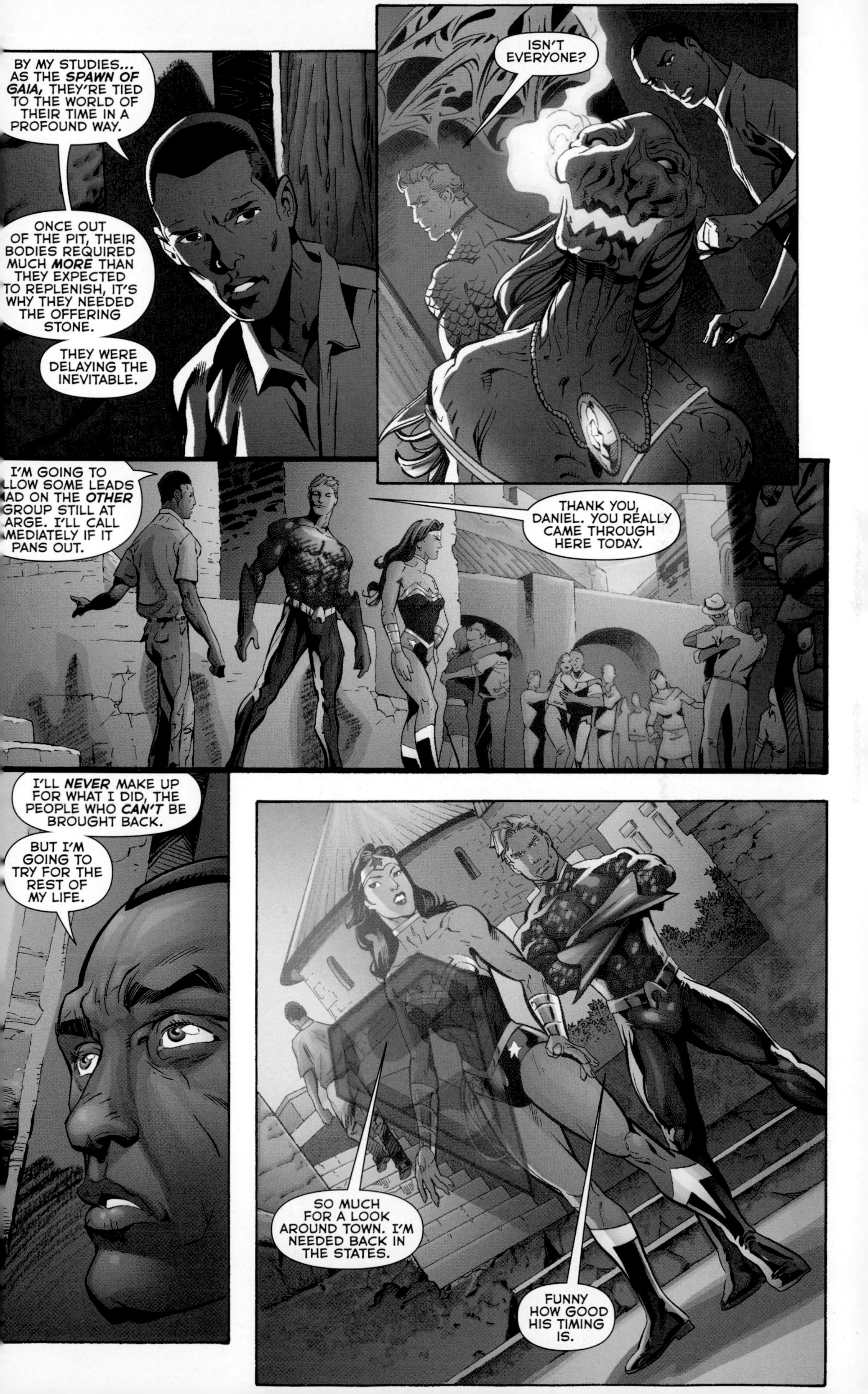
BY MY STUDIES... AS THE SPAWN OF GAIA, THEY'RE TIED TO THE WORLD OF THEIR TIME IN A PROFOUND WAY.
ONCE OUT OF THE PIT, THEIR BODIES REQUIRED MUCH MORE THAN THEY EXPECTED TO REPLENISH, IT'S WHY THEY NEEDED THE OFFERING STONE.
THEY WERE DELAYING THE INEVITABLE.
ISN'T EVERYONE?
I'M GOING TO LLOW SOME LEADS AD ON THE OTHER GROUP STILL AT ARGE. I'LL CALL MEDIATELY IF IT PANS OUT.
THANK YOU, DANIEL. YOU REALLY CAME THROUGH HERE TODAY.
I'LL NEVER MAKE UP FOR WHAT I DID, THE PEOPLE WHO CAN'T BE BROUGHT BACK.
BUT I'M GOING TO TRY FOR THE REST OF MY LIFE.
SO MUCH FOR A LOOK AROUND TOWN. I'M NEEDED BACK IN THE STATES.
FUNNY HOW GOOD HIS TIMING IS.

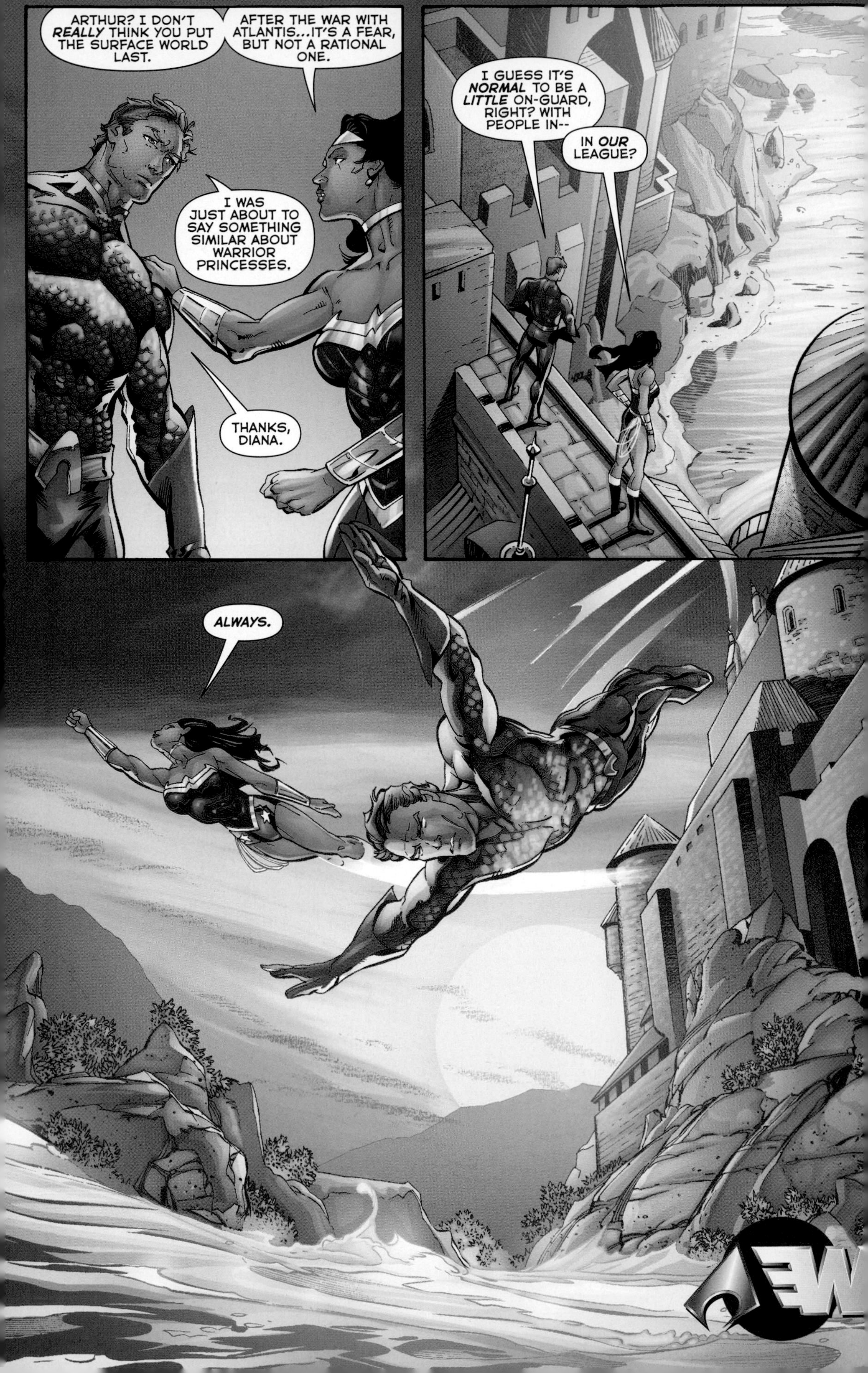
ARTHUR? I DON'T *REALLY* THINK YOU PUT THE SURFACE WORLD LAST.
AFTER THE WAR WITH ATLANTIS...IT'S A FEAR, BUT NOT A RATIONAL ONE.
I WAS JUST ABOUT TO SAY SOMETHING SIMILAR ABOUT WARRIOR PRINCESSES.
THANKS, DIANA.
I GUESS IT'S *NORMAL* TO BE A *LITTLE* ON-GUARD, RIGHT? WITH PEOPLE IN--
IN *OUR* LEAGUE?
ALWAYS.

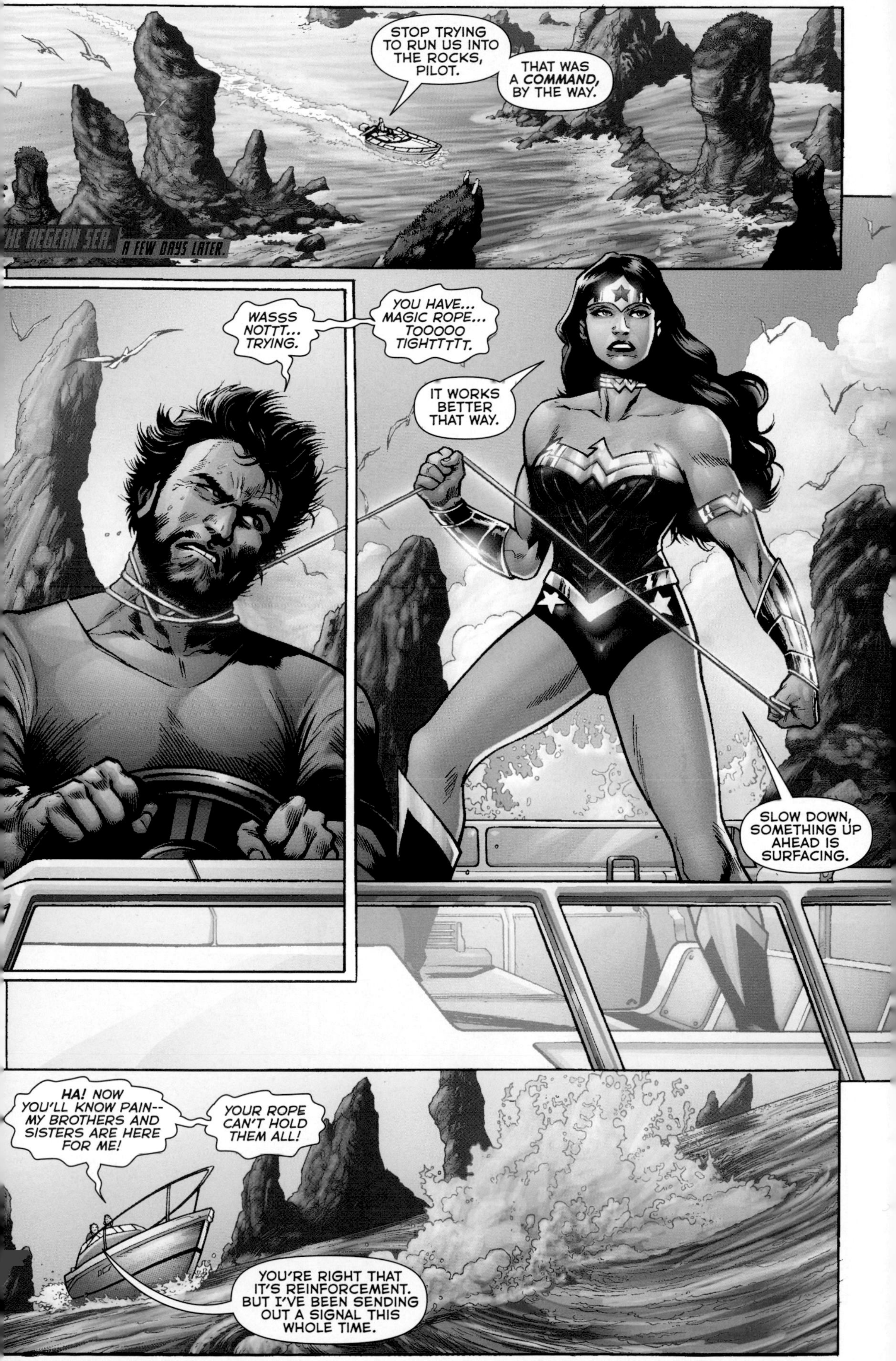
STOP TRYING TO RUN US INTO THE ROCKS, PILOT.
THAT WAS A COMMAND, BY THE WAY.
HE AEGEAN SEA.
A FEW DAYS LATER.
WASSS NOTTT... TRYING.
YOU HAVE... MAGIC ROPE... TOOOOO TIGHTTTTTT.
IT WORKS BETTER THAT WAY.
SLOW DOWN, SOMETHING UP AHEAD IS SURFACING.
HA! NOW YOU'LL KNOW PAIN-- MY BROTHERS AND SISTERS ARE HERE FOR ME!
YOUR ROPE CAN'T HOLD THEM ALL!
YOU'RE RIGHT THAT IT'S REINFORCEMENT. BUT I'VE BEEN SENDING OUT A SIGNAL THIS WHOLE TIME.

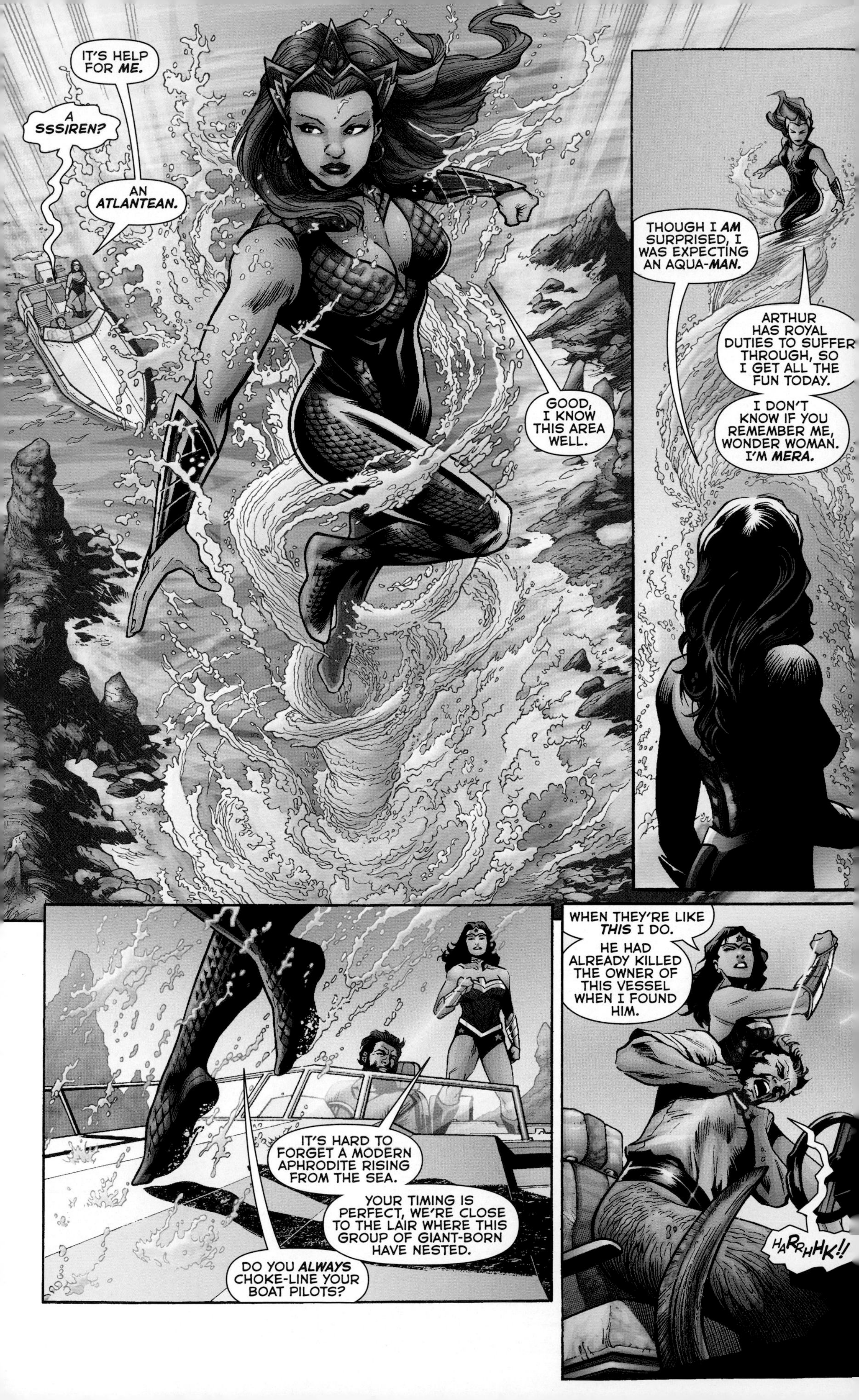

A SSSIREN?
IT'S HELP FOR ME.
AN ATLANTEAN.
GOOD, I KNOW THIS AREA WELL.
THOUGH I AM SURPRISED, I WAS EXPECTING AN AQUA-MAN.
ARTHUR HAS ROYAL DUTIES TO SUFFER THROUGH, SO I GET ALL THE FUN TODAY.
I DON'T KNOW IF YOU REMEMBER ME, WONDER WOMAN. I'M MERA.
IT'S HARD TO FORGET A MODERN APHRODITE RISING FROM THE SEA.
YOUR TIMING IS PERFECT, WE'RE CLOSE TO THE LAIR WHERE THIS GROUP OF GIANT-BORN HAVE NESTED.
DO YOU ALWAYS CHOKE-LINE YOUR BOAT PILOTS?
WHEN THEY'RE LIKE THIS I DO.
HE HAD ALREADY KILLED THE OWNER OF THIS VESSEL WHEN I FOUND HIM.
HARRHHK!!

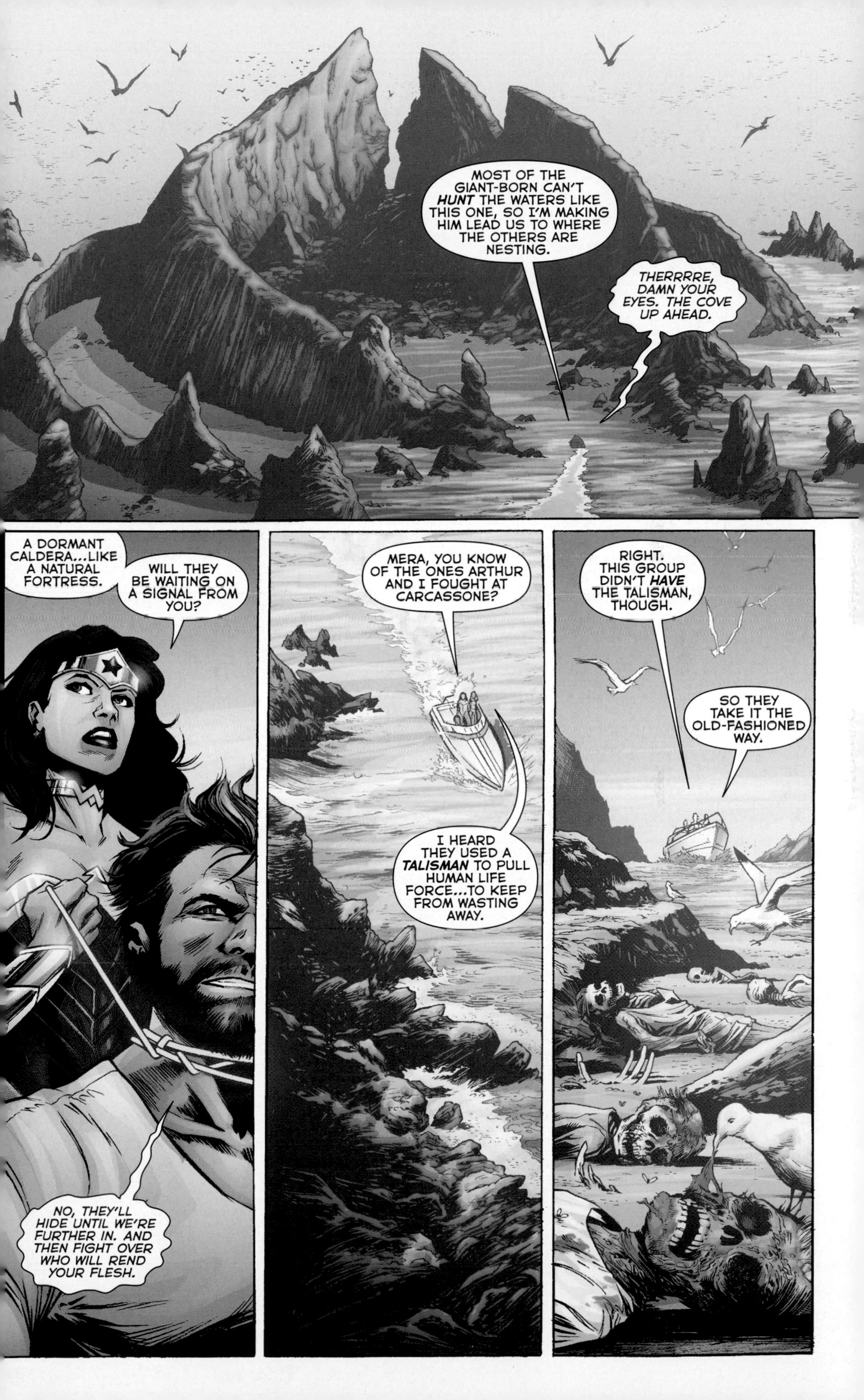
MOST OF THE GIANT-BORN CAN'T HUNT THE WATERS LIKE THIS ONE, SO I'M MAKING HIM LEAD US TO WHERE THE OTHERS ARE NESTING.
THERRRRE, DAMN YOUR EYES. THE COVE UP AHEAD.
A DORMANT CALDERA...LIKE A NATURAL FORTRESS.
WILL THEY BE WAITING ON A SIGNAL FROM YOU?
NO, THEY'LL HIDE UNTIL WE'RE FURTHER IN. AND THEN FIGHT OVER WHO WILL REND YOUR FLESH.
MERA, YOU KNOW OF THE ONES ARTHUR AND I FOUGHT AT CARCASSONE?
I HEARD THEY USED A TALISMAN TO PULL HUMAN LIFE FORCE...TO KEEP FROM WASTING AWAY.
RIGHT. THIS GROUP DIDN'T HAVE THE TALISMAN, THOUGH.
SO THEY TAKE IT THE OLD-FASHIONED WAY.

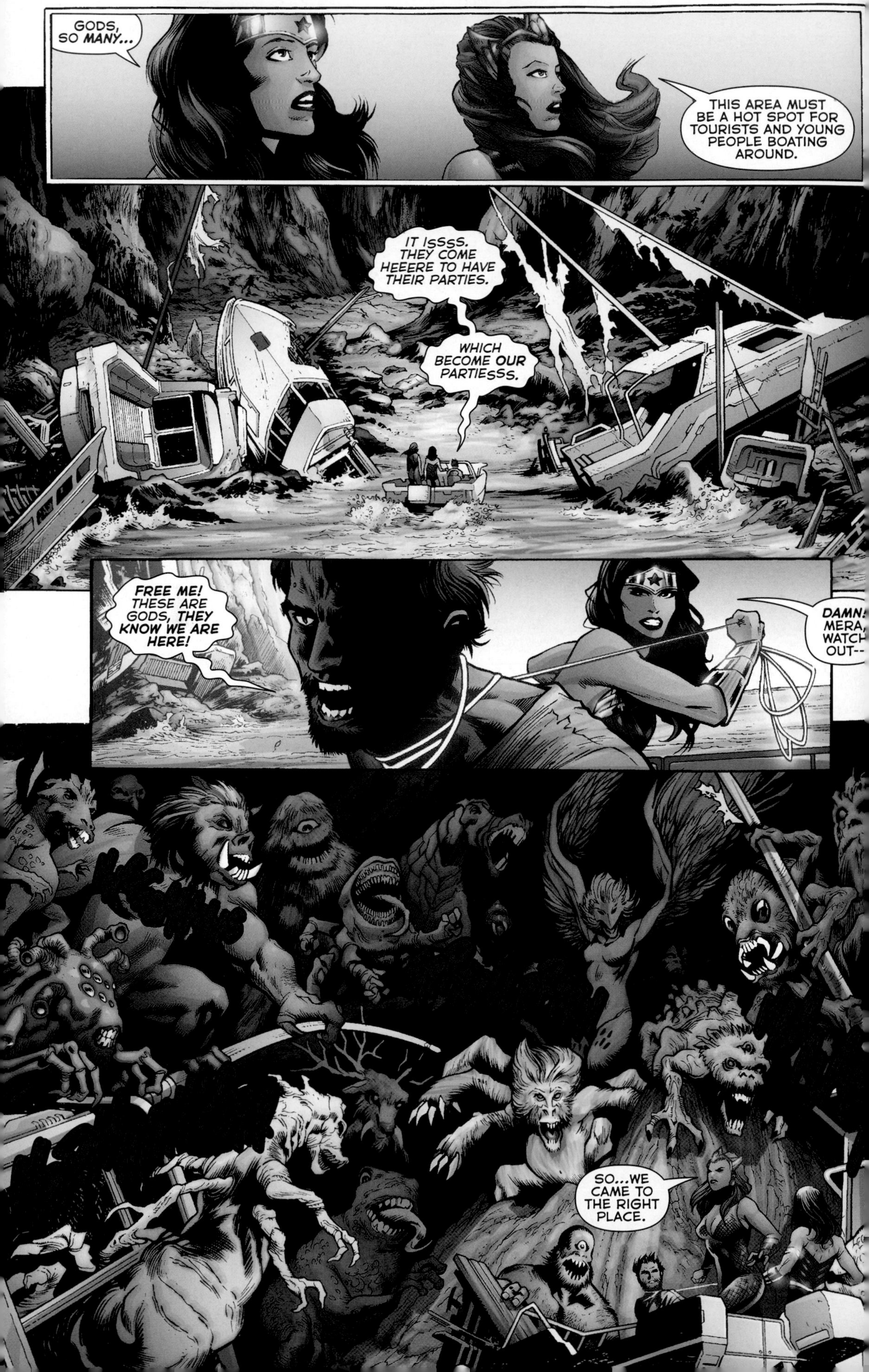
GODS, SO MANY...
THIS AREA MUST BE A HOT SPOT FOR TOURISTS AND YOUNG PEOPLE BOATING AROUND.
IT ISSSS. THEY COME HEEERE TO HAVE THEIR PARTIES.
WHICH BECOME OUR PARTIESSS.
FREE ME! THESE ARE GODS, THEY KNOW WE ARE HERE!
DAMN! MERA, WATCH OUT--
SO...WE CAME TO THE RIGHT PLACE.

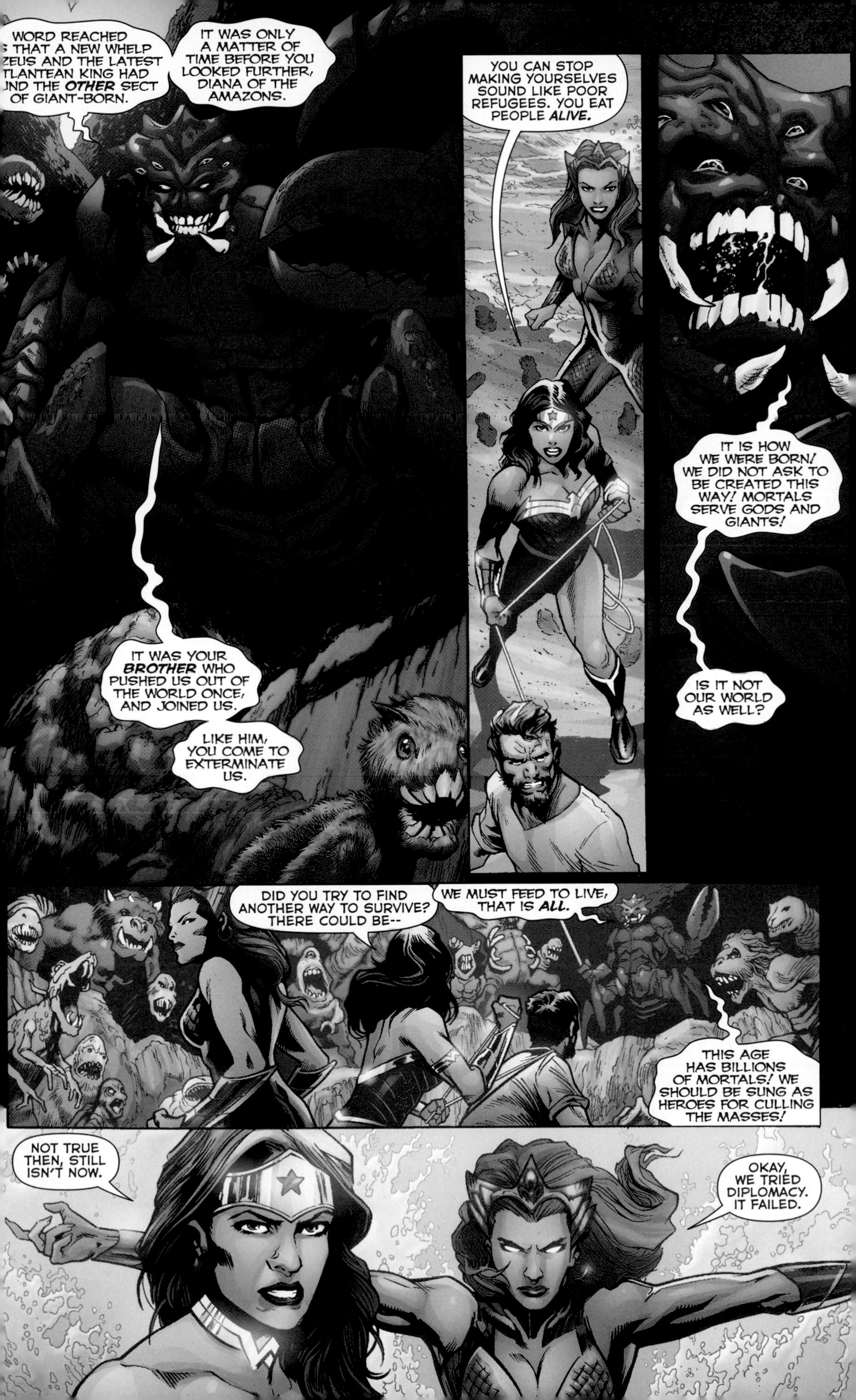
WORD REACHED S THAT A NEW WHELP ZEUS AND THE LATEST TLANTEAN KING HAD UND THE *OTHER* SECT OF GIANT-BORN.
IT WAS ONLY A MATTER OF TIME BEFORE YOU LOOKED FURTHER, DIANA OF THE AMAZONS.
IT WAS YOUR ***BROTHER*** WHO PUSHED US OUT OF THE WORLD ONCE, AND JOINED US.
LIKE HIM, YOU COME TO EXTERMINATE US.
YOU CAN STOP MAKING YOURSELVES SOUND LIKE POOR REFUGEES. YOU EAT PEOPLE ***ALIVE.***
IT IS HOW WE WERE BORN! WE DID NOT ASK TO BE CREATED THIS WAY! MORTALS SERVE GODS AND GIANTS!
IS IT NOT OUR WORLD AS WELL?
DID YOU TRY TO FIND ANOTHER WAY TO SURVIVE? THERE COULD BE--
WE MUST FEED TO LIVE, THAT IS ***ALL.***
THIS AGE HAS BILLIONS OF MORTALS! WE SHOULD BE SUNG AS HEROES FOR CULLING THE MASSES!
NOT TRUE THEN, STILL ISN'T NOW.
OKAY, WE TRIED DIPLOMACY. IT FAILED.

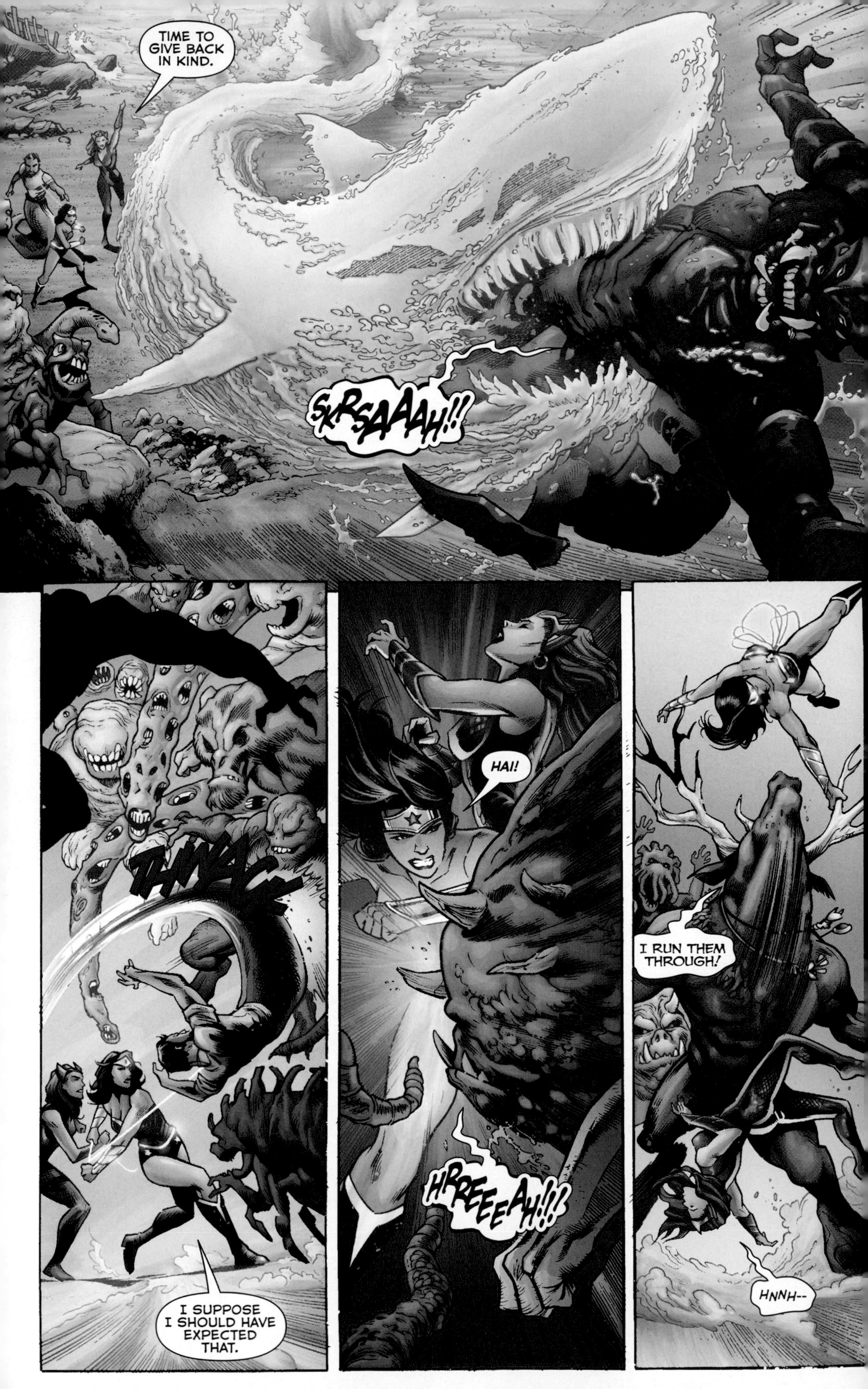
TIME TO GIVE BACK IN KIND.
SKRSAAAAH!!!
THWAC
I SUPPOSE I SHOULD HAVE EXPECTED THAT.
HAI!
HRREEEEAH!!!
I RUN THEM THROUGH!
HNNH--

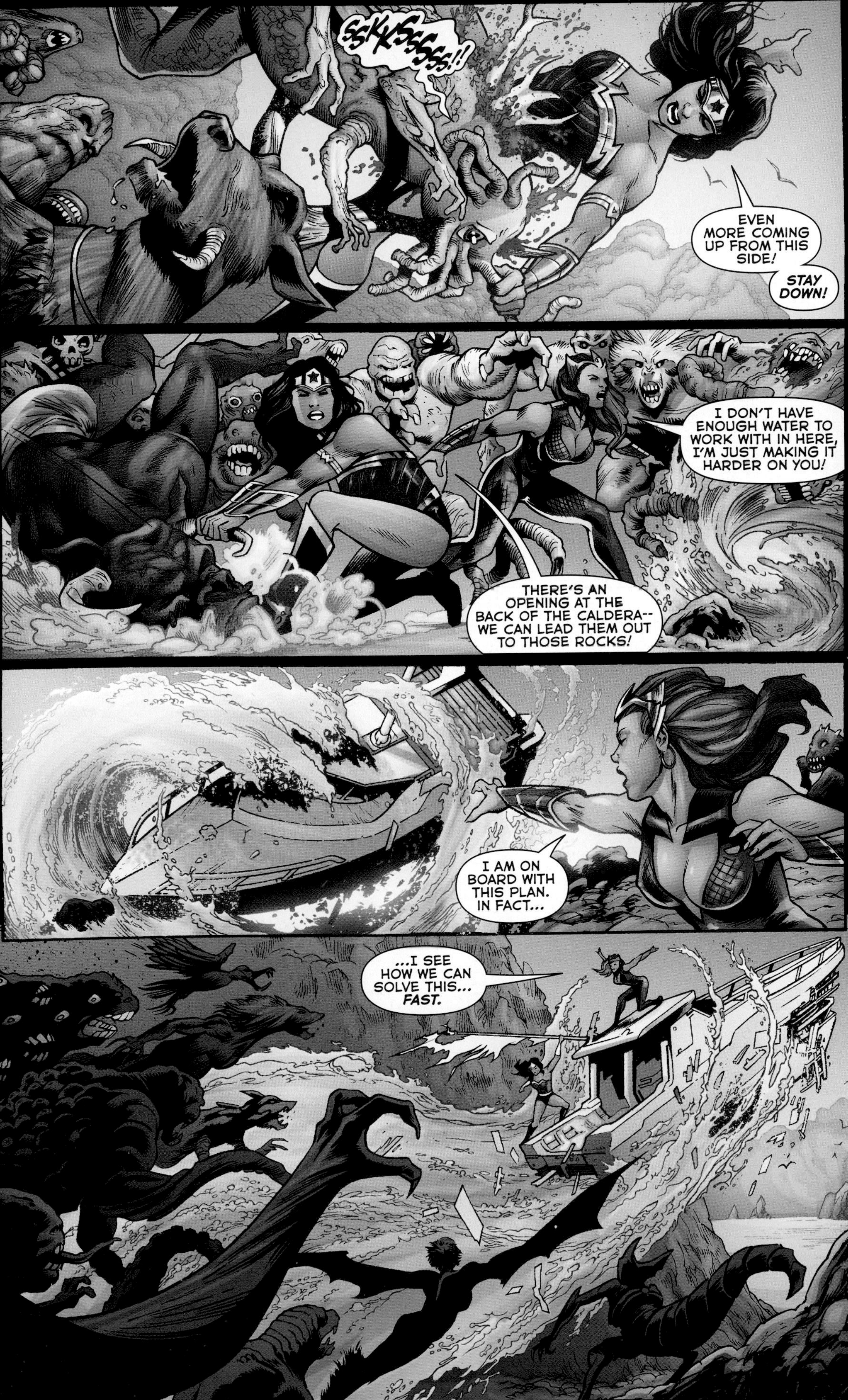
SSKKSSSSSS!!
EVEN MORE COMING UP FROM THIS SIDE!
STAY DOWN!
I DON'T HAVE ENOUGH WATER TO WORK WITH IN HERE, I'M JUST MAKING IT HARDER ON YOU!
THERE'S AN OPENING AT THE BACK OF THE CALDERA-- WE CAN LEAD THEM OUT TO THOSE ROCKS!
I AM ON BOARD WITH THIS PLAN. IN FACT...
...I SEE HOW WE CAN SOLVE THIS... FAST.

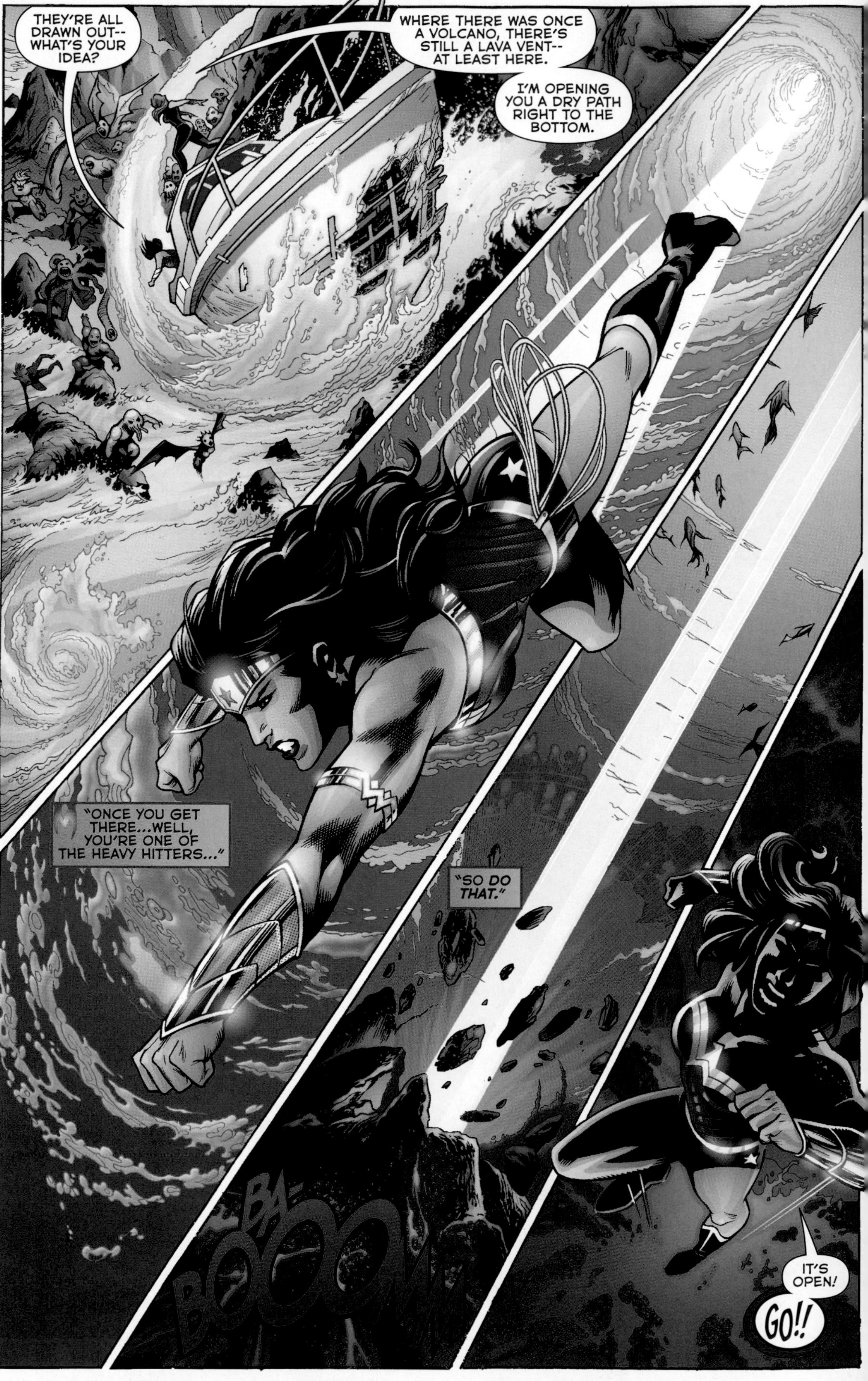
THEY'RE ALL DRAWN OUT-- WHAT'S YOUR IDEA?
WHERE THERE WAS ONCE A VOLCANO, THERE'S STILL A LAVA VENT-- AT LEAST HERE.
I'M OPENING YOU A DRY PATH RIGHT TO THE BOTTOM.
"ONCE YOU GET THERE...WELL, YOU'RE ONE OF THE HEAVY HITTERS..."
"SO DO THAT."
BA-BOOOOM
IT'S OPEN!
GO!!

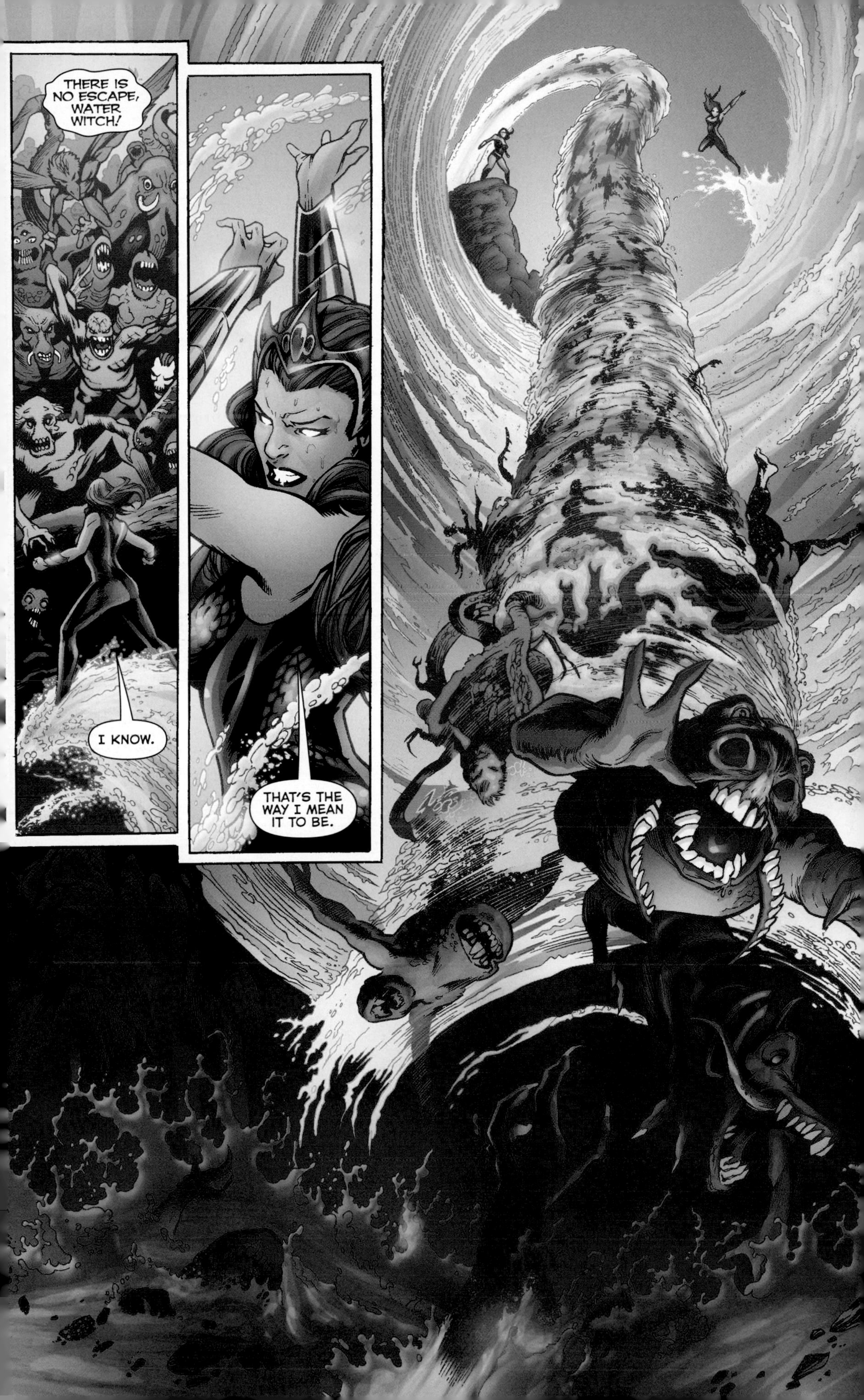
THERE IS NO ESCAPE, WATER WITCH!
I KNOW.
THAT'S THE WAY I MEAN IT TO BE.

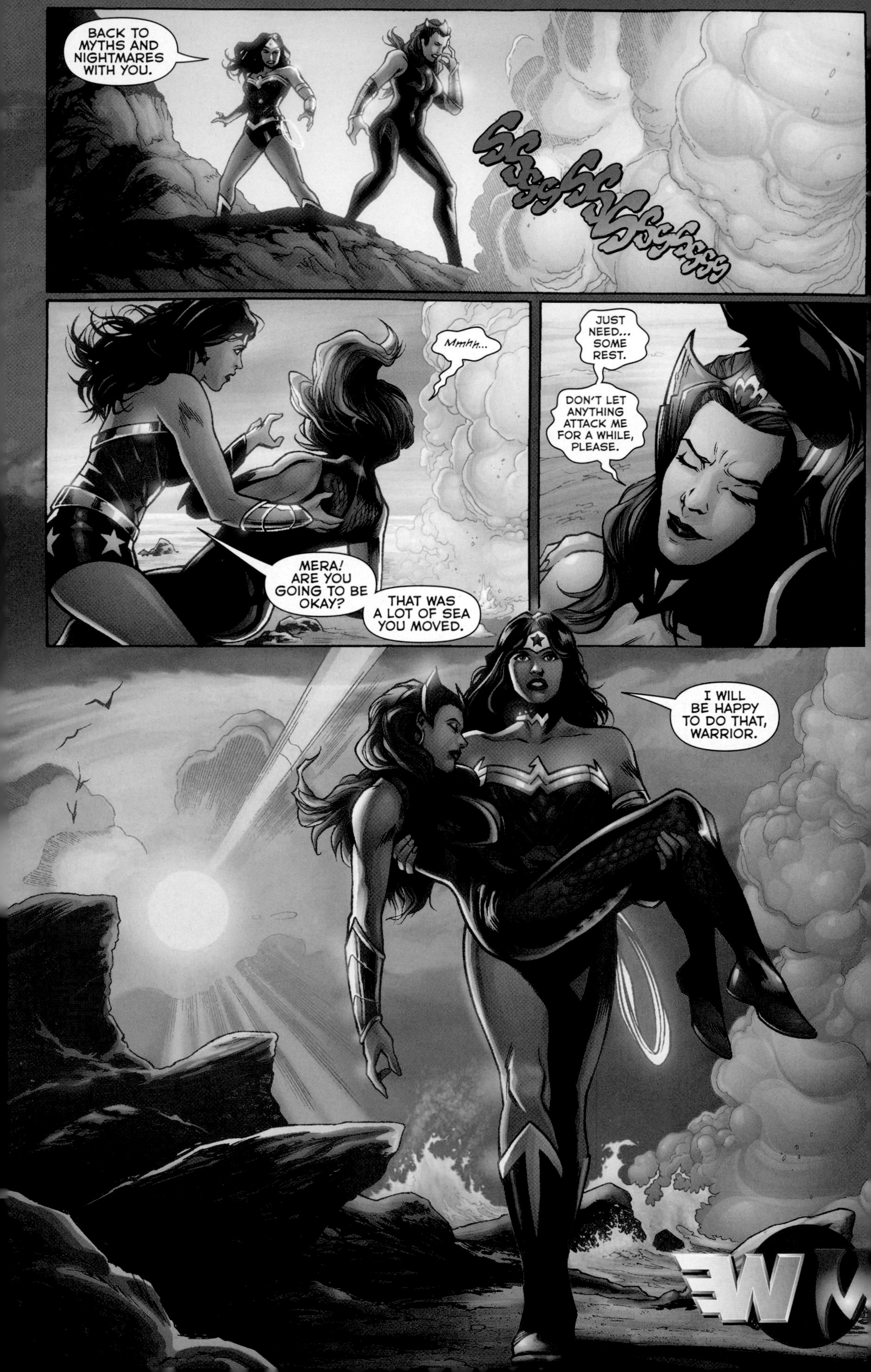
BACK TO MYTHS AND NIGHTMARES WITH YOU.
SSSSSSSSSSSSSSSSSSS
Mmhh...
MERA! ARE YOU GOING TO BE OKAY?
THAT WAS A LOT OF SEA YOU MOVED.
JUST NEED... SOME REST.
DON'T LET ANYTHING ATTACK ME FOR A WHILE, PLEASE.
I WILL BE HAPPY TO DO THAT, WARRIOR.

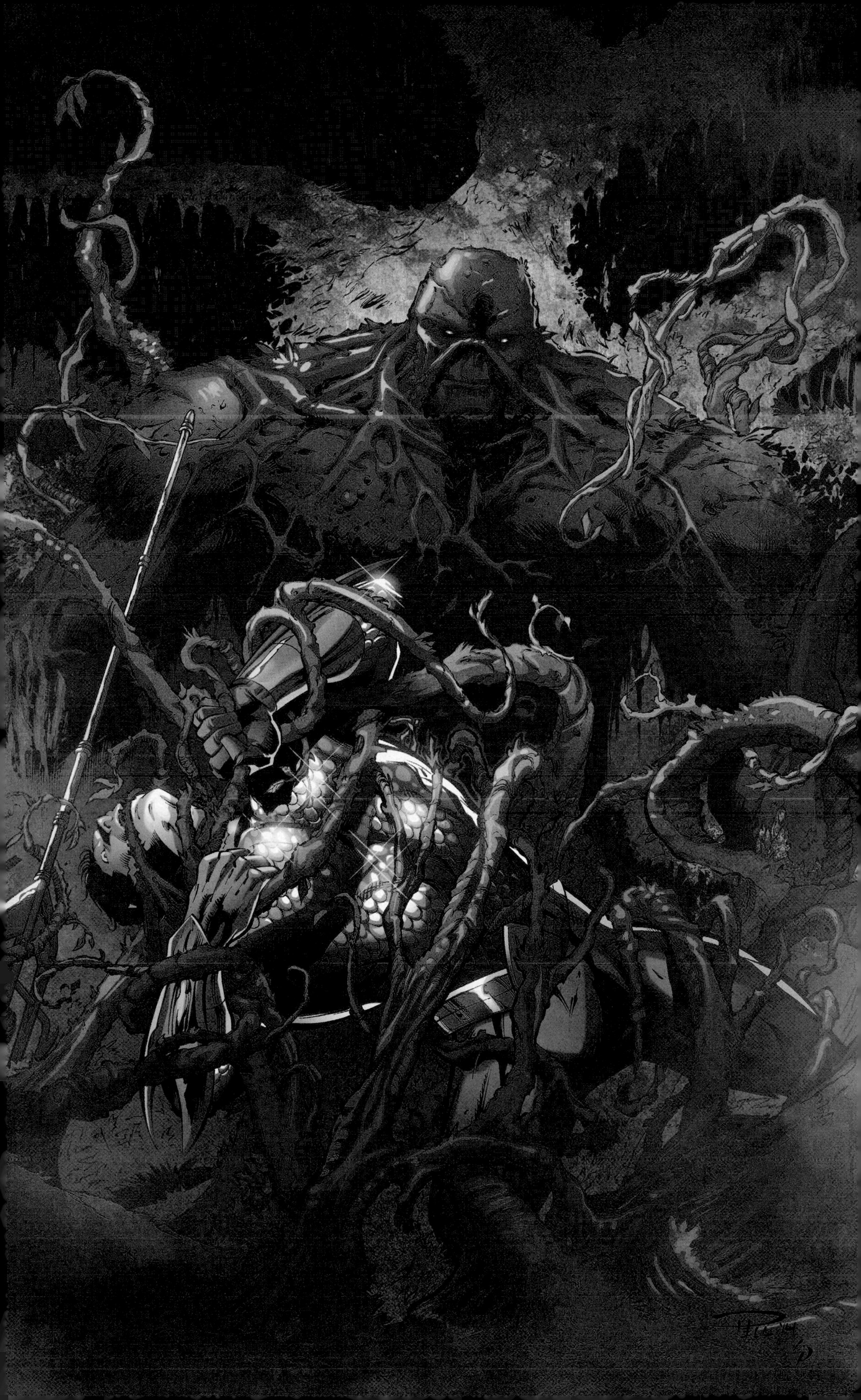

IN THE MUCK

JEFF PARKER writer **PAUL PELLETIER ALVARO MARTINEZ** (pgs 165-170) pencillers **SEAN PARSONS RAUL FERNANDEZ** (pgs 165-170) inker
RAIN BEREDO colorist **TRAVIS LANHAM** letterer cover by **PAUL PELLETIER, SEAN PARSONS** and **WIL QUINTANA**

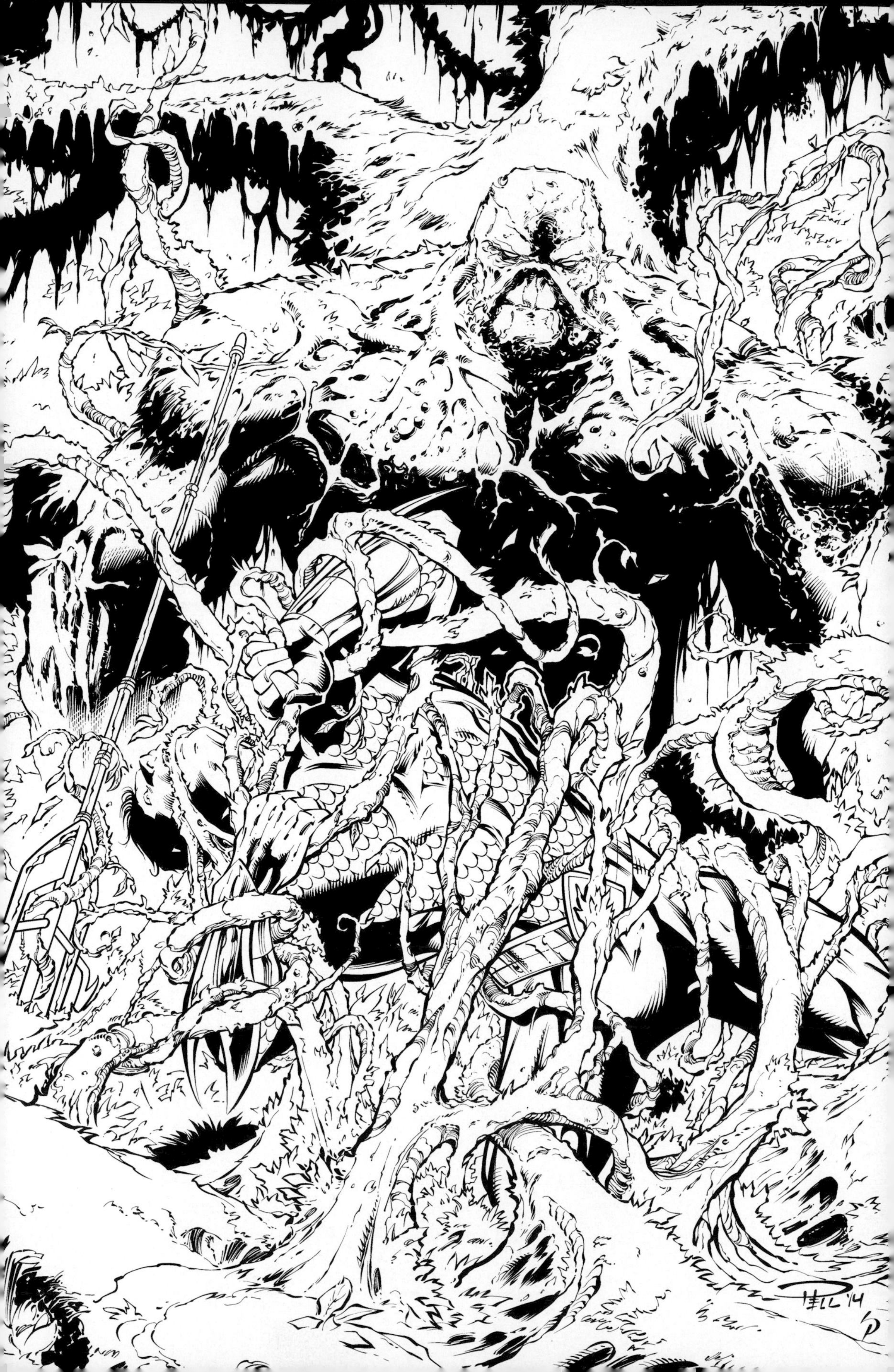
PELL '14

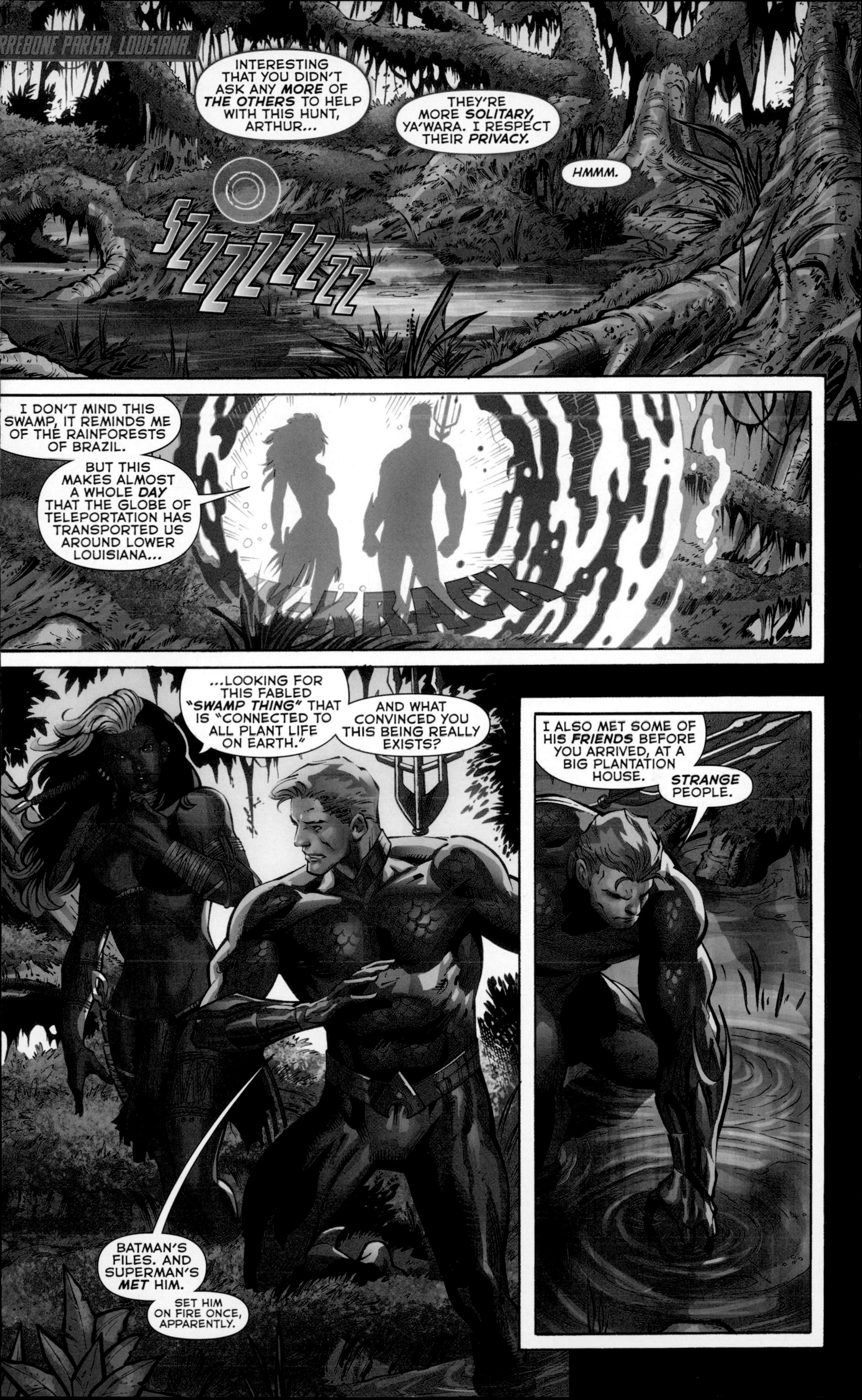
RREBONE PARISH, LOUISIANA.
INTERESTING THAT YOU DIDN'T ASK ANY MORE OF THE OTHERS TO HELP WITH THIS HUNT, ARTHUR...
THEY'RE MORE SOLITARY, YA'WARA. I RESPECT THEIR PRIVACY.
HMMM.
SZZZZZZZZ
I DON'T MIND THIS SWAMP, IT REMINDS ME OF THE RAINFORESTS OF BRAZIL.
BUT THIS MAKES ALMOST A WHOLE DAY THAT THE GLOBE OF TELEPORTATION HAS TRANSPORTED US AROUND LOWER LOUISIANA...
KRACK
...LOOKING FOR THIS FABLED "SWAMP THING" THAT IS "CONNECTED TO ALL PLANT LIFE ON EARTH."
AND WHAT CONVINCED YOU THIS BEING REALLY EXISTS?
BATMAN'S FILES. AND SUPERMAN'S MET HIM.
SET HIM ON FIRE ONCE, APPARENTLY.
I ALSO MET SOME OF HIS FRIENDS BEFORE YOU ARRIVED, AT A BIG PLANTATION HOUSE.
STRANGE PEOPLE.

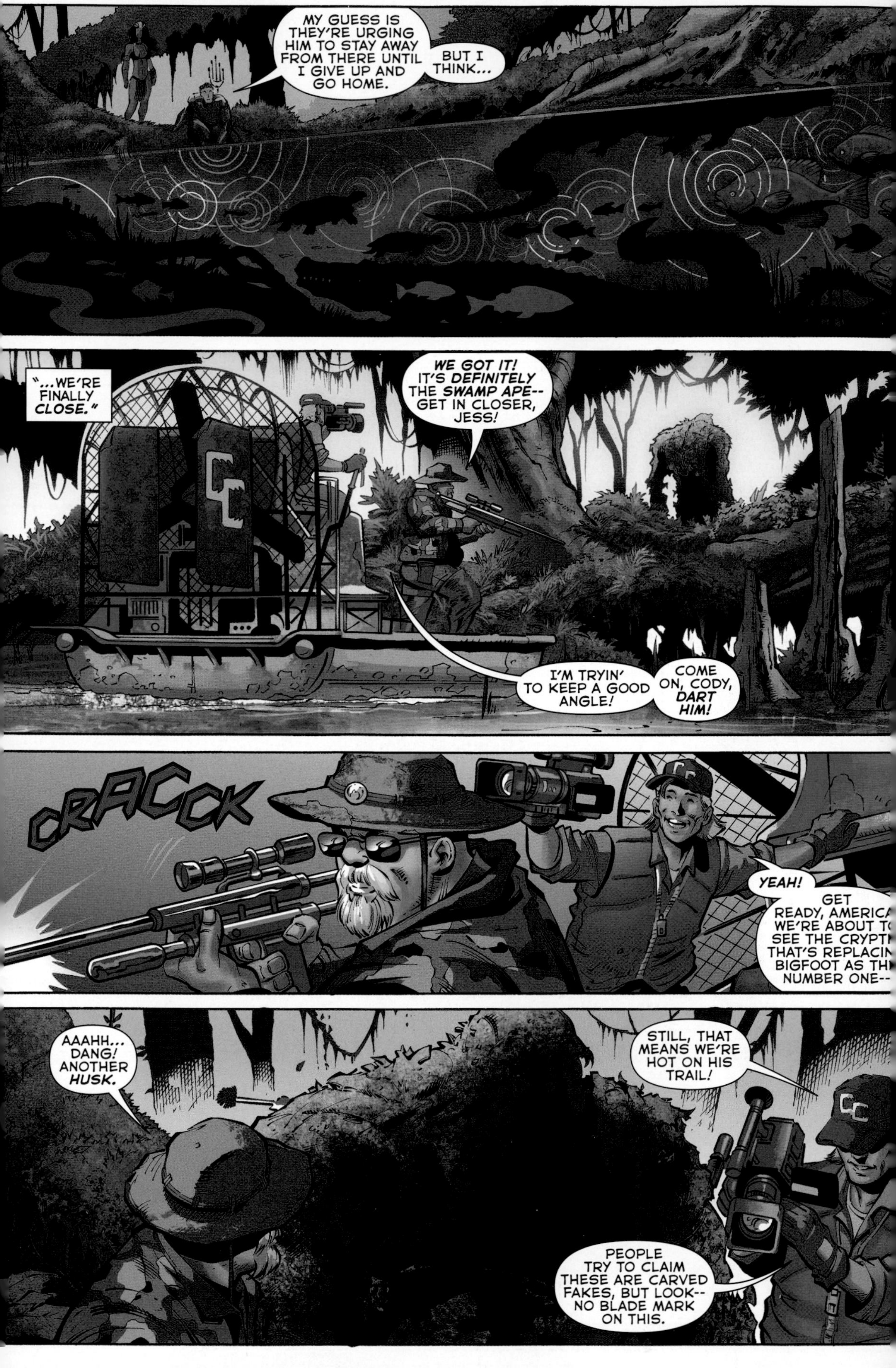
MY GUESS IS THEY'RE URGING HIM TO STAY AWAY FROM THERE UNTIL I GIVE UP AND GO HOME.
BUT I THINK...
"...WE'RE FINALLY CLOSE."
WE GOT IT! IT'S DEFINITELY THE SWAMP APE-- GET IN CLOSER, JESS!
I'M TRYIN' TO KEEP A GOOD ANGLE!
COME ON, CODY, DART HIM!
CRACCK
YEAH!
GET READY, AMERICA WE'RE ABOUT T SEE THE CRYPTI THAT'S REPLACIN BIGFOOT AS TH NUMBER ONE--
AAAHH... DANG! ANOTHER HUSK.
STILL, THAT MEANS WE'RE HOT ON HIS TRAIL!
PEOPLE TRY TO CLAIM THESE ARE CARVED FAKES, BUT LOOK-- NO BLADE MARK ON THIS.

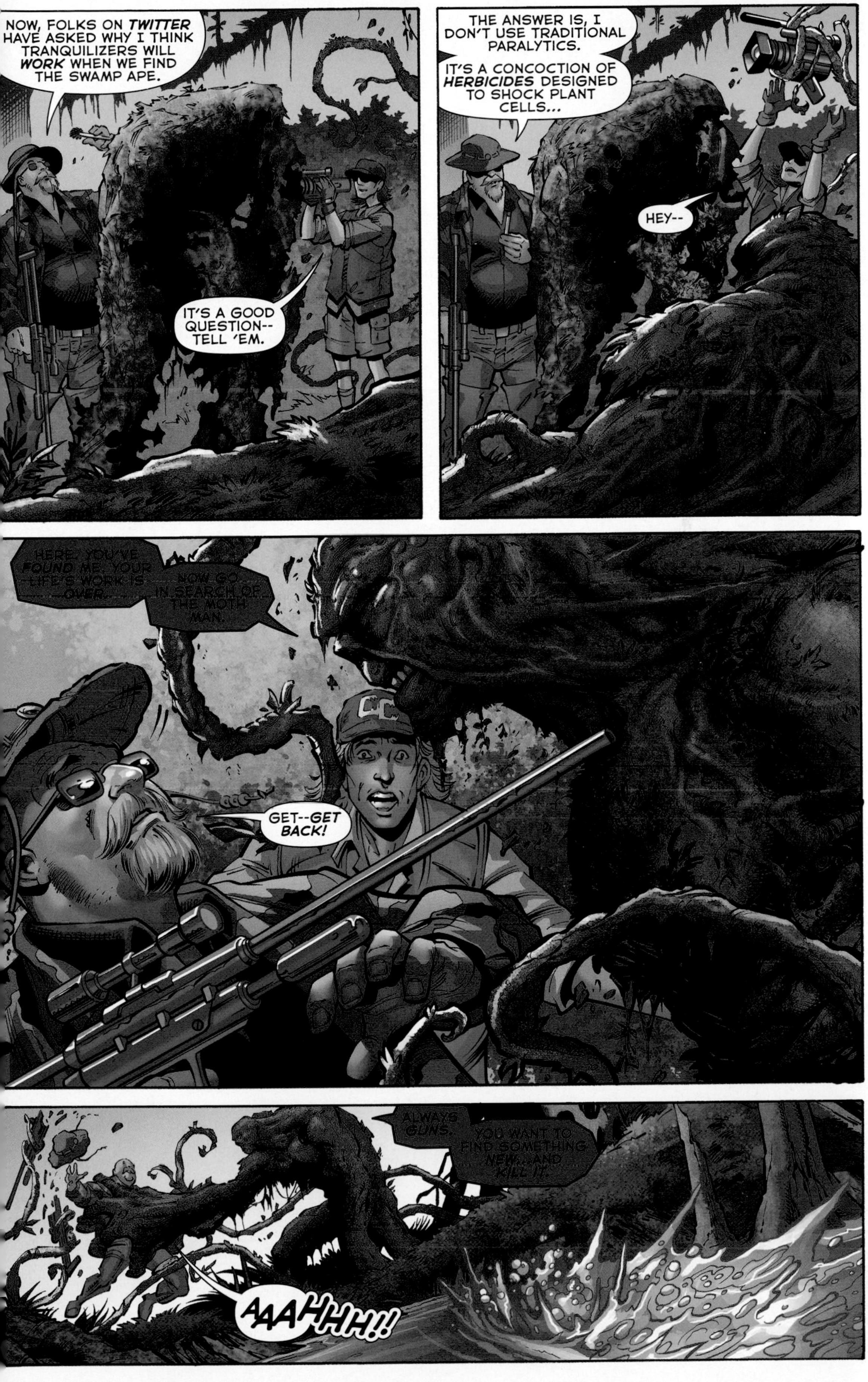
NOW, FOLKS ON TWITTER HAVE ASKED WHY I THINK TRANQUILIZERS WILL WORK WHEN WE FIND THE SWAMP APE.
IT'S A GOOD QUESTION-- TELL 'EM.
THE ANSWER IS, I DON'T USE TRADITIONAL PARALYTICS.
IT'S A CONCOCTION OF HERBICIDES DESIGNED TO SHOCK PLANT CELLS...
HEY--
HERE. YOU'VE FOUND ME. YOUR LIFE'S WORK IS OVER.
NOW GO IN SEARCH OF THE MOTH MAN.
GET--GET BACK!
ALWAYS GUNS.
YOU WANT TO FIND SOMETHING NEW...AND KILL IT.
AAAHHHH!!

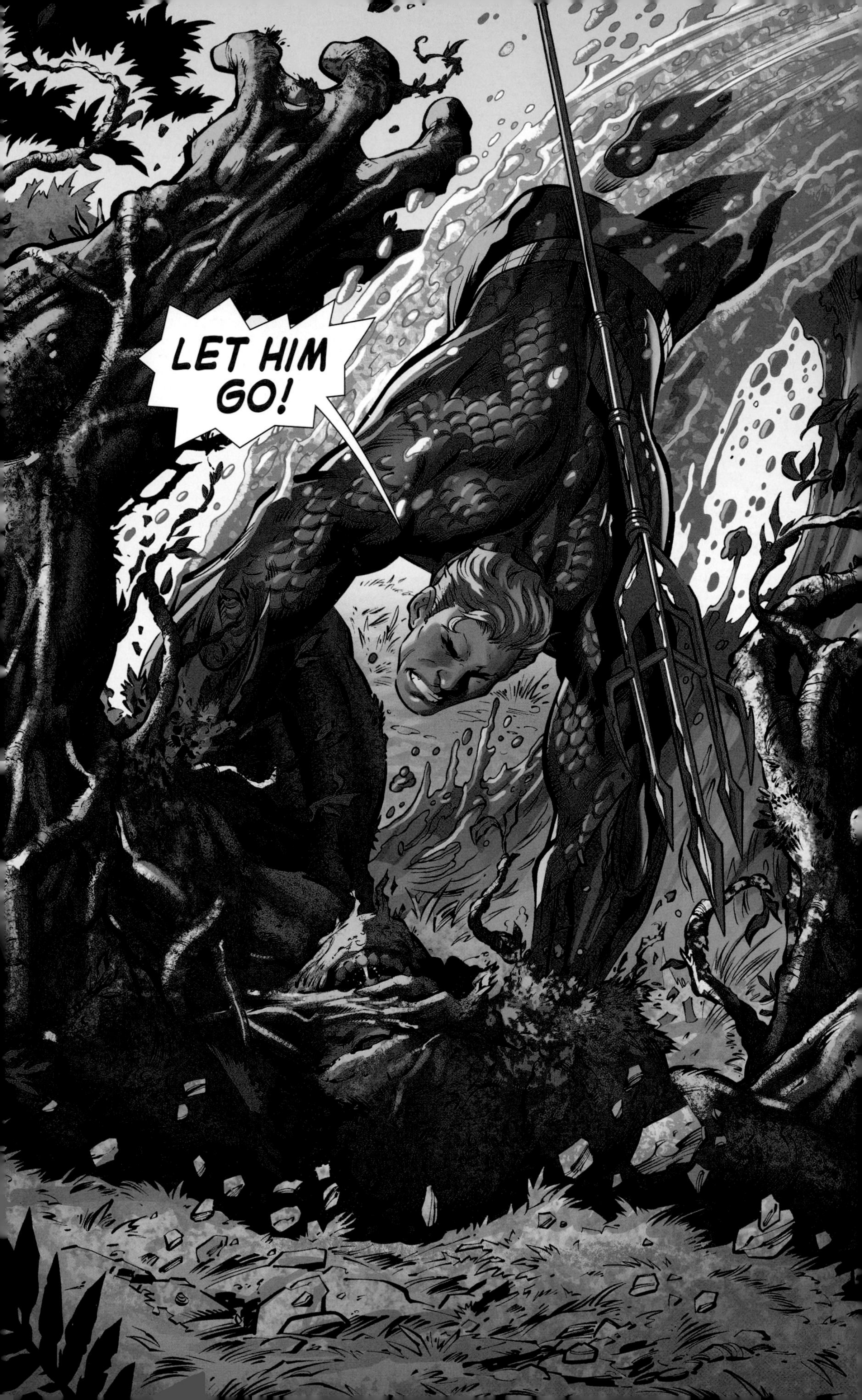
LET HIM GO!

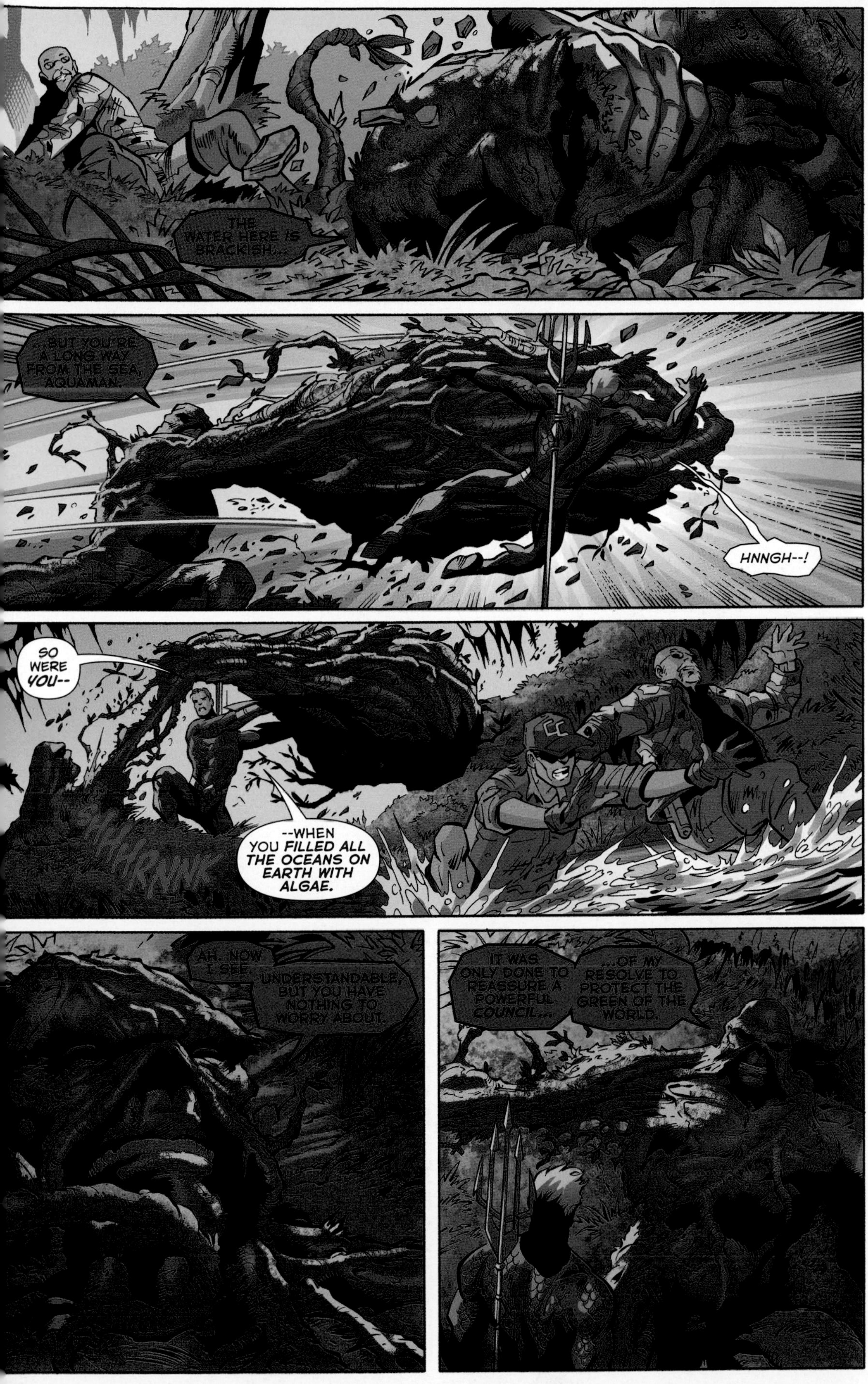
THE WATER HERE IS BRACKISH...
...BUT YOU'RE A LONG WAY FROM THE SEA, AQUAMAN.
HNNGH--!
SO WERE YOU--
--WHEN YOU FILLED ALL THE OCEANS ON EARTH WITH ALGAE.
SHHHRNNK
AH. NOW I SEE.
UNDERSTANDABLE, BUT YOU HAVE NOTHING TO WORRY ABOUT.
IT WAS ONLY DONE TO REASSURE A POWERFUL COUNCIL...
...OF MY RESOLVE TO PROTECT THE GREEN OF THE WORLD.

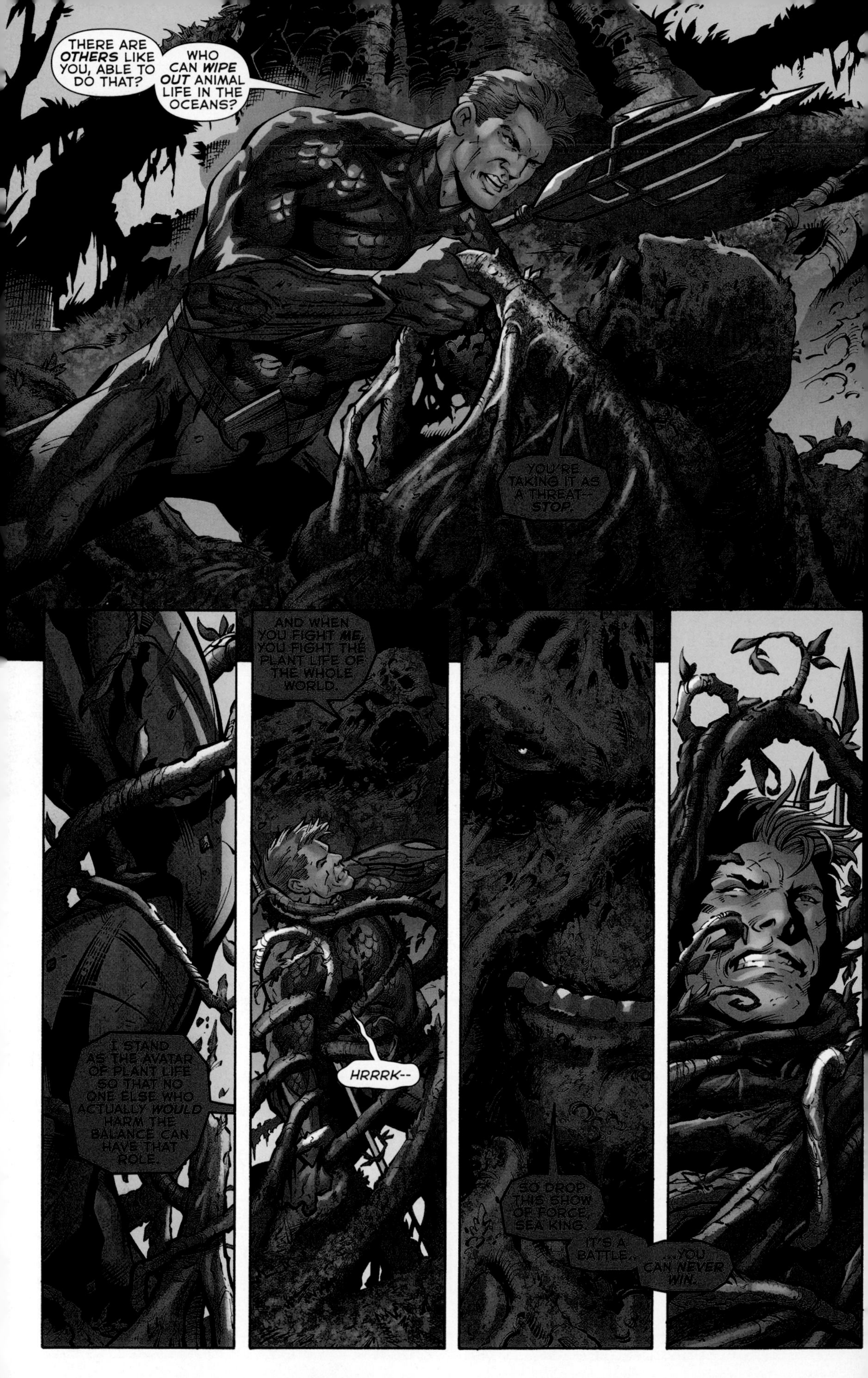
THERE ARE OTHERS LIKE YOU, ABLE TO DO THAT?
WHO CAN WIPE OUT ANIMAL LIFE IN THE OCEANS?
YOU'RE TAKING IT AS A THREAT-- STOP.
I STAND AS THE AVATAR OF PLANT LIFE SO THAT NO ONE ELSE WHO ACTUALLY WOULD HARM THE BALANCE CAN HAVE THAT ROLE.
AND WHEN YOU FIGHT ME, YOU FIGHT THE PLANT LIFE OF THE WHOLE WORLD.
HRRRK--
SO DROP THIS SHOW OF FORCE, SEA KING.
IT'S A BATTLE...
...YOU CAN NEVER WIN.

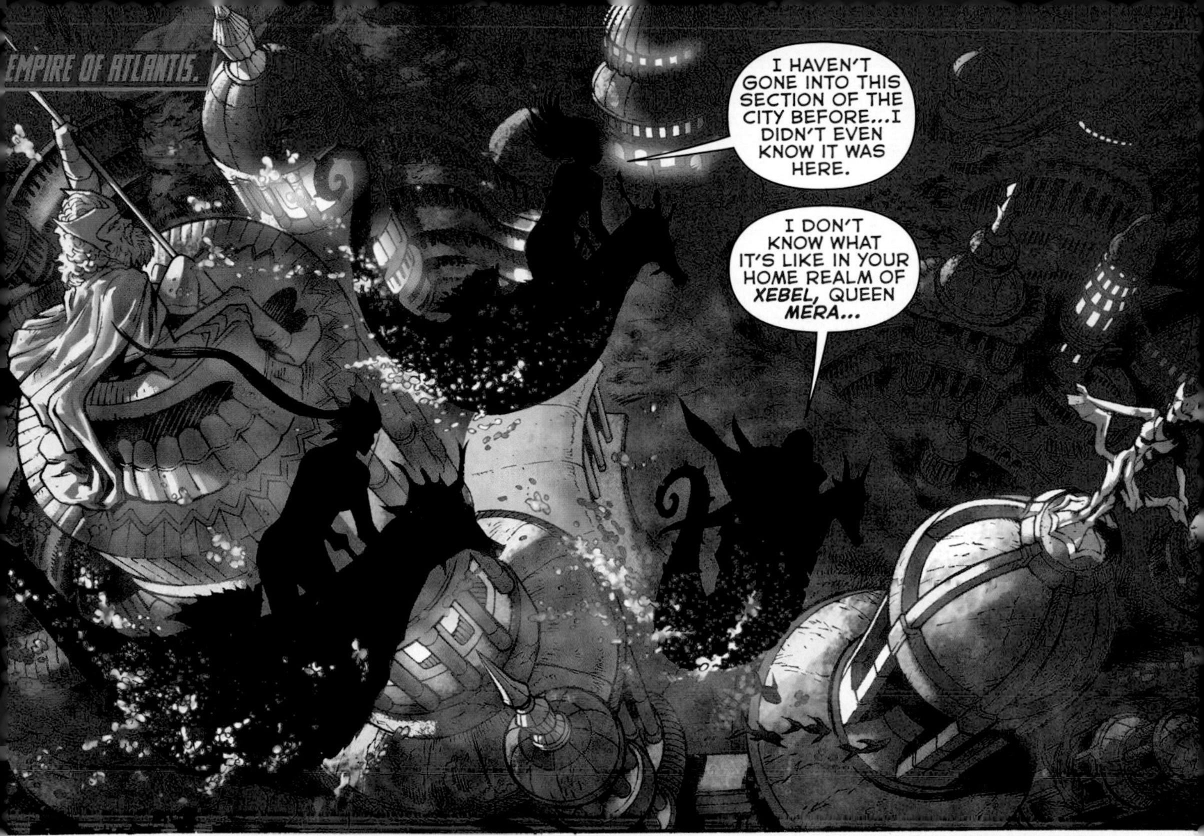
EMPIRE OF ATLANTIS.
I HAVEN'T GONE INTO THIS SECTION OF THE CITY BEFORE...I DIDN'T EVEN KNOW IT WAS HERE.
I DON'T KNOW WHAT IT'S LIKE IN YOUR HOME REALM OF XEBEL, QUEEN MERA...

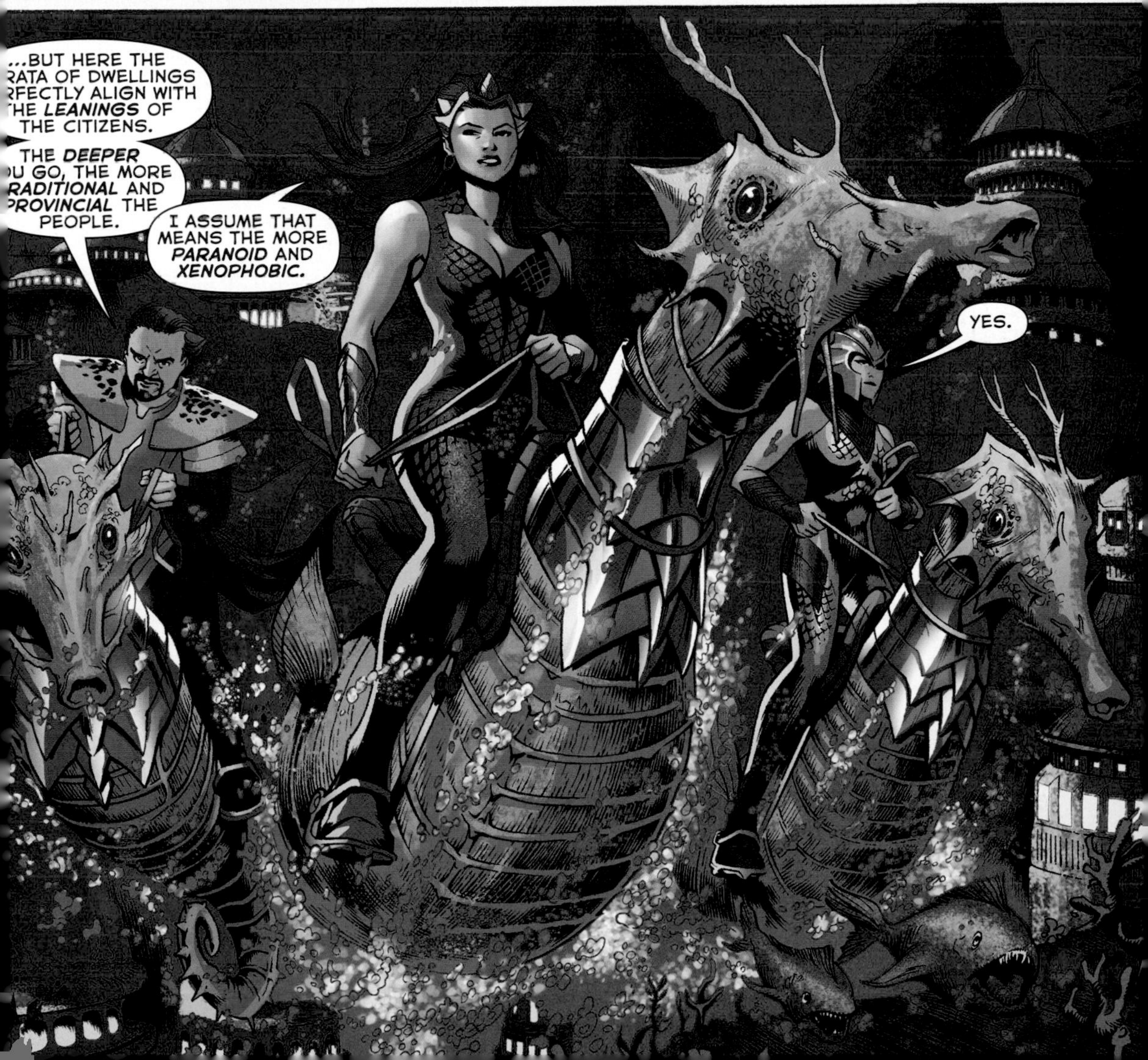
...BUT HERE THE RATA OF DWELLINGS RFECTLY ALIGN WITH HE LEANINGS OF THE CITIZENS.
THE DEEPER U GO, THE MORE RADITIONAL AND PROVINCIAL THE PEOPLE.
I ASSUME THAT MEANS THE MORE PARANOID AND XENOPHOBIC.
YES.

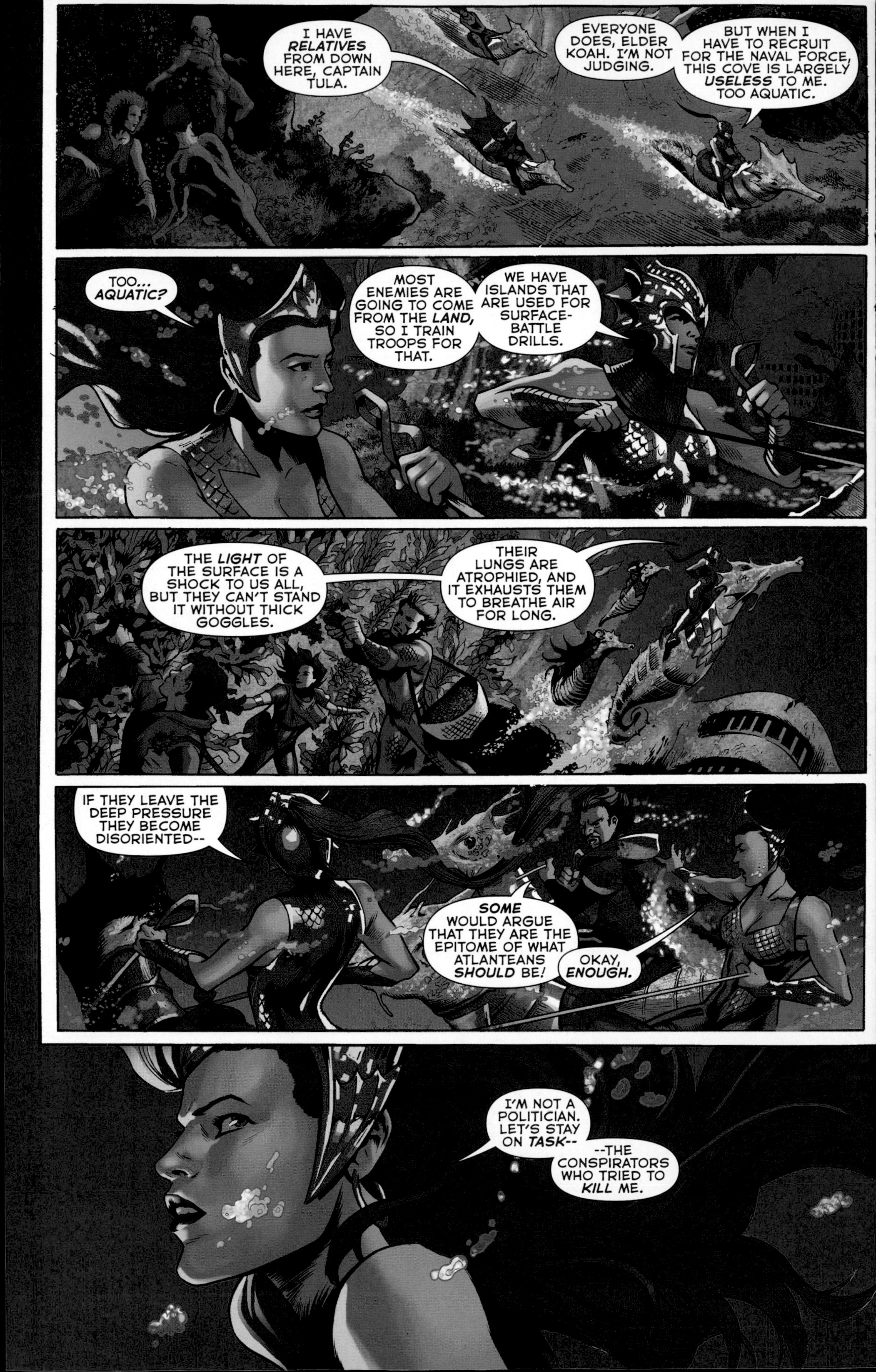
I HAVE *RELATIVES* FROM DOWN HERE, CAPTAIN TULA.
EVERYONE DOES, ELDER KOAH. I'M NOT JUDGING.
BUT WHEN I HAVE TO RECRUIT FOR THE NAVAL FORCE, THIS COVE IS LARGELY *USELESS* TO ME. TOO AQUATIC.
TOO... *AQUATIC?*
MOST ENEMIES ARE GOING TO COME FROM THE *LAND,* SO I TRAIN TROOPS FOR THAT.
WE HAVE ISLANDS THAT ARE USED FOR SURFACE-BATTLE DRILLS.
THE *LIGHT* OF THE SURFACE IS A SHOCK TO US ALL, BUT THEY CAN'T STAND IT WITHOUT THICK GOGGLES.
THEIR LUNGS ARE ATROPHIED, AND IT EXHAUSTS THEM TO BREATHE AIR FOR LONG.
IF THEY LEAVE THE DEEP PRESSURE THEY BECOME DISORIENTED--
SOME WOULD ARGUE THAT THEY ARE THE EPITOME OF WHAT ATLANTEANS *SHOULD* BE!
OKAY, *ENOUGH.*
I'M NOT A POLITICIAN. LET'S STAY ON *TASK*--
--THE CONSPIRATORS WHO TRIED TO *KILL* ME.

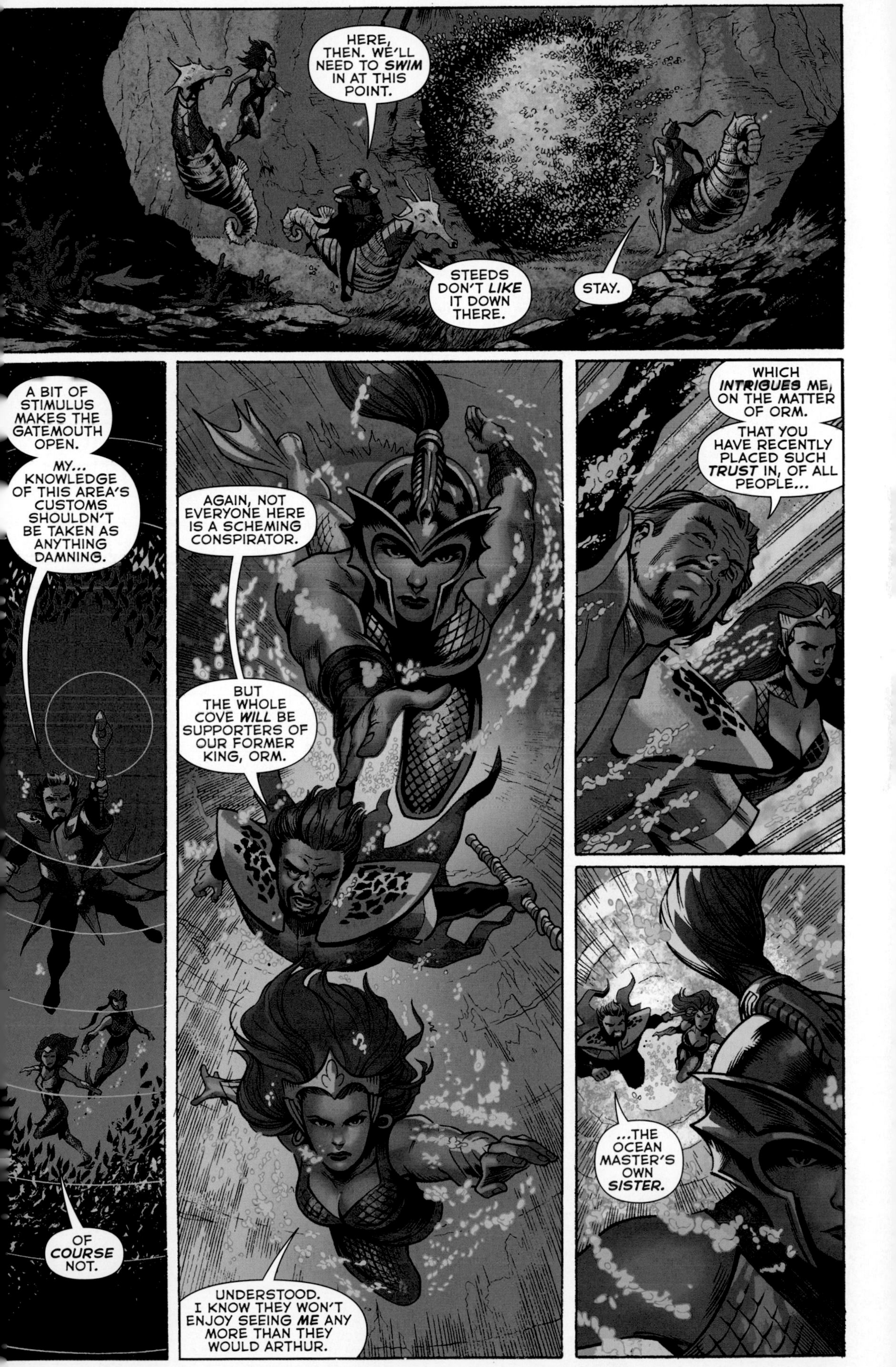
HERE, THEN. WE'LL NEED TO SWIM IN AT THIS POINT.
STEEDS DON'T LIKE IT DOWN THERE.
STAY.
A BIT OF STIMULUS MAKES THE GATEMOUTH OPEN.
MY... KNOWLEDGE OF THIS AREA'S CUSTOMS SHOULDN'T BE TAKEN AS ANYTHING DAMNING.
OF COURSE NOT.
AGAIN, NOT EVERYONE HERE IS A SCHEMING CONSPIRATOR.
BUT THE WHOLE COVE WILL BE SUPPORTERS OF OUR FORMER KING, ORM.
UNDERSTOOD. I KNOW THEY WON'T ENJOY SEEING ME ANY MORE THAN THEY WOULD ARTHUR.
WHICH INTRIGUES ME, ON THE MATTER OF ORM.
THAT YOU HAVE RECENTLY PLACED SUCH TRUST IN, OF ALL PEOPLE...
...THE OCEAN MASTER'S OWN SISTER.

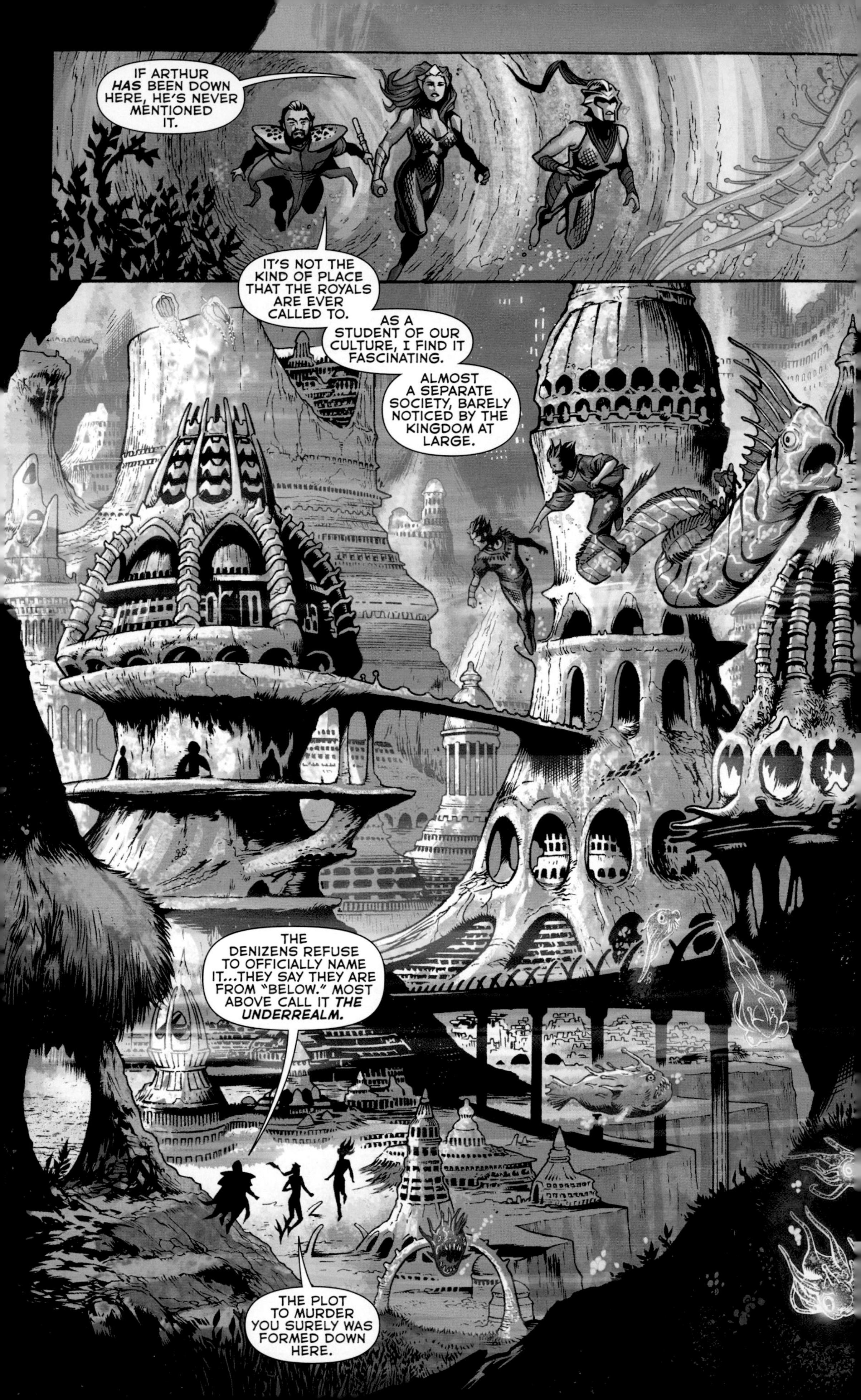
IF ARTHUR HAS BEEN DOWN HERE, HE'S NEVER MENTIONED IT.
IT'S NOT THE KIND OF PLACE THAT THE ROYALS ARE EVER CALLED TO.
AS A STUDENT OF OUR CULTURE, I FIND IT FASCINATING.
ALMOST A SEPARATE SOCIETY, BARELY NOTICED BY THE KINGDOM AT LARGE.
THE DENIZENS REFUSE TO OFFICIALLY NAME IT...THEY SAY THEY ARE FROM "BELOW." MOST ABOVE CALL IT THE UNDERREALM.
THE PLOT TO MURDER YOU SURELY WAS FORMED DOWN HERE.

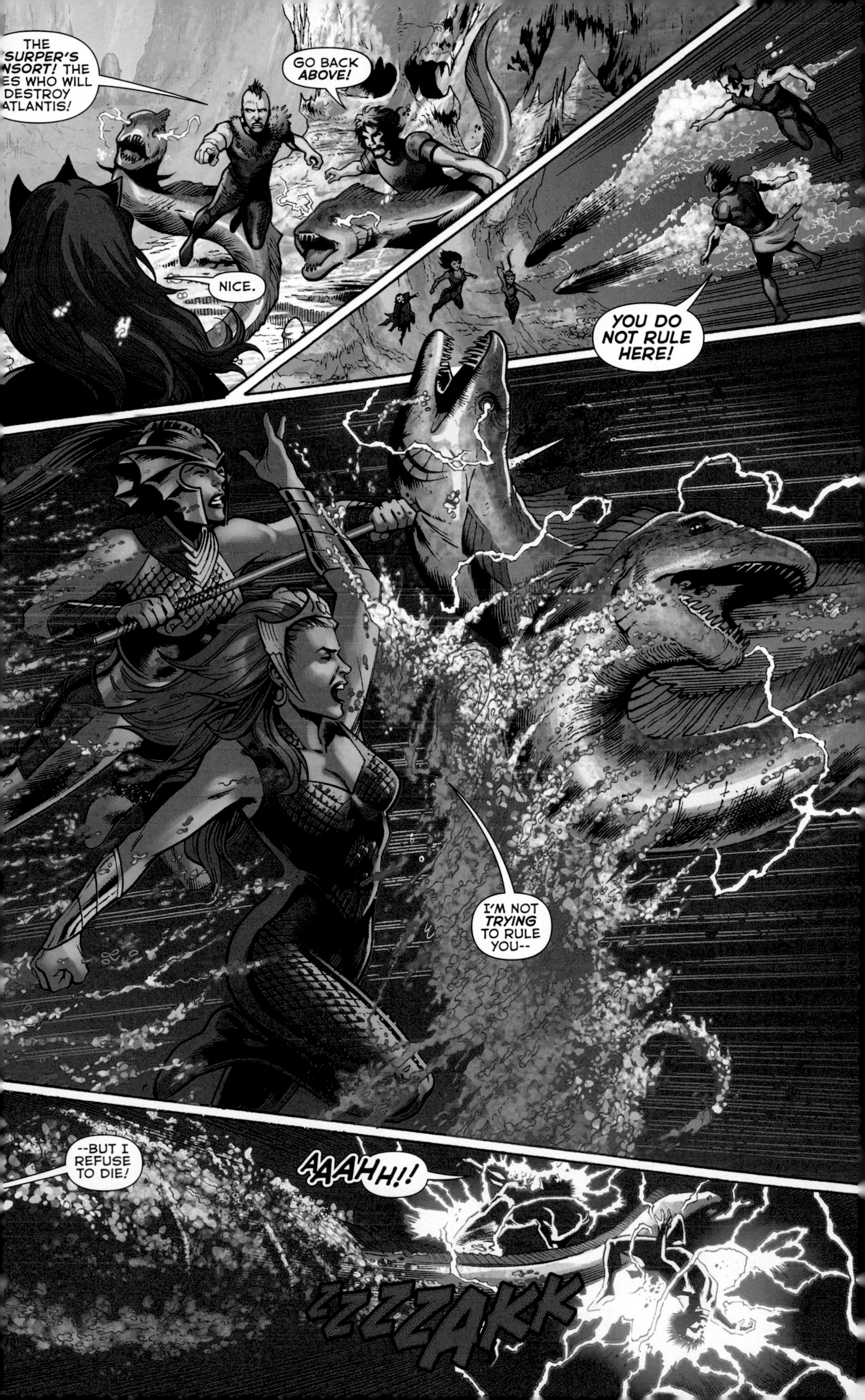
THE SURPER'S NSORT! THE ES WHO WILL DESTROY ATLANTIS!
GO BACK ABOVE!
NICE.
YOU DO NOT RULE HERE!
I'M NOT TRYING TO RULE YOU--
--BUT I REFUSE TO DIE!
AAAHH!!
ZZZZAKK

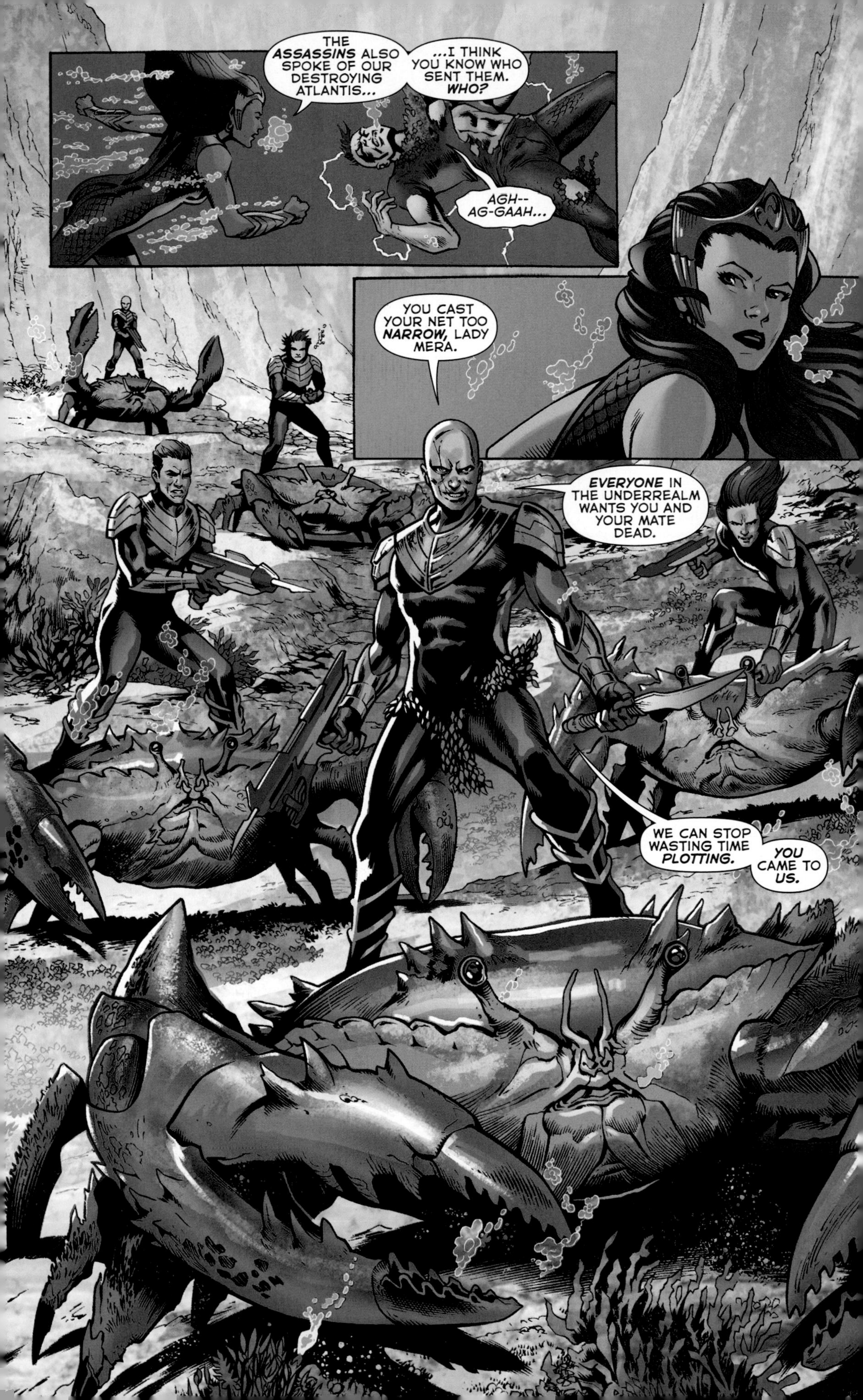
THE ASSASSINS ALSO SPOKE OF OUR DESTROYING ATLANTIS...
...I THINK YOU KNOW WHO SENT THEM. WHO?
AGH-- AG-GAAH...
YOU CAST YOUR NET TOO NARROW, LADY MERA.
EVERYONE IN THE UNDERREALM WANTS YOU AND YOUR MATE DEAD.
WE CAN STOP WASTING TIME PLOTTING.
YOU CAME TO US.

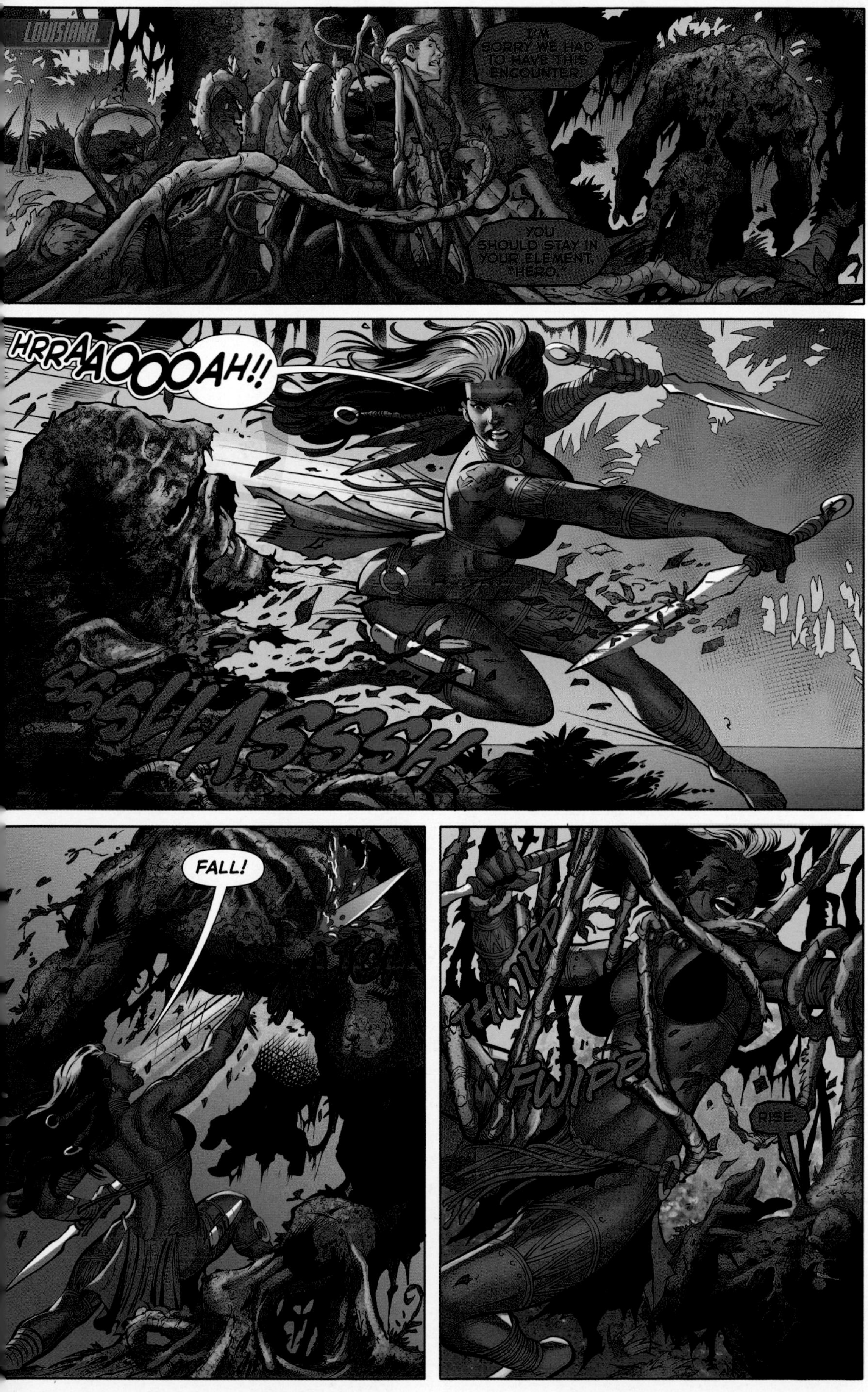
LOUISIANA.
I'M SORRY WE HAD TO HAVE THIS ENCOUNTER.
YOU SHOULD STAY IN YOUR ELEMENT, "HERO."
HRRAAOOOOAH!!
SSSLLASSSSH
FALL!
THWIPP
FWIPP
RISE.

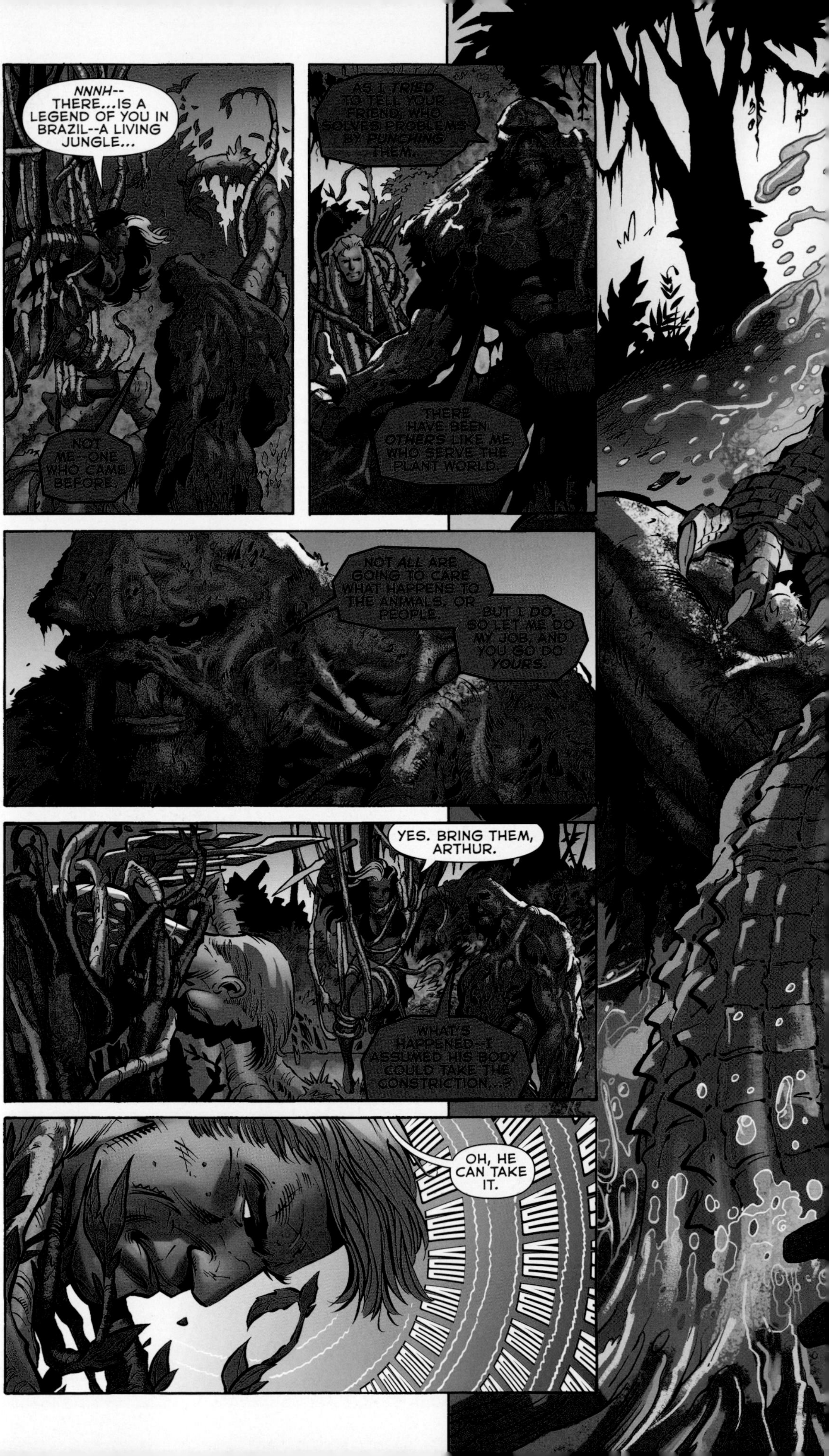
NNNH-- THERE...IS A LEGEND OF YOU IN BRAZIL--A LIVING JUNGLE...
NOT ME--ONE WHO CAME BEFORE.
AS I TRIED TO TELL YOUR FRIEND, WHO SOLVES PROBLEMS BY PUNCHING THEM.
THERE HAVE BEEN OTHERS LIKE ME, WHO SERVE THE PLANT WORLD.
NOT ALL ARE GOING TO CARE WHAT HAPPENS TO THE ANIMALS. OR PEOPLE.
BUT I DO. SO LET ME DO MY JOB, AND YOU GO DO YOURS.
YES. BRING THEM, ARTHUR.
WHAT'S HAPPENED--I ASSUMED HIS BODY COULD TAKE THE CONSTRICTION...?
OH, HE CAN TAKE IT.

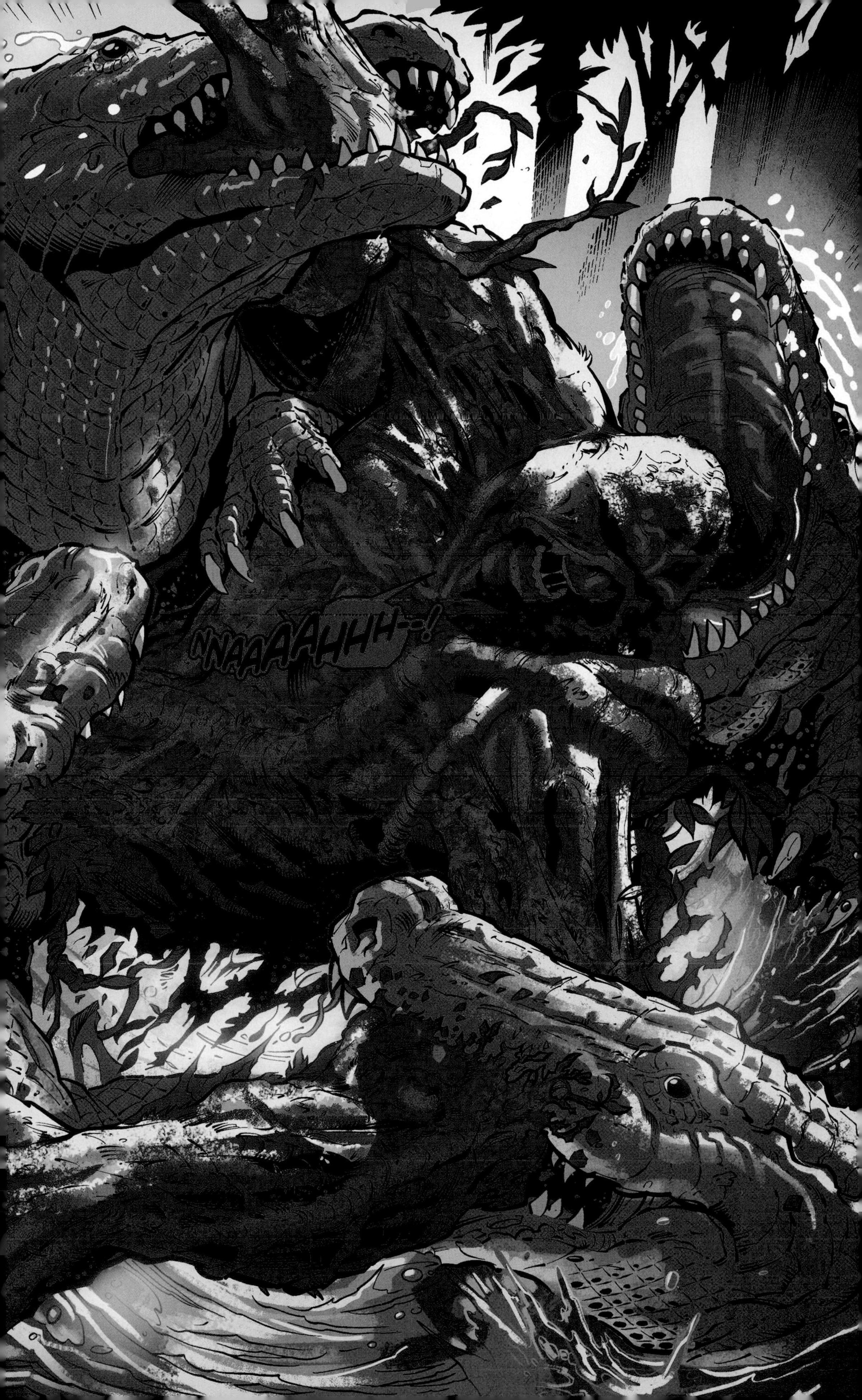
NNAAAAHHH--!

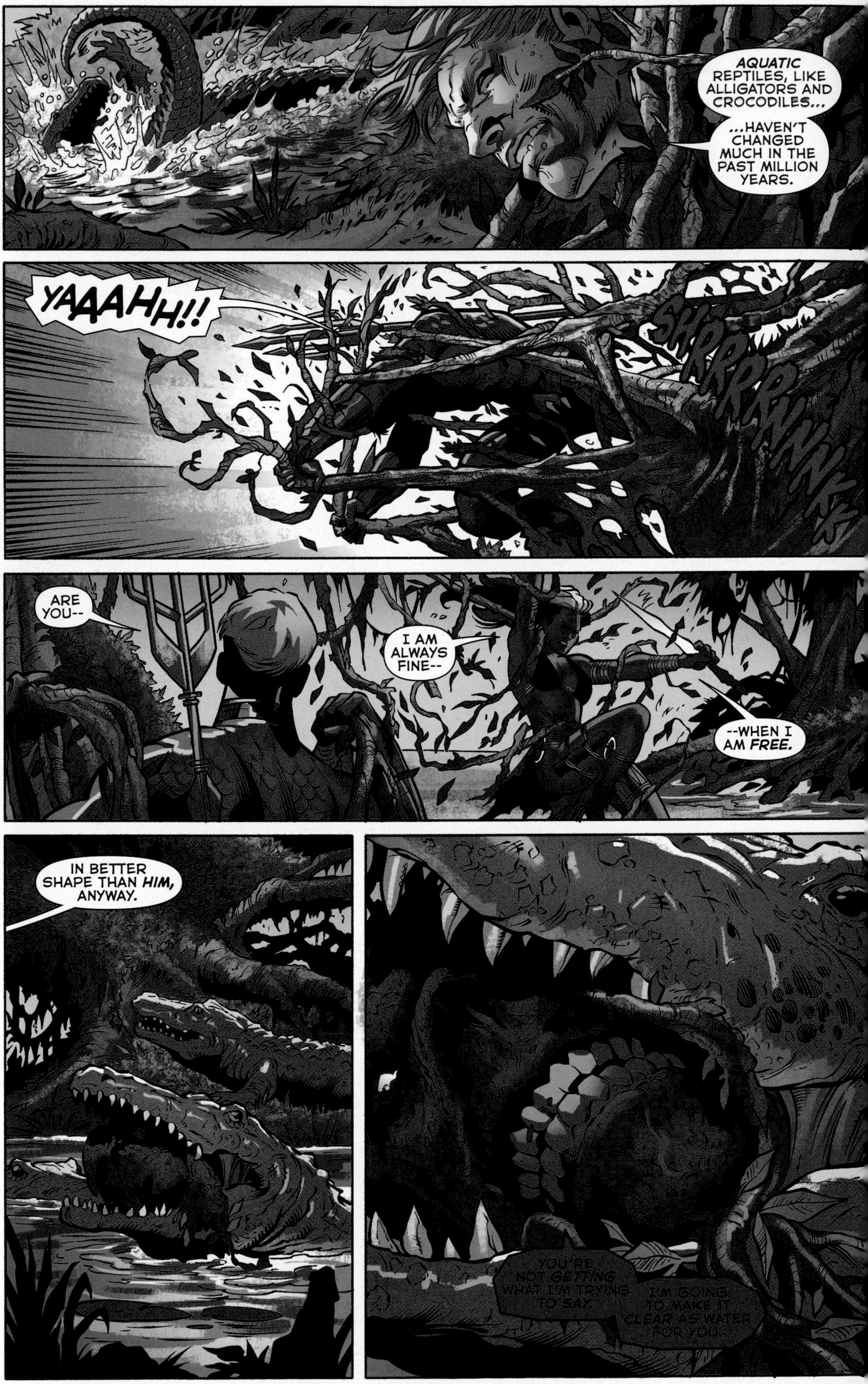
AQUATIC REPTILES, LIKE ALLIGATORS AND CROCODILES...
...HAVEN'T CHANGED MUCH IN THE PAST MILLION YEARS.
YAAAHH!!
SHRRRNNNKK
ARE YOU--
I AM ALWAYS FINE--
--WHEN I AM FREE.
IN BETTER SHAPE THAN HIM, ANYWAY.
YOU'RE NOT GETTING WHAT I'M TRYING TO SAY.
I'M GOING TO MAKE IT CLEAR AS WATER FOR YOU.

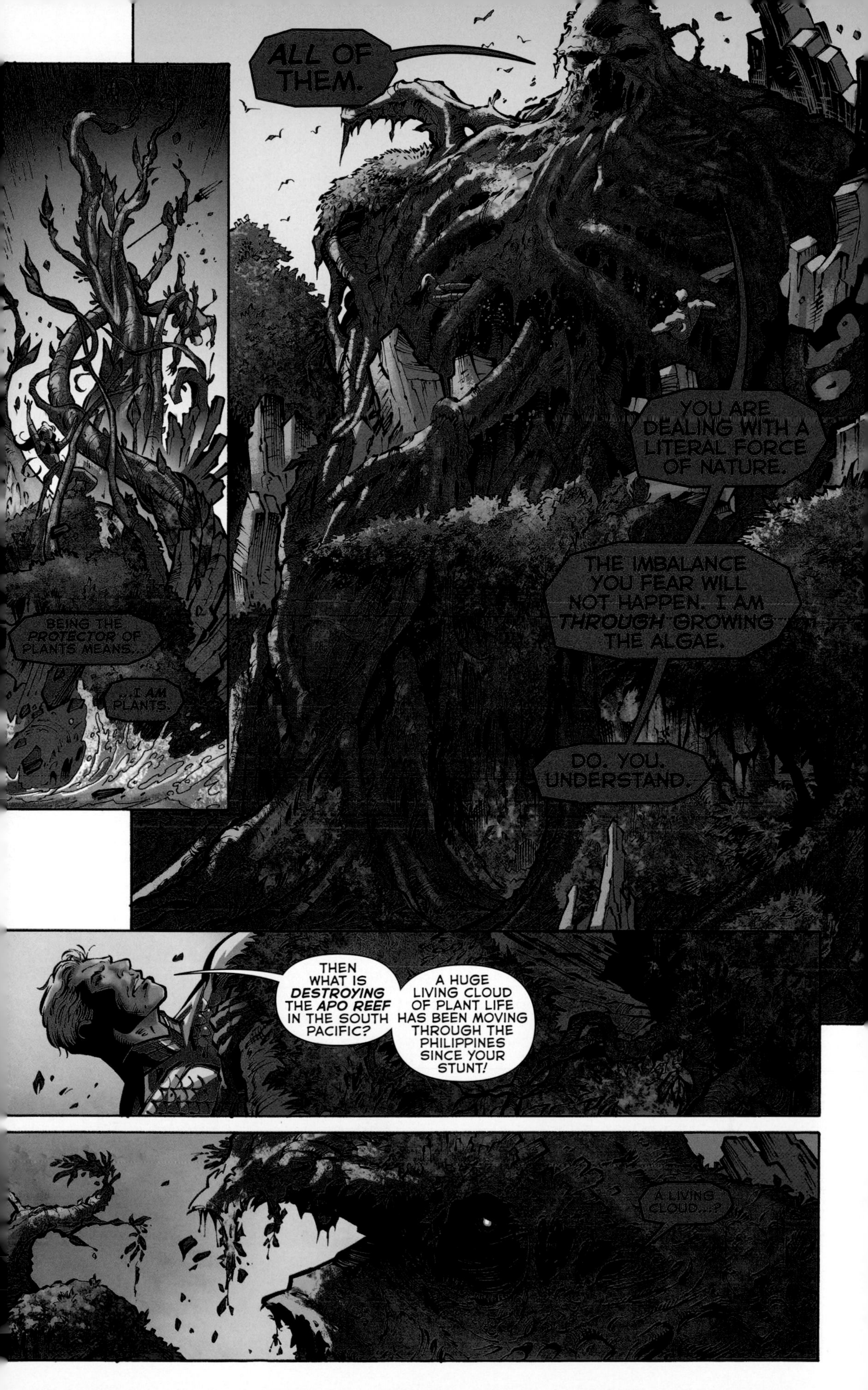
ALL OF THEM.
BEING THE PROTECTOR OF PLANTS MEANS...
...I AM PLANTS.
YOU ARE DEALING WITH A LITERAL FORCE OF NATURE.
THE IMBALANCE YOU FEAR WILL NOT HAPPEN. I AM THROUGH GROWING THE ALGAE.
DO. YOU. UNDERSTAND.
THEN WHAT IS DESTROYING THE APO REEF IN THE SOUTH PACIFIC?
A HUGE LIVING CLOUD OF PLANT LIFE HAS BEEN MOVING THROUGH THE PHILIPPINES SINCE YOUR STUNT!
A LIVING CLOUD...?

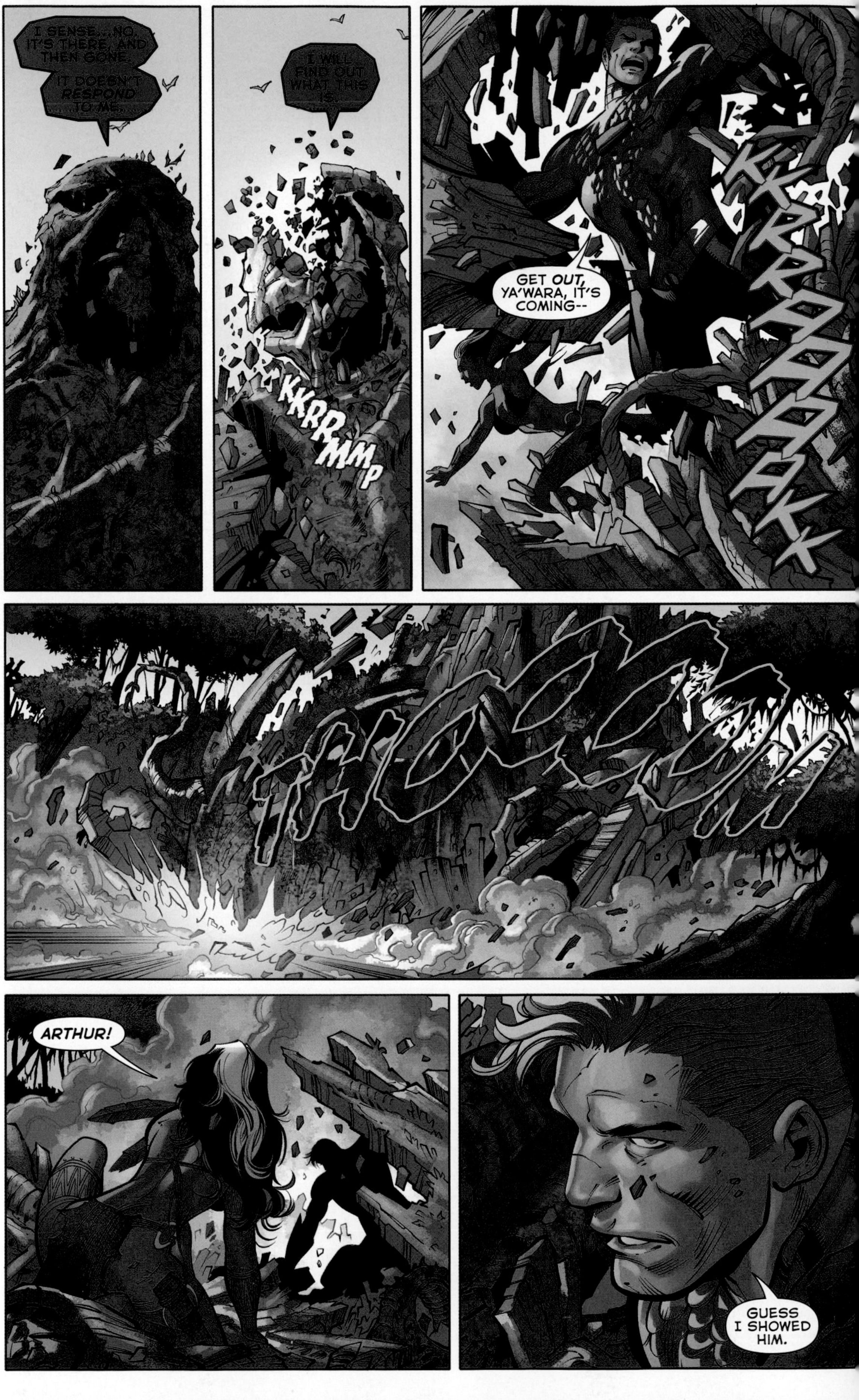
I SENSE... NO. IT'S THERE, AND THEN GONE.
IT DOESN'T *RESPOND* TO ME.
I WILL FIND OUT WHAT THIS IS.
KKRRMMMP
GET *OUT*, YA'WARA, IT'S COMING--
KKRRAAAAKK
THOOOM
ARTHUR!
GUESS I SHOWED HIM.

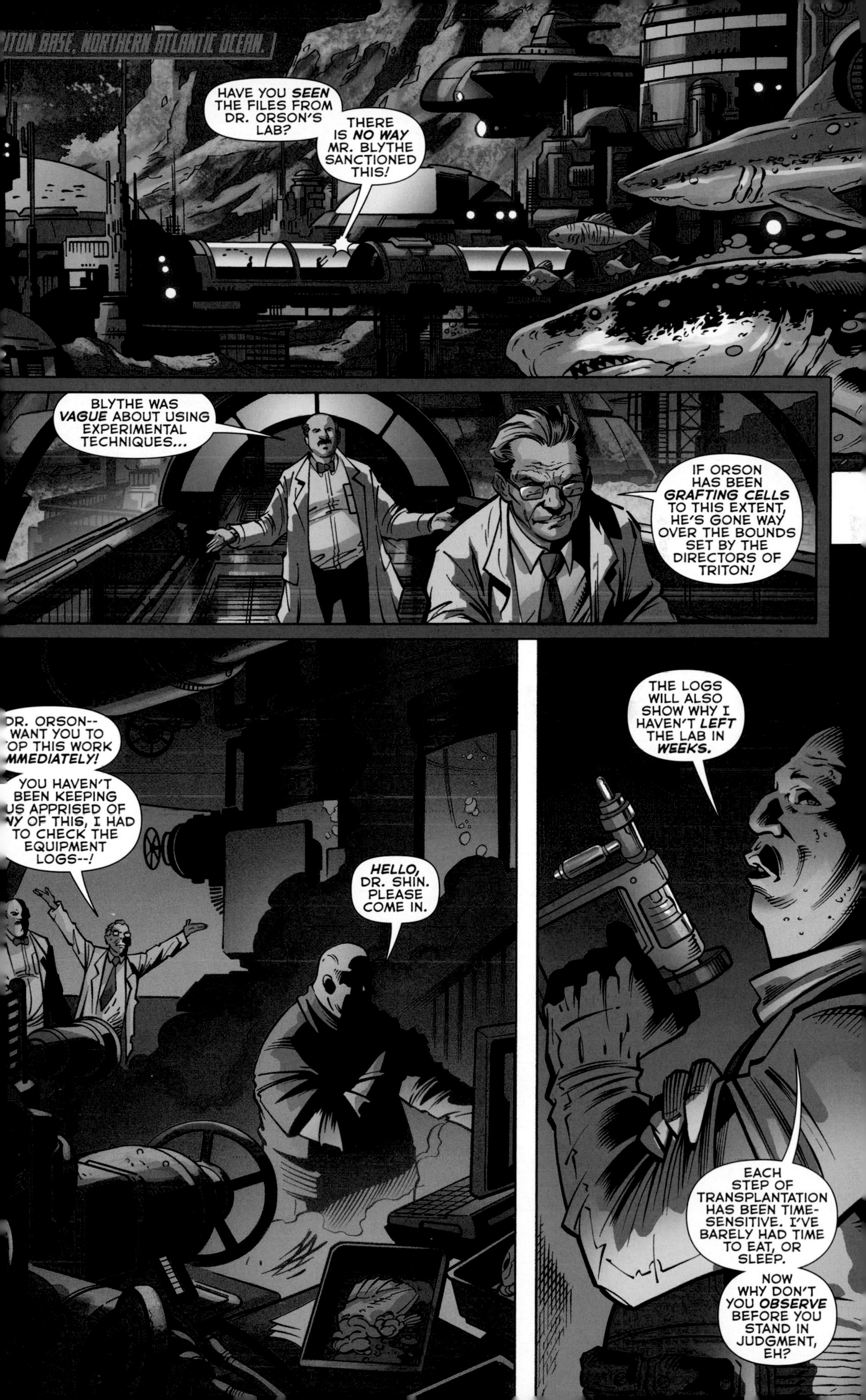
ITON BASE, NORTHERN ATLANTIC OCEAN.
HAVE YOU SEEN THE FILES FROM DR. ORSON'S LAB?
THERE IS NO WAY MR. BLYTHE SANCTIONED THIS!
BLYTHE WAS VAGUE ABOUT USING EXPERIMENTAL TECHNIQUES...
IF ORSON HAS BEEN GRAFTING CELLS TO THIS EXTENT, HE'S GONE WAY OVER THE BOUNDS SET BY THE DIRECTORS OF TRITON!
DR. ORSON-- WANT YOU TO OP THIS WORK MMEDIATELY!
YOU HAVEN'T BEEN KEEPING US APPRISED OF NY OF THIS, I HAD TO CHECK THE EQUIPMENT LOGS--!
HELLO, DR. SHIN. PLEASE COME IN.
THE LOGS WILL ALSO SHOW WHY I HAVEN'T LEFT THE LAB IN WEEKS.
EACH STEP OF TRANSPLANTATION HAS BEEN TIME-SENSITIVE. I'VE BARELY HAD TIME TO EAT, OR SLEEP.
NOW WHY DON'T YOU OBSERVE BEFORE YOU STAND IN JUDGMENT, EH?

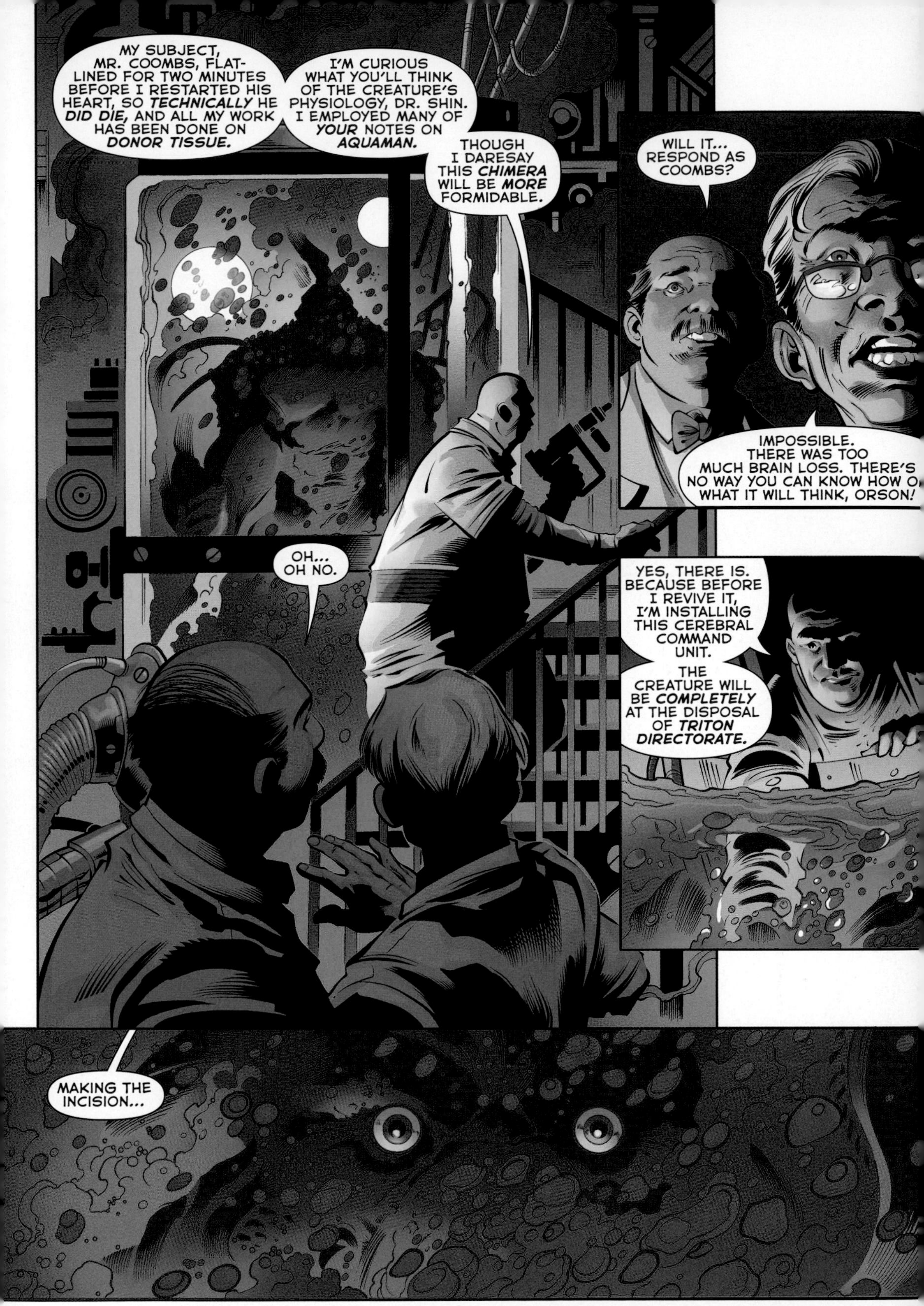
MY SUBJECT, MR. COOMBS, FLAT-LINED FOR TWO MINUTES BEFORE I RESTARTED HIS HEART, SO TECHNICALLY HE DID DIE, AND ALL MY WORK HAS BEEN DONE ON DONOR TISSUE.
I'M CURIOUS WHAT YOU'LL THINK OF THE CREATURE'S PHYSIOLOGY, DR. SHIN. I EMPLOYED MANY OF YOUR NOTES ON AQUAMAN.
THOUGH I DARESAY THIS CHIMERA WILL BE MORE FORMIDABLE.
WILL IT... RESPOND AS COOMBS?
IMPOSSIBLE. THERE WAS TOO MUCH BRAIN LOSS. THERE'S NO WAY YOU CAN KNOW HOW O WHAT IT WILL THINK, ORSON!
OH... OH NO.
YES, THERE IS. BECAUSE BEFORE I REVIVE IT, I'M INSTALLING THIS CEREBRAL COMMAND UNIT.
THE CREATURE WILL BE COMPLETELY AT THE DISPOSAL OF TRITON DIRECTORATE.
MAKING THE INCISION...

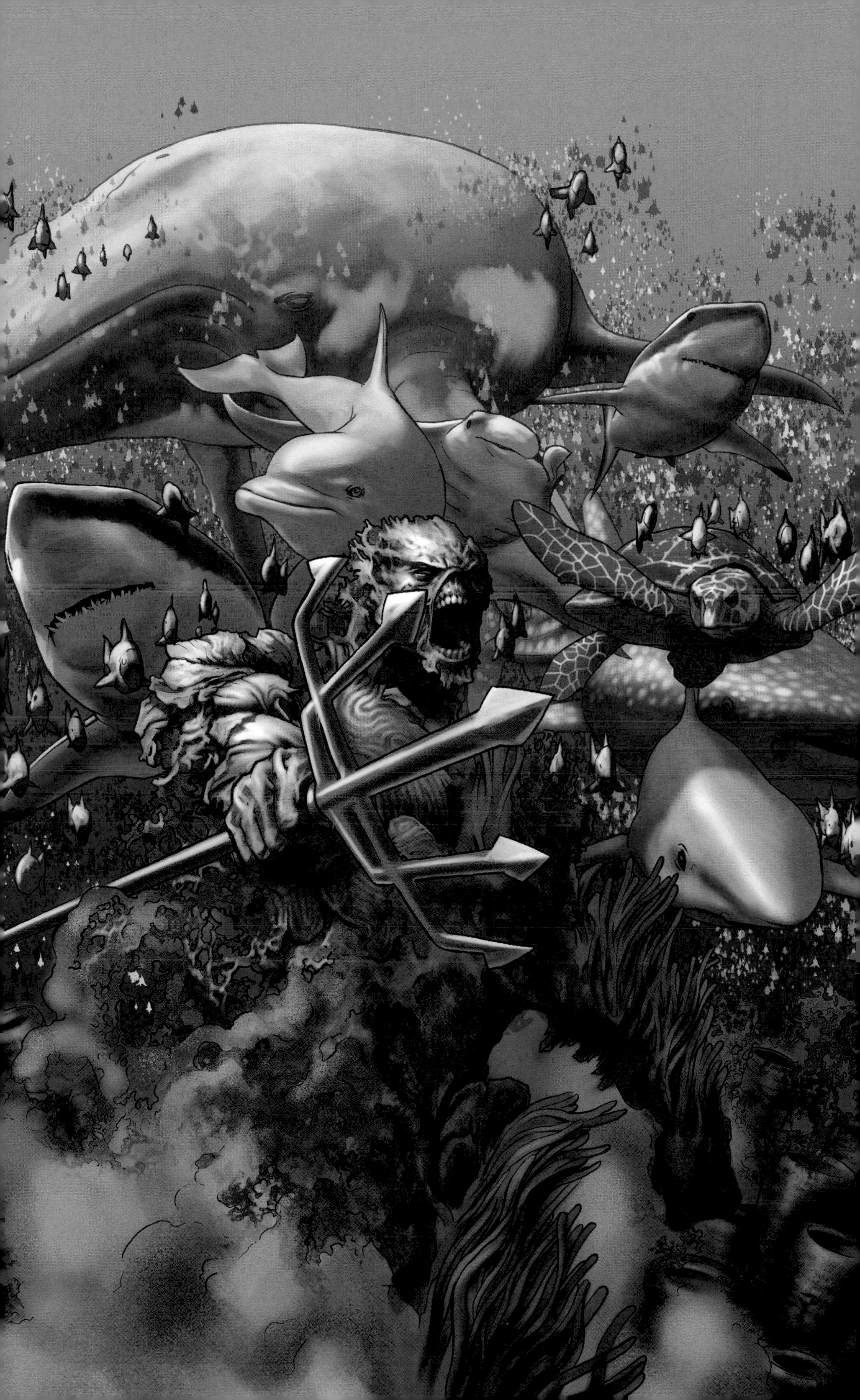

BLUE/GREEN

CHARLES SOULE writer JESUS SAIZ artist MATTHEW WILSON colorist
TRAVIS LANHAM letterer cover by JESUS SAIZ

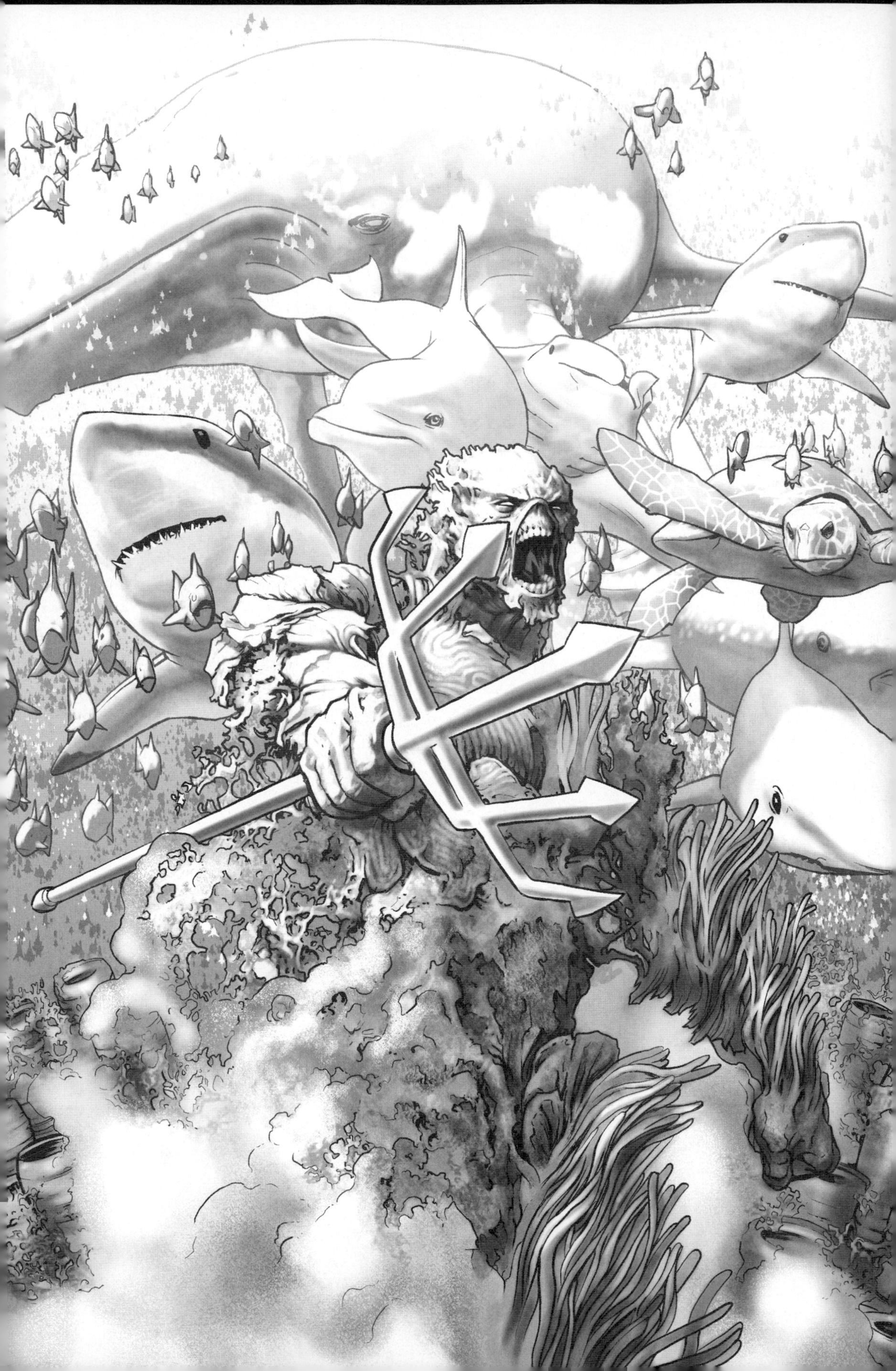

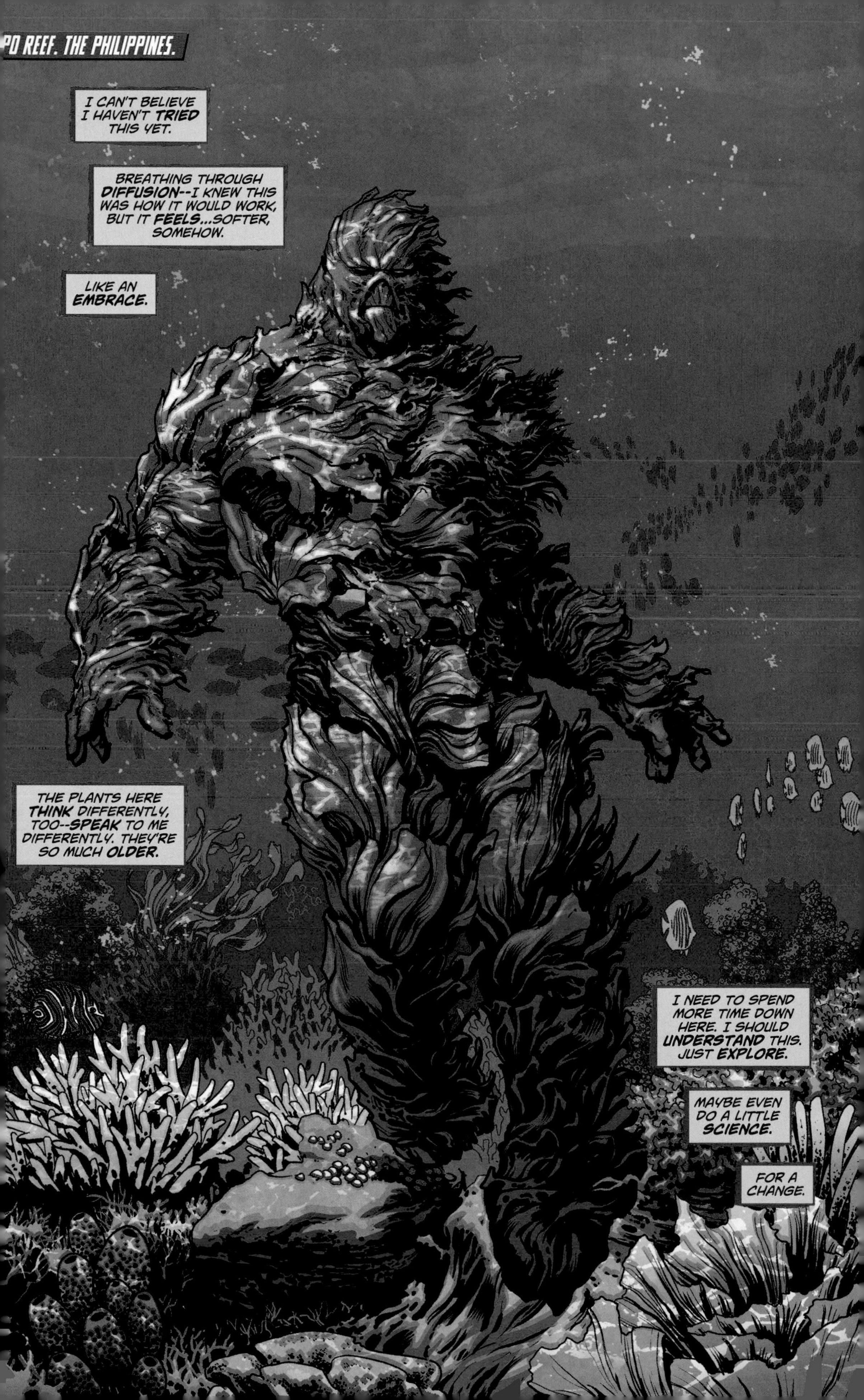
PO REEF. THE PHILIPPINES.
I CAN'T BELIEVE I HAVEN'T TRIED THIS YET.
BREATHING THROUGH DIFFUSION--I KNEW THIS WAS HOW IT WOULD WORK, BUT IT FEELS...SOFTER, SOMEHOW.
LIKE AN EMBRACE.
THE PLANTS HERE THINK DIFFERENTLY, TOO--SPEAK TO ME DIFFERENTLY. THEY'RE SO MUCH OLDER.
I NEED TO SPEND MORE TIME DOWN HERE. I SHOULD UNDERSTAND THIS. JUST EXPLORE.
MAYBE EVEN DO A LITTLE SCIENCE.
FOR A CHANGE.

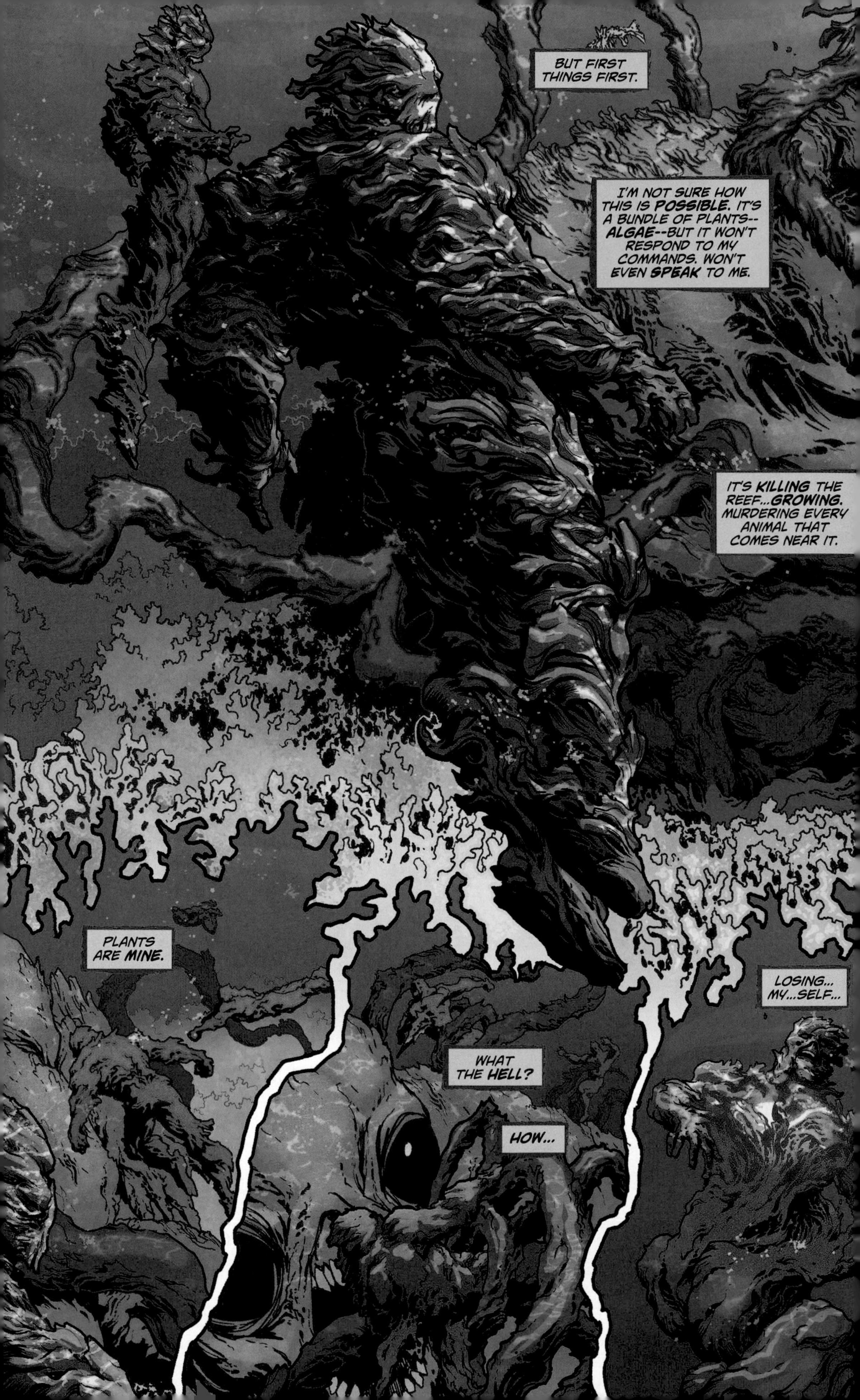
BUT FIRST THINGS FIRST.
I'M NOT SURE HOW THIS IS POSSIBLE. IT'S A BUNDLE OF PLANTS--ALGAE--BUT IT WON'T RESPOND TO MY COMMANDS. WON'T EVEN SPEAK TO ME.
IT'S KILLING THE REEF...GROWING. MURDERING EVERY ANIMAL THAT COMES NEAR IT.
PLANTS ARE MINE.
WHAT THE HELL?
HOW...
LOSING... MY...SELF...

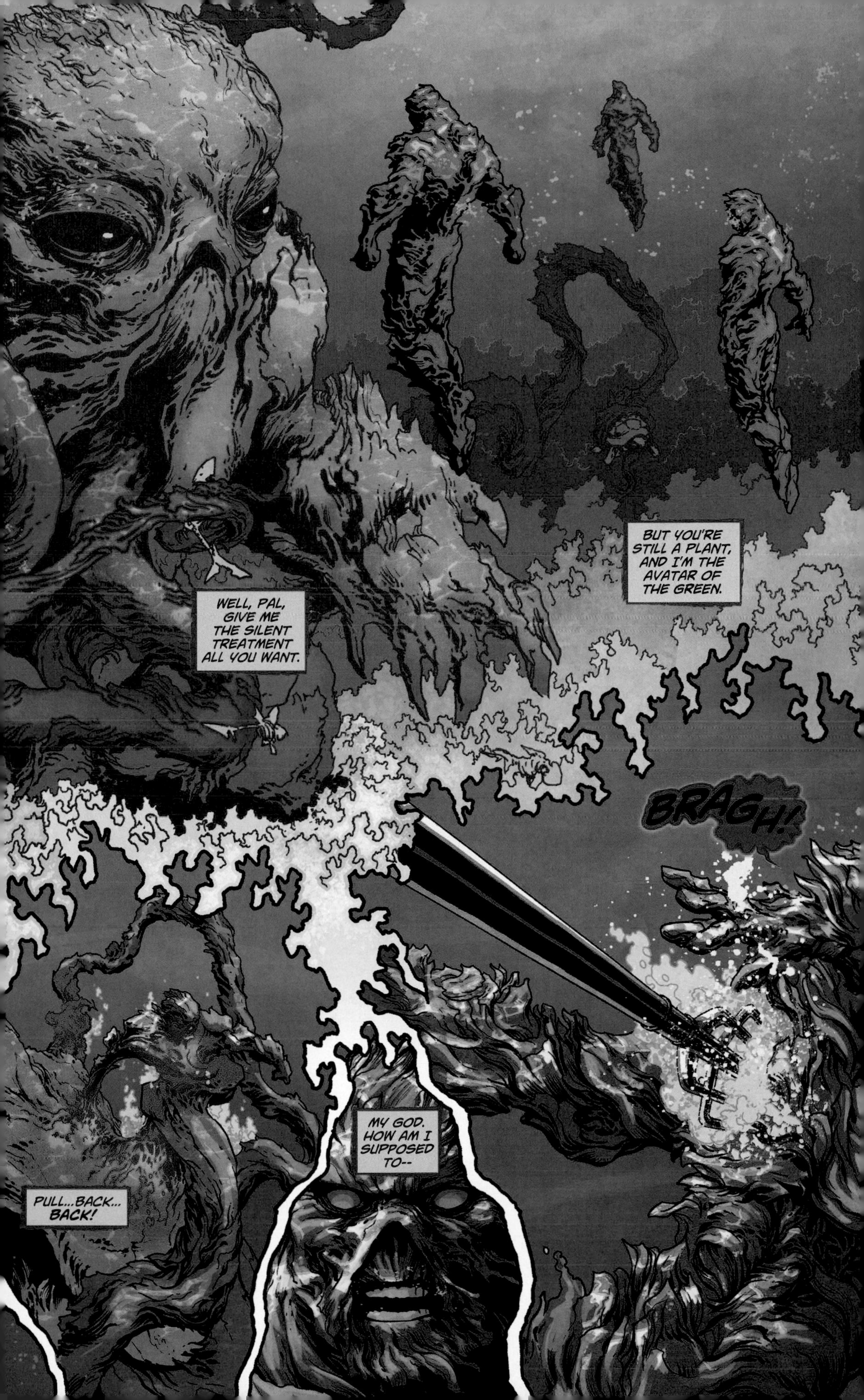
WELL, PAL, GIVE ME THE SILENT TREATMENT ALL YOU WANT.
BUT YOU'RE STILL A PLANT, AND I'M THE AVATAR OF THE GREEN.
BRAGH!
MY GOD. HOW AM I SUPPOSED TO--
PULL...BACK... BACK!

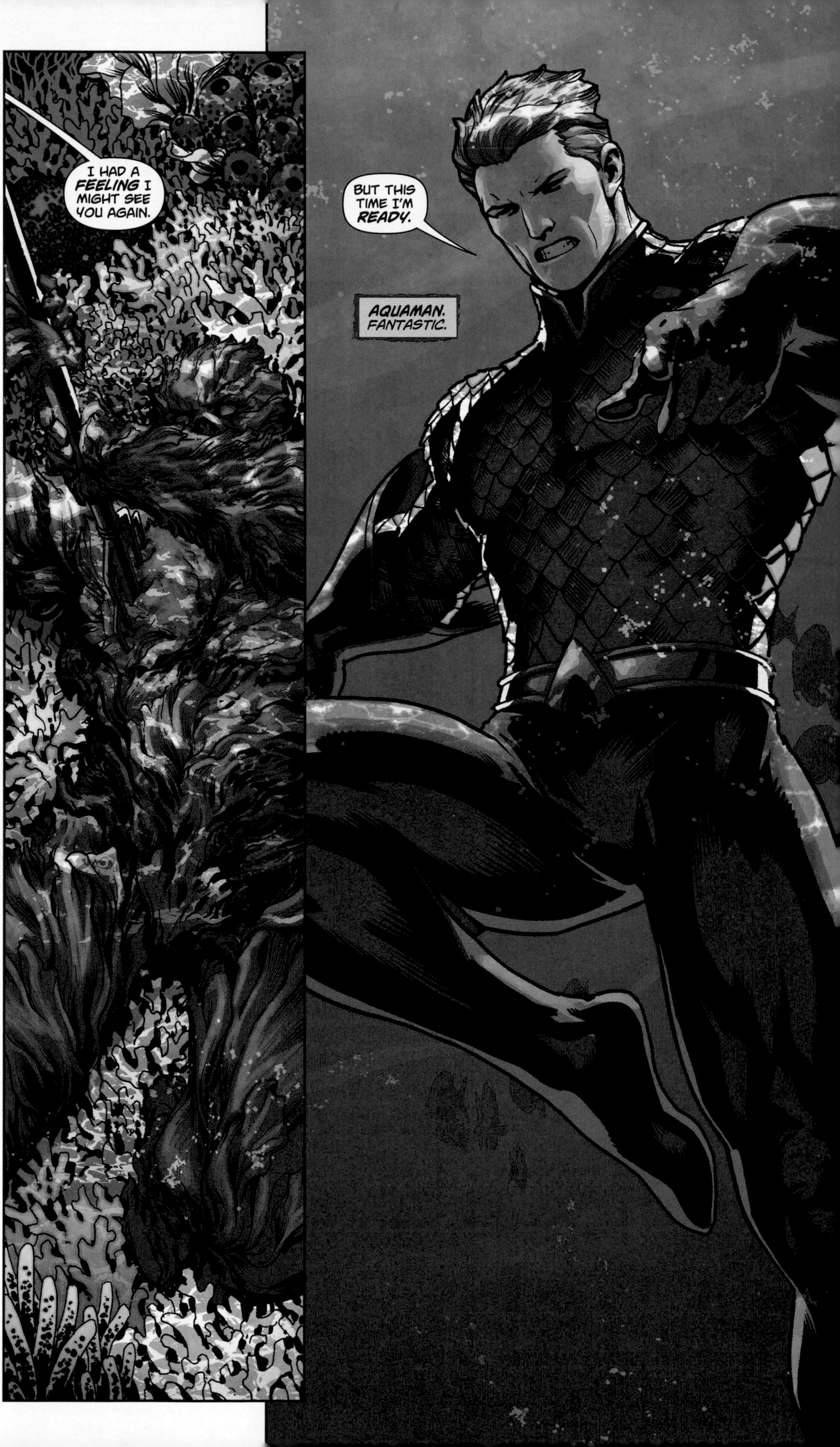
I HAD A FEELING I MIGHT SEE YOU AGAIN.
BUT THIS TIME I'M READY.
AQUAMAN. FANTASTIC.

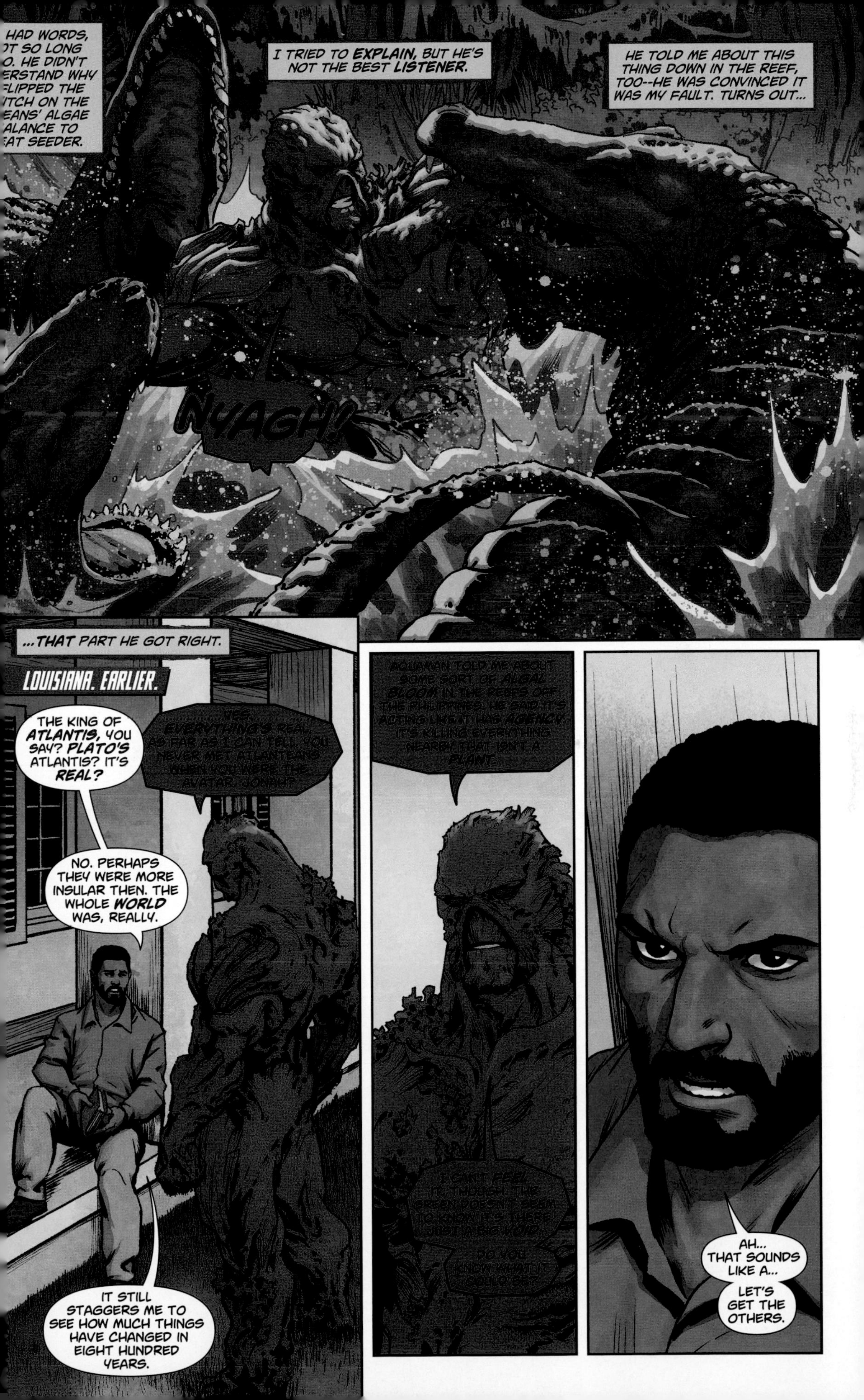

HAD WORDS, OT SO LONG O. HE DIDN'T ERSTAND WHY FLIPPED THE ITCH ON THE EANS' ALGAE ALANCE TO EAT SEEDER.
I TRIED TO EXPLAIN, BUT HE'S NOT THE BEST LISTENER.
HE TOLD ME ABOUT THIS THING DOWN IN THE REEF, TOO--HE WAS CONVINCED IT WAS MY FAULT. TURNS OUT...
NYAGH!
...THAT PART HE GOT RIGHT.
LOUISIANA. EARLIER.
THE KING OF ATLANTIS, YOU SAY? PLATO'S ATLANTIS? IT'S REAL?
YES. EVERYTHING'S REAL, AS FAR AS I CAN TELL. YOU NEVER MET ATLANTEANS WHEN YOU WERE THE AVATAR, JONAH?
NO. PERHAPS THEY WERE MORE INSULAR THEN. THE WHOLE WORLD WAS, REALLY.
IT STILL STAGGERS ME TO SEE HOW MUCH THINGS HAVE CHANGED IN EIGHT HUNDRED YEARS.
AQUAMAN TOLD ME ABOUT SOME SORT OF ALGAL BLOOM IN THE REEFS OFF THE PHILIPPINES. HE SAID IT'S ACTING LIKE IT HAS AGENCY. IT'S KILLING EVERYTHING NEARBY THAT ISN'T A PLANT.
I CAN'T FEEL IT, THOUGH. THE GREEN DOESN'T SEEM TO KNOW IT'S THERE. JUST A BIG VOID.
DO YOU KNOW WHAT IT COULD BE?
AH... THAT SOUNDS LIKE A...
LET'S GET THE OTHERS.

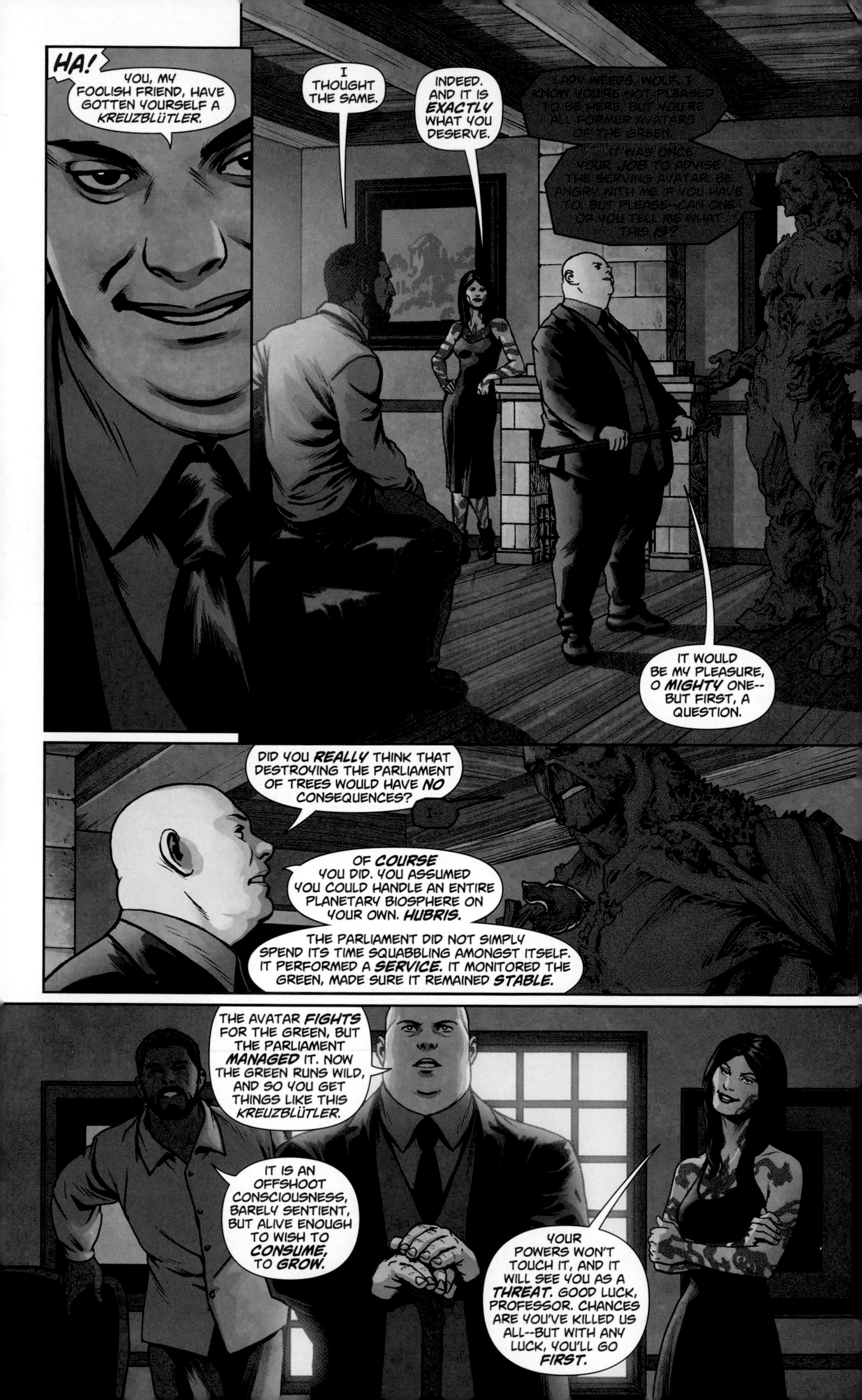
HA! YOU, MY FOOLISH FRIEND, HAVE GOTTEN YOURSELF A KREUZBLÜTLER.
I THOUGHT THE SAME.
INDEED. AND IT IS EXACTLY WHAT YOU DESERVE.
LADY WEEDS, WOLF, I KNOW YOU'RE NOT PLEASED TO BE HERE, BUT YOU'RE ALL FORMER AVATARS OF THE GREEN.
IT WAS ONCE YOUR JOB TO ADVISE THE SERVING AVATAR. BE ANGRY WITH ME IF YOU HAVE TO, BUT PLEASE--CAN ONE OF YOU TELL ME WHAT THIS IS?
IT WOULD BE MY PLEASURE, O MIGHTY ONE--BUT FIRST, A QUESTION.
DID YOU REALLY THINK THAT DESTROYING THE PARLIAMENT OF TREES WOULD HAVE NO CONSEQUENCES?
I--
OF COURSE YOU DID. YOU ASSUMED YOU COULD HANDLE AN ENTIRE PLANETARY BIOSPHERE ON YOUR OWN. HUBRIS.
THE PARLIAMENT DID NOT SIMPLY SPEND ITS TIME SQUABBLING AMONGST ITSELF. IT PERFORMED A SERVICE. IT MONITORED THE GREEN, MADE SURE IT REMAINED STABLE.
THE AVATAR FIGHTS FOR THE GREEN, BUT THE PARLIAMENT MANAGED IT. NOW THE GREEN RUNS WILD, AND SO YOU GET THINGS LIKE THIS KREUZBLÜTLER.
IT IS AN OFFSHOOT CONSCIOUSNESS, BARELY SENTIENT, BUT ALIVE ENOUGH TO WISH TO CONSUME, TO GROW.
YOUR POWERS WON'T TOUCH IT, AND IT WILL SEE YOU AS A THREAT. GOOD LUCK, PROFESSOR. CHANCES ARE YOU'VE KILLED US ALL--BUT WITH ANY LUCK, YOU'LL GO FIRST.

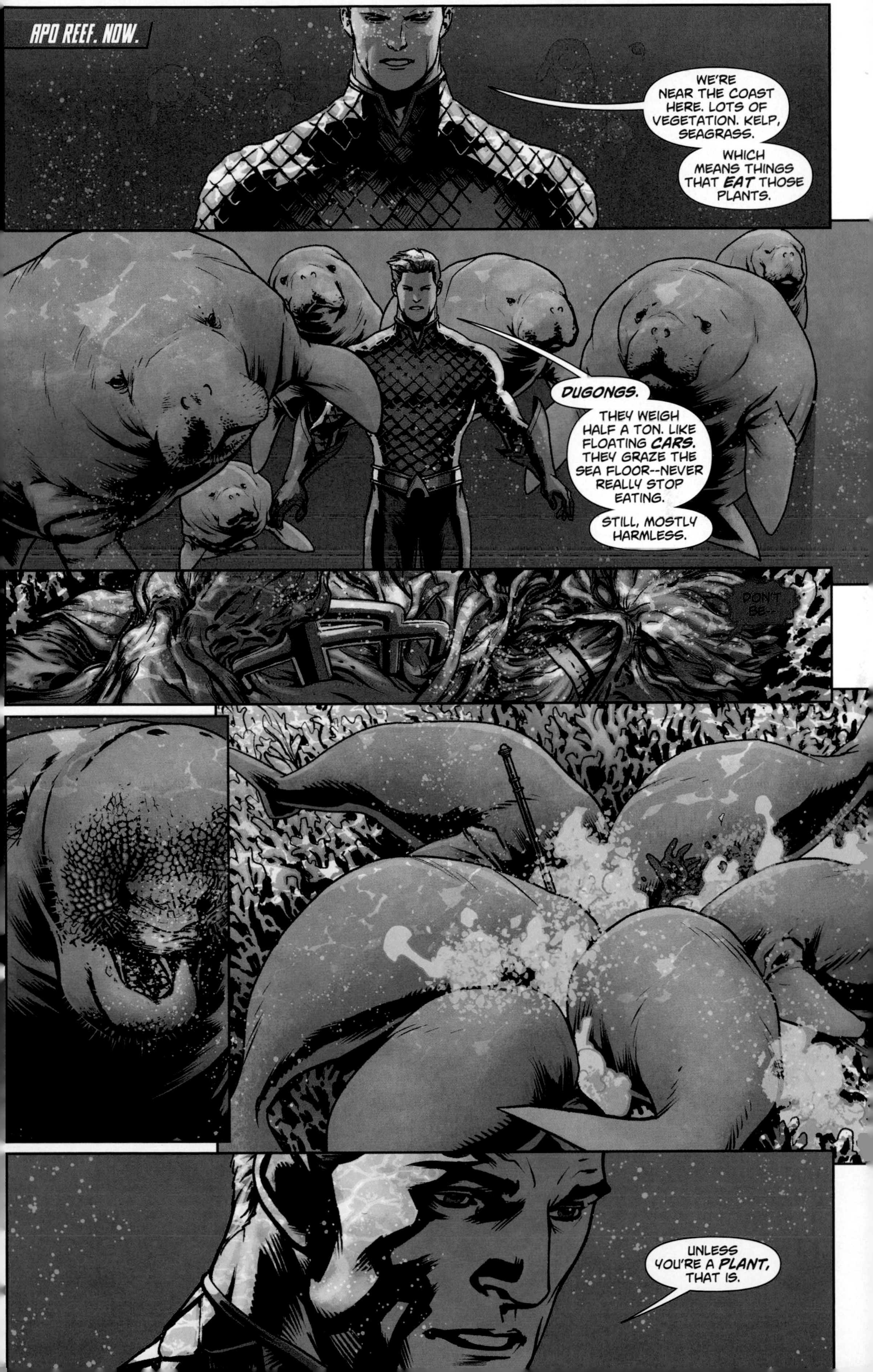
APO REEF. NOW.
WE'RE NEAR THE COAST HERE. LOTS OF VEGETATION. KELP, SEAGRASS.
WHICH MEANS THINGS THAT EAT THOSE PLANTS.
DUGONGS.
THEY WEIGH HALF A TON. LIKE FLOATING CARS. THEY GRAZE THE SEA FLOOR--NEVER REALLY STOP EATING.
STILL, MOSTLY HARMLESS.
DON'T BE--
UNLESS YOU'RE A PLANT, THAT IS.

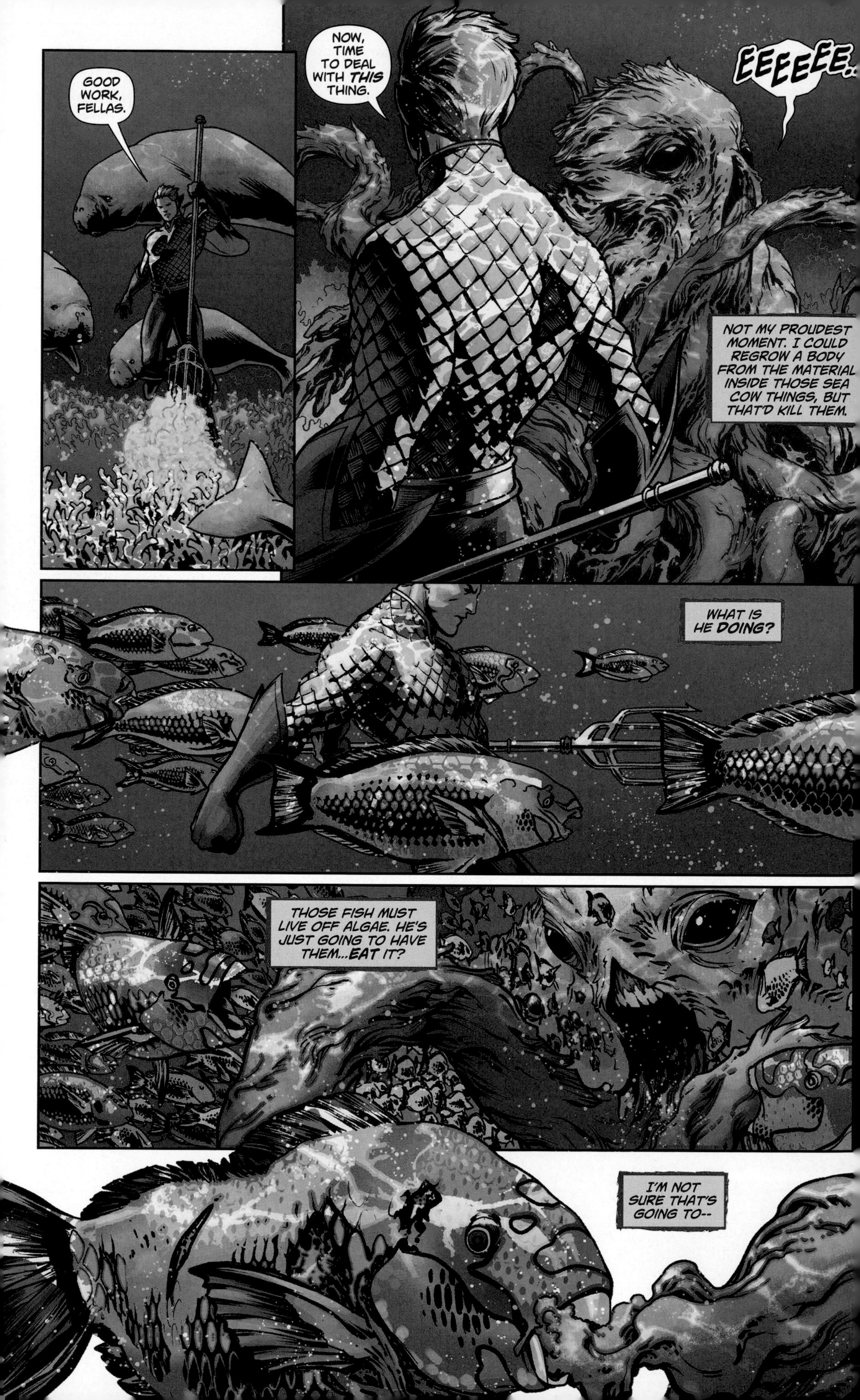
GOOD WORK, FELLAS.
NOW, TIME TO DEAL WITH THIS THING.
EEEEEE...
NOT MY PROUDEST MOMENT. I COULD REGROW A BODY FROM THE MATERIAL INSIDE THOSE SEA COW THINGS, BUT THAT'D KILL THEM.
WHAT IS HE DOING?
THOSE FISH MUST LIVE OFF ALGAE. HE'S JUST GOING TO HAVE THEM...EAT IT?
I'M NOT SURE THAT'S GOING TO--

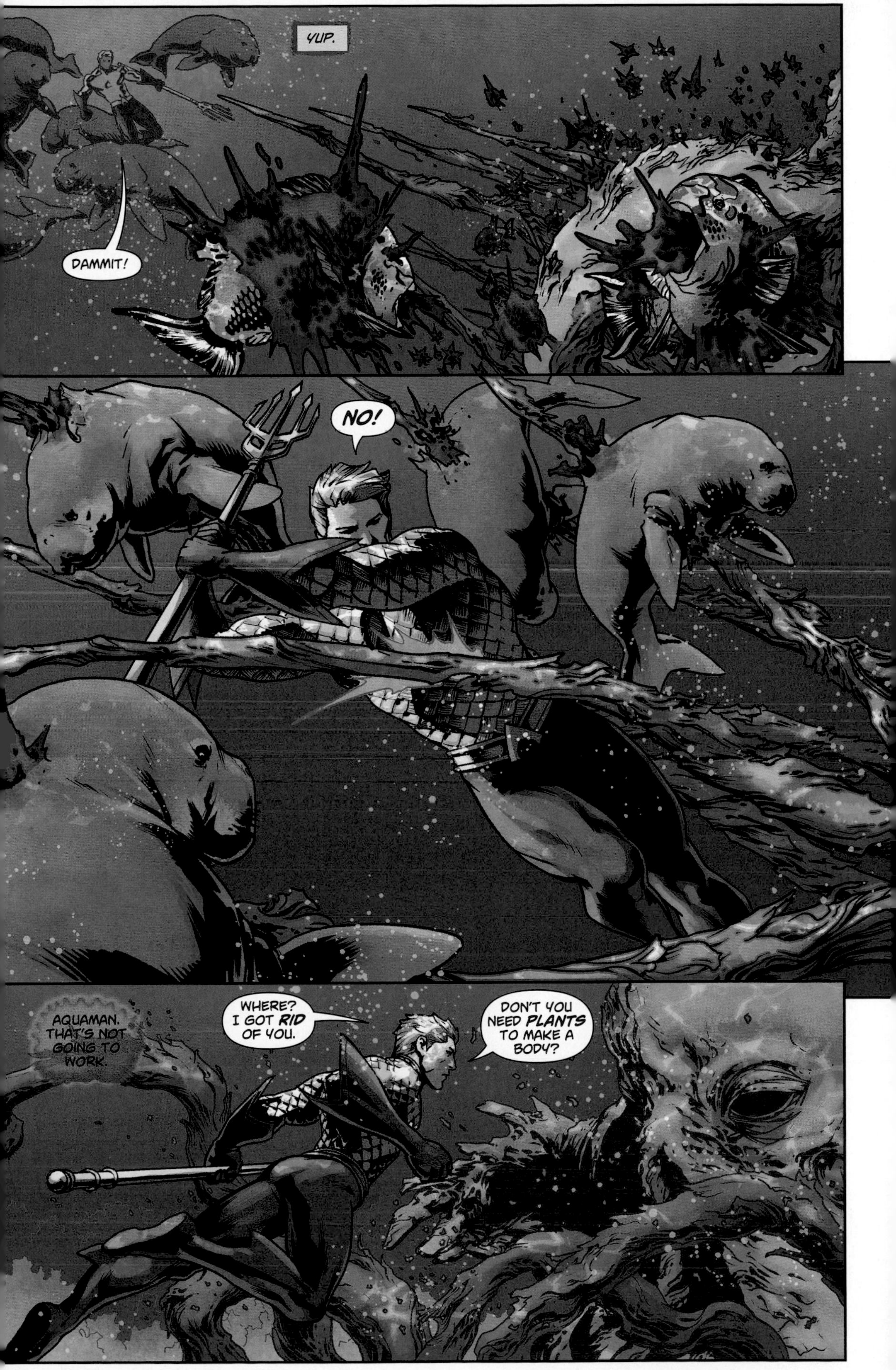
YUP.
DAMMIT!
NO!
AQUAMAN. THAT'S NOT GOING TO WORK.
WHERE? I GOT RID OF YOU.
DON'T YOU NEED PLANTS TO MAKE A BODY?

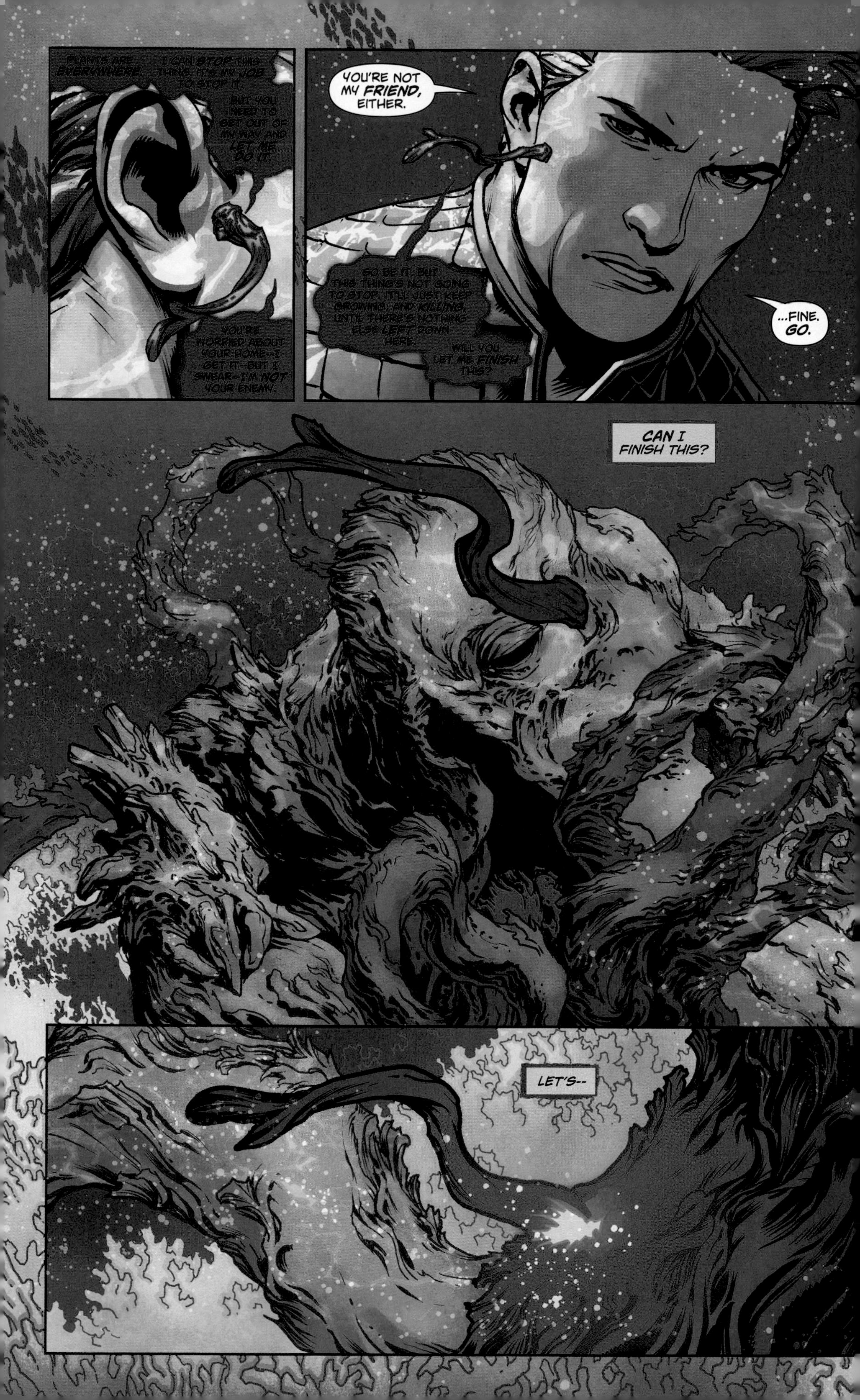
PLANTS ARE EVERYWHERE.
I CAN STOP THIS THING. IT'S MY JOB TO STOP IT.
BUT YOU NEED TO GET OUT OF MY WAY AND LET ME DO IT.
YOU'RE WORRIED ABOUT YOUR HOME--I GET IT--BUT I SWEAR--I'M NOT YOUR ENEMY.
YOU'RE NOT MY FRIEND, EITHER.
SO BE IT. BUT THIS THING'S NOT GOING TO STOP. IT'LL JUST KEEP GROWING. AND KILLING. UNTIL THERE'S NOTHING ELSE LEFT DOWN HERE.
WILL YOU LET ME FINISH THIS?
...FINE. GO.
CAN I FINISH THIS?
LET'S--

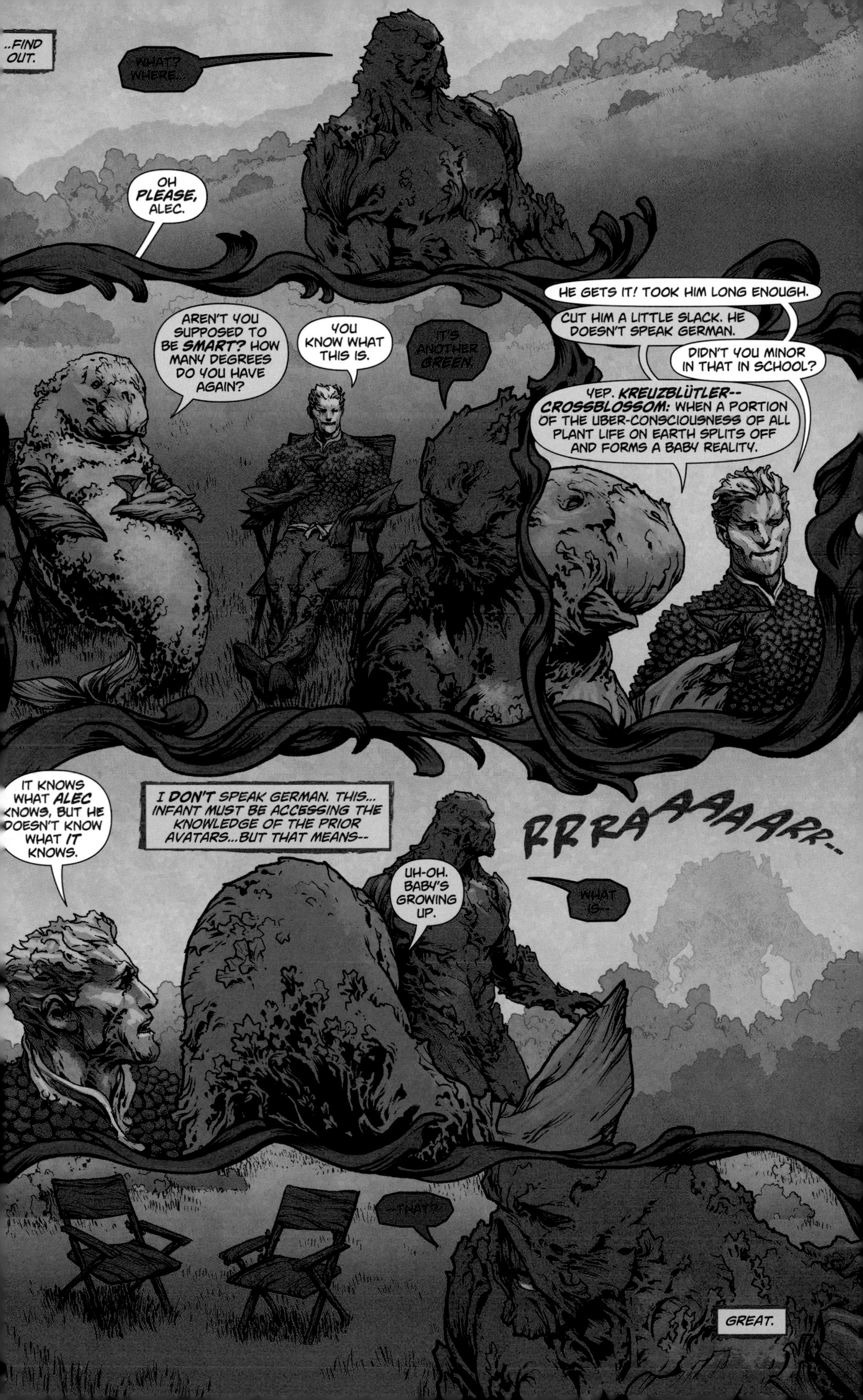
..FIND OUT.
WHAT? WHERE...
OH PLEASE, ALEC.
AREN'T YOU SUPPOSED TO BE SMART? HOW MANY DEGREES DO YOU HAVE AGAIN?
YOU KNOW WHAT THIS IS.
IT'S ANOTHER GREEN.
HE GETS IT! TOOK HIM LONG ENOUGH.
CUT HIM A LITTLE SLACK. HE DOESN'T SPEAK GERMAN.
DIDN'T YOU MINOR IN THAT IN SCHOOL?
YEP. KREUZBLÜTLER--CROSSBLOSSOM: WHEN A PORTION OF THE UBER-CONSCIOUSNESS OF ALL PLANT LIFE ON EARTH SPLITS OFF AND FORMS A BABY REALITY.
IT KNOWS WHAT ALEC KNOWS, BUT HE DOESN'T KNOW WHAT IT KNOWS.
I DON'T SPEAK GERMAN. THIS... INFANT MUST BE ACCESSING THE KNOWLEDGE OF THE PRIOR AVATARS...BUT THAT MEANS--
UH-OH. BABY'S GROWING UP.
RRRAAAAAARR..
WHAT IS--
--THAT?
GREAT.

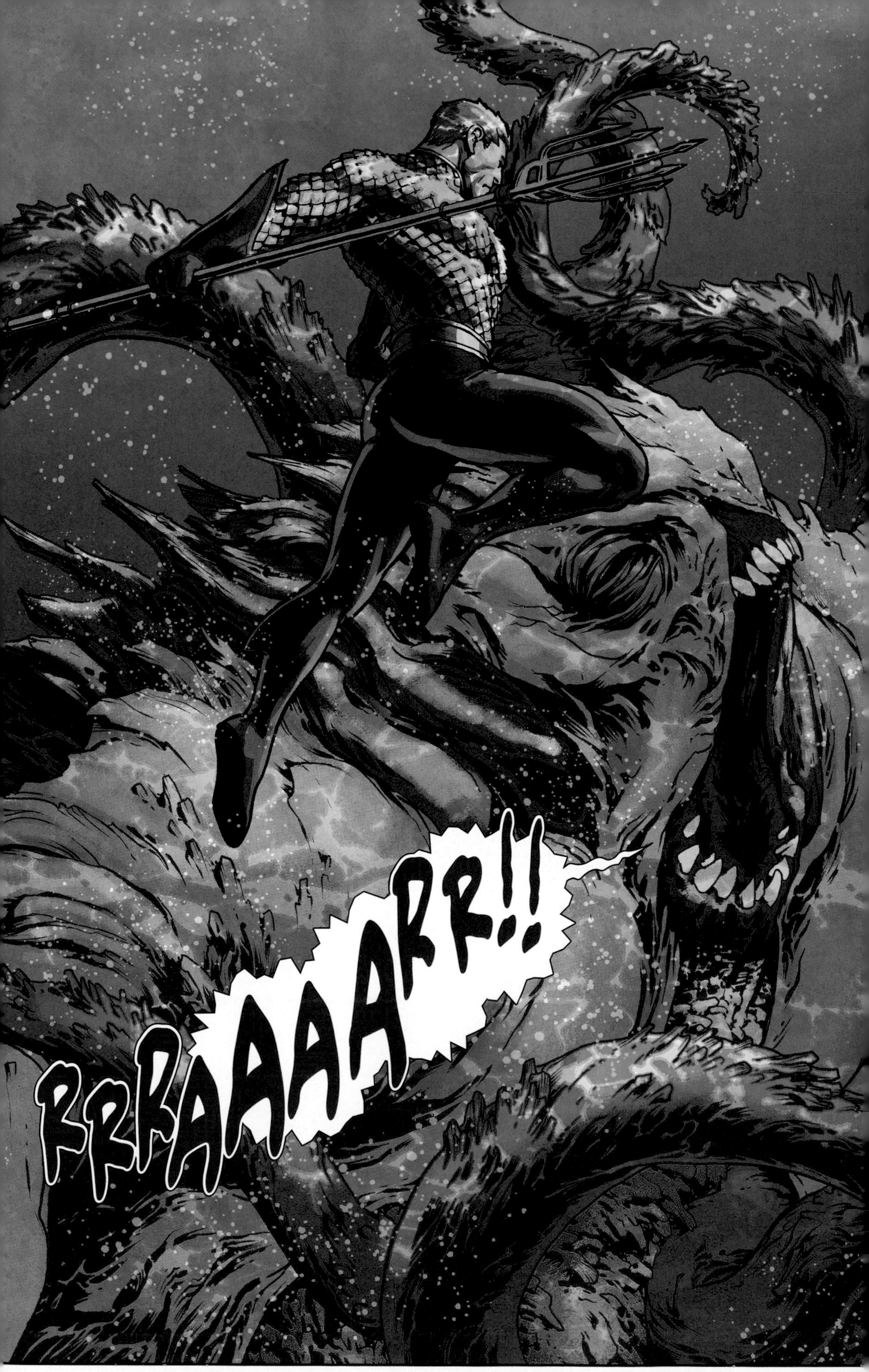
RRRAAAAARR!!

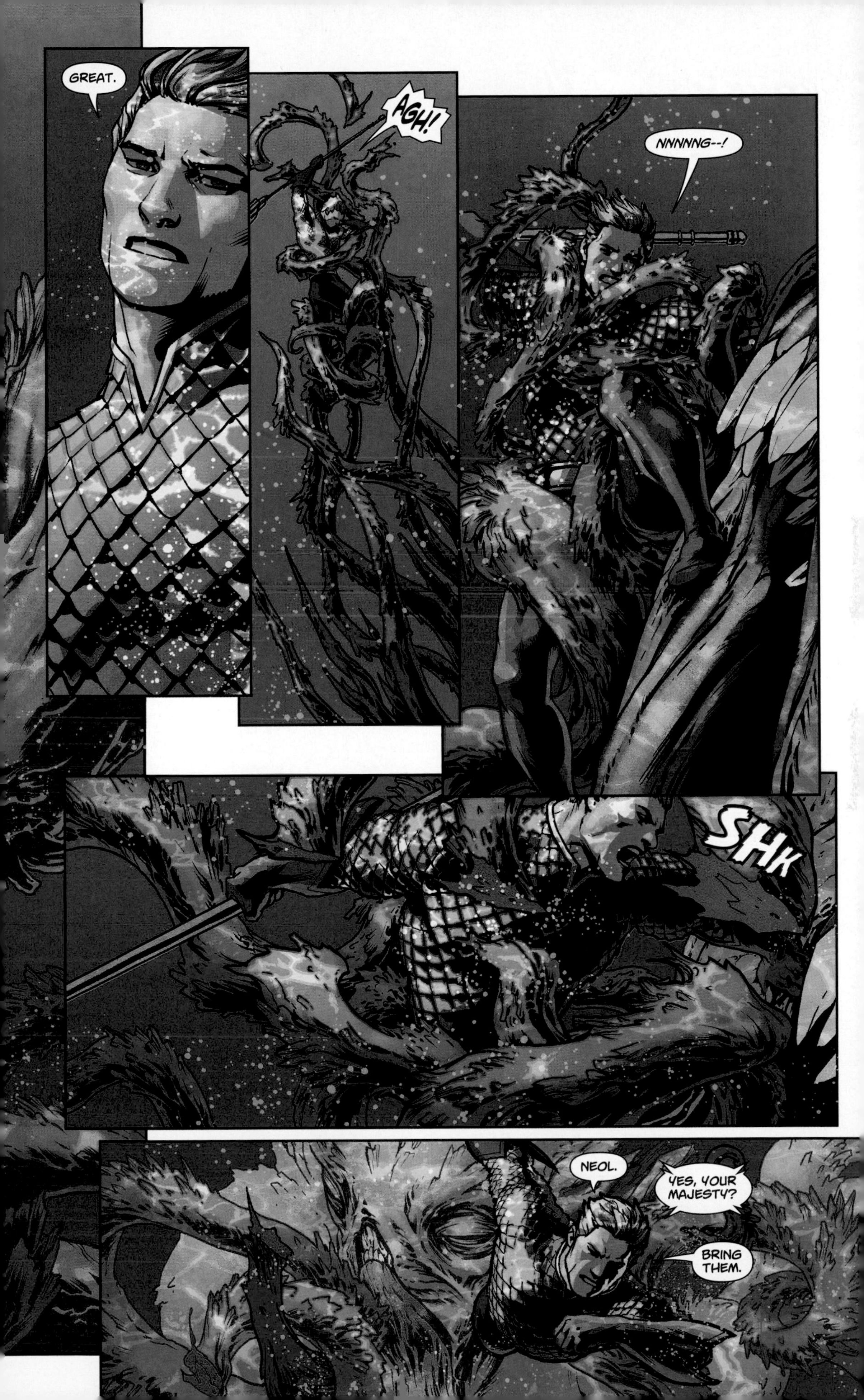
GREAT.
AGH!
NNNNNG--!
SHK
NEOL.
YES, YOUR MAJESTY?
BRING THEM.

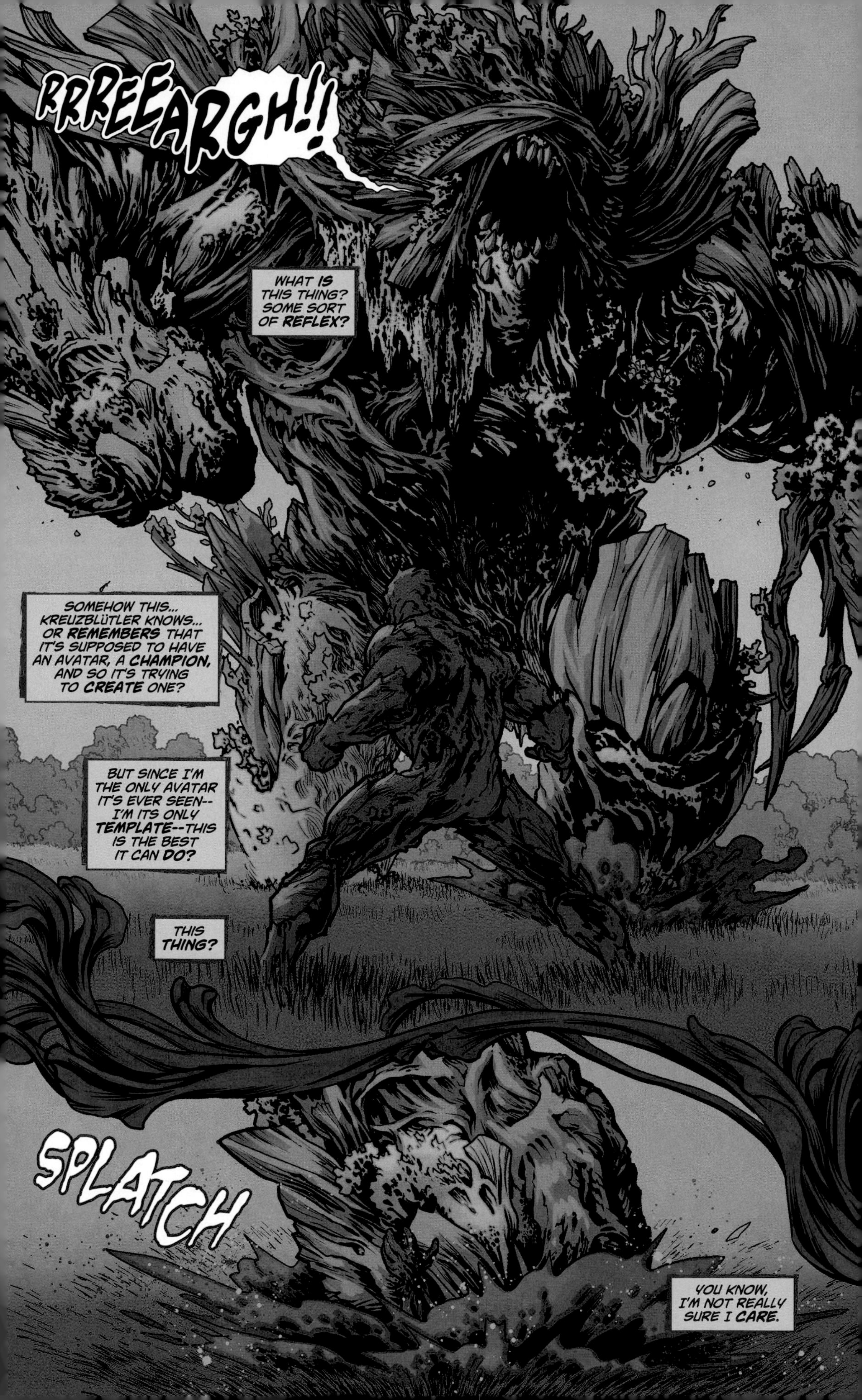
RRREEARGH!!
WHAT IS THIS THING? SOME SORT OF REFLEX?
SOMEHOW THIS... KREUZBLÜTLER KNOWS... OR REMEMBERS THAT IT'S SUPPOSED TO HAVE AN AVATAR, A CHAMPION, AND SO IT'S TRYING TO CREATE ONE?
BUT SINCE I'M THE ONLY AVATAR IT'S EVER SEEN--I'M ITS ONLY TEMPLATE--THIS IS THE BEST IT CAN DO?
THIS THING?
SPLATCH
YOU KNOW, I'M NOT REALLY SURE I CARE.

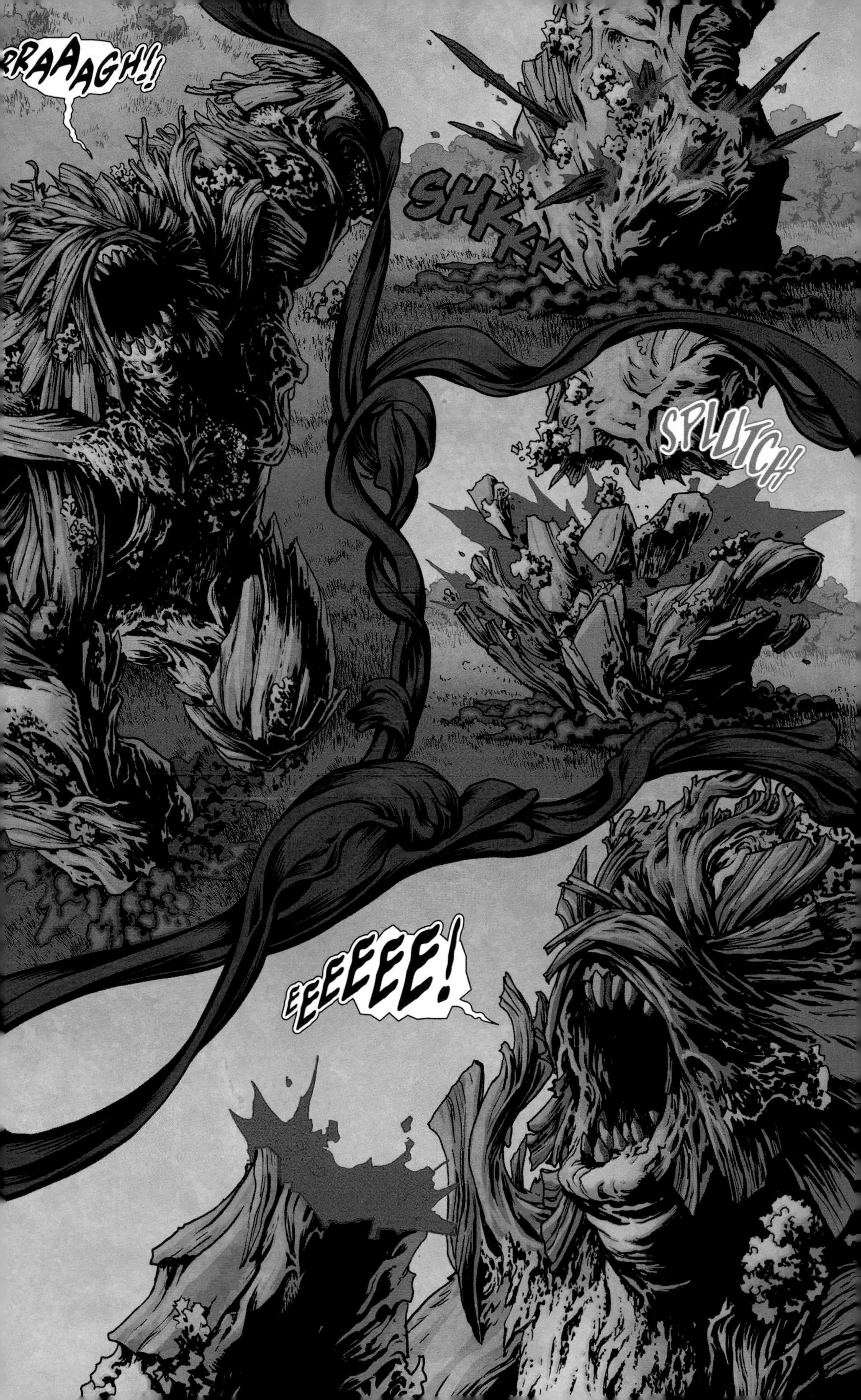
RAAAGH!!
SHKKK
SPLUTCH
EEEEEEE!

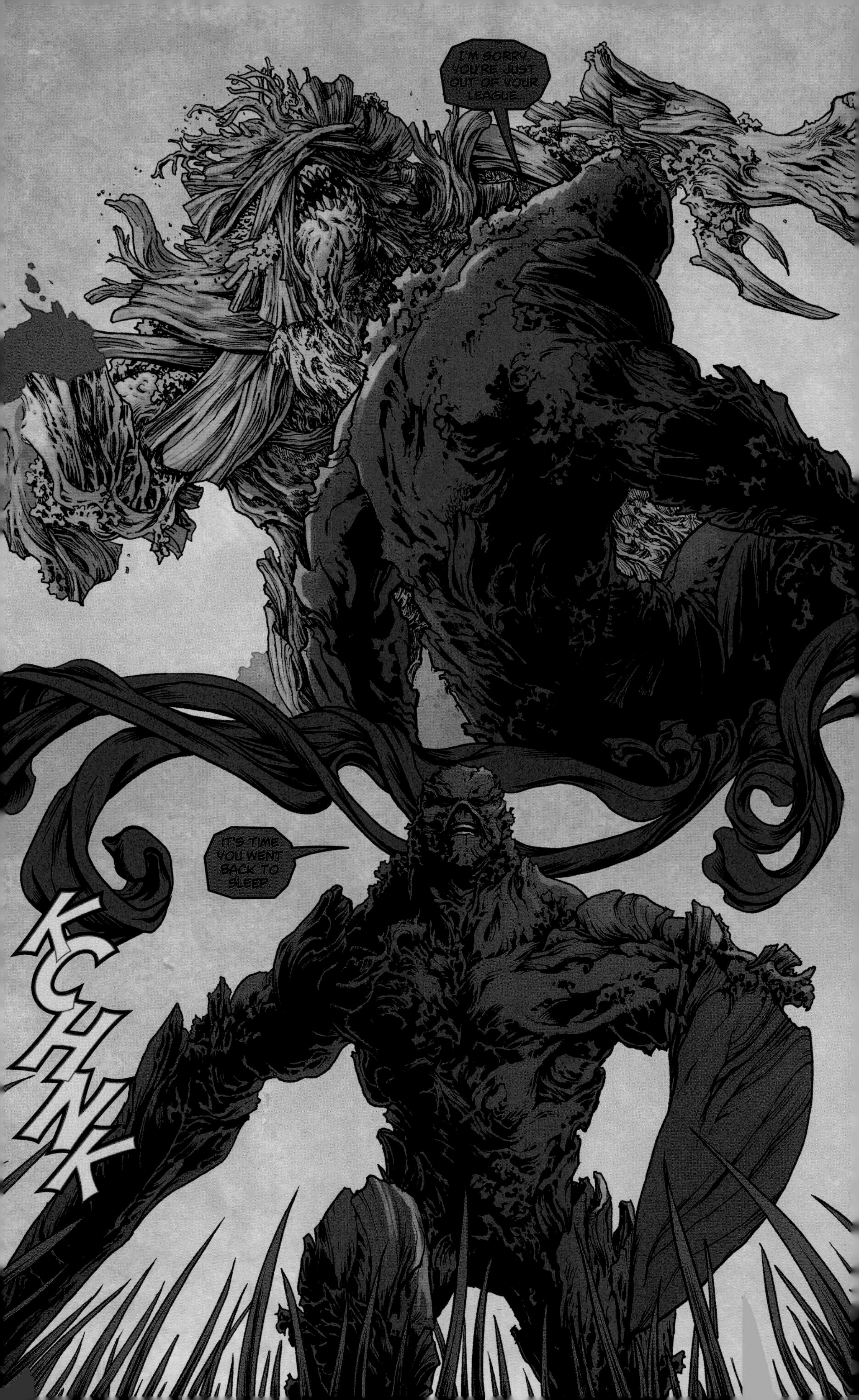
I'M SORRY. YOU'RE JUST OUT OF YOUR LEAGUE.
IT'S TIME YOU WENT BACK TO SLEEP.
KCHNK

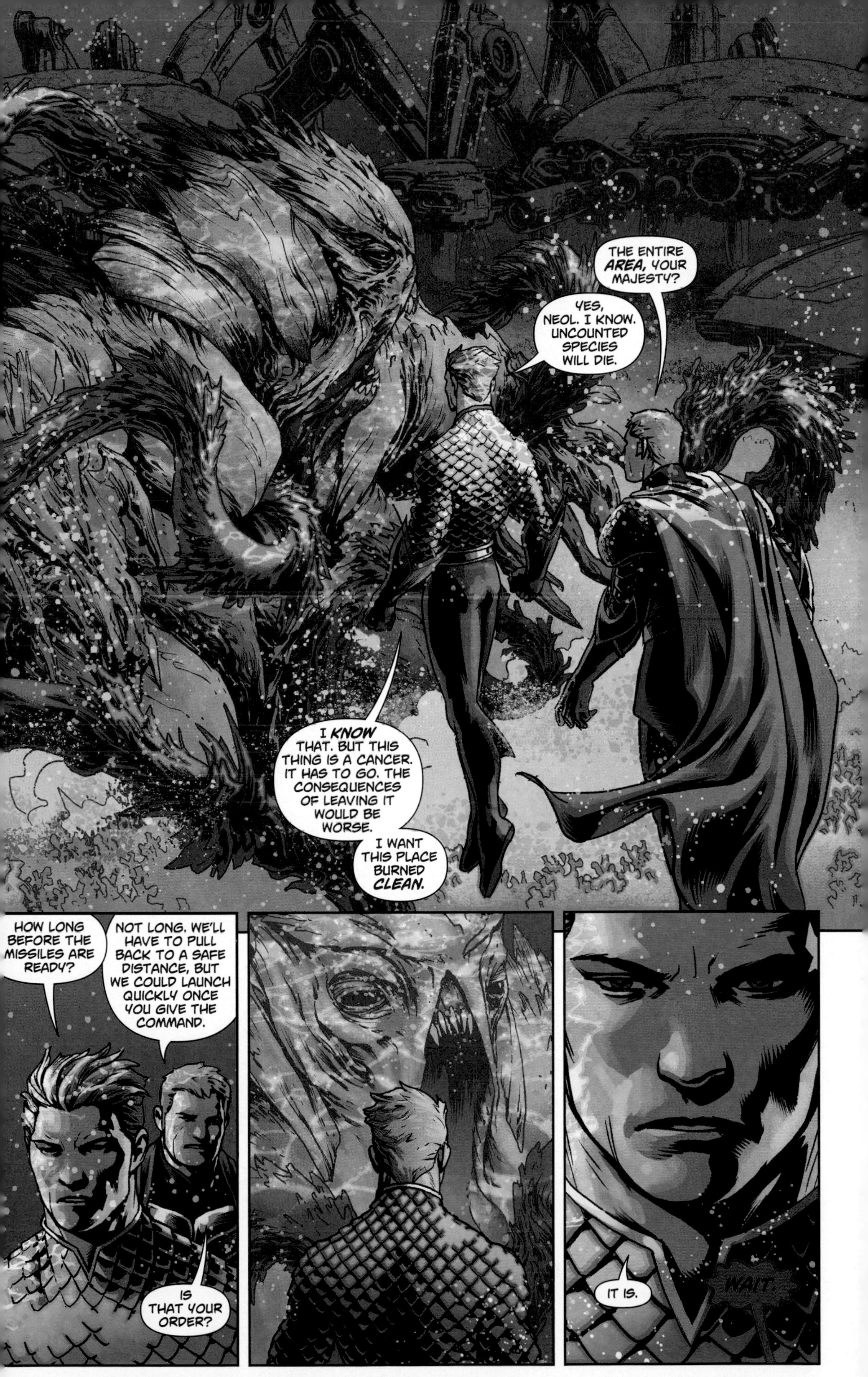
THE ENTIRE AREA, YOUR MAJESTY?
YES, NEOL. I KNOW. UNCOUNTED SPECIES WILL DIE.
I KNOW THAT. BUT THIS THING IS A CANCER. IT HAS TO GO. THE CONSEQUENCES OF LEAVING IT WOULD BE WORSE.
I WANT THIS PLACE BURNED CLEAN.
HOW LONG BEFORE THE MISSILES ARE READY?
NOT LONG. WE'LL HAVE TO PULL BACK TO A SAFE DISTANCE, BUT WE COULD LAUNCH QUICKLY ONCE YOU GIVE THE COMMAND.
IS THAT YOUR ORDER?
IT IS.
WAIT.

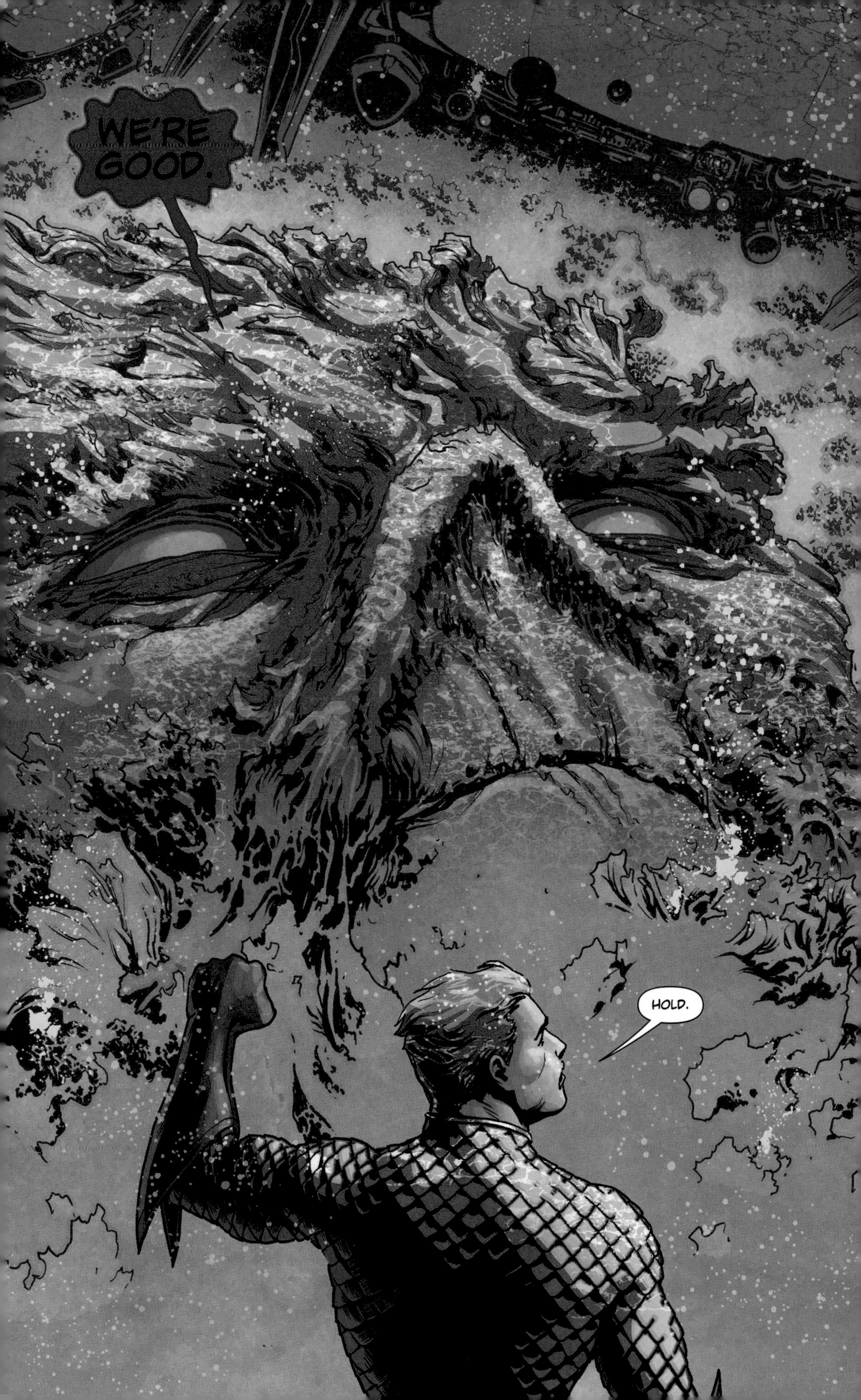
WE'RE GOOD.
HOLD.

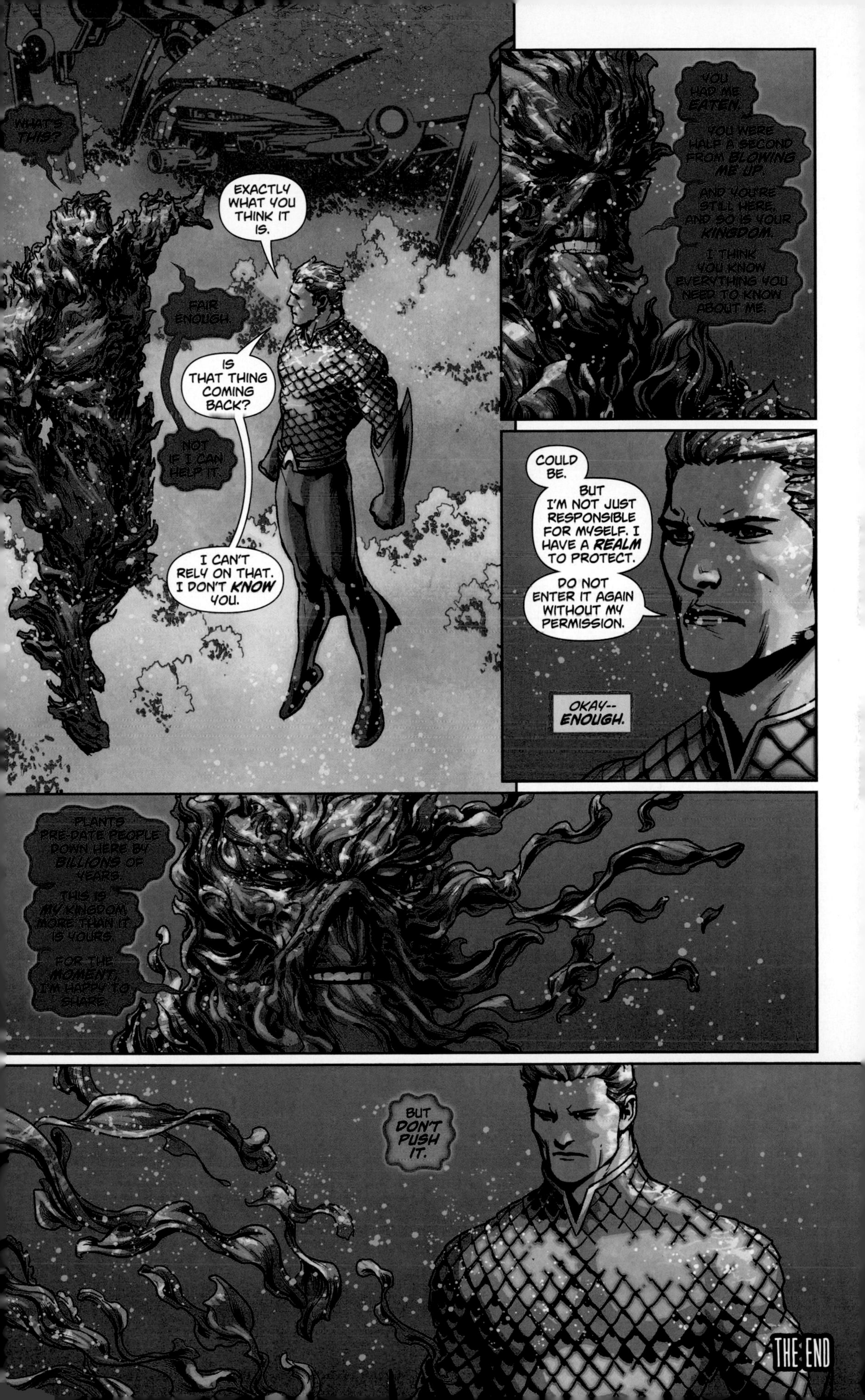
WHAT'S THIS?
EXACTLY WHAT YOU THINK IT IS.
FAIR ENOUGH.
IS THAT THING COMING BACK?
NOT IF I CAN HELP IT.
I CAN'T RELY ON THAT. I DON'T KNOW YOU.
YOU HAD ME EATEN.
YOU WERE HALF A SECOND FROM BLOWING ME UP.
AND YOU'RE STILL HERE, AND SO IS YOUR KINGDOM.
I THINK YOU KNOW EVERYTHING YOU NEED TO KNOW ABOUT ME.
COULD BE.
BUT I'M NOT JUST RESPONSIBLE FOR MYSELF. I HAVE A REALM TO PROTECT.
DO NOT ENTER IT AGAIN WITHOUT MY PERMISSION.
OKAY-- ENOUGH.
PLANTS PRE-DATE PEOPLE DOWN HERE BY BILLIONS OF YEARS.
THIS IS MY KINGDOM MORE THAN IT IS YOURS.
FOR THE MOMENT, I'M HAPPY TO SHARE.
BUT DON'T PUSH IT.
THE END

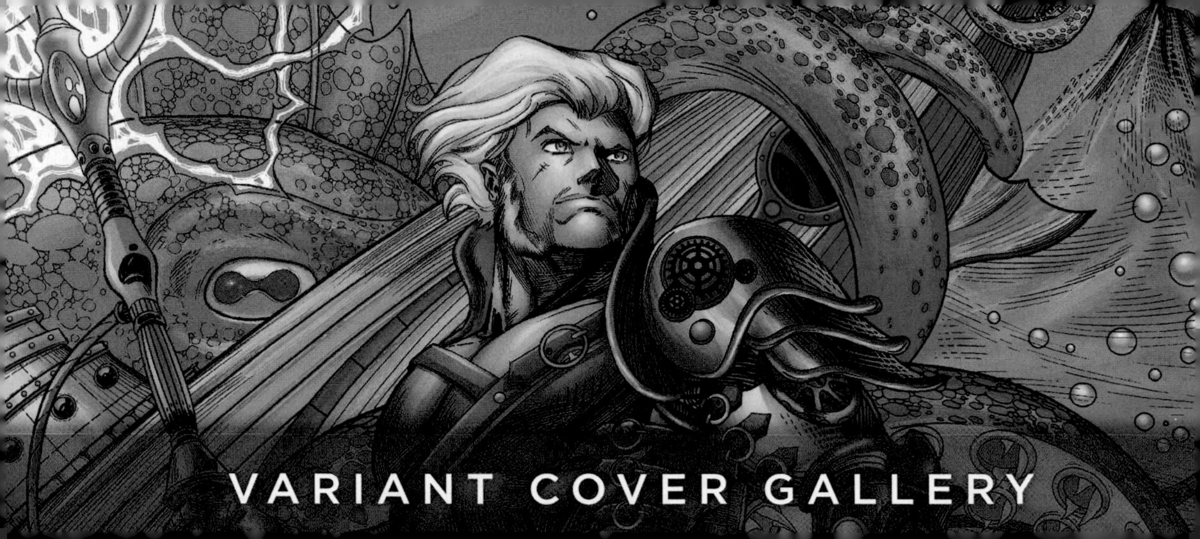

VARIANT COVER GALLERY

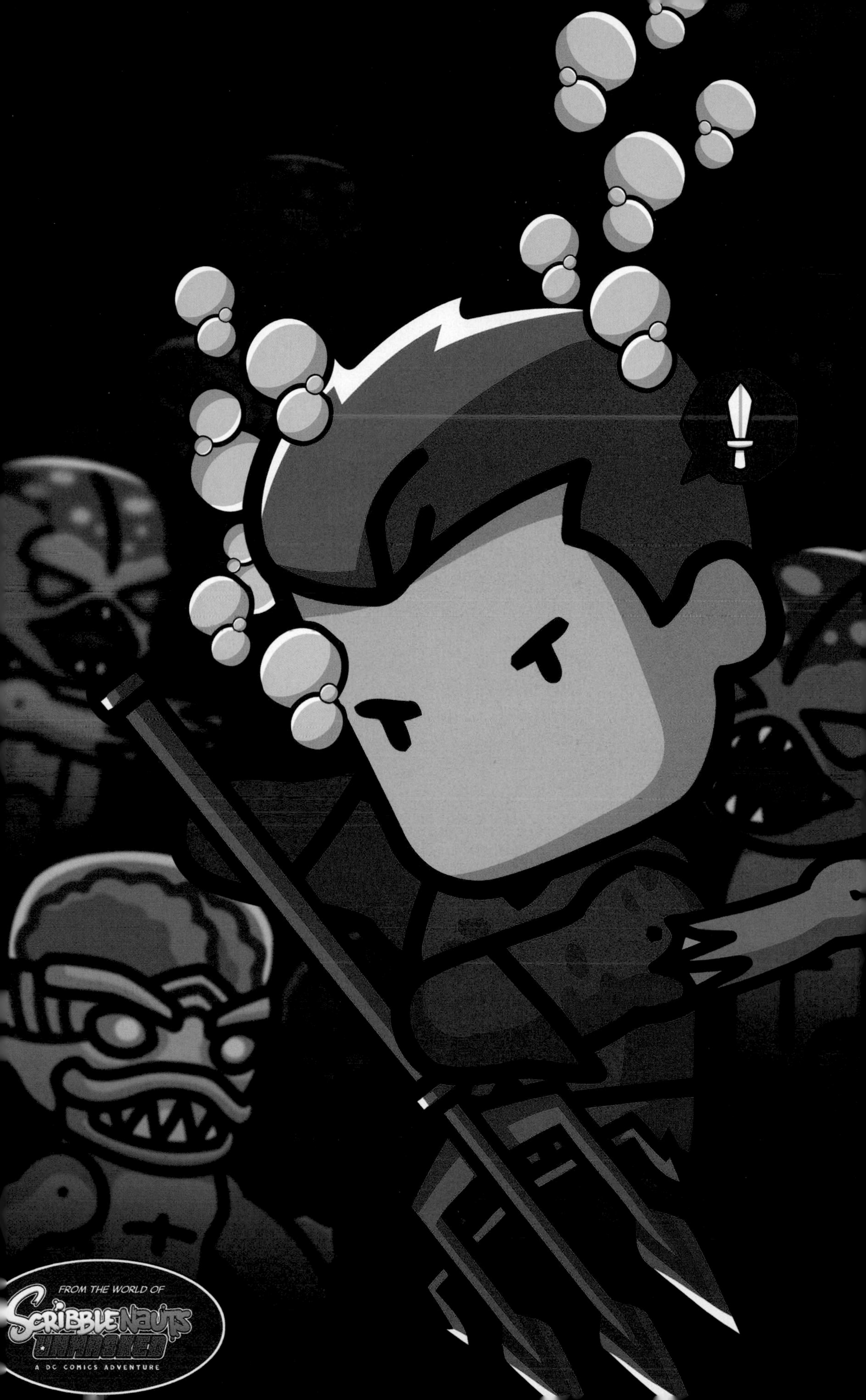
FROM THE WORLD OF
SCRIBBLENAUTS
UNMASKED
A DC COMICS ADVENTURE

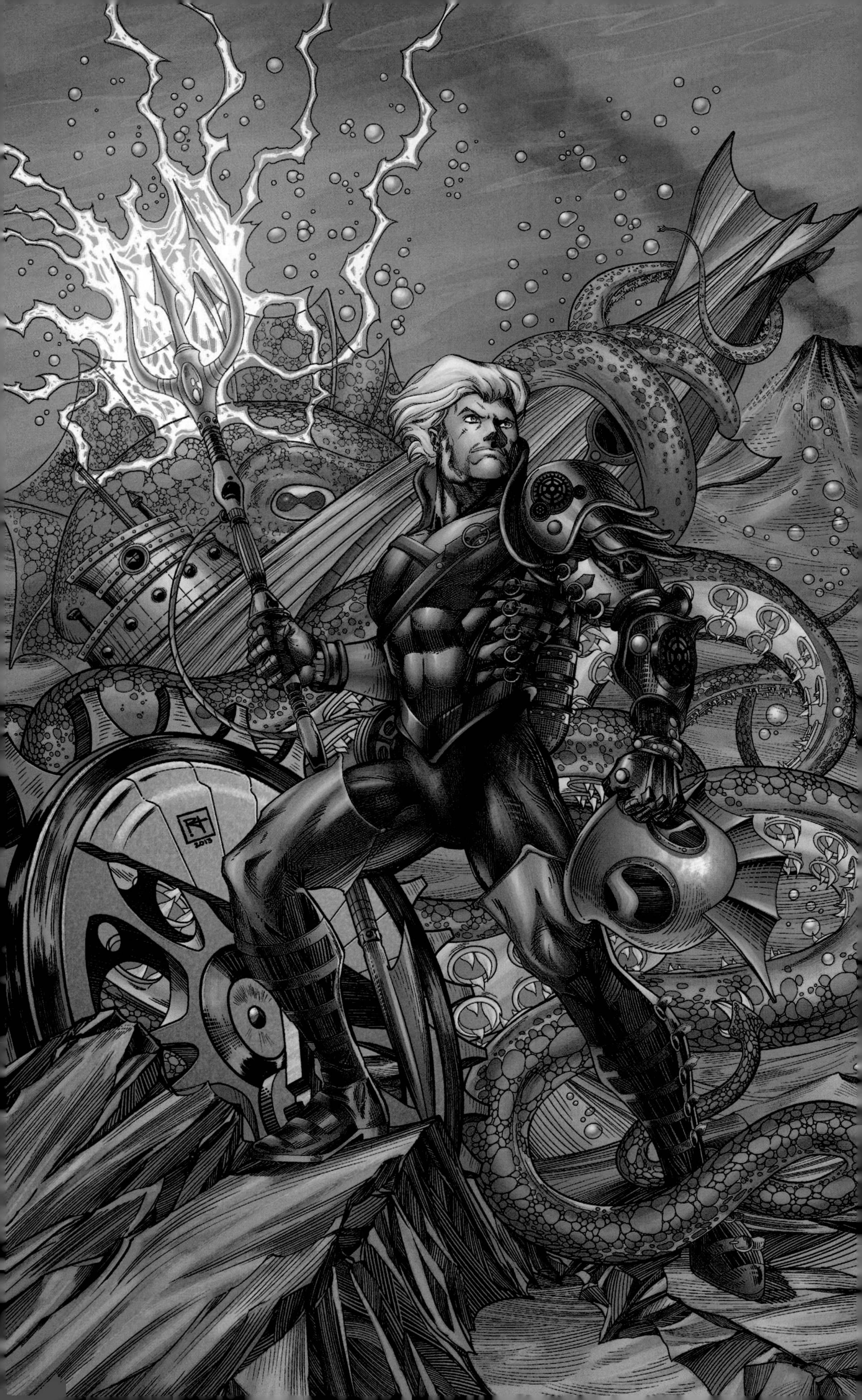

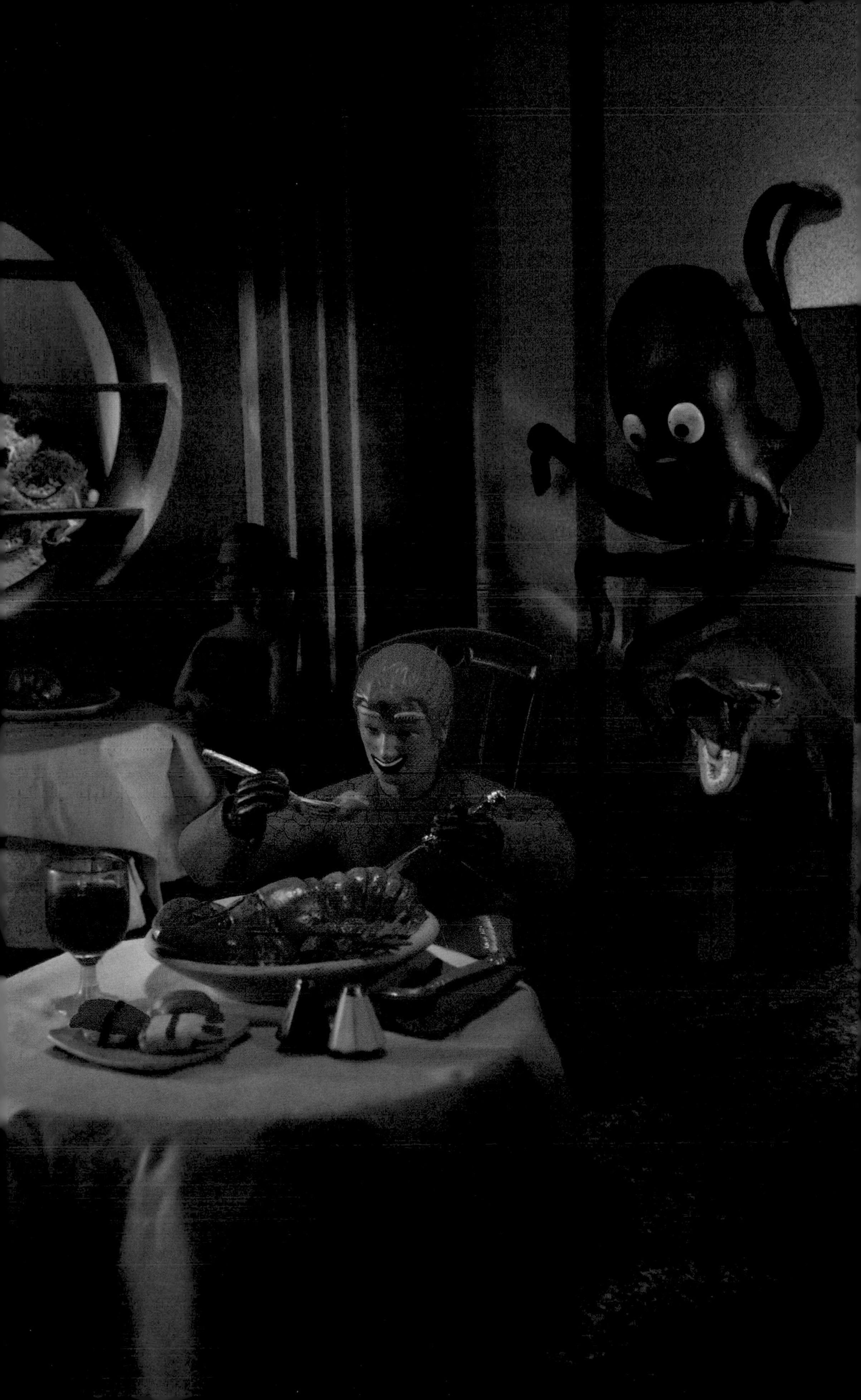

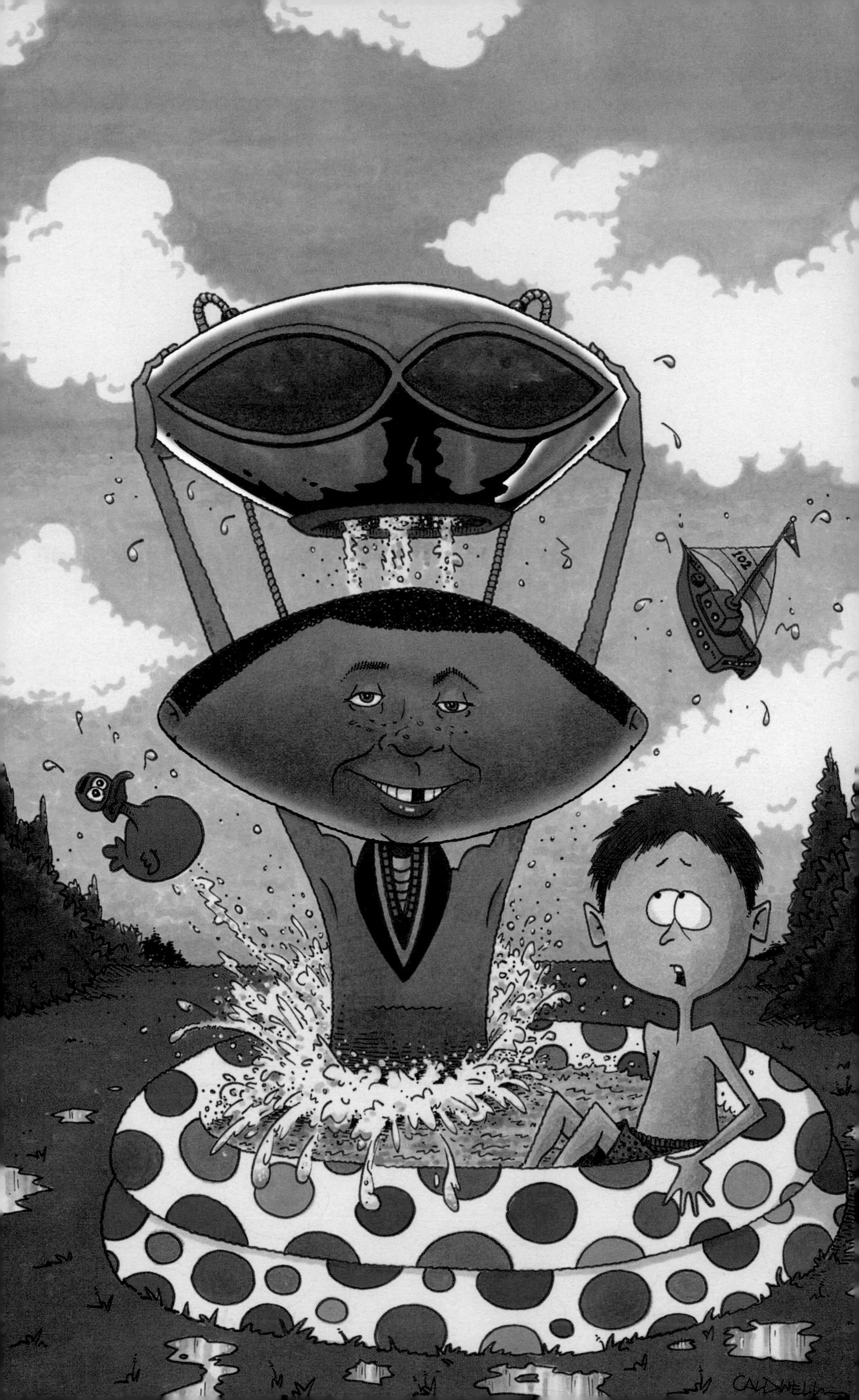
102

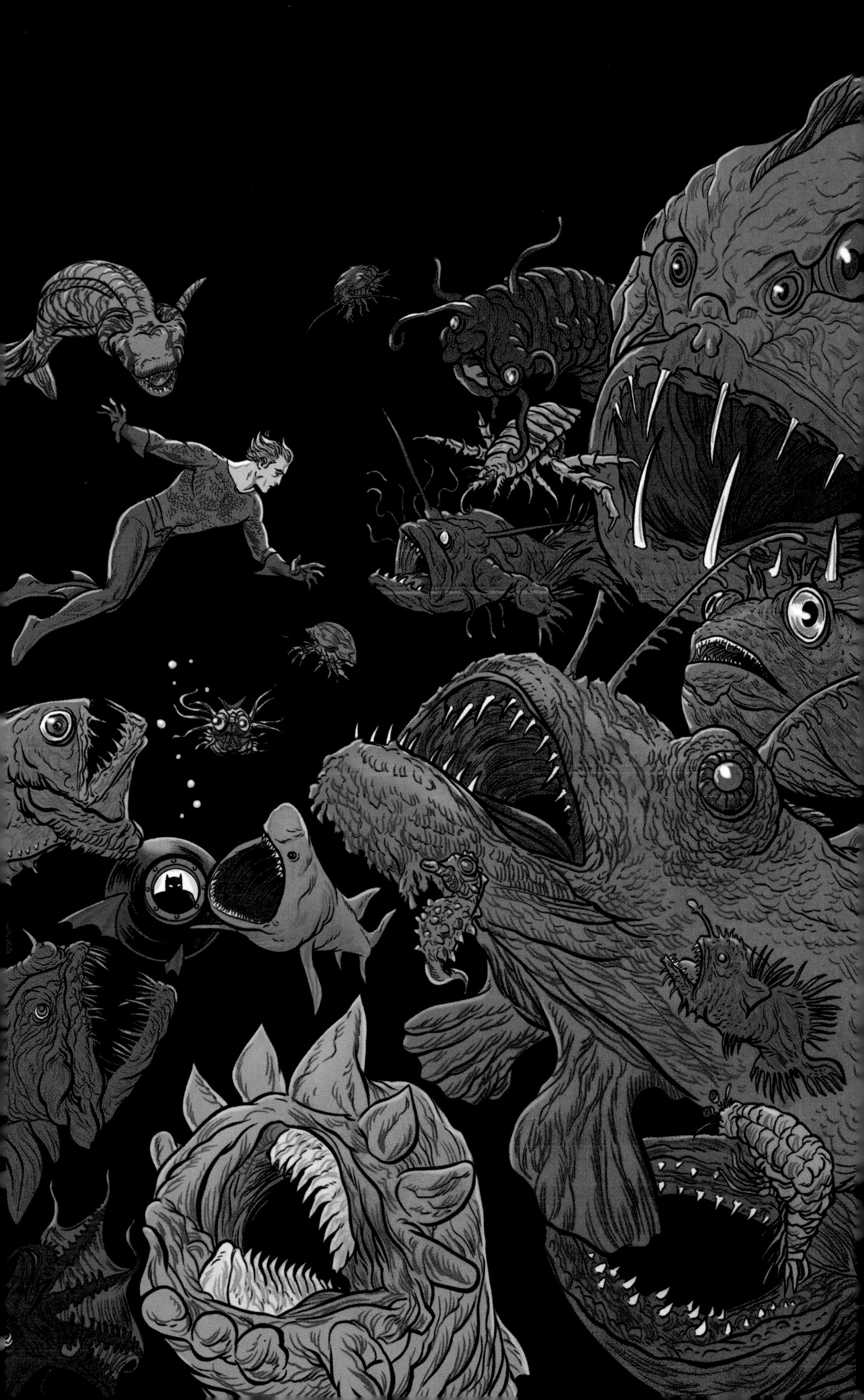

DC COMICS™

START AT THE BEGINNING!
AQUAMAN
VOLUME 1: THE TRENCH
GEOFF JOHNS and IVAN REIS

AQUAMAN VOL. 2: THE OTHERS

AQUAMAN VOL. 3: THE THRONE OF ATLANTIS

JUSTICE LEAGUE VOL. 3: THE THRONE OF ATLANTIS

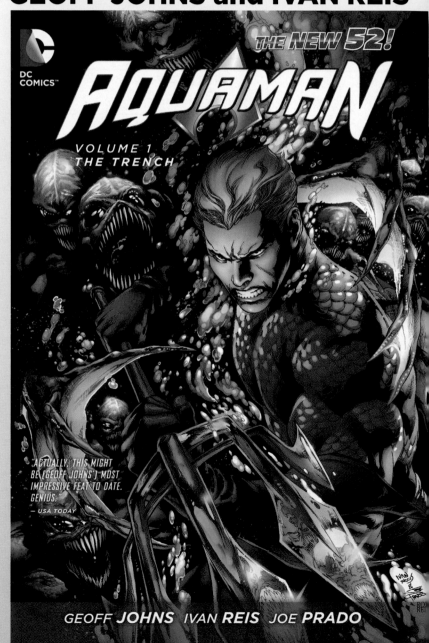

THE NEW 52!

DC COMICS™

AQUAMAN

VOLUME 1
THE TRENCH

"ACTUALLY, THIS MIGHT BE [GEOFF JOHNS'] MOST IMPRESSIVE FEAT TO DATE. GENIUS."
— USA TODAY

GEOFF JOHNS   IVAN REIS   JOE PRADO

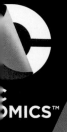

"Writer Geoff Johns and artist Jim Lee toss you–and their heroes–into the action from the very start and don't put on the brakes. DC's über-creative team craft an inviting world for those who are trying out a comic for the first time. Lee's art is stunning."—USA TODAY

"A fun ride."—IGN

START AT THE BEGINNING!

JUSTICE LEAGUE VOLUME 1: ORIGIN

GEOFF JOHNS and JIM LEE

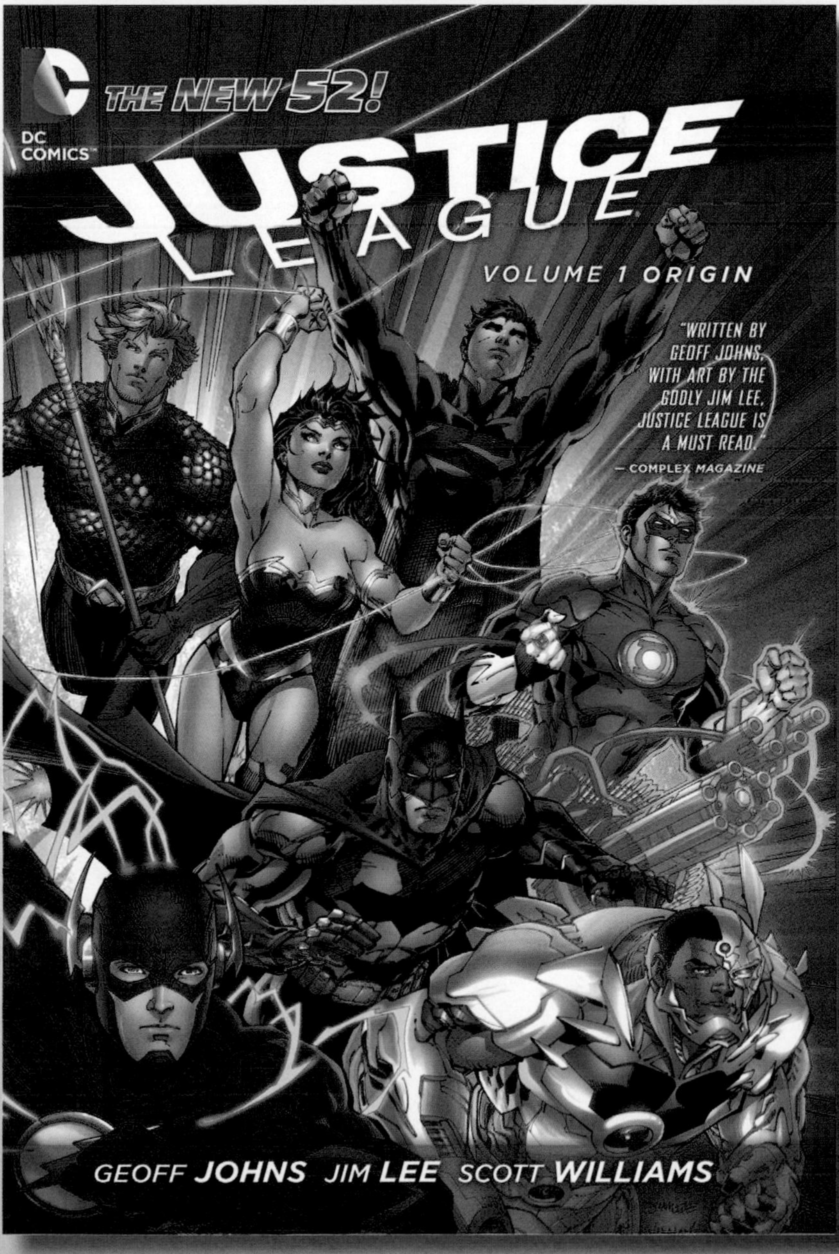
THE NEW 52!
DC COMICS
JUSTICE LEAGUE
VOLUME 1 ORIGIN
"WRITTEN BY GEOFF JOHNS, WITH ART BY THE GODLY JIM LEE, JUSTICE LEAGUE IS A MUST READ."
– COMPLEX MAGAZINE
GEOFF JOHNS JIM LEE SCOTT WILLIAMS

JUSTICE LEAGUE VOL. 2: THE VILLAIN'S JOURNEY

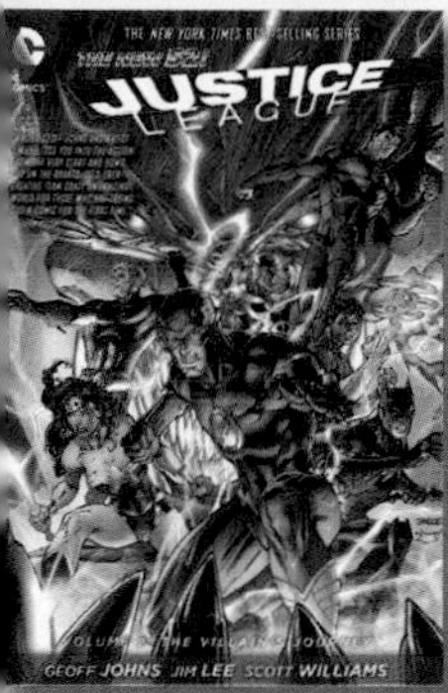
JUSTICE LEAGUE
GEOFF JOHNS JIM LEE SCOTT WILLIAMS

JUSTICE LEAGUE VOL. 3: THRONE OF ATLANTIS

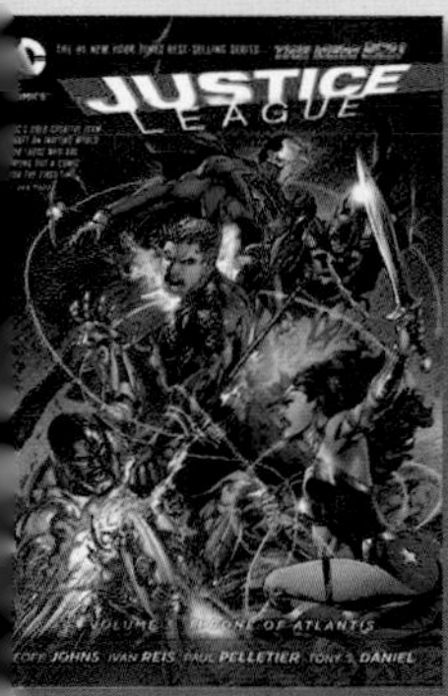
JUSTICE LEAGUE

JUSTICE LEAGUE OF AMERICA VOL. 1: WORLD'S MOST DANGEROUS

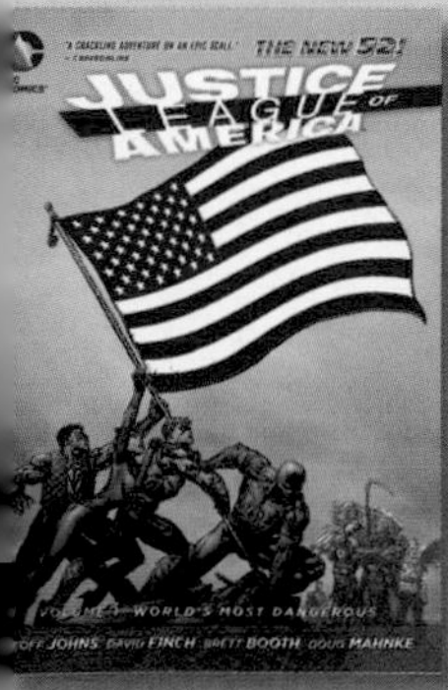
THE NEW 52!
JUSTICE LEAGUE OF AMERICA

"Widescreen. Jaw-dropping action.
a surefire hit
—CB

"Extremely cool and exceptionally crafted.
—AIN'T IT COOL NEW

READ THE FOLLOW-UP TO THE *NEW YORK TIMES* #1 BEST-SELLING BLACKEST NIGHT

BRIGHTEST DAY

GEOFF JOHNS and PETER J. TOMAS

BRIGHTEST DAY
VOL. 2

BRIGHTEST DAY
VOL. 3

GREEN LANTERN:
BRIGHTEST DAY

GEOFF JOHNS
PETER J. TOMASI
IVAN REIS
PATRICK GLEASON **FERNANDO PASARIN**
ARDIAN SYAF **SCOTT CLARK** **JOE PRADO**